WOMEN
and the
PSYCHIATRIC
PARADOX

WOMEN
and the
PSYCHIATRIC
PARADOX

P. Susan Penfold
& Gillian A. Walker

Eden Press
Montréal · London

WOMEN AND THE PSYCHIATRIC PARADOX

P. Susan Penfold and Gillian A. Walker

© copyright 1983 Eden Press Inc.
4626 St. Catherine St. West, Montréal, Canada H3Z 1S3
and
3 Henrietta Street, London WC2E 8LU England

ISBN: 0-920792-09-X

First Edition

Printed in Canada by the John Deyell Company

Dépôt légal — deuxième trimestre 1983
Bibliothèque nationale du Québec

Cover design and original artwork by J.W. Stewart

≡ *TABLE OF CONTENTS*

Acknowledgements

The research for this work was made possible by grant No. 1208-0-75 from the Non Medical Use of Drugs Directorate, Department of Health and Welfare, Canada. Our thanks are due to Betty Wong, Robbie Simpson, Margo Sanderson, and other staff of the Western Regional Office. Our findings and conclusions do not necessarily represent the views of the Department, but are those of the authors of this manuscript.

Chapter VIII is reprinted, by permission, from *The Canadian Journal of Psychiatry*, Vol. 26, No. 1, pp. 24-31, where it appeared under the title "Women and Depression." Acknowledgements are also due to *Bioethics Quarterly*, where a shortened version of Chapter VII, entitled "Psychotropic Drugs and Women," appeared in Vol. 2, No. 1, pp. 20-38, in 1980. *The CPA Guidelines for Therapy and Counselling with Women* are reprinted with the permission of the Canadian Psychological Association.

This manuscript was typed and retyped by Amy Lariviere, Lillian Lim, Betty Jones, Susan McLintock, Ruby Toren, Mary Walmsley, and Maureen Rothwell.

Feedback, advice and suggestions were given by Joann Robertson, Ingrid Pacey, Ruth Cooperstock, Alison Griffith, Judy Gold, and Helga Jacobson. Our work was also catalysed by a variety of suggestions and encouragement from a number of our colleagues in the Department of Psychiatry and the Women Students's Office, both at the University of British Columbia, and Women's Movement friends in the community.

A vital element in our lives is our past and present women's group: Marie Campbell, Alison Griffith, Susan Innes, Ingrid Pacey, and Joann Robertson. Support and tolerance have been provided by Paul, Mary and Robert Stephenson, Kevin and Jeremy Walker, Ellen Trick, Bill Horne, David Hinks, Trudy Cowan, our parents, and other family and friends.

We are particularly indebted to Dr. Dorothy E. Smith both for her work, which has provided a basis for much of our thinking, and for her personal support and encouragement.

P. Susan Penfold
Department of Psychiatry, University of British Columbia and Department of Psychiatry, Children's Hospital, Vancouver

Gillian A. Walker
School of Social Work, Carlton University, Ottawa

WOMEN AND PSYCHIATRY

AS WOMEN WORKING WITH WOMEN and with children we have become increasingly concerned over the past few years with the disjunctions and difficulties which become apparent when using traditional psychiatric models of diagnosis and treatment. Our concern stems from the recognition that psychiatric theories fail either to explain or to provide solutions for many of the dilemmas which we encounter in our lives or in the lives of those who come to us for help. In this we are not alone; women's dissatisfaction with the psychiatric profession is well documented. This dissatisfaction arises from women's growing awareness of their oppression, and the role that traditional psychiatric theories about women play in that oppression.

Over the past decade a new women's movement has built on the work of earlier feminists to produce compelling evidence of women's oppression at all levels of society. It is no longer a fact that must be argued in each and every context. Reports on the status of women in every industrialized country indicate the same pattern of under-representation in low paying, low status positions. A recent report on poverty in Canada shows women to be vulnerable to poverty as low income wives, single parents and senior citizens. Their situation at the bottom of the economic picture both reflects and maintains the view of women as less important and less deserving in society than men. It has been fashionable in the last year or two for men, and some women, to present women's inferior status as a thing of the past; as an issue now resolved. Actually, the gap in wages between women and men is increasing and many hard won gains in the areas of affirmative action, alternative social services, health care and child care are being eroded.

The statement of women's oppression is both simple and far reaching. It is a statement which, while it requires no defending, needs to be amplified. To say that women have been and still are oppressed, are treated as objects, as "other," as less than fully human, is to say that women are purely victims. This falls into the trap of seeing ourselves as a monolithic group over all time; passive, helpless bystanders throughout history, acted upon by the men and events which shape it. This is how we have been portrayed. The range and diversity of women's oppression defies such simplistic categorization. Women have been more or less oppressed and have participated in and struggled against oppression in many different ways, times, and places.

Whether or not the roots of oppression are historically grounded in physical/biological differences is unclear. That such differences have been equated with inferiority is no longer a matter for debate but a reflection of the perception which views as inferior all that belongs to or is assigned to women. That same perception assigns to women all that has been already devalued as inferior. Our concern here is with the specific and particular ways in which women in our time and in our society continue to be oppressed. The manifestations and practices which maintain that oppression, and the part which psychiatry plays in it, are the themes which unite the chapters in this collection.

The ways in which the basic oppression of women is woven into the very fabric of our society are wide ranging. An understanding of this must be achieved if the situation of women with regards to psychiatry is to become in any way comprehensible. Similarly the part which psychiatry plays in the social system must be recognized in all its complexity if we are to come to grips with its role vis-à-vis women. Although critics of psychiatry have existed as long as the institution itself, it is only recently that women have developed a perspective which illuminates their experience. What is beginning to be revealed in doing thi work goes far beyond the bounds of the institution itself, since the institution reflects and perpetuates the society of which it is a part.

Initial criticism by women pointed out that psychiatry treats women in stereotypic ways and reinforces existing inequalities. Since psychiatry is in its own terms the very place where we turn for help and healing, it is impossible to reconcile this contradiction without attributing to the institution a mammoth and malign conspiracy to oppress, which is clearly beyond the bounds of reason. To reconcile the contradiction we have to examine psychiatry from outside the framework of its own discipline. Psychiatric expertise is called as evidence in legal proceedings, contributes to the formulation of social policies, and informs texts on parenting, education, sexuality and many other areas. It has been suggested, by men themselves, that much of what is presented in theories as the "psychology of women" is merely patriarchal rhetoric and represents the desires and disappointments of men. It is also significant that only in recent feminist criticism has it become apparent that the "psychology of women" correlates closely with the "characteristics of oppression," a connection entirely overlooked in traditional psychiatric approaches.

When we look at the institution of psychiatry from a perspective of women and seek to understand some of the issues which concern us, we find that there is no way to answer the questions that arise. There is little within the framework of the discipline itself to account for the presence in a "helping profession" of theories which represent women as inferior, destructive or untreatable. There is no explanation for studies that indicate that women receive psychiatric diagnoses when presenting symptoms identical to those for which men receive physiological diagnoses. Nothing accounts for the prevalence of sexual abuse of female patients by their male therapist, or for the high incidence of the prescription of psychotropic drugs to women as compared to men. As "domestic" violence becomes an open issue we are finding many women who have received medical and psychiatric treatment for years without the doctors concerned recognizing that they were being regularly and severely beaten by their husbands. In many areas, such as rape, incest, and wife abuse, we find psychiatric intervention seemingly more concerned with "blaming the victim" and protecting the perpetrators than with helping the women who turn to psychiatrists for aid.

Although there has been considerable debate on the subject of women and psychiatric treatment over the past few years, the debate has remained on the periphery of the discipline. Books, periodicals and articles are often presented as if they represent the new but minor branch of the psychiatric enterprise. Major training texts, such as Freedman, Kaplan and Sadock's *Comprehensive Textbook of Psychiatry,* contain minimal reference to the concerns raised by women or to the new material which they have produced. Indeed, as much energy now seems to be going towards disproving as unfounded the feminist critique as went into attempting to understand or respond to it.

Within the discourse of psychiatry, that is the texts, journals, conferences and literature which are the means by which knowledge is disseminated, there is evidence of much confusion and self-questioning. Critics from within and from without the institution have drawn attention to the lack of effective treatment of many disorders. Practising psychiatrists talk of the "narcissistic depletion," or lack of morale they experience when their work seems ineffective and patients fail to recover. The proliferation of theories and therapeutic methods contributes to confusion. (For example, a count made in 1975 revealed 140 forms of psychotherapy.) So far, however, these difficulties have generally been conceived of as simple contradictions between opposing philosophies. In a contradictory situation there is a choice between one course or another to resolve the dilemma. The choices and solutions offered by psychiatrists include: a more adequate redefinition of the medical model of treatment; stricter adherence to that model; stricter standards of professional control, peer review and monitoring of professional ethics; disengagement from involvement with other institutions which are clearly agencies of the state, such as the penitentiaries and armed services; and better practice and research to counteract the biases which have been uncovered.

Starting our enquiry from the perspective of women leads to the conclusion that the range of solutions proposed from within the psychiatric discourse arises from an inadequate analysis of the nature and mandate of the institution and will not provide the answers women seek. Our consideration of the relation of women to the institution has led us to examine psychiatry as a part of the apparatus through which society is organized and ordered. This facet is obscured by an ideology which presents the legal system, business interests and the professions as neutral bodies outside the domain of the state. The extent to which government, state, and these institutions are interrelated and represent the interests of those in a dominant power position is not evident in our everyday understanding of how society functions.

Psychiatry does not fully acknowledge the nature of this relation to the system. By presenting, and indeed viewing, itself as a profession grounded in the tenets of scientific medicine, it is able to lay claim to an objective body of knowledge with which it purports to cure those ills which are "mental" in nature. As such it represents itself as an "expert service model." Closer examination of the definitions of mental illness and the theory and function of psychiatry reveals a situation fraught with confusion. The conceptualization of dilemmas as resulting from different treatment philosophies, lack of adequate funding and facilities, and a conflict between the needs of the individual and the society mask an intrinsic contradiction. Psychiatry is both part of the ideological and coercive mechanisms of industrial society and at the same time is committed to the resolution of the very tensions and strains which that society and its institutions produce. It is from this central contradiction that many other difficulties stem and this makes it possible for psychiatry to take a part in the oppression of some of the very people it purports, and intends, to help.

Having said this it is important to make it clear that a critique of the structure of the institution is not necessarily a criticism of the individual psychiatrist. It is our experience that most psychiatrists have a deep concern for the well-being of their patients and express disappointment and dismay if some of their interventions are less than effective. The "bad apple" theory so often advanced to explain cases of gross abuse is not sufficient, however, to account for the negative experience of psychiatric interventions reported by numbers of patients. In the chapters that follow we are attempting to show some of the ways that the structure of the institution mitigates against the attempts of individual practioners trying to ensure that their practice is therapeutic. It is our hope that the perspective we offer will provide a context which will allow individual psychiatrists to develop a broader understanding of the dilemmas which they face. Individual solutions, like the solutions offered from within the psychiatric discourse as a whole, avoid the political implications of the location of the institution within the system.

Women's critiques, along with those from medical sociology, critical sociology, and the radical therapy movement, confront us with issues of the social definition of reality, issues of class, race, and sex; the social construction and use of knowledge, history and ideology. These are fundamental issues and ones which we are only beginning to tackle. This presents us with a particular dilemma; as women we are in some very specific ways outside the "frame." This is not accidental, although it may indeed not be deliberate. It arises from the nature of a society which places the power to construct and transmit knowledge in the hands of men; not all men, but those men in the dominant position. This position includes, as its right, power over the very way in which our lives are made sensible, made rational, made comprehensible. It is in this sense that we use the term "ideology"; not as a set of biased and self-interested beliefs, but as a socially produced construction of ideas and explanations; a set of procedures and practices which both accounts for and organizes the social system. In the process, ideology provides an explanation that obscures actuality by providing an alternative view which legitimizes the position of those who create it. Thus, if women's reactions to oppression can be explained in terms of individual pathology, or as a function of feminine psychology, the objective facts of oppression are obscured and need not be changed.

There is a further dimension to the dilemma. Ideology obscures the absence of alternative explanations which might become apparent if those not concerned in its creation had a voice. Women have been excluded from the production of knowledge, the very language of which is full of the relevancies of men. We have not been admitted to the ranks of philosophers, academics and politicians in numbers sufficient to make our voices heard. As women in the mental health profession we have some access to the discourse but when we search for ways of introducing the work of women who are producing other forms of knowledge about women's actual lives and experience, we face the allegation that their testimony is invalid because it is not "psychiatry," it is subjective or unfounded, unscientific. An examination of the sociology of knowledge indicates that in every era the pursuit of "objective" and "unbiased" scientific truth leads to a rationalization of the power relations of that era. Women have not as yet had access to the power structures in ways which would allow them to be equal partners with men in society.

Psychiatry is an institution in a society in which women are oppressed. It plays a specific role in that oppression. Our emphasis in this work is on the interplay of psychiatric ideas and practices which both reflect and influence the perception and treatment of women in society as a whole and by the institution of psychiatry in particular.

This work is a beginning in which we seek to rejoin some of the dimensions of women's experience which the polarizing, typifying and categorizing procedures of conventional modes of thought have rent apart into distinct disciplines and domains. We hope to sketch the outlines for a more holistic approach to women and our experiences which will put the relation of women to psychiatry into a broader context.

The book is divided into three parts which consider first psychiatry as an institution, then women in relation to this institution and, finally, some of the alternative resources and services which we as women are providing for ourselves. Focusing on areas of relevance and concern to women leads us to a rather different organization of material from that which is available in conventional psychiatric texts. There is little in such texts, for example, on violence toward women, or women and "the family," or sex-role stereotyping. This lack in itself reflects the relevancies of those who control the production and dissemination of knowledge. We have not, however, been able to cover in one volume the many and diverse areas in which vital material about women is being developed. Issues such as women's sexuality and lesbianism have already evoked many volumes in their own right; they have barely been touched on here. We have developed a framework for exploration which could be used in considering such issues, but must leave to others the ongoing task of putting together the knowledge vital for our growth and power.

The first two chapters examine how the need for the presentation of an "expert service model" has resulted in the construction of a history of psychiatry to support this position. The increasing use of medical practices as solutions to social problems highlights the contradiction between this model and the actual relation of psychiatry to the state. Seeing the direct and indirect relation of psychiatry to the way in which society is organized and ordered makes evident how the confusion, repressive treatment and injustice which critics have pointed out can exist within a profession which is committed to humanitarian ideals and a model of healing. This perspective locates the current crisis in the psychiatric discourse within the framework of the broader sphere of the ideological, political and economic crises of our times.

In Chapter III we attempt to show how psychiatry as an "expert service model" provides a method for understanding, and in some ways coping with, socially organized situations as personal and individual problems. This method functions to locate and contain within the individual and family unit the distress, damage and dysfunctional aspects of the system in which we live. As such it involves an elaborate framework for "blaming the victim" for her or his troubles. This framework obscures the variety of experiences of those who are differently located in and articulated to society. The dominant group in a society based on unequal power relations perceives its position and its views as normative, and all other groups as either sharing the same interests or as deviant through some lack or fault of their own. The dominant group controls the production and dissemination of ideas and is seldom aware that the voices and experiences of other groups are silent and invisible. Psychiatry, as part of the dominant group in this social setting, has been unaware, at least until recently, of the ideological nature of its position. This has contributed to the proliferation of accounts and modalities which purport to deal with a variety of syndromes but which, in many cases, have evolved to counteract or normalize the disjunctures between the experiences of different groups by relating distress and disruption to personal pathology.

The fourth chapter stresses that the recognition of a dominant group position in psychiatry is of particular significance for women. Women have never had a major place in the production of ideas and their experience is represented only through the eyes of the predominantly male dominant class. Certainly, and ironically, there have been theorists among women in psychiatry as perhaps nowhere else. This has been offered as proof that psychiatry is a non-discriminatory institution. The particular place of women theorists in psychiatry is illuminating. They have, in the main, worked to elaborate or reinforce originally male tenets of the nature of feminity or the role of women as mothers in the genesis of mental illness. Some theorists have disputed some of the teachings as being androcentric, but few have as yet introduced an understanding of women's experience as women present it. Much psychiatric theory regarding women is revealed as more ideological than scientific. It contains images and symbols of women which, when examined, prove to be archetypes and stereotypes. These have changed and developed but have always been presented in a mythical manner as representing the actual nature of women for all times. Such images and symbols are part of the network of ideas which have been used to enforce women's roles and to control the activities of women through the centuries. In appropriating them as scientific theory, psychiatry functions as a form of social control through, over, and above its actual practices of treatment and incarceration.

Chapter V contains a review of the widespread and confusing array of literature on sex and gender identity. This material highlights the fact that "masculinity" and "femininity" are social constructs which have little necessary relationship to maleness or femaleness but which vary according to the political demands of the time. Psychiatric theories both produce and reflect the political realities of social organization and provide a method for their enforced internalization as self-image or gender identity. This chapter examines the debate between traditional theories, which stress the absolute necessity for rigid and polarized sex roles, and recent work which suggests that a flexible and androgynous self-definition is fundamental to the realization of human potential.

Theories about the family, described in Chapter VI, commonly attribute problems in the children or in family relationships to the "bad mother" who has failed to meet her children's needs or to catalyse appropriate relationships in the family. Less frequently are absent fathers, deviant children or total families held responsible. Despite much evidence to the contrary, these theories and related attitudes are still pervasive. The ascendancy of various theories in different time periods can be understood if they are studied in relation to predominant social, political and economic trends. Set in its historical perspective, the family as an institution is seen to change in relation to the economic structuring of society. Although the family is seen to be a private place where individual emotional needs are met, the fact is that experiences, patterns and attitudes evolve in a direction that best meets the needs of society. Families are forced to absorb tensions that arise in the "public" realm. Mothers, in turn, are expected to be the emotional mediators and organizers of families. The stage is set for theories which, reflecting popular beliefs, blame individual families or individual family members, and obscure the root of problems within our social structures.

Violence towards women is an aspect of our society which is barely considered; its prevalence is such that it is almost commonplace. In many instances it is concealed in issues such as "domestic" or "family" violence or pornography. Psychiatric theories and attitudes, the penal system, and other institutions of society reflecting and reinforcing stereotypes of femininity and masculinity, serve to condone or to minimize the serious nature of violence towards women. Rape is the major focus of Chapter VII, and serves as a paradigm for examining other forms of violence towards women. In rape, as in wife beating and incest, it is the victim who is presented as the cause of the act. To understand society's primitive stance toward women and children who are the victims of assault, it is necessary to look at historical and cross-cultural views of women, and to take into account their enforced dependency in the family structure.

There is a high incidence of depression in women, especially among mothers of young children. The rate of prescription of anti-depressant drugs to women is correspondingly high. Chapter VIII examines the ambiguities which surround the definitions and classifications of depression and the effect of the variety of definitions on the treatment of women. Despite the possible relevance of some existing theories, their focus on individual women obscures other issues. The effect of a woman's daily experience, while living out her expected role in the family and subject to stresses generated by present social structures, is seldom considered. Recent theoretical work by women demonstrates a link between women's social situation and clinical depression. It is the work of the non-psychiatric writers, however, that fully illuminates women's misery, the drudgery of their lives, their self-abnegation and reliance on others for their identity.

An examination of the use of psychotropic drugs in the management of a variety of conditions highlights the relationship of psychiatry to the broader social context of which it is a part. The focus in the ninth chapter is on the use of mind-altering drugs in the treatment of women, and draws attention to the close connection between drug prescription and stereotyped views of women's role. Physician's attitudes, stimulated and reinforced by drug company advertising, seem to be based on traditional expectations of women rather than on scientific evidence of the efficacy of drug treatment. The place of prescription drugs in patient managment is often seen to be a function of control as opposed to treatment. It is this aspect of drug use which throws doubt on the claim that more effective treatment procedures have been the moving force behind the community health approach and the decline of the large mental hospital. Women, as the most frequent users of psychotropic drugs, are predominant among those whose distress and dysfunction is minimized and individualized by the current trend in drug usage.

A feminist perspective and the various analyses which grow out of it leads to a different view of both the problems and treatment of women from that held by traditional psychiatry. Feminism is by no means a party line, but it is a political vision which recognizes the vital and essential humanity of women. There are a number of stances within the philosophy. Chapter X looks at some of these and the measures which have developed from them. Many women who seek psychiatric help do so because it is the only kind of help that appears to be valid and is also covered by medical insurance. This is a major factor, since women are seldom affluent. Feminists believe that much of the misery and distress that women experience does not require therapy or treatment in the traditional sense. The consciousness of oppression has implications for alternative approaches such as those developed in self-help groups, women's studies, political action and consciousness raising. The significance of existing alternatives which women have developed becomes clear in this context.

This chapter is also concerned with the appropriateness of feminist therapy. The task of reclaiming what feminist theorists have described as the "colonized territory" of our bodies and minds involves dealing with the internalization and perpetuation of oppression which has heretofore been described as the "psychology of women." The Women's Health Movement has been in the forefront of this action and feminist therapists are providing the impetus for new areas of exploration. This involves discovering new ways of thinking; reviewing old concepts and developing new ones which serve rather than rule our thinking. We need to reassess such concepts as shame, guilt, autonomy, actualization, individuation, homosexuality and above all "femininity" and its relation, if any, to femaleness.

The implications for psychiatry of a recognition that many of its theories are worse than irrelevant for women (who form almost two-thirds of its constitutents) are grave and far-reaching. There is little within the traditional discourse to build upon. What we as women know about ourselves we know from each other, from our novels, diaries, poetry, films, art, the work of our scholars, and from our sharing of the struggle towards a "common language." Those engaged in formulating knowledge of women will have to be prepared to tap these resources as well as their own clinical experience if their work is to prove itself relevant to women's needs.

Looking at the issues faced by women, not as merely individual or psychological, but as embedded in the social construction of reality leads to a questioning of the very basis of the institution of psychiatry. It has been suggested that the social sciences, including psychiatry, are at a pre-paradigm level of knowledge. We suggest that a paradigm of mental illness as individual pathology exists, but that epistemologically it is gravely flawed. The history of psychiatry is often described as consisting of a number of revolutions. The crisis, as illuminated by women's perspective, indicates the need for a new paradigm which could provide for the greatest revolution yet.

≡ ≡ ≡

PART ONE

PSYCHIATRY
AS AN
INSTITUTION

≡*CHAPTER I*

A CRITIQUE OF THE
HISTORY OF PSYCHIATRY

IN EXAMINING THE HISTORY OF PSYCHIATRY
as an institution it is important to appreciate the ways in which mental
health services are integrated into the overall health care system. All
societies typically respond to disturbed and disturbing behaviour "by
designating individuals and evolving social institutions whose primary
function is to evaluate, interpret, and provide corrective measures.
Medicine as an institution and as a discipline, and physicians as professionals, evolved as one form of response to such social needs."[1] The
institutions of law, religion and education serve a purpose, either by
disseminating information and understanding deemed relevant for effective social organization, or by furnishing sanctions and corrective
measures when an area of functioning is threatened. In our society
these institutions are, in the main, operated by those individuals or
groups who have access to education, training and status, and who,
therefore, occupy a social location within the dominant class. This is a
determinate position in, and relationship to, the political and economic
systems through which the society is organized and run.

When the medical enterprise is seen solely as an independent professional endeavour, drawing its authority not from its relationship to
the ruling structures but from access to scientific practices, objective
truths, healing powers and humanitarian ideals, the elements of its
functioning that stem from the requirement that it enforce social rules
become puzzling and problematic, if they are visible at all. What could
be described as merely a contradiction, a debate between whose needs
are to be served, the individual or those in power in the society to

which he or she belongs, can be seen as a paradoxical injunction for medicine if it undertakes to serve both needs as its central mandate.[2] The "objective" medical position assumes that the needs of the individual will correspond to those of society if the individual is healthy; thus the equation of health with conformity to a particular set of beliefs becomes a moral issue in which ". . . judgements are made not in the name of virtue or legitimacy, but in the name of health."[3]

What is obscured by the presentation of medicine as an independent profession is not only the potential for oppression in the relationship between the physician and those seeking help, but also the manner in which the relationship between medicine and political, administrative and bureaucratic structures affect the form of the profession, its independent and entrepreneurial aspects and the services its delivers.

The nature of this paradox and the current crisis in scientific medicine can both be traced to roots in the development of the medical and mental health professions as we understand them today. One of the difficulties in doing so, however, arises from the recognition that much of what obscures the relation of medicine to the social system is the way in which the history of science, medicine and psychiatry have been presented. The body of current and historical material used in training physicians and mental health personnel downplays or takes little account of the elements of social control and moral sanction which have been convincingly delineated by critics of the institution.

THE TRADITIONAL VIEW OF THE HISTORY OF PSYCHIATRY

The history of psychiatry is usually presented as a complex picture of an elaborate and essentially medical system. This system is traced back to the earliest records of western civilization and beyond.[4] The historical process is shown to be an accumulation of a body of scientific knowledge and skill in treatment which has developed from roots in classical Greek and Arab teachings. It reveals the ways in which the mentally ill have been treated by psychiatrists and their direct equivalents or counterparts. Psychiatry is depicted as an aspect of the "march of progress"; a scientific enterprise motivated by the search for knowledge and the evolution of increasingly humanitarian ideals. It is now seen as taking its rightful place as the crucial and leading component in the multi-faceted mental health institution of today. The institution is thus equipped to handle an ever-broadening range of personal and social problems which are the result of individual inability to deal with the increasing complexity and rapid change of modern industrial society.

This view of psychiatry as an orderly accumulation of knowledge and skill presents those seeking to understand its function with a number of difficulties. The way in which the conventional picture has been drawn conveys an understanding of the institution that does not account for the frequent contradictions and anomalies which are evident in the critical writings of many commentators. Before we attempt to develop an understanding that would better illuminate the nature of the institution, it is important to recognize how the conventional view is arrived at, and why it continues to hold sway. In doing so, we are by no means suggesting that events have been falsified to fit the picture in any deliberate sense, only that their selection and emphasis distorts the image by presenting a part as the whole.

Kuhn formulates a similar argument when discussing the difficulties involved in understanding the nature of the overall scientific enterprise from an examination of the accounts of historians.[5] He draws attention to the method by which an orderly, developmental account of the progress of scientific endeavours is created. Kuhn maintains that the images drawn from the study of finished achievements, presented as they are in the classics and in textbooks, are fundamentally misleading. They bear, he suggests, no more resemblance to the enterprise that produced them "than an image of a national culture drawn from a tourist brochure or a language text."[6]

By this process of historical reconstruction, Kuhn suggests, science is depicted as the constellation of facts, theories and methods collected in current texts, and scientists as the men [sic] who have struggled, with or without success, to contribute to it. The task of the scientific historian then becomes one of chronicling contributions to the ever-growing stockpile of knowledge and noting which obstacles have interfered with that accumulation. This two-fold task involves determining which man [sic] at which time discovered or extended a law, theory, or fact, and also describing and explaining the errors and myths that inhibited the more rapid acceptance and accumulation of such laws and theories.

A brief review of the history of psychiatry taken from texts in current use and readily available articles,[7] indicates that a similar process is at work. Psychiatry is characterized as being the result of the melding of three streams; the custodial, the medical, and the behavioral science, or alternatively couched in terms of Mental Health's Three Revolutions.[8] Progress in understanding and treating mental illness becomes a cumulative matter, an implementation of rudimentary psychiatric theories beginning with prehistoric and primitive medicine men who "undoubtedly added native psychologicial wit to magical science."[9] This tradition was carried on by the priestly attendants of the Greek god Aesculapius, by Hippocrates, the Father of Medicine,[10] by St. Augustine,[11] and many other early figures.

"The First Revolution" is depicted as following a period of ignorance and superstition during the middle ages, when lunatics, if cared for at all, were incarcerated in asylums such as Bethlehem Priory — from which the term bedlam originates. This revolution in care was initiated by great men such as Tuke, the Quaker philanthropist who founded The Retreat near York, and Pinel, the physician who struck the chains off the lunatics in Paris. They and their supporters were instrumental in initiating various forms of the Moral Management mode of treatment under which lunatics were treated with dignity and concern, and with the expectation that they would learn to behave in a manner that would allow them to return to their lives outside the asylum. This custodial treatment modality had considerable influence and was employed in Britian, Europe and on the eastern seaboard of North America, but it was short-lived. During this same period, in the early nineteenth century, Rush, known as the Father of American Psychiatry, recognized that lunacy and alcoholism were caused by disease and were thus the purview of the physician. In the mid-nineteenth century, reformers such as Dorothea Dix campaigned for changes in custodial conditions, which produced bigger, better and separate asylums for the care of the insane.

"The Second Psychiatric Revolution" is generally attributed to Freud and his contemporaries, who were responsible for the introduction of psychotherapy. Although mainly concerned with the outpatient treatment of neurotic disturbances, this movement was extremely influential as a general treatment modality for the mentally ill. Sullivan and Fromm-Reichman pioneered the use of psychotherapy with psychotic or more severely disturbed patients; and Sullivan's work on the interpersonal aspects of the development of identity had a marked impact on the conceptualization of personality, and led to a return to the recognition of interactive components in both illness and treatment. This coincided with the advent of certain physical therapies such as electroconvulsive and insulin shock treatment and psychosurgery. These developments led to a re-emphasis on treatment rather than on purely custodial care. Also, a part of this stream was the informational input from the rapidly expanding fields of the behavioural sciences, chiefly psychology but including sociology and cultural anthropology.

Psychiatry's "Third Revolution" is considered by historians and commentators to have been produced by new discoveries in psychopharmacology. This fortuitous development occurred at a time of rapid advance in the knowledge of genetic and biochemical factors in mental illness. A growing national and political concern with the plight of the mentally ill and the effect of long-term incarceration in asylums and mental hospitals combined with the medical advances to create a climate of hope and dedication to change. Tenets and concepts from the public health model showed the way for the growth of the community mental health movement, and the availability of psychotropic medication opened up the possibility of early treatment and the cure or maintenance and care of mental patients in their own communities. The avowed intent in many programs at this stage was the closure of all of the large and isolated asylums and mental hospitals.

Historians acknowledge some regrettable but unavoidable lapses in this orderly progression. These are dutifully recorded in the chronicle, just as Kuhn predicts in his analysis of traditionally presented histories of science. The setbacks are usually portrayed as due to external pressures in the form of historical forces, and are often presented as the precipitating factors in each era of reform or evolution. For example, during the dark ages after the fall of the Roman Empire, superstition is presented as having superseded classical wisdom. Historians suggest that many unfortunates who would now be recognized as mentally ill were treated as possessed by demons or burnt at the stake as witches, and those who survived were imprisoned in chains until the more enlightened policies of Tuke, Pinel and Chiarugi provided humane alternatives.

The Industrial Revolution is seen as producing an upheaval in social conditions which led to rapid change and to the urbanization of large sections of the population. This divorced lunatics from their communities and led to the building of large warehouse-like asylums which became overcrowded and unmanageable. The ignorance and brutality of attendants is held to have contributed to an unfortunate lack of care for the insane. Similarly, the depressed economic conditions in late nineteenth-century Europe, which drove masses of deprived (or depraved) immigrants to North America, is seen as the cause of further intense overcrowding of asylums as fast as they were built. This, combined with the concurrent emphasis on hereditary factors in etiology, backed up by theories based on Social Darwinsim, is seen as having a moribund effect on treatment and on the morale of psychiatrists, or alienists, as they were more often called at that time.

The climate is then recognized as right for the revolution sparked by Freud and his followers, but this in turn is viewed as tending to excess and leading to a preoccupation with intrapsychic processes. Therapists of all disciplines gravitated to the office desk. The limitations of universal psychoanalytic treatment, a slow, time-consuming process, are assumed to have become evident in the face of the large numbers of potential patients revealed by the screening methods developed during the Second World War, and the undeniable success of short-term crisis intervention which was pioneered in that context. Broader social definitions of mental illness are identified as indicators of the need for widespread programs and an increase in trained personnel, and the stage is thus set for the "Third Revolution";[12] that of the community mental health movement.

This brief outline is, of course, condensed and simplified. The texts studied cover, in varying degrees of detail, many schools, movements and theoretical stances that held sway in different countries, and deal with the development of categorization of disease phenomena, diagnostic schema and external influences, such as the lay organizations which worked for reform, like the Mental Hygiene Movement. The overall impression is still congruent with Kuhn's description of the image gained by writing with the particular kind of hindsight which selects from the broad canvas of events those which contribute to an ever-increasing stockpile of knowledge, expertise and skill. Psychiatry is thus shown to have surmounted all setbacks and enlarged its scope, and the scope of its attendant disciplines, to the point where it can offer solutions to the problems that face the world in the declining years of the twentieth century.[13]

Caplan suggests a further reason for this particular form of historical image.[14] She draws attention to the traditional method of presenting history through biographies of the careers and theories of such eminent figures as Pinel, Kraepelin, Freud and Meyer. This tended to produce a narrowing of focus and a distortion of perspective in which ". . . the development of the care of the insane appeared as a teleological growth from the healing shrines of antiquity and the superstitious cruelty of the Middle Ages to the scientific and humanitarian attitudes of the nineteenth and twentieth centuries. This traditional focus on outstanding individuals implied undemonstrated connections between [their] ideas and obscured the relationship between men whom we now regard as enlightened leaders, and the prevailing practices and ideas of their own time."[15]

In a detailed chapter on the historical and theoretical trends in psychiatry, in the *Comprehensive Textbook of Psychiatry*, Mora deplores the "old-fashioned view of history as the unfolding of the great man theory — that is, as a succession of unrelated creative flashes by individual men, quite often in the assumption of unproved teleological postulates."[16] He sees psychiatrists so far as being "ill equipped to deal with historical matters because of their amateurish historical perspective, a tendency to focus on great men . . . and even more important an inclination to view history . . . from the biased adherence to a particular school."[17] Mora points out that the study of the history of psychiatry actually developed concurrently with psychiatry itself in the Age of Englightenment of the eighteenth century, during the time when men were concerned with learning from their own history. He sees it as having become insular and inadequate with the rise of nineteenth-century nationalism. Mora welcomes the return of a broader focus on the mid-twentieth century, and offers his own chapter as recognition of "events that anticipated modern methods of physical psychiatric therapy, psychopharmacology, and hospital care as well as those that led to the focus on psycho-dynamics [in the hope] that each reader will be able to identify the historical antecedents of his own philosophy of psychiatry and, thus, to acquire a deeper and broader understanding of it."[18]

The new approach which Mora represents emphasizes the importance of considering historical events within the cultural configurations and climate of opinion in which they occurred. This would seem to be compatible with Kuhn's description of the approach of a new group of scientific historians who are endeavoring "to display the historical integrity of science in its own time." From this perspective, Kuhn suggests, "Science does not seem altogether the same enterprise as the one discussed by writers of the older historiographic tradition. By implication, at least, these historical studies suggest the possibility of a new image of science."[19] To do so, Kuhn proposes that distortions be avoided by abandoning the procedures that seek out permanent contributions of ideas from older science to "our present vantage."[20]

Mora, however, embraces the conclusion reached by Agassi[21] "that history should be viewed from the perspective of a continuity — that is, a slow development of events, each occurring in the context of a given historical background, characterized by the prevalence or, conversely, inhibition of particular themes or clusters of prescriptions." What Mora depicts as a radical departure from old-fashioned treatments of history turns out, however, to read very much like a combination of the "great man" approach and Kuhn's rejected science textbook approach; tied together but made more complicated than ever by reference to the cultural climate of the times in which the events occurred.

While recognizing that "the field of psychiatry is now in the state of uncertainty and restlessness"[22] and that "a great variety of contrasting trends and assumptions are at the base of psychiatry's theoretical and practical formulations,"[23] Mora still views these oppositional trends as a cumulative entity. He proposes that history, ". . . by pointing to similarities between now and the past, and the apparent cyclic occurrence of attitudes and customs and the basic consistency of human needs and ways of solving problems — may offer much needed guidelines."[24]

As an eloquent elaboration of the methods indicted by Kuhn, Mora's account bears that relationship to the actual psychiatric enterprise which Kuhn likened to the image of a country drawn from tourist brochures or language texts. Study of such a descriptive chronicle does not offer the possibility of a critical analysis of the enterprise. A critical analysis is necessary, however, to allow for an alternative understanding from which to proceed. Mora suggests that psychiatry's current broadmindedness and openness to new ideas and influences is a sign of hope in a time of confusion. If it leads to a further proliferation of competing theories, schools and ideas, it seems unlikely that the outcome will be either a clarification or a change in the image of the essential nature of the institution.

The historical method discussed is not entirely fortuitous, or merely inadequate, however. It is, as Kuhn points out, "deeply and probably functionally, ingrained in the ideology of the scientific profession." He suggests that the temptation to write history backwards is greater for scientists, although it is an omnipresent tendency in all disciplines. The inclusion of certain historical details and scientific accounts may give "artificial status to human idiosyncrasy, error and confusion [and] dignify what science's best and most persistent efforts have made it possible to discard."[25]

There is a deeper level of ideological functioning here that Kuhn intimates. The process of writing history backwards promotes an assumption of the absolute truth of current formulations, and thus attributes a moral tone of "rightness" to the scientific enterprise. Psychiatry's adherence to a historical tradition that is identified with scientific endeavour serves to emphasize the discipline's position, and so carves out a territorial claim to a particular expertise and a legitimate function and status within the realm of science. With this position goes access to the moral sanctions subsumed under the aegis of scientific truth. The kind of historical perspective that implies an orderly progression is an eminently justifiable attempt by historians to bring systematic and logical order to a diverse and complex field. However, this method requires that all consideration of human behaviour, thought processes and disorders from time immemorial be subsumed under the label of "psychology." Almost any historical figure who was concerned with the individual is, or can then be called, a psychiatrist or psychologist, even though these terms as we know them were not used until the nineteenth century.[26] Bomberg, for example, is particularly proficient at intellectual "sleight-of-phrase." He notes that psychotherapy, as a definitive discipline, did not exist until the latter part of the eighteenth century, and admits that it is only from a modern vantage point that forces can be traced from classical times to the present fabric of society. At the same time he offers such summaries of historical trends as: "Psychology (metaphysics) beckoned students . . .," and ". . . the moral (emotional) factors underlying insanity . . ."[27]

Through an orderly progression, the assumption of the mantles of law and religion by medicine in general and psychiatry in particular are seen to proceed virtually without question. The equation of scientific diagnoses of sickness and health with moral judgements of legitimacy and virtue leads to the recognition of physicians as the moral and spiritual guardians of physical and mental health. Bomberg accomplishes this impression with two words: "Monkish physicians." He manages to imply, in his discussion of this aspect of historical development, that lay overseers were responsible for all punishment and neglect while godly and/or medical men were concerned only with justice, humanity and medical treatment.[28] By attributing solely humanitarian motives to members of the institution, such historians ignore the entrepreneurial aspects of the profession's development and its struggle for status. This obscures the actual relationship of that status to the physician's location as part of the agencies of social control in society.[29] In this way the profession appears as independent of the institutional constraints exercised by the administrative and bureaucratic procedures involved. The extent to which these procedures organize and limit the freedom to work as a "professional" is obscured. Record-keeping, referral procedures, and the diagnostic procedures necessary to maintain payment schedules, for example, are seldom considered to be factors in treatment practices, which are presumed to stem directly from theoretical precepts. It is also impossible to see, in this form of account, that the institution of psychiatry is part of the organization and operation of the social system in which we live. As such it represents and enforces the interests of those who rule and administer the system.[30]

The supposition of a consistent and cohesive scientific knowledge base delineates psychiatry as being in possession incontrovertible truth about human development, behaviour and personality, and the nature of pathology. According to this schema, the institution has progressed to the point where mental illness can be prevented by public health methods such as early screening, parent effectiveness training, and consultation with the education system. A number of therapeutic modalities can be used to cure or, if chronic, control and care for those cases where prevention proves impossible. This is seen as a result of the availability of a range of treatment methods which can be adapted to the individual skills and preferences of the psychiatrist and to the needs of the patient.

Such a supposition is based on the assumption that psychiatry has developed an unambiguous definition of an unambiguous phenomenon, mental illness, which is universal and cross-cultural. Whatever the cause, mental illness is seen as intrapsychic in manifestations and amenable to accurate diagnosis from discrete symptomatology. Diagnostic procedures thus dictate appropriate treatment, under the objective medical direction of the psychiatrist. Since the phenomenon is general, this diagnostic and treatment procedure is held to be equally applicable to any patient regardless of race, class or sex.

Most psychiatrists and commentators will recognize that this is a somewhat "tourist brochure" picture of what actually happens. The anomalies in this position are evident on all sides. Studies of diagnosis, referral and treatment, such as that done by Hollingshead and Redlich, show clear differences which relate to socio-economic class.[31] Rosenhan's pseudopatient experiment throws grave doubt on the ability of mental hospital staff to distinguish between "normal" behaviour and mental illness.[32] The studies which have failed to prove diagnostic reliability are too numerous to list. Men and women have received different diagnoses and treatment for the same symptoms.[33] Yet, in spite of these difficulties, failure to correspond to current models or to respond to a particular treatment mode is frequently characterized as a function, not of the inadequacy of the formulation available, but of the internal differences or deficiencies of the individual patient or group of patients. The so-called "verbal therapies," for example, are generally recognized to be less effective for certain groups, such as immigrant or working-class people, because members of such groups are seen to be deficient in language skills, less articulate, and less educated. The possibility that they may face problems, such as unemployment or poverty, which are not amenable to verbal solutions, is seldom considered. The definition of deficiency or inability to make use of the verbal model is used to explain the use of drug therapy, incarceration, etc., as the appropriate treatment for these groups. It is virtually impossible for the patient in this system to challenge the psychiatrist and express, or even come to understand, that which happens in her or his life experience; problems or distress do not conform to the formulations offered by the experts. The professional has a monopoly on diagnosis and supervision of appropriate treatment. Patients who do not fit categories or respond to treatment are thus seen as recalcitrant or resistant, both of which can then be categorized as symptoms of their illness. This circular process maintains the power relation of "doer" and "done to."

Available forms of history have produced an image of psychiatry which has been described as an "expert service model." It is a model that contains so many contradictions that psychiatrists can be described by their proponents as the rightful champions of the mentally ill, an oppressed group in society, and by their detractors as the major oppressors of that self-same group. An example of both points of view was provided at the 1977 World Congress of Mental Health in Vancouver. Bertram Brown challenged mental health professionals to act as advocates for their patients, who are an oppressed group in society, while Rosemary Brown spoke of the consistent use of psychiatric ideas and practices as a method of oppression for people throughout the world.[34] Psychiatrists who experience the strains and contradictions of the current state of the profession, struggle to find solutions to the many dilemmas they face. Because the image of the institution provided within its own texts and discussions is limited to the "expert service" analysis, however, these solutions often propose measures that remain within the bounds of that analysis. Abuses can only be conceived of in terms of the incompetent practices of individual psychiatrists, lack of strict professional controls, incomplete theoretical knowledge, or an inadequate definition of disease. Solutions offered so far include a more adequate re-definition of the medical model, stricter standards and professional controls, disengagement from involvement with other institutions which are clearly agencies of government control, such as prisons and the armed services, and better practice and research to counteract any biases which may have been uncovered.[35]

A more comprehensive understanding of the institution of psychiatry in relation to the social system in which it operates is necessary in order to account for the difficulties it faces. Without such an understanding, it is not possible to answer the criticism that has arisen both inside and outside the framework of the discipline. This criticism comes from a variety of forces. Sometimes it is voiced by disillusioned psychiatrists themselves;[36] sometimes by sociologists and psychologists;[37] sometimes by historians, philosophers and scholars of other disciplines.[38] There are numerous accounts of the destructive experience of being a mental patient, written by patients themselves or recreated in fictional form by novelists and filmmakers. Recent criticism from a feminist perspective has the added dimension of drawing attention to the normative and prescriptive content of psychiatric theory and practice.[39]

It is from this last perspective that a broader view can be assembled; one that makes it possible to sketch an outline into which the experience of women in general, and as patients in particular, can be entered. In doing so, it also becomes possible to see how other members of the mental health profession fit into a picture that usually focusses on the psychiatrist-patient relationship alone. That relationship itself takes on a different aspect when seen as an interaction between proponents of different class, race or sexual status. Finally, bureaucratic constraints and influences can be taken into account. From this viewpoint, it is

— 15

hoped that more comprehensive solutions to the current crisis will become apparent, solutions that meet not only the needs of the profession, but also the needs of those who are its victims.

≡   ≡   ≡

CHAPTER TWO

TOWARD A BROADER
VIEW OF THE INSTITUTION

TO WRITE AN ALTERNATIVE HISTORY of psychiatry that locates the development of the institution within the context of the development of the social system of which it is a part would require a full-length text in itself. What follows is a brief summary of some of the factors involved. It indicates the direction that such an enterprise might take in detailing the rise of the institution and its place in contemporary industrial society.

The authority for the state's exercise of power over the "person of the insane" is traced by Kittrie to three distinct conceptual sources that are fundamental to the Anglo-American political system. He provides a historical context and definition of what he terms the "therapeutic state," which is used here, along with the work of other critics already cited.[1]

First, the state as protector of the peace may exercise its general policing powers in all cases where public order is disturbed or threatened. Next, the power of *Parens Patriae* provides for the guardianship of the property of the legally disabled; a function performed in medieval England by the feudal lord of the area in which a lunatic resided. As the power of the Crown was consolidated in the thirteenth century, this function was assumed by the officers of the state in the name of the King. The third consideration is the power of the Crown over the indigent insane as members of the pauper community. Kittrie notes that the social control exercised through these functions has developed from a penal to a therapeutic model, which is congruent with an increase in the responsibility of the state for total public welfare.

Tracing the roots of the "therapeutic state" to the Middle Ages, as Kittrie suggests, uncovers the foundations of modern society and its ruling structures. Scull[2] also sees a progression from the Middle Ages to modern times in approaches to problems posed by the need to control the difficult and the dangerous. He suggests three features of modern society which, although analytically distinct, are empirically closely connected. These features cannot be accounted for without a historical perspective. They are: the state's substantial involvement in direct social control and the emergence of a highly rationalized and centrally administered apparatus; the creation of institutions largely segregated from the surrounding community, committed to the treatment of many types of deviance; and the emergence of professional and semi-professional "experts" in the "helping occupations," each charged with ministering to increasingly differentiated sorts of deviance.[3] Scull's analysis allows for a consideration of the implication of the profession in the process of social control. How that relation developed is crucial to an understanding of the dilemmas of modern psychiatry.

Prior to the sixteenth century, those who could not or would not be useful to their community, and could not be cared for in the community, tended to be cast out. Lazariums (leper colonies) and marginal lands were populated by vagabonds, lepers, madmen and other unfortunates. Those housed within cities were kept in the gatehouses, and archers were employed to keep the unwanted away from the cities. The ship of fools, in which lunatics were cast adrift, was a practical and symbolic solution, water and madness having been seen as connected since the Grecian era. Only the most unmanageable were treated in this manner; church hospices, hospitals and other simple institutions provided custodial care for some poor, orphaned, aged, sick or lost souls who were beyond the care of the community.

By the early sixteenth century, the upheavals caused by the struggles of European monarchies to consolidate the power of the Crown over the power of the Catholic Church effectively undermined ecclesiastical responses to the needs of the indigent. This happened at a time when demands for internal order were increasing. In England, the Reformation and the dissolution of the monasteries weakened the role of the church in civil society. Under the Poor Law Act of 1601, ecclesiastical responsibility was replaced by the principle of secular involvement, with parishes empowered to levy taxes for the support of the indigent. Parochial systems continued to provide for many unfortunates, chiefly through "household relief," a form of pension paid to relatives or others perepared to care for them. The growing commercialization of agriculture pauperized large numbers of people, who became an increasing burden on the parish and a threat to order. Although "houses of confinement" existed during the sixteenth and seventeenth centuries, it was not until the late eighteenth and early nineteenth centuries that a sizeable part of the indigent population was housed in institutions. The population of most institutions, prior to the nineteenth century, was somewhat mixed. Little attenton was paid to the precise categorization of deviants, except in a few specialized charity asylums and private madhouses. Workhouses, almshouses and asylums received young and old, men and women, the decrepit, dependent, and the unmanageable of all types.

A major thrust of the nineteenth-century reform movement was directed towards the provision of separate institutions for different categories of deviance. It has been argued that the Industrial Revolution and its concomitant urbanization was responsible for the institutional response to the rapid breakdown of social structures and the corresponding increase in mental illness. Scull, however, shows that pressures to differentiate and institutionalize the deviant occurred before the vast industrial cities contained more than a minority of the population.[4] It is his contention that the development of institutional methods of control arises, in large part, from the profound change in social relations brought about by the economic upheavals caused by the growth of a capitalist market system. The economic dominance and subordination of a feudal society contained a dimension of personal ties and responsibilities. Now paternalism, deference, dependence and a sense of obligation towards the unfortunate was replaced by a system in which employers owed only wages to employees.

The care and control of the unemployed unemployables became the concern of the state, since it was beyond the capacity of most working people to care for incapacitated members of the community. The middle and upper classes were required to take up the social costs of the market system through taxes and philanthropy. They became increasingly concerned with accurate differentiation between the deserving and undeserving poor: those who must be forced to work by the withholding of relief payments and those whose disabilities made them legitimate objects of charitable concern. With the majority of the working class living at a bare subsistence level, the payment of a "household relief" form of pension was seen as an encouragement to idleness at the expense of the middle classes. This climate of fiscal awareness fostered a ready response to the efforts of reformers such as Dorothea Dix, whose aim was to differentiate the forms of institutions in order to provide distinct and humane care for the mentally ill and incapacitated.

Once the massive capital outlay required to build asylums, hospitals, orphan homes, reformatories and prisons had been committed, successive waves of reformers had little success in attempting to prove the perils of institutionalization. Banishing unproductive or difficult family members to warehouse-like institutions, where they were isolated from the community, remained the major solution until such time as the conditions that had brought the institutions into being had been superseded by various forms of welfare state. By the middle of the twentieth century, changes in social organization and the physical decay of many large facilities built in the previous century made the process of "decarceration" feasible. Scull suggests that the availability of welfare payments and spiralling costs of maintaining an inmate population were the main impetus behind the community mental health and other decarceration movements. Strong trends towards emptying the state's mental hospitals and returning patients to the community are evident prior to the discovery of psychotropic drugs, which traditional history cites as the precipitating factor.[5]

PSYCHIATRY AND THE DEFINITION OF MENTAL ILLNESS: A CASE OF CONCEPTUAL IMPERIALISM

From the perspective briefly outlines here, the history of psychiatry is seen to be something other than an orderly "march of progress" of the ideas and methods involved in caring for the mentally ill. It is closely interwoven with the social and economic development of modern capitalist society; a process far more complex, and even chaotic, than the term "march of progress" implies. Mora suggests that developments within the institution of psychiatry should be related to the cultural considerations and climate of opinion of the times in which they occurred. This approach will only be useful if an understanding of cultural configurations includes the changing economic structure in which they are embedded.[6]

Within this framework it is possible to correlate the actual differentiation of psychiatry as a profession with the first uses of the title and the separating out of categories of institutional population in the early nineteenth century.[7] Scull suggests that psychiatry provides the clearest example of that differentiation and the concomitant development of "expert" professions. As "mad-doctors," a number of physicians had begun to evolve an elaborate rationale for their treatment procedures. The somewhat loose cultural construct of madness was transformed by them into an ostensibly scientific, coherent phenomenon produced by underlying pathology.[8] It is clear that Navarro refers to the same process of development when he shows that bureaucracy precedes the scientific revolution.[9] Grob points out that asylums and mental hospitals, even in the nineteenthcentury, were never entirely the monolithic institutions that critics portray.[10] They always performed a rag-bag function of caring for senile, aged and otherwise impaired inmates, and experimented with various institutional forms, some of which approximated current ideas of community care.[11]

The re-definition of "madness" as "mental illness" is a crucial component of subsequent development. It introduces a strand in the historical process which is germane to the search for a broader understanding of the psychiatric enterprise. In tracing this element, however, it is fruitless to engage in a debate on the nature and existence of mental illness. As Grob states, little is really known about what is designated as mental illness.[12] Neither its acceptance as a discrete phenomenon nor its relegation to a mere label used in the organization of bureaucratic forms of social control furthers the kind of understanding necessary for a broader analysis. Such dichotomizing of positions results in an oversimplification of the existing situation and forces a polarization of views of psychiatry. The debate then becomes focussed on the issue of therapy versus control, with a resultant stalemate from which there are only two courses of action: improving the institution along existing lines, or abolishing it entirely.

Charting a course between the two poles allows for the possibility that both therapy and control exist side-by-side in the complexity of the overall picture. What then becomes apparent is a process by which the care or control of the dysfunctional members of society, among whom were numbers of madmen or lunatics, has been differentiated into separate areas. The care and control of those defined as mentally ill has become the province of psychiatry. Once this definition exists, it has particular implication for those so designated, regardless of their actual condition. It is not the definition itself, but the power to define which is the key.

The history of medicine, presented as the march of progress and the triumph of science, offers the same "tourist brochure" image which Kuhn attributes to the history of science in general. This image leaves no room for the recognition that its expert, professional status was originally based not in knowledge, but in power. Much of the authority of medicine and, by extension, of psychiatry, arises from the equation of moral judgement of virtue and legitimacy with scientific definitions of health and illness. The transformation of mad-doctors into psychiatrists, the only legitimate experts on mental illness, is a prime example of the process whereby this authority evolved.

The struggle between proponents of medical treatment and moral management in the early nineteenth century provides an illustration of the process at one of its most crucial stages. Medical definitions of illness at this time were based largely on nosologies derived from the observation of symptoms, and physicians differed as to the forms of underlying pathology indicated. A basic cluster of treatments was applied to most conditions. A number of physicians inclined to the opinion that forms of insanity were diseases of the brain, abdominal and nervous systems, and medical treatment, where given, was much the same as for any other illness. Treatment consisted largely of bleeding, blistering, purges and powders. Benjamin Rush, often referred to as the father of American psychiatry, boldly declared that all disease stemmed from a single underlying pathology. He defined, among other conditions which were manifestations of that pathology, insanity, alcoholism, murder, suicide, lying, revolutiona (opposition to the American Revolution), anarchia (over-commitment to liberty following the Revolution), and failure to believe in the utility of medicine or the tenets of Christianity. Rush added to the general medical remedies a number of measures that were designed to produce a salutary terror. An extreme example of Rush's deductive powers is to be found in his discovery of the disease of Negritude. On coming across the case of a black man suffering from vitiligo, which had caused his skin to turn white, Rush concluded that all black people suffer from a form of congenital leprosy, from which this man had made a spontaneous recovery.[13]

22 —

Some asylums and madhouses were run by medical men, often society physicians, who relied on the profits to augment their incomes. Most institutions were administered by lay people, either on behalf of charity societies or for local authorities. A physician was in attendance to minister to bodily illness where necessary. From the eighteenth century onward, recurring enquiries and reports revealed the brutal and degrading conditions that prevailed in both privately owned and state-run institutions. Commissions were empowered to inspect all asylums, but were made up of members of the Royal College of Physicians and did little other than reinforce the link between state and medical involvement in setting standards for the care of the insane.

A serious challenge to the emerging medical commitment to the insane arose with the founding of the York Retreat at the end of the eighteenth century. The Retreat was set up by a Quaker group under William Tuke as an alternative to the brutal conditions at York's asylum. It was devoted to the humane and "moral" treatment of the insane, on the assumption that a firm, kindly approach would provide an environment in which the mentally deranged could recover their senses. Although Tuke had an understandable distrust of the medical profession of his day, he allowed visiting physicians to attempt to cure patients under his care; they met with virtually no success, and confessed disillusionment with their own practices. There ensued a long battle between supporters of Tuke's concept of moral management and those convinced that medical treatment was the only proper response to the care of the insane. The medical profession then kept up constant pressure on licensing bodies, local asylum boards and committees, the government and individual magistrates in order to advance their hegemony in the field. Among other things, they retained control of the commissions that inspected asylum conditions by insisting on a predominance of medical representation. By the middle of the nineteenth century, the asylum doctor had transformed dominance over the field of mental illness into a monopoly. At no point was medical efficacy effectively demonstrated; the process was, to all intents and purposes, social and political, not based in any technical advancement of knowledge.[14]

Certain aspects of this struggle are particularly illuminating for the puposes of this survey. Scull[15] points to the particular elements that led to the defeat of the moral managment protagonists. Tuke and his successors resisted all attempts to persuade them to develop a theoretical base for their work at the Retreat. They insisted that each patient be seen as an individual and treated as such; a process which they felt would be rendered impossible once theoretical speculation as to the cause or nature of the derangment was undertaken. They also refused to train a specialized staff to work with the patients, maintaining that the very effectiveness of their work was based on the lay character of their "helpers." Despite the firm denial of the efficacy of medical practices in instances of mental derangment, however, the moral management movement had no vocabulary of its own and relied on such medical terms as "mental illness," "patient" and "treatment." These three factors: lack of a theoretical knowledge base, lack of a trained body of experts, and a language that contradicted its fundamental tenets by using medical terms while denying medical validity, combined to prevent the development of an alternative profession to compete with medicine. Thus, almost by default, medicine was able to make a case for being the only profession in the field. There ensued a final compromise, whereby the effectiveness of moral management was acknowledged and absorbed into the professional framework of the physician as one of a number of treatment modalities available to the newly emerging specialization of psychiatry. This merger was epitomized by the injunction that all asylums should be under the control of men of sound character and ability, namely medical men, who were morally unimpeachable and therefore fit to provide moral treatment. By the end of the nineteenth century, virtually all asylum directors were medical men.

PSYCHOLOGY PROVIDES A THEORETICAL BASE FOR "RATIONAL MAN"

The significance of the moral management movement can better be appreciated by viewing it in conjunction with the development of psychology later in the same century. Here, the "science of the rational mind" provided a theoretical basis for the moral position. Tuke's idea that moral treatment could re-educate the lunatic into something resembling the newly emerging, middle-class ideal of the rational individual was closely approximated as the basis of a discipline that typified those ideals as the natural, normal model for civilized man [sic]. The characteristics of rational man, thus defined, were those necessary to produce individuals capable of operating in the abstract rational mode of organization and administration by which society was now ordered and ruled.

The relationship of psychiatry to the newly emerging disciplines of the behavioral and biological sciences was at first somewhat ambiguous. Some medical men saw psychology as a branch of medicine. They sought to avoid further splits and specializations by maintaining it within their discipline and insisting that even moral treatment was never satisfactorily implemented except by physicians. Others bitterly resisted the inclusion of such "metaphysical" propositions in the realm of medical practice.

Eventually, however, a number of psychological precepts and theories were absorbed into the psychiatric domain. Freud, for example, maintained his medical affiliations and subscribed to a disease model of pathology, even though most of his constructs were psychological in nature. The circle was closed by the work of Stack Sullivan and Fromm Riechman, who applied therapeutic techniques to the severely disturbed in medical settings. The most significant aspect of the absorption of ideas from the behavioural and social sciences into the mainstream of psychiatric theory is not, however, their manifestation in forms of psychotherapy, but their relation to normative values. Locating underlying pathology in the developmental processes of early childhood opened up a whole new field of expertise. Psychologists produced theories concerning human nature, development, behaviour and personality, which became not just theoretical constructs based on descriptive practices, but normative, prescriptive ideologies that purported to define normality in all areas of thought and action. Indeed, Smith suggests that Freud's work, for example, represents a major technical advance. He extended the imperialism of "rationality" into the realm of personal experience, providing one of the forms of "indepth" organization of consciousness required to operate in the abstract, rational mode of organization. He developed a set of techniques for examining life and experience in relation to an ideology that legitimates and enhances conformities of feeling and disposition as well as action. This ideology also offers an elaborate technique for separating out what is "healthy" from what is not.[16] Private and office practice of individual psychotherapy was one of the outcomes of this development.

The true conceptual imperialism set in motion by the power to define mental illness came into full flower, especially after the Second

World War, when treatment and the labels "healthy" and "ill" were made relevant to the ever-increasing areas of human existence. The various helping professions, with medicine still in the forefront as principal authority, were now fully entrenched as the core of the "therapeutic state" to which Kittrie draws attention.[17] In less than a century, the phenomenon that Zola and other critics[18] refer to as the "medicalization of life" had become a paramount force, one which Pitts insisted, in 1968, was the most effective means of social control, destined to become the main formal mode.[19] The issue of the "medicalization of life" has been dealt with from a number of standpoints by writers such as Illich, LaLonde and Conrad, and their views have been challenged, clarified and identified as ideological by such critics as Starr, Navarro and Engel, among others.[20]

Bazelon and many others[21] draw attention to some of the most negative aspects of the medicalization of social problems. If problems are defined in medical terms, it can be left to medical experts to find solutions, allowing the rest of society to abdicate responsibility. Thus, if poverty, racism and crime are considered mental health issues, society does not have to look for social causes or solutions. A further implication is that, once defined as a mental health issue, the social problem is located in the personal realm of the individual's state of consciousness. Thus, it is considered appropriate to deal with it as an individual problem for which there should be an individual solution. Even treatment approaches that recognize interactional components in people's activities restrict the milieu for treatment to the individual, the family, and the most immediate environment.

THE MEDICALIZATION OF LIFE AND ITS PARTICULAR SIGNIFICANCE TO WOMEN

The recognition of two strands — the increasing medicalization of life's problems, and the growth of normative theories that provide one of the bases for such medicalized definitions — allows us to begin to consider the experience of women. When we look to the conventional psychiatric framework for explanations that would speak to our concern about the position of women in relation to the institution, we find significant blanks. The commonplace linguistic convenience of using "he" as both the general and the masculine pronoun in the English language makes it easy to assume that women are present throughout the account, as professionals and as patients. They are, in fact, virtually invisible in either role. Apart from occasional mention of outstanding lay figures, like reformers Dorothea Dix or Elizabeth Packard, there is scant reference to women until the twentieth century, when their occasional appearance as psychoanalysts and patients seldom excites comment. Szasz remarks that if Packard is considered at all, she is usually treated in a denigrating manner.[22] One (female) historian offers tantalizing, brief descriptions of occasional nineteenth-century debates concerning the propriety of allowing female attendants on male wards or the controversy surrounding the appointment of a female physician to the women's wing of an asylum.[23] In general, however, there is no discussion of the predominance of "great men" as opposed to "great women," and this leads to the impression that women's experience is subsumed under the neutral title of "patients."

The historical introduction to a recently published text on *Women in Therapy* fails to expand much on this picture. The authors explicitly propose what is usually tacitly assumed. They suggest that a woman's biological function rendered her unfit for any role other than that of patient until medical advances freed her from the burden of frequent pregnancies and the risk of childbed mortality. Consequently, the chapter is sprinkled with sentences such as ". . . for reasons which are not wholly clear, most witches were women," "curiously enough, the development of psychoanalysis . . . was concerned almost exclusively with women patients," and ". . . ironically, members of their own sex seem to have played . . . a formidable part in propagating the misleading and damaging notion of the schizophrenogenic mother."[24] As an account of why women in North America currently number less than 10% of the psychiatrists and more than 60% of the patients, "curiously enough" and "ironically" seem woefully inadequate.[25] Above and beyond its woeful inadequacy, however, this view contributes to the "march of progress" school of thought. It obscures an important aspect of the struggle for professional ascendancy that has already been illustrated as being largely social and political rather than based in the accumulation of actual knowledge. The part that sex and class played in the struggle has been obliterated in existing accounts.

Long before the rise of psychiatry *per se,* various streams of medical practice were engaged in a battle for status. The main protagonists in the initial stages were the male physicians who ministered to the

Court and the upper classes; and the barber-surgeons, the apothecaries and the folk-healers who served the remaining population. In the Middle Ages, at least, most folk-healers were "wise women," or witches. Many of the millions of women accused of witchcraft and burnt at the stake were not the pitiful victims of senility and mental illness, as Zilboorg[26] and others have suggested. They were healers and midwives, whose skill was based on empirical knowledge of anatomy, herbology, and what could be described as nursing care. As such, they were often more effective than the physicians whose "expertise" was drawn from the study of classic Greek and Arab texts. Eventually, as the physicians sought to expand their sphere of influence, the surgeons and apothecaries were absorbed into the mainstream of the profession. The old practices of folk-healers were ruthlessly suppressed on the grounds that they were magical, superstitious, and harmful "old wives' tales." Gradually, the territory that remained in the hands of women, namely childbirth, was taken over, first by male midwives and then by the medical specialities of obstetrics and gynaecology.

The history of women and medicine is now being written by feminist scholars.[27] It is evident from this work that women have consistently struggled to take an active part in health care, both as part of various popular health movements and as physicians. The late nineteenth century saw women in the U.S.A. and elsewhere founding their own medical schools and hospitals and occasionally even representing as much as half the graduating classes in mixed medical colleges. The acceptance of women in mixed colleges led to the closing of most women's colleges but gains were short-lived. The establishment of quota systems and the introduction of such institutional practices as compulsory internship for hospital practice, combined with restricted access to internships for women, actively and effectively excluded the majority of women from the medical profession.[28] Those who have entered its ranks have often had to make considerable compromises in order to succeed. As part of the process of professionalization they have been expected to take a position with regard to their own sex that is no more sympathetic or informed than that of their male colleagues. With the advent of the recent feminist revival, the proportion of women entering the profession is once again increasing and awareness of women's concerns are being brought to the fore.

Over the past two centuries, however, women also re-entered the medical field in less prestigious occupations: as attendants, nurses, social workers and, in more recent times, as psychologists. Their role was often largely seen as an extension of the womanly role in the home. They were expected to act as helpmates to the doctor, carrying out the everyday tasks required to present the patient as ready for the doctor's expert intervention.[29]

This is, of necessity, a brief and condensed summary. Even so, it indicates the reasons for women's invisibility in the forefront of medical history; they were systematically excluded from the profession until comparatively recent times. The fact of their absence has implications beyond the actual loss of participatory rights and status for women as physicians. It also means that the experts who took over the power to define women's lives have been, almost exclusively, men. This second aspect is of major significance in the search for the reasons that underlie women's relationship to the psychiatric profession. The power to define mental illness and to create normative theories concerning almost all aspects of life gave men of science the power to prescribe and proscribe both the "nature" and the role of women in society.

In a world where religion no longer provided absolutes on which to rely, science was seen as the only viable alternative. Pursuit of the scientific method was assumed to be leading towards the discovery of the absolute and fixed laws of nature that govern the universe. Science became "the new religion," and people turned to scientific experts for guidance in every sphere of their lives. Since scientists, by their very position, were assumed to produce objective knowledge, untainted by the interests of any particular group in society, they were seen to be the best people to guide the world for the good of all. In the case of women, the better educated the woman, the more aware of scientific progress, the more inclined she was to see salvation in the scientific truth that the experts could provide for her. Experts in the field of medicine and the behavioural sciences took it for granted that biological functions, psychological processes and social roles were one and the same for women. The role that society demanded of women was assumed to be that dictated by the laws of nature. In the absence of any other authoritative view, such as might have been provided by women themselves as "experts" on their own lives and experiences, the pejorative content of expert opinion and, indeed, the fact that the experts were men, went unchallenged.

The medicalization of the physical aspect of women's lives was virtually complete by the end of the nineteenth century. "Male doctors

. . . asserted that menstruation, pregnancy, childbirth, and menopause were illnesses. Healthy men certainly never experienced them."[30]
Once classified as illnesses, they properly fell under the physician's care.
Medical experts, for example, felt it within their domain to publicly oppose higher education for women, since the development of the intellect
was believed to be invariably counter-balanced by the atrophy of the
organs of reproduction. Thus it was felt that educated women were unfit to fulfill their fundamental social and natural function of procrea-
tion. By the middle of the twentieth century, a variety of experts had
claimed dominion over all aspects of women's existence, providing
definitive instruction on how they should feel, think and act, as daughters, wives, mothers, sexual beings, and even, where necessary, as
members of the work force. Corea, in a chapter entitled "Medicine and
Social Control," presents a powerful discussion of the ways in which
control over women's bodies has been both medically and morally
enforced. Psychologists even produced studies which confirmed that
women's "innate" capacity for patience and endurance makes them
biologically fit for boring, mundane and exploitative tasks in factories
and offices.[31]

The pretensions of "the experts" reached a peak in statements such
as that made by the president of the American Psychiatric Association
in 1968. He declared that the entire world and its problems were the
proper area for psychiatric intervention. Nor, he insisted, should psychiatry be daunted by the task.[32] At the same time, however, the
groundswell of disillusionment with the promises of scientific progress
was becoming evident. In the context of the medical and social sciences,
this disillusionment manifested itself in several areas and from several
sources. Perhaps the most pragmatic questioning has come from within
the political structures responsible for funding the ever-proliferating
programs designed to solve problems through therapeutic intervention.
As the costs of such programs soared, there was a corresponding demand for evidence of their effectiveness. Such evidence was not forth-
coming. Statistics showed increasing incidence of mental illness, delinquency, crime, family breakdown, and general social disorganization.
The economic crises of the 1970's has produced a time of fiscal con-
straint. This, in turn, has led the various forms of state and third-party
payment systems for health care to demand more accountability from
the services they fund. For psychiatry in particular, this has had widespread repercussions. Faced once again with the need to rationalize and

justify treatment procedures, some psychiatrists have increasingly abandoned their allegiance to scientific models, and voice complaints about the difficulties of applying strict evaluative criteria to what is, after all, the "art" of healing. Others have retreated to stricter definitions of the medical model in an attempt to provide diagnostic and prognostic tools that are responsive to the administrative practices of scientific management. This is one of the sources of much of the self-questioning within the profession. Peer reveiw procedures, tightening of licensing and upgrading of education are, in some measure, responses to the demands of government that psychiatry justify its expert status by proving that what it does is the most effective way of dealing with the areas it purports to serve.

Another source of questioning of the validity of the psychiatric institution has come from the societal reaction and labelling theorists, and is mainly sociological in approach. Although this criticism has provided a valuable impetus for the sociological study of the nature of psychiatry, it has had two unfortunate consequences. One is to produce a view that is somewhat iatrogenic: that psychiatrists actually create mental illness by a process of definition, independent of any actual phenomena, and out of an intrinsic malevolence born of a hunger for coercion and control. The other is more complex. By seeking to understand the nature and function of the institution from an examination of its impact on individuals, it fails to provide conceptualizations that allow for a broader analysis. For, while society is made up of individuals, it cannot be understood in terms of individual experience alone. This again leads to a view of psychiatry in which its functions of social control appear arbitrary, and can only be accounted for by some immediate perversity or self-interest on the part of the controllers.[33] Some of the impetus to eliminate all psychiatric hosptials has had this position as its theoretical base, but again, as an analysis it has failed to provide direction for solutions to current social problems.

The third source of criticism is the one on which considerable focus has already been placed. It draws some strength from the insights of labelling and societal reaction theory, but its main concern is rather different. The position held by a number of radical therapists, racial minorities, feminists and other critics takes issue with psychiatry as an institution in which the ideology (as well as the practices) has an intrinsic potential for oppression. It is the contention of this critical position that psychiatry has proposed, as scientific truths, theories that actually embody the social norms of those in a position of power in modern society. From this perspective, the "tourist brochure" image of psychiatry is seen as that image of the institution produced by a small section of its members. This section is empowered by its status, education and, to a large extent, its sex, to present as the true nature of psychiatry that carefully selected body of knowledge that forms the ideology of the institution. That ideology presents an alternative rationale for the social costs of living in a society based on hierarchical orders of organization and their attendant institutionalization of inequality and exploitation. This rationale locates the damage and dysfunction of dominant and subordinate status, not within the system that produces it, but within the individual who experiences it. Since the psychiatric ideology both reflects and takes part in producing this interpretation, it follows that the situation cannot be fully understood or explained by focussing on the impact of the institution on the individual alone. The impact of institutions on individuals may provide an excellent indicator of the kind of problems to be dealt with, but an exclusive focus on this relationship neglects both the structure of the organization itself and the overall context in which a particular institution operates. The current tendency to cast the dilemmas of psychiatry as those of therapy versus control, or the individual versus society, generates little possibility for understanding or change.[34] The real concern of psychiatry is not so much with the individual as with the creation and maintenance of individualism as an ideology.

CONCLUSIONS

This chapter began as an exploration of the nature of the institution of psychiatry and an attempt to understand both its relation to the broader social system and its implication in the oppression of women. What has become evident in the search is a far broader and more complex picture than that presented in traditional histories of the profession. Significant factors appear to be missing from traditional accounts. Or rather, what is present in those accounts takes on a different significance when viewed in conjunction with what is absent. When women themselves start to provide a critique of the institution, they draw attention to the missing factors. They begin by delineating their own exclusion from the production of psychiatric ideology. If, however, the debate is cast only in terms of the exclusion of women, it allows for a very partial response to the critique. Psychiatry has the option of seeing the matter as one of an unfortunate historial bias against women which no longer operates. The "changing role of women" can then be added as an extra field of study and specialization: another chapter in the compendium of psychiatric formulations. This has already happened to some extent with the inclusion of one short chapter on the women's movement, by a female author, in the 1975 edition of the *Comprehensive Textbook of Psychiatry*.[35] Feminist therapy itself has been characterized as a new type of psychotherapy to be considered along with the 140 or so other "schools" identified in a recent survey.[36] Separate sessions on women's issues have been included in many annual conferences and meetings. Although this approach may well provide a wider range of options for women seeking help and for those female psychiatrists who want to focus on working with them from a feminist perspective, it does not deal with the full implication of the critique.

When it becomes evident that moral judgements, containing those pejorative and oppressive elements of social control through which women have been kept in a subordinate position in society, have been advanced as an objective, scientific knowledge base by psychiatry, the entire ideology of the institution is called into question.

Psychiatry can be seen to have a place in the history of ideas. Concepts such as "enlightenment" and "the dignity of the person" advanced by philosophers such as Rousseau, Locke and Montesquieu influenced the treatment practices of such men as Tuke, Pinel and Chiarugi. It presented a particularly difficult dilemma with regard to those defined as mentally ill, however, since they were, by virtue of their condition, seen as being less than human.[37] With the development of normative medical and behavioural theories, which increasingly prescribed the qualities and beliefs of the dominant class as the prototype for being fully human,[38] everyone thus excluded can equally be viewed as somehow less than human. When they become psychiatric patients, whether they be women, minority racial groups, or of the working class, the potential for oppression is endemic to the system. Women, as over half the general population and almost two-thirds of the patient population, are the most visible and specific examples of the issues upon which we have chosen to focus.

Elements of the struggle for status and position which begin to surface in the alternative account of psychiatric history, are obscured in conventional accounts. What is presented as the orderly accumulation of expertise, engaged in the overthrow of ignorance, brutality and superstition, can also be seen as a process whereby the newly emerging middle classes carved themselves a buffer position between the lower classes and the plutocracy. Experts, who by virtue of their status as men of science were deemed to be totally objective and representative of no one interest group within the system, saw themselves as those most fit to guide society in the direction of progress. The progessions are hierarchically organized, however, and increasingly part of the machinery of government in its broadest sense. When this is not accounted for in the conventional image of the institution, it is impossible to understand how the relation of psychiatry to the social system affects its professional practices.[39] Neither is it possible to see that the ideology of psychiatry defines as healthy or normal the ability of the individual to operate in ways necessary to make our particular social system function. Psychiatric practices filter out as amenable to psychiatric intervention any activity or state of consciousness that is contrary to that requirement. This only becomes visible, however, when a critique from the standpoint of women, or any group outside the dominant framework, begins to broaden an understanding of the situation of psychiatry beyond its relation to ideas and examines its relation to the overall social and economic organization of society. Although this provides a more covert form of control than the abuses of psychiatric treatment in the USSR, its elements are based on uncomfortably similar principles. Western ideals of political freedom and civil rights make abhorrent the idea that divergent political beliefs could be classified and treated as mental illness, Benjamin Rush notwithstanding. Yet certain forms of failure to conform to social expectations are regarded as symptomatic of mental illness in our system.

The crisis of confidence in psychiatry, both from within its ranks and from outside, is partly a reflection of the broader crisis in science itself and in the world's economic, political and social organization. Society is in the process of re-defining its relationship with the "new religion" of science, which has not yet produced the solutions promised at the height of its most optimistic phase. Scientific and technological definitions of progress are being questioned by increasing numbers of the population, who have recognized that the scientific enterprise and even its methodologies are not immune from human bias and self-interest. They have not necessarily produced ultimate, objective and absolute truths by which to guide and govern the best of all possible worlds. The involvement of psychiatry in the process whereby society is organized, administered and ruled can no longer be obscured by claims of professional and scientific objectivity. The issues of dominance, subordination, and institutionalized inequality will have to be made part of the psychiatric debate.

≡   ≡   ≡

CHAPTER III

PSYCHIATRIC
IDEOLOGY AND ITS FUNCTIONS

PSYCHIATRY IN ITS PRESENT FORM IS NOT a random undertaking, a political plot, or a bad case of intellectual indigestion — although critics have made convincing arguments to these effects. In looking at how psychiatry takes its place among the institutions through which society is organized and governed, we have examined how it performs a specific function in the way in which people and events are ordered and controlled. It does so, as has been suggested, both by treating people and by taking part in creating the very terms through which human realities come to be seen in ways that make them the appropriate subject for psychiatric control.

The psychiatric ideology exists to organize, categorize, and make observable certain kinds of activities, in such a way that they become amenable to action or explanation in psychiatric terms.[1] It is in this sense that we use the term "ideology," not as a set of biased and self-interested beliefs, but as the socially produced construction of ideas and explanations: a set of procedures and practices that both accounts for and organizes the social system. In the process, ideology provides an explanation that obscures actuality by providing an alternative view that legitimizes the position of those who create it.

The institution of psychiatry, then, has a dual relation to the structures through which society is organized and governed. It cares for and controls those termed mentally ill, and provides the sorting mechanisms for deciding who those shall be. The professional training of practitioners includes learning how to filter out of the complex, contradictory, indefinite and diverse real world those activities which

35

can be seen as relevant to psychiatric intervention. The psychiatrist must deal with what is defined as irrational, pathological or abnormal. It would be logical, therefore, to look to definitions of normality to see what standards exist against which the psychiatrist must judge how to sort out the everyday world to fit psychiatric ideology.

PSYCHIATRIC DEFINITIONS OF NORMALITY

Evidence can be cited to show that there are notions that are generally held and taken for granted of what is or is not "normal" in human activities.[2] This is part of the "invisible judgemental work" included in psychiatric diagnostic procedures. It is an area that has provoked increasing comment in psychiatric circles, and one that is crucial to this discussion. Gaylin suggests that, prior to recent re-assessment of the relation between society and science, psychiatry was able to ignore the immense ethical and moral implications of its activities. The psychiatrist ". . . by building a body of psychology that defined normalcy in all areas of behaviour and action, . . . constructed a coercive tool and [used it] to fashion a mode of behaviour for others."[3] Newberger and Bourne see this not as a historical factor but as an ongoing process, which escalates with the increasing tendency to draw social issues into the medical domain, so that the physician "becomes a moral entrepreneur, defining what is normal, proper or desirable."[4]

Closer examination of the concept of "normalcy" or "normality," however, reveals confusion and contradiction on all fronts. The *Comprehensive Textbook of Psychiatry* devotes an entire chapter to the subject. In it, Offer and Sabshin begin by stating that psychiatrists have a "trained incapacity" to recognize, let alone conceptualize, the "normal." They attribute this to a training process that concentrates on manifestations of abnormality.[5] Offer and Sabshin attempt to clarify a number of ways in which normality is identified. They advance four perspectives on normality, the first of which, "normality as health," proposes that "behavior is assumed to be within normal limits when no manifest pathology is present."[6] This definition carries considerable propensity for circular reasoning. The authors quote Romano as stating "that a healthy person is one who is reasonably free of undue pain, discomfort and disability"; who defines "reasonably" and "undue," and how this is done, is not discussed.[7] The second perspective is "normality as Utopia," a definition that sees it as "that harmonious and optimal blending of the diverse elements of the mental apparatus that culminates in optimal functioning."[8] This perspective is subject to the same problem as to who has the power to define "optimal and harmonious functioning," and how possible it is by this definition to achieve "normality." Freud's view of the concept of normality as "an ideal fiction" is referred to in this context.[9] Discussing the same definition in his consideration of the topic, Eysenck states: "We call a person normal the more he approaches the ideal, whether it be ideally high intelligence, good looks, or uninterrupted health."[10]

The third perspective, one most frequently used in psychology and biology, is that of "normality as average" or, in Eysenck's phrase, "the statistical definition."[11] It is based on the mathematical principle of the bell-shaped curve: the middle range of the curve is conceived of as normal, while both extremes are seen as deviant. Offer and Sabshin point out that this application, "in developing model personalities for different soceities . . . assumes that the typologies of character can be statistically measured."[12] Eysenck, while considering the usage "clear, straightforward and intelligible," draws attention to areas of ambiguity, particularly with regard to definitions of health. "The normal person is one who has the average number of illnesses and fractures and whose life is ended by one of the more common diseases. The person who is completely healthy and lives to a ripe old age . . . would be exceedingly abnormal from this point of view."[13] The final definition offered by these authors is that of "normality as transactional systems": a functional description that "stresses changes or processes rather than a cross-sectional definition of normality . . . [encompassing] variables from biological, psychological and social fields."[14]

As an antidote to problems that they see as arising from definitions of normality extrapolated from clinical studies of abnormality, Offer and Sabshin propose a more rigorous use of non-patient, cross-sectional, follow-up, longitudinal and predictive research. This suggested redress of balance does not deal with the problems of definition, however, and presents further difficulties. In reviewing research of this nature they discover that all the studies discussed were done on middle-, if not upper-class, populations. Also, the majority of subjects studied were males. "The danger," they state, "is obvious. There may be a tendency to use the middle-class, white male as a model."[15] A careful reading of this quotation in its context reveals no irony on the authors' part in the understatement of their conclusion.

It is only after considering as a separate issue "normality and emergent social movements," that Offer and Sabshin touch on a further definition of normality that correlates with one offered by Eysenck: one which, he suggests, has played an important part in the development of psychology. This definition involves the procedure of naming as normal that which is considered to be "natural." Such a view can be held despite statistical evidence to the contrary; Eysenck suggests, "the tendency to regard certain forms of conduct as naturally or biologically innate . . . seems to be based, in many cases, . . . on an erroneous identification of that which is natural with that which is current in our society."[16]

Eysenck, along with Offer and Sabshin, eventually comes to the conclusion that normality and health are relative terms that include within them the function and judgement of the definer and the use to which the definition is to be put. This leads to an understanding that the terms cannot be considered in the abstract: "they depend on the cultural norms, society's expectations and values, professional biases, individual differences, and the political climate of the time, which sets out the tolerance for deviance."[17] Offer and Sabshin take note of strong reactions from special-interest groups to the use of racial, sexual, geographic and age-related stereotypes as the equivalent of norms for these groups, and recognize that "institutional racism has pervaded psychiatry in many ways and has influenced the concept of normality in black as well as other minorities."[18]

The remedies that the authors propose arise from an analysis based on the assumption that the problems and confusion lie in a lack or misuse of information, and an over-commitment to a particular view or bias on the part of the protagonists. The solutions they propose include: more studies; more subjects; better sampling; and more stringent safeguards against bias. This is a principle that Watzlawick, Weakland and Fisch have delinated as "more of the same" in problem-solving: adding more information or attempting solutions along the same lines as those already tried. Such solutions become part of the problem by adding to its complexity, when what is required is a "re-framing" of the problem to allow for new perspectives and approaches.[19] A similar point is made by de Bono in discussing conceptual prisons. A conceptual prison exists because, like a hole dug in one place, a theory or theories can only be enlarged and elaborated upon to respond to anomalies that become evident. If the hole is in the wrong place to begin with, its actual location cannot be altered by this method. Much the same conclusion, in relation to the physical sciences, is drawn by Kuhn in his description of scientific revolutions as paradigm shifts. When a major changes takes place, it is usually the result of the over-elaboration of a theoretical position to include too many anomolies. It often requires someone not committed to the initial paradigm to shift the approach to the problem to an alternative perspective.[20]

In order to unravel the problems raised in the discussion of normality as a concept, it is necessary to "re-frame" the issue by looking beyond the ideological boundaries laid out by Eysenck, Offer and Sabshin, and other writers attempting solutions from the psychiatric perspective. What is needed is a broader approach that gives a better account of what is actually happening to cause such confusion: one that attempts to sort out ideology from knowledge. What Offer and Sabshin and Eysenck have discovered in their examinations is that no one of the definitions of normality available does the work of laying bare, let alone accounting for, the lived actualities of human beings in this or any other society. The problem of what is normal is seen by them as that which must be discovered, not as what needs to be explained. Normality is taken as a "fact," a concrete thing that we have not yet learned to distinguish properly. Yet what they propose is a better process for "naming" the presumed phenomenon, not an explanation of how the concept of normality is constructed and used. This work can be attempted if it is approached from a different starting place, one that does not assume that everyone is somehow articulated to society in the same manner, with accidents of birth, race, sex or class as variables that impinge on a universal, normal or natural developmental process. An alternative starting place is one that proposes that human growth, development and consciousness are shaped and given definite form by the experience of living in a particular location within the social structure. This is a view that allows for the consideration of different experiences of domination and subordination, power and powerlessness , not as a matter of personal fault, misfortune or choice, but as the outcome of living out the structuring of social relations in a group or society where power and resources are not equitably distributed.

NORMALITY AS AN INVISIBLE JUDGEMENT

There is a body of work that does begin to approach human experience from this perspective. It is, as Offer and Sabshin seem to discover almost by serendipity, from the discontent and protest of less powerful groups in society that the most cogent criticism of concepts of normality as they coincide with cultural stereotypes arises. It is from this perspective that institutions that are ostensibly neutral and objective can be seen to contain elements that are racist, sexist or class-based. Such an understanding is seldom apparent from within the institution or discipline itself, since its procedures maintain its own conceptual boundaries inviolate until such time as representatives of these groups gain entrance, or make an impact from without. Thus the writings of Fanon, a black psychiatrist, provide a view of colonial oppression as it is experienced by the oppressed and as it is explained in psychiatric terms.[21] The pedagogical work of the Brazilian educator, Freiere, reveals the consciousness of both oppressor and oppressed as generated by their relationship within the social structure.[22] Hegel, in examining the relationship between master and servant, provides a basis for an understanding of class relations and the relations between women and men.[23] Allport, in his influential book on prejudice, treats a similar theme but does so in terms of values, attitudes and cultural influences: themselves concepts that limit the usefulness of his work for an understanding of the power structure of society and how people produce and live it.[24]

Much of this work has been developed by Miller and Mothner for the purpose of understanding women's situations and experience. In a more general sense, their summary begins to approach the different perspective we are seeking. Although we will follow their usage of the descriptive terms of "dominants" and "subordinates," it is important to remember throughout that these terms refer to the activities of living people who are in a dominant or subordinate relation to each other.

In stressing this relational aspect, Miller and Mothner start by confirming that "both parties are tied to each other in many ways and affect each other profoundly. Indeed, they need each other."[25] However, those in the dominant group "tend to be destructive to the less powerful group. (There are also destructive effects on the dominant group.)"[26] This destructiveness can take a number of forms; the subordinate group are often labelled as defective, their unequal status often attributed to despised characteristics. While the dominant group has little need to truly understand the subordinate group, the latter group must know how to please and placate those with power. Subordinates, therefore, tend to have a much clearer understanding of their unequal status and of the characteristics of the dominant group. The subordinate group may, on the other hand, accept as true the dominant view of itself as inferior, since it is the prevailing view of society.

Miller and Mothner point out that "since the dominants determine society's ethos, its philosophy, morality, social theory, and its science, they legitimize the unequal relationship and incorporate it into all of society's cultural concepts."[27] The dominant group sees itself as the model for "normal human relationships" and can therefore regard it as "normal" to treat others destructively or derogate them, obscure what is being done, create false explanations and rationales (such as racial and sexual inferiority) and oppose action towards equality.

What becomes evident in this exploration is that there is no single, clear concept of normality in the reified form in which Offer and Sabshin and Eysenck seek to define it. Normality is not a thing that can be plucked out of its surroundings and identified. It depends on an interaction between the definer, the context, and that being defined. Beyond this, moreover, it is evident that the definition is not objective but merely agreed upon: linked to social conformity rather than to scientifically verifiable knowledge. Further, we have seen that ideas about what is "normal" come from the consciousness of those with the power to define: the dominant group of Miller and Mothner's analysis. The power to define, as we have seen, is an effective means of social control. "One of the most powerful ways to control others is to control the meaning of what is valid information. The basic act of creating a concept whose meaning is given by us to others and whose validity is defined by us for others is a powerful control over others."[28]

There is another aspect of the power to create and provide concepts which is at the root of the ability to create ideology as opposed to knowledge. If a concept, created to name and make comprehensible some activity or process, is detached from the context of that activity or process, it can be reified: that is, seen as something in its own right. From there it is a short step to seeing it as having "agency," or causal efficacy. Once this is the case, the concept can easily be seen as causing the very activity or process it was created to name or make comprehensible. For example, in the case of psychiatry it is possible to identify procedures by which the statements people make about certain thoughts, feelings or activities, and the conceptual forms used to name them, such as anxiety, dependency, or aggressiveness, are constituted as symptoms of mental illness. One of the ways in which this is accomplished is by disregarding the fact that the process is an interaction. "Symptoms are not observable independent of actual settings in which people are related to one another. There are always two parties to a symptom."[29] When one of the parties is a psychiatric professional, we generally ignore their part in the procedure because they occupy a position of objectivity in "examining" someone. Yet, as Smith points out, "being objective is a special way of relating to people. Examining someone is a special kind of interaction."[30]

Once the symptoms, or set of symptoms, have been formulated and detached from the person's account, they can be arranged to establish an order among them which provides an explanation for what is observed. This is the kind of procedure accomplished by diagnosis. "The psychiatrist already works with an array of different pictures of the kind of person who is schizophrenic, who is neurotic, who is alcoholic, etc. The types include notions of behaviour appropriate for women and for men. They include judgements about people's physical appearance. And so on, and so on. Diagnosis includes this *invisible* judgemental work on the part of the psychiatric professionals."[31] (Emphasis in the original.) The symptoms can be attached to the diagnosis, and need no longer account for the original relationship in which they were generated.

The arrangement of symptoms within a diagnostic category, a particular theoretical formulation, or a conceptual model, then allows them to be constituted as a "distinct entity," for example, schizophrenia or depression, which can be seen to cause the symptoms in the first place. Thus the *person* has become a *patient* whose mental illness determines her thoughts, feelings or behaviour. She is a schizophrenic, or a manic depressive, or a neurotic, or whatever. A further process strengthens the procedure: once a person is suspected or diagnosed as mentally ill, she becomes someone who is not expected to make sense in terms of the social definition of rationality or normality. She is also not to be related to in the same way as someone who is not mentally ill, and what she says is not given the same credence. "It is discredited as a basis for action."[32] Smith gives the example of a woman who tells her doctors that she will go crazy if confined to her domestic routine, and she is thus confined and does "go crazy." Her statement appears among the list of her symptoms.[33]

THEORETICAL MODELS, ILLUSTRATED BY
A COMPARATIVE CASE HISTORY

The current practice of psychiatry actually provides a number of ways of filtering out the particulars of people's lives in order to see them as appropriate to psychiatric treatment. In attempting to system-ize an understanding of how clinicians operate in a psychiatric setting, Lazare[34] proposes the existence of four implicit models which, he suggests, account for how a patient is diagnosed and treated. That Lazare considers these models "hidden" is indicative both of the con-fusion and the competition between various schools of thought, and of the lack of attention psychiatry itself pays to how psychiatric inter-vention is actually accomplished. He outlines the development of the models as follows:

The medical model, which gave nineteenth-century psychiatry its classification of mental illness, provides the conceptual basis for: more recent focus on the use of psychotropic medication; studies of the genetic transmission of mental illness; and metabolic disorders as a factor of psychiatric illness, particularly depression.

The psychologic model, Lazare suggests, has had a widespread ef-fect, not only on psychiatry but on everyday thinking in general. Psychotherapy, its derivative, has become the most popular method of treatment, especially for personality disorders and the neuroses.

The behavioural model, with theoretical foundations that devel-oped early in this century, has had a period of rapid growth since the late 1950s. Behavioural therapy, its derivative, has evoked considerable interest in the clinical field. It offers shorter duration of treatment, and applicabilities to a broader range of patients than the psychologic or medical models.

The social model views the psychiatric ward as a social system, and has enjoyed a revival since the 1950s. The establishment of a relation-ship between social class and mental illness, and the passing of legisla-tion to provide psychiatric care in the community have allowed for a number of treatment modalities that offer services to the mentally ill patient, with minimal separation from the community. Although the model has a social focus, mental illness and patient status are taken as given.

Lazare then goes on to make the models explicit, and identifies their internal consistency, proceeding by illustrating how the actualities of a particular patient's situation would be regarded according to medical, psychological, behavioural and social formulations. For Lazare's case history we are substituting the story of a woman called Linda. What follows is how she might be described and treated on the basis of the four conceptual models.

The medical model: case history. L., a twenty-five-year-old married woman, gave a history of acute panic attacks dating back to shortly after the birth of her third child. The frequency and severity of the attacks have varied over the intervening five years, with some remission during periods of hospitalization. In the last year, the attacks have increased in frequency, and are currently an almost daily occurrence. They show a diurnal variation, manifest in increased anxiety in the late afternoon. Her speech is hurried, disjointed, and thought process is erratic. She shows some fixative ideation on religious topics, and patterns of fear of phobic intensity. The patient reports recent weight loss, difficulty in sleeping, sexual impairment, and frequent, severe headaches. Sensations of suffocation accompany her attacks. There is no history of mental illness in the family, and the patient describes herself as competent and content before the onset of the attack.

The physician using the medical model regards psychiatric illness as a disease like any other, and concerns himself with etiology, pathogenesis, signs and symptoms, differential diagnosis, treatment and prognosis. If, in this case, no organic damage is discovered, the patient will be given a diagnosis, perhaps psychotic depression or schizo-affective psychosis, be told that she is suffering from a psychiatric illness, and treated with psychotropic medications and rest.

The psychologic model: case history. L., a twenty-five-year-old married woman, reported having acute anxiety attacks over a five-year period, since the birth of her third child. Her parents divorced when she was six years old, and she had no further contact with her father. Her relationships with her mother and stepfather were poor. She married an older man, who had been deserted by his first wife and children. She expresses severe guilt over her failure to maintain high standards of housekeeping and child care, and over her frigidity towards her husband.

She has acute panic attacks in reaction to open space, knives, and travelling in cars or busses, both to speed and to enclosure. She also reports the desire to throw herself through large windows. She describes her anxiety attacks as consisting of loss of breath, violent headaches, fear of blackouts and falling, and extreme agitation, combined with irrational fears for the safety of her husband and children. She is eager to receive help in the hospital setting.

The therapist using a psychological model will see such psychiatric disturbance as a manifestation of unconscious conflict. The child's instinctual drive, her smooth progress through the oral, anal and genital stages of development, must mesh with appropriate parenting. Trauma such as deprivation, separation, rejection, seduction, and over-protection leads to fixation at a certain stage of development, or regression to an earlier stage and the related formation of various sets of pathological defenses against anxiety, and deviation of personality development. The patient's problems with her children will be related to her own mother's failure to meet her needs in the oral stage, her high expectations for herself and the preoccupation with cleanliness seen as a fixation in the anal stage. Failure to resolve her oedipal conflict will account for her choice of an older man, her unconscious incestuous feelings towards him, and her frigidity. Phobias may be seen as a displacement of the anxiety aroused by conflict over incestuous longings. The fact that her anxiety attacks started after the birth of her third child may be equated with murderous rage towards yet another rival for her husband's affection (particularly if the third child is a girl). Her irrational fears about the safety of her husband and children are reaction formation, a defense against this underlying murderous hostility. The patient-therapist relation will provide a means for her to remember, re-experience, and abandon pathological ways of coping by experiencing these feelings towards the therapist and having the opportunity for a "corrective emotional experience."[35]

The behavioural model: case history. L., a twenty-five-year-old married woman, gave a history of phobic reactions, ranging from panic attacks to fear of windows, also insomnia, anorexia, and sexual impairment. These panic attacks began shortly after the birth of her third child, and her fear was at first intensified by the lack of medical help available in the remote community. Later, her behaviour brought her attention, and medical, psychiatric and housekeeping assistance when it interfered with her prior ability to cope with her household tasks. She complained of her husband's failure to respond to her needs and those of the children, and continued to try to impress on him the severity of the situation, in an effort to enlist his support and approval.

The therapist using a behavioural approach would see both neurosis and psychosis as learned behaviour resulting from aversive events and maintained to secure positive effects or avoid negative ones. Symptoms of the problem are to be treated as such, and not considered the manifestation of disease or unconscious conflict. The patient's behaviour might be seen as the result of a lack of positive reinforcement from her husband for her attempt to maintain high standards in performing her household tasks. A typical therapeutic course might include: "1) determining the behaviour to be modified; 2) establishing the conditions under which the behaviour occurs; 3) determining the factors responsible for the persistence of the behaviour; 4) selecting a set of treatment conditions; and 5) arranging a schedule of re-training . . . the conditions that result from the behaviour may be modified by positive reinforcement, negative reinforcement, aversive conditioning, and extinction."[36] Treatment might consist of enlisting the patient's husband as a "significant other" to respond positively to her positive coping, and give her encouragement while not responding to her negative behaviour. A variety of other methods might be tried on individual behaviours.

The social model: case history. L., a twenty-five-year-old married woman, had been experiencing severe anxiety attacks since shortly after the birth of her third son. The first attack happened in an isolated region, where there was no doctor available to treat what appeared to be physical symptoms. The attacks persisted after her return to the city, where she and her family settled in a remote suburban housing area. Because of her fear of leaving the house, she was unable to form contacts with her neighbours, and her family of origin rejected her over-demanding behaviour. Few of her earlier friends were able to travel to see her. Her dependence on her husband for support and help in the household caused friction in the relationship. Subsequent hospitalization produced temporary improvement, indicating that the isolation of the home aggravates, if not causes, her symptoms. Prolonged isolation has intensified her fears of the unfamiliar.

A therapist with the social model orientation would see Linda's symptoms as an index of social disorder, and focus on the way she, as an individual, functions in the social system. "Treatment consists of reorganizing the patient's relation to the social system. If others do not seem to care, how can she get them to care? If the patient's behaviour is irrational, how can she learn to stop acting irrationally, or how can her family better tolerate her behaviour? If the therapist wants to re-structure the 'nuclear' social system, he may see the patient with her family. If the therapist wants to assess the broader social system, he may attempt to influence major social issues, such as housing or educa-tion."[37] In Linda's case the therapist using the social model might note the correlation between isolation and the patient's symptoms, and intervene at the nuclear level to clarify relations in the family, and per-haps also to repair estrangements with the family of origin. Noting that Linda has lost access to many of the people to whom she previously related, the therapist might intervene at the social level by suggesting that the family move closer to the city. There, contact might be estab-lished by invitations to the home, and the gradual initiation of visiting those close at hand. Individual or group therapy might provide a transi-tional support system and a place to learn social skills that may not have developed in the marital situation.

HOW PSYCHIATRIC FORMULATIONS ARE DERIVED AND APPLIED

Lazare acknowledges that it is hard "to understand how a psychi-atrist selects the clinical data that he consideres relevant, how he formu-lates a case, and how he chooses the treatment he prescribes."[38] In discussing this problem, Lazare suggests a number of explanations. He proposes a logical selection process, since certain conditions respond more readily to certain forms of treatment. This implies that the clinician therefore chooses to work with patients whose symptoms indicate that they will benefit from his approach, or chooses his ap-proach to fit the patient's needs. Lazare is aware, however, that the administrative and bureaucratic practices of psychiatry have a role in the selective process, and that "the available treatment resources are an important determinant of the choice of model. Psychotherapy clinics . . . attempt to apply psychotherapy in understanding patients. Walk-in and emergency clinics, in responding to large numbers of patients, approach [them] from social and medical perspectives. . . . There are many psychiatric hospitals that specialize in the application of electro-convulsive treatments . . . [and] frequently over-diagnose syndromes as responsive to this form of therapy. . . . Psychiatric hospitals that specialize in social . . . or psychologic techniques . . . may regard medical treatment . . . as offering 'only' symptom relief, even when it is likely that such treatment will produce marked clinical remission."[39] Indeed, it seems that prior even to these considerations, simply going to a psychiatric facility with a complaint or problem will result in receiving a psychiatric diagnosis. Exactly which diagnosis is given may depend on factors such as those outlined by Lazare.

A confusion in Lazare's argument becomes apparent when he comments on the correlation between socio-economic factors, types of illness diagnosed, and treatment prescribed. This implies that the socio-economic status of patients determines the particular illnesses from which they suffer, and this in turn dictates the choice of treatment to be offered. Yet, Lazare himself has indicated that the methods prevalent in the particular facility are a deciding factor, and has demonstrated that it is possible to fit the actualities of a patient's life to any one of a number of orientations or frameworks.

Lazare sees the problem as one of incomplete information and professional over-commitment to a particular approach. He suggests that this is not confined to psychiatrists alone, but affects medicine as a whole, and reflects "limitations in our understanding of human behaviour." To counteract this he proposes: "In good clinical practice, a psychiatrist will employ several conceptual models with the knowledge that all reflect some aspects of the truth but all are incomplete versions of the truth." He sees that "the test of clinical skill is the assemblage of an appropriate mix for a particular case," and recommends that "to accomplish this best, the clinician should be explicit about the models that he employs in addressing a case, and about the principle upon which he bases his treatment."[40] This is a straightforward and pragmatic approach, which springs from the hope of discovering "the comprehensive set of general 'laws' "[41] of human behaviour, towards which Lazare sees a steady progress, despite evident and inherent contradictions.

Lazare's summary of the models seeks to place them in a historic framework within the institution. He does so, however, in a way that locks them in as parallel or alternative ideas, and obscures their relation to the development of the institution of psychiatry itself as a part of the governing apparatus of society. By doing this, he is able to present the models as part of the developing understanding of human behaviour. What is missing from this presentation is exactly that relation to the institutional structure which would allow us to see the models as a particular way of understanding human behaviour in psychiatric terms, as opposed to any other terms in which we might understand it. An example of this kind of ideological trap is given by Fanon in his critique of Manoni's "Prospero and Caliban."[42] Fanon shows how the actual objective conditions of colonial exploitation and oppression in Madagascar are transformed in Manoni's work into a picture in which an innate dependency complex in colonized peoples accommodates an innate authority complex in the colonizers. This produces an arrangement that satisfies everyone's deep-rooted and innate psychological needs; a veritable *folie à deux*. Such a psychological explanation obscures the actual historical conditions and the social relations between the colonized and their colonizers. It allows us to think of the situation in terms of human behaviour, as if this can be isolated from the settings in which it occurs. Thus it provides an explanation which both legitimates and justifies oppression.

Psychiatric models, hidden or not, have a place in the development of an institution that provides for certain kinds of human difficulties to be seen as the domain of psychiatrists and other mental health professionals. What they have in common is the assumption that takes "the 'individual' as both the *unit of study* and as the *unit of meaning*."[43] (Emphasis in the original.) This can be characterized as merely an extension of the Western ideology of "individualism." It is more accurately understood as a function of the way that "the social and economic organization of society generates typical situations for people to endure *as individuals* because they have no power to change them and do not see them as matters which can be changed."[44] (Emphasis in the original.) It is this assumption that results in the further assumption that individually experienced difficulties are indeed individual problems, regardless of cause. This leads to the expectation that a person's problems can be understood and defined in terms of individual functioning, perhaps in an immediate network or environment, and remedied within the same context.

Such assumptions take little or no account of the fact that in complex, modern society "the everyday world is not fully understandable within its own scope. It is organized by social relations not fully apparent in it or contained in it."[45] Many decisions that directly affect people's lives are made at state and corporate levels. The way in which people are able to live their everyday lives is dependent on a multitude of factors which are beyond the power of individual control. Few of us are able to change such things as the availability of jobs or housing, supermarket prices, the content of media presentations, the policies of corporate or bureaucratic bodies, and the numerous issues that affect both action and experience at the everyday level. Those who, like psychiatrists, intervene at the level of individual experience, must restrict their interventions to the immediate environment. They are only able to work towards changing the individual's action and experience within that local setting. Hence, the focus on adaptation or adjustment of the individual to the circumstances, for which psychiatry has often been criticized, can be seen as both a reflection of, and a justification for, the ideology of individualism — which obscures the actual structuring of society. The work of psychiatry is to make individual experience comprehensible in individual terms, and not in any other way in which we might understand it. What is true for the patient as an individual is also true for the individual psychiatric professional whose work is organized outside the local and particular setting of the office or ward. However much individual psychiatrists may try to change their ways of working with patients, the constraints of location within the institution maintain them on opposite sides. The psychiatrist cannot be other than "agent of the state." It is easier to see this relation in agencies and settings that are directly articulated to state policy and funding,[46] but it is also a result of the ideological practices of individual definitions and diagnoses that have been outlined. These practices function by working on social reality to shape it into what is psychiatrically relevant. The same practices are used by those who see themselves as operating outside the "institution" *per se,* as private practitioners or therapists with non-traditional orientations.

The four models that have been considered all have a similar message and function. They present us with an individual woman whose life experience may be a little out of the ordinary, but whose continued over-reaction, though comprehensible, can only be seen as abnormal in some definite ways. Whether we see Linda's difficulties as caused by her early childhood relationships, learning patterns, isolation, or even a bio-chemical imbalance, the end result is the same. Linda is a psychiatric patient whose symptoms, however interpreted, can be relieved by intervention at the individual level. That intervention may attack her thoughts, feelings, behaviour or even, in the case of the social model, her immediate environment, but what is visible is an individual who is not coping with her relatively normal life.

Linda is a real person and indeed a psychiatric patient. Her story is the same story, regardless of the pieces that have been filtered out to form the content of the various models interpreted here. Her life can be made over into a case history, however inadequately, because we know how to do the work of filtering out the psychiatric relevancies. What we do, who we are and how we do this is not visible in the account; it has been rendered invisible in the very procedure involved in its construction. This could probably be done with anybody's story. Rosenhan's study, "On Being Sane in Insane Places," shows how a perfectly ordinary young man, who had been admitted to hospital because he said he heard voices, was transformed into a patient with a case history that accounted for his condition, even though in this situation his "condition" did not in fact exist. This is one of the somewhat sinister aspects of a particularly interesting pseudo-patient experiment which draws attention to the kinds of issues we are raising here.[47]

LINDA'S STORY

The real Linda did not become a case history as conceptually coherent as those presented by using Lazare's hidden models. Her "psychiatric career," as Chesler would call it,[48] contains many of the elements that have been outlined because they are already filtered through Linda's account and the memory and reorganization of what she told as her story.

Linda repeatedly telephoned a crisis service for help in dealing with her panic and discomfort, her fits of shaking, fear of fainting, fear of leaving the house and, most of all, her fear of being crazy. When we talked to her and helped her to calm down, we were able to have a number of conversations about her current situation and her past experiences. Most of this she told us in terms of her adolescent difficulties at home, her early marriage and successes or failures as a wife and, subsequently as the mother of three young children. She also talked of her husband's successes or failures in providing for the family, helping with the household, and relating to the children. She had known for some time that she urgently needed help and had sought it for physical complaints, emotional states and spiritual yearnings, from her family doctor, from psychiatrists and social workers, and from a fundamentalist religious group. When the solutions offered by these sources provided temporary relief at best, she saw this as proof of her diminishing sanity and was afraid that she would eventually be "locked up."

Linda first recognized the psychiatric nature of her difficulties when her family doctor was unable to find any organic cause for her headaches, blackouts and attacks of suffocation. Referring her to a psychiatrist was the obvious next step in dealing with what must therefore be an emotional problem. She then spent several short spells in the psychiatric wards of local hospitals and a longer time in the provincial mental hospital when she could no longer cope with her domestic duties and was overwhelmed by her agitation and fear. Although she felt relieved during these hospital stays, they failed to "cure" her and she became confused about what was wrong. She tried a number of alternatives: the religious group, a lay therapist, and a self-help association of ex-mental patients. Nothing really helped, and she came to the conclusion that she had not yet received the right kind of psychiatric treatment. Contiained in Linda's assessment of her situation was an awareness that having a psychiatric problem was part of her psychiatric problem. She felt that she was not listened to or taken seriously because of her status as a mental patient. Her husband frequently threatened to have her committed and to use her psychiatric record as a means to deny her custody or even access to her children should she ever leave him. This contributed to her anxiety and to her conviction that she must, in truth, be going crazy.

By a variety of energetic manoeuvres, Linda managed to get herself admitted to a prestigious urban teaching facility, in spite of the fact that it did not serve her geographic locality and her physician did not have admitting privileges there. While she was in this hospital, members of the crisis service attended her case conference. The brief discussion between the psychiatric resident, psychologist and a psychiatric nurse was couched in terms of the patient's inadequate personality, acute and undifferentiated anxiety, emotional lability, hysterical reaction, panic attacks, phobic neurosis, disorganized thought processes, insomnia, frigidity and chronic headaches.

Linda and her various therapists over the years saw her situation in psychiatric terms. Her emotional state was irrational and could be defined and treated as mental illness. At various times she was given: medication for anxiety, headaches and insomnia; behaviour modification techniques for phobic reactions; relaxation training for tension; and some individual and group therapy to help her sort out her thoughts more clearly. Her inability to manage the home was remedied by the provision of home-helps and housekeepers. When the results of these treatments were short-lived, the therapists were reluctant to treat her again. She was seen as chronic, resistant, a "re-admission" at one facility or another, and "difficult." Linda remembered that while hospitalized, the message she most frequently received from everyone — friends, social worker, therapists, and staff — was that she had a good husband who stood by her and visited regularly, lovely children, and a nice home. She should count herself lucky and stop making such a fuss — fuss about what never seems to have been seen as an issue.

Through our contact with Linda we had developed a strong sense of the terror and entrapment she experienced in her life, and yet, to our knowledge what was happening to her was never considered as anything other than a function of her emotional state and her instability. It was taken for granted by her therapists, and by Linda herself, that as a mental patient with a psychiatric history she was predictably having problems in coping with her life. The method by which a diagnosis had been arrived at, and a case history written, was not apparent from the manner in which she was discussed at the case conference. The particular nature and function of the document from which the descriptions were read was that of shaping Linda's story into a standardized form, an objective account that would convey the essential "facts" of her "case" to anyone with the correct training to read it.

Our direct involvement with Linda ceased at this time and we do not know which of the available theoretical formulations was used by her therapists to explain her situation or dictate her treatment in that setting. The important point here is not so much whether Linda was given adequate treatment, but that she was, in some ways, typical. What is missing from her story is crucial in recognizing how it is that her life had come to be understood as that of a psychiatric patient. Linda herself struggled to speak about her life in psychiatric terms. She could not see, and indeed had never been offered, any other way of explaining what was happening to her, except that she must be going crazy. Nothing else accounted for her terror, panic, and array of symptoms.

If theories and models are to be accepted as valuable to the extent that they provide an adequate explanation and conribute to actual knowledge, then certainly the social-environmental model comes closest to providing an explanation for the actual circumstances of Linda's daily life. It still, however, treats her as an individual, subject to unusual circumstances and unable to cope with them on an individual basis. It does not do the full work of laying bare Linda's story as lived in the complex society where she was unable to function. Even so, it would undoubtedly be an improvement on what actually happened. The alternatives given her were to be crazy at home or rather less crazy in a hospital. Of the two, Linda finally chose feeling safe and being cared for in hospital, and was therefore seen as a recalcitrant patient who did not want to get better. It never seems to have occurred to anyone to question: better, for what? Nobody ever asked her what really went on at home; her husband was never included in the picture; everything was interpreted as Linda's state of mind, her inability to cope with her life being seen as a symptom of her craziness.

To the extent, then, that the social-environmental model would seem to provide a way of asking these questions, it comes closest to seeking out a broader context in which Linda's story could be told. It does not, however, make visible the invisible judgements that have gone into all the diagnostic processes which have been reviewed. It does not account for the assumption that, apart from a few irregularities, Linda's life was the normal life for a woman of her age, class and circumstances, and that if she could not live it she must be abnormal. The irregularities, and her response to them, then become a focus for the production of her case history, in which they must be seen as the cause of her problems. Although this shifts the "blame" somewhat from Linda's state of mind to certain events that proved beyond her individual capacity to handle, it remains within the framework of her individual response to her particular environment.

It would need a completely different procedure to make Linda's life and her actual responses comprehensible in any other way. We would need to see not one set of causes, one effect and one solution, but the full range of circumstances that bring a woman like Linda to the "career" of psychiatric patient. What we need to know is how it comes about that certain types of experiences that are common to many women in our society are structured as individual and seen, felt and treated as such. We need to know what women's lives as subordinates are really like. We need to recognize what women's work in the home accomplishes for society at large, as well as for the immediate family. We need to speak of the realities of Linda's life in different terms. We need to question how it is that a seventeen-year-old woman would regard marriage, to a man with a history of violence towards his first wife, as the best option available for escaping from a poor home life. We need to know what her early married life was like, as she struggled to fulfill her ideas of the perfect wife and mother. We need to be able to describe what happened on that long car journey north, during which Linda was responsible for three tiny children, and which preceded her first panic. We need to understand what the isolation of living in a mobile home in a company town does to a woman's work of maintaining the family. We need to see how modern social organization creates situations where women have no control over the aspects that affect their life and work; for example, where jobs are available, where housing is available, what help is available to a woman who is terrified of her husband but afraid to lose her children. This kind of in-depth understanding of women's lives and the forms of their oppression is only now being put together. Until it is generally available to women, they will only have the terms created for them by the "experts" with which to explain their experiences.

When there is a disjunction between the world as women experience it and the terms given them to understand the experience, women have little alternative but to feel crazy. "Psychiatry deals with the disjunctions between how women are supposed to feel and respond in their situation and how women actually do feel and respond and what their situation is in their experience. Psychiatry creates and authorizes for women ways of thinking about their unhappiness and despair, their sense of oppression, of being trapped by husband and children, or being stifled by subordination to the house."[49] Evidence suggests that as many as five out of six people diagnosed as depressed are women. Many of them are married, and those at home with young children are at high risk. Most agoraphobics, who fear leaving the house, open spaces and crowds, are women, again, mostly married women, few of whom were fearful before marriage.[50] This evidence is not generally used to question what is actually happening to women in this society but to point

to women's inadequacy. Linda's expression of despair was labelled as a
symptom of her mental illness. Her symptoms were real: she was fearful,
distraught, in physical pain, suffocating. Talking with her was like trying
to calm a frantic animal caught in a cage. The bars on her cage were not
visible as such: she had a good husband, lovely children, a nice home.
Linda's "symptoms," then, were highly symbolic. She created tangible
bars to her cage in the form of fears of going outside, fear of the picture
windows through which she might throw herself, fear of cars in which
she might leave, fear of knives with which she might kill herself or those
around her. Inside those bars she was not safe, for the terror also lay
within. The only relief, the only alternative, was the hospital. It was a
refuge from fear, but at the cost of being a psychiatric patient. In the
hospital Linda was "better," calm and peaceful, except that her agitation would return if threatened with discharge. Her personal solution
was the best she could manage in order to survive, though she still had
some hope that she could be "cured," and would eventually cope with
her life. Since nothing was done to change this life, however, she had
little alternative but to resist getting "better."

SUMMARY

There is apparent confusion in the psychiatric texts as to the
definition of normality against which mental illness is to be judged. It is
evident, in fact, that there is implicit agreement among professionals
that what is normal is that which is socially acceptable as "that version
of the world which has been sanctioned as 'reality.' "[51] The dominant
group in any society controls the meaning of what is valid information.
For women and other subordinate groups, the version of the world
which has been sanctioned as reality does not address their lived experience; but because they have no accepted terms of their own, women
have had few opportunities to understand this disjunction. The opportunities offered to them within the framework of the institution of
psychiatry provide a way to experience the disjunction as proof of
mental illness. That is, in some sense, its purpose: to present someone
who has broken down under the strain of an intolerable existence,
which must not be seen as intolerable, as someone to be "fixed up"
with pills, treatment, and psycho-therapy in order to go on living with
the strains, or else as someone to be put away and cared for as incapa-
ble.[52] In the words of Caplan and Nelson: "Train a person in psychological theory . . . and suddenly a world disastrously out of tune with
human needs is explained as a state of mind."[53]

≡ *PART TWO*

WOMEN
and
PSYCHIATRY

CHAPTER IV

WOMAN: THE UNIVERSAL SCAPEGOAT

"SINCE EVE, WOMEN HAVE BEEN BLAMED FOR THE problems of man, mankind, and themselves. The pressure to internalize feelings of guilt is enormous."[1]

In the previous chapters we considered the relationship of psychiatric theory to the practices of the institution. This relationship can be seen as part of the location of psychiatry in the broad social structure of which it is a part. When examining some of the ways in which models of mental health and illness serve to obscure and even to regulate the social costs of living in our particular form of society, we dealt in general terms with women and men alike. We did not focus on our major concern — the particular relation of women to psychiatry. To do so will require an examination of the position of women in society as a whole and especially their relation to the ideological structures through which western industrial society is ordered, regulated and governed.

Women do not have a direct relation to the formation of these ideological structures. In fact, they have been systematically excluded, sometimes inadvertently, but often deliberately.[2] They have not had an equal voice in the development of the theoretical formulations which are the basis of the social sciences and psychiatric theory. This is the result both of the generation of theory by those who occupy particular positions in the institution and who, by virtue of their dominant status, are usually men, and of the actual situation and status of women among those whose voices are not considered relevant or authoritative in this society. As women we only have those ways of making experience comprehensible which were created by men for their own use. This second-hand relation of women to the ideas and language which help us to order and make sense of our experience means that women are doubly vulnerable to having their reality invalidated. Like other minority groups, we have no voice in how we are represented, but beyond that we lack the direct relationship of male experience to male images and symbols.

The particular relation of women to the ideological structures of psychiatry is not visible from within its framework. It is not visible in the theories themselves unless they are examined in a manner which locates them and the institution within the social system as a whole. It then becomes possible to see that much of what is presented as the psychology of women has been justifiably described as "patriarchal rhetoric."[3] There are quite concrete difficulties in knowing women in any other terms, however. Control of the ideological apparatus of society has allowed men to incorporate as knowledge an array of symbols and images of women which both represent, and to some degree create, the way that women are visible to men and to themselves.

Certain images of women occur across time, race and culture. Most reflect the profound ambivalence which men feel towards women. Because of this common theme, myths and ideas concerning women and the symbols through which they are represented appear to be relatively consistent throughout the ages. These images are seen as a universal part of a collective human consciousness (or unconsciousness) and as therefore representative of deep and universal truths about the nature of women; all women for all time. Closer examination of the relation of themes and images to their context, however, reveals that they are not mere free-floating ideas which are ever-present. They are an integral part of how life is ordered, regulated and given meaning in any given society.

In our present society the images which are invoked to record and regulate the position and status of women are in part those which psychology, psychiatry, and the social sciences in general, have built up from the images of the past. These are presented as an explanation of "the natural order of things." The existence and function of such images goes unquestioned; it is simply assumed that the nature of women is known. The knowledge exists in the myths, folklore, literature and religious teachings which we embrace. Scientific study begins from this assumption and examines the parameters and particulars of this known nature. In this manner psychiatry in particular has taken on a function previously carried out to a large degree by organized religion;

that of providing a rationale and an explanation for the inevitability of the way things are for women. Tracing the details of women's lives throughout recorded history, in order to assess the relationship of prevalent images to women's actual status, presents something of a difficulty. Recorded history itself is a measure of the control which men exert over the means and methods of understanding social structures. It is the history of *mankind* and reflects the relevances of *men's* experience. Feminist historians are now working to reclaim what can be salvaged of women's own history but much is lost to us forever. By comparing what we do know of women's lives with the prevalent images, archetypes and stereotypes, we can begin to identify how it is that these themes both grow out of, and become part of, the view of women held and enforced at a given time.

From comparisons between what was actually happening and the ideas which gave it its particular historical meaning, we will look at how psychiatric theories have been used to control women. They function to provide a way of seeing distress, misery, and the disjunction between experience and understanding as individual pathology. There is a particular disjunction between reality as women experience it and reality as it is explained by the ideas present in the culture in general and in psychiatric theory in particular. It is this disjunction that is at the root of the distress which often initially sends women in search of psychiatric help. Smith describes how women's protests, once they have been classified as symptoms, come to be seen as ". . . merely 'expressive,' merely a movement — or a gesture, a raving, a hysteria, an attack on the dark in the dark, a bellow of rage or anguish, a horror of not being — that hole in the world through which its sense finally leaks away."[4]

EARLY WESTERN HISTORY

Much of what we understand of the lives of women in early and pre-recorded history is based on supposition drawn from fossils and artifacts. Although this also applies to the lives of men, we are limited with regard to women by the relevancies of those who have collected and interpreted historical and anthropological data. Recent attempts to reconstruct this early history from a feminist perspective provide an interesting counterbalance, although there is little evidence on which to base any theories or reconstructions. Morgan provides one such theory, which is also a lively critique of the male popularizers of ethological and sociobiological schools of thought. She dismisses them with asperity, naming them "The Tarzanists."[5] A recent academic contribution is that of Zilman and Tanner who use the tools of sociobiology to challenge the sexist nature of the speculative reconstructions of many leading male members of these disciplines, and to present their own feminist theories.[6] Images which have survived from these early times are those of fertility symbols, earth-mother goddesses, and priestesses concerned with seasonal rituals and rites. Early taboos connected with menstruation and childbirth contain seeds of the kind of ambivalence with which women have come to be regarded, but there is little evidence to show that they were instituted by men. Indeed, it is possible that women developed taboos for reasons of their own, such as a defense against untimely childbearing. Although it is possible to surmise from these images that women were powerful figures in pre-history, it is important to remember that we do not know the nature of the actual relation between the images and women's position in society.

The development of a written language which has survived to this day provides us with glimpses, through myths and legends, of women warriors and goddesses who, like their male counterparts, were the embodiment of many contradictory qualities. Some, like the Hindu goddess, Kali, were symbols of both creation and destruction. Others championed men or deceived them, were wise, foolish, vengeful, faithful, capricious, loving or vain. It is not until predominantly dualistic forms of thought appear that we begin to get a clear image of women as the opposite of men. Polarities such as day and night, black and white, good and evil, also encompass as a basic component, male and female. To see women as the opposite of men does not in itself, however, account for the negative valuation of their position. Women were intitially characterized as powerful in their own right and in their own ways.

Scholars and commentators offer a number of explanations for why images of women gradually diminished in their powerfulness and were reduced to views of women considered only in relation to men. The most popular and consistent seem to be those which suggest that the development of forms of society in which property was held by individuals, rather than in common by a tribe, led to the need to establish inheritance rights. The realization that males contributed to reproduction meant that children were no longer seen as related to the mother alone. From needing a man to sire *her* children, women then moved to being the vessel which produced *his* children. As such she became man's property and, where inheritance was concerned, his exclusive property, since this was the only way of ensuring true blood-related heirs. It is postulated that extreme sanctions on women's sexuality relates to this development. A woman had to be a virgin until married, and faithful after marriage, to ensure legitimate heirs. Thus the ownership of women's sexuality and reproductive functions by men was enforced. In some cultures, adultery or even fornication were punishable by death for women, though seldom for the man involved. This is still the case in some cultures and certainly most rape laws clearly reflect their origins in the definition of women as property.[7] These changes in women's status may be reflected in images and symbols which represent women as wives and mothers and no longer as fertility goddesses, priestesses, and warriors.

The more that western social organization came to be conceptualized in polar terms, the more evident it became that certain poles were considered more valuable, important, or correct than their opposites. The opposition of Nature and Civilization, Body and Soul, and Emotion and Reason, which comes to us from classical Greek thought, paved the way for a change in the images of women. Women's identification with nature had initially been seen as a civilizing force, one which led to the cultivation of crops, the maintenance of permanent or semipermanent dwellings, the makings of vessels and clothing, as well as the bearing and rearing of children. With the conceptualization of nature as the opposite of civilization and as a factor to be transcended or controlled by "civilized man," came an era in which women seem to have been identified with those aspects of life which had to be most rigidly ordered and regulated. Women, therefore, were assigned those human attributes which were considered an impediment to man's struggle towards a higher form of being or civilization. Whereas the older supernatural forces had been conceived of as powerfully and often positively female, femaleness now represented negatively conceptualized powers such as carnality and evil magic. The supernatural force to which people now aspired was that of a male, omnipotent god who required a "higher" form of spiritual worship, manifested in ways which included the denial of sexuality. It has been suggested that the transcendence of "nature" in a civilization in which spiritual values were paramount was accomplished, at the level of ideas, by splitting mystical experience from its basis in sexuality.[8] True spirituality had as its essence the mysticism achieved through "denial of the flesh" and asceticism carried to extreme lengths. Sexuality and everything identified with it, particularly its symbol, woman, then represented temptation, a failure of will, a lapsing of faith, a fall from grace, and the succumbing to the baser desires of the body. Woman as symbol in this context, in her archetypal role of seductive, licentious and destructive physical nature incarnate, could only be seen as evil, or as a vessel of the forces of evil, allied with the powers of damnation.

The ideal of manhood in this scheme was the maintenance of celibacy. Those who could not attain the ideal must marry rather than burn in hell for the sin of fornication. Although theoretically the options were the same for women, those who sought a celibate life faced considerable opposition. Man striving for a nonsexual life dedicated to spiritual values and enterprises was aspiring to realize his true being in the likeness of god. Woman, whose being was carnal, temporal and profane, must deny her true nature and become a pseudoman in order to live a virginal life.[9] However, since these ideas existed in a world of principalities and powers in which the continuation of the race and peoples was also of paramount importance, it is easy to see that they do not represent the total reality of peoples' lives. They do, however, give a background which helps to account for the ways in which women were viewed as sexual beings whose nature and freedom must be curbed both to ensure the legitimacy of heirs and to safeguard man's spiritual survival in the hereafter. The power of these views can be inferred from the stature of such influential theologians as St. Augustine who suggested that sexual activity be eliminated so that there would be no more children and the end of the world would come in one generation. This he regarded, none too hopefully, as the perfect way to transcend the wretched physical world and gain the everlasting realm of spiritual existence. Some of the contradictions which such disjunctions must precipitated are illustrated by the development of movements such as the tradition of "Romance and Courtly Love" and the worship of women as pure, nonsexual beings, exemplified by the Virgin Mary. The lengths to which the church went to detach "Our Lady" from the taint of carnal knowledge is an illustration of this.[10]

THE PERSISTENCE OF ARCHETYPES AND
THEIR STEREOTYPIC COUNTERPARTS

This highly condensed summary is not meant to outline a simple, linear progression of ideas and images through the centuries. It does, however, give us a background against which to examine in more detail the later developments which are our concern. In the "modern" era (which we consider to begin with the transition from feudal to industrial social organization), factual material in the form of records, publications, laws, and a written literature is more readily available. We enter it, however, with a wealth of legend, law, myth, and religious teaching on the nature and status of women. Most of what is written or recorded was done so by men, and there is little concrete information about women's actual situation. What we do know is gleaned chiefly from the laws which confine women to the position of property and from what historians call "prescriptive literature." This is written material in the form of domestic management manuals, moral primers, educational treatises, religious tracts, and cautionary or instructional tales or fables. As such, this body of material has some of the same problems as records in general. It is hard to tell how much it relates to women's actual lives and how much is merely the reflection of the authors' ideas on how women should behave.

From these various representations of women through the ages we can draw a general idea of the kind of archetypal images present in western culture and their relation to stereotypical views of women. An archetype, in the sense in which we are using the term, refers to a pervasive and recurring image of women on a universal scale, sometimes different in manifestation but often remarkably consistent in theme and symbols. It is usually a particular *figure* — mythical, legendary or actual. Archetypes can be a powerful, if unacknowledged, influence on the way we understand our own experience and the actions of those around us.

To preserve the dichotomy of thought-process which men's images of women illustrate, we will organize a summary of archetypes around two themes which illustrate the ambivalence of the images. There are only two distinct kinds of women: good and bad. Both can further be described as weak or strong. "Good women," who are also powerful, are earth-mothers and fertility symbols; symbols of moral rectitude and creative muses for men's inspiration. There are few of them. More frequent are women who are "good" because of their purity, innocence, loyalty, and need of protection. What power they possess comes from their ability to influence men by their gentle goodness. Myths and fairytales abound with such damsels. "Bad women," whose danger lies in their power, are insatiable temptresses and destroyers, often both, and occasionally monsters of evil in their own right. They are devourers, polluters, and child killers. Weaker women on the bad side of the dichotomy are untrustworthy, shrewish, seductive, and licentious whores.

Nowhere is the ambivalence towards women more apparent than with respect to the role of beauty in images of women. It is a woman's beauty which makes her a prize to be sought, the symbol of her goodness and purity, yet it is her beauty which entraps men and leads them to destruction. Snow White and Rose Red typify this dichotomy. Both are beautiful (where is the fairytale heroine who is as good as she is ugly?); one is pure and virginal, the other sexual and wicked. Sometimes the dichotomy is expressed as two sides of the same woman, as with the little girl with the curl on her forehead, but more commonly qualities are polarized. Ugly women are almost invariably portrayed as stupid, silly or wicked, as are the ugly sisters in *Beauty and the Beast* or in *Cinderella.*

If we consider stereotypes as those typifications and generalizations which serve to categorize and simplify a basically chaotic and incomprehensible world, we can see that they also have the quality of ordering and regulating that world. They do so by providing shoulds and oughts, prescriptions for how things should be as well as descriptions of the way things are. Stereotypes change with circumstances and different archetypes are incorporated into them at different times. This becomes very clear when considering the range of characteristics and activities attributed to women in the number of stereotypic views which have been advanced over the ages. A checklist will reveal both the prescriptive and sanctioning functions of the stereotypes and the influence of archetypal images. The Feminine Principle, Eternal Feminine, and True Womanhood, have been invoked to require that women be obedient, submissive, chaste, clean, nurturant, diligent, self-effacing, self-sacrificing, serene, tender, intuitive, feeling, fertile where appropriate, and altruistic. A woman who is not all of these things is destructive, manipulative, lascivious, licentious, irresponsible, greedy, tricky, nagging, irrational, emotional, vain, self-centred, and selfish.

Whereas the early archetypal figures represented both creation and destruction, birth and death, fertility and famine, those that followed were increasingly defined directly by and through their relation to men. (Even the word "woman" comes from the Saxon for "wife of man.") Eve and Pandora did not give birth to men as early mother goddesses had done, but were fashioned by male gods for men's use. Through sexuality, defined in biblical terms as knowledge of good and evil, they were the downfall of all mankind, responsible for sin, sickness, corruption, pain and death. Hope for the world remained in Pandora's box; Eve's travail in childbirth gave women a way to redeem themselves through suffering and the production of a saviour for mankind. In these two figures it is possible to see women being held responsible for the ills of the world and for its redemption.

How the many images and their incorporation into the stereotypes which prescribe and describe women's role at any given time actually relate to women's lives over the ages is work which is only now being undertaken. Historians propose the study of this aspect of history; "a recognition of the multivalence of sexual symbols can help interpret the complex and seldom unilinear relationship between cultural images of women and the status of women within a given society."[11] Women's history may indeed diverge from that of men. It is apparent from recent studies that eras assumed to represent great progress for mankind, such as Hellenic Greece, the Renaissance, or the French Revolution, had quite different implications for women. In Classical Greece, women and slaves were excluded, as a matter of course, from most of the democratic principles, ideals and practices. The Renaissance, which has long been considered by historians to be a period which saw great advances in cultural and material conditions, "was marked by increasing inequalities of social power between men and women."[12] Women who demanded that the Revolutionary goals of liberty, equality, and fraternity be extended to include them were firmly rebuked and their more militant spokeswoman guillotined.[13] During the Reformation, when Europe writhed in chaos as church and state fought to maintain their identities and powers, millions of women were burned as witches. Great ages for men, including the Age of Reason or Enlightenment, have not coincided with a marked rise in the status of women, although they may indeed have made for changes. The goal of men has been defined as "progress" and progress as a concept includes the subduing and exploitation of the natural world and the acquisition of property.

Women, long identified with nature and still in many legal senses the property of men, can only exist in the relation of "other" to men in such a man's world, in the sense in which de Beauvoir has conceptualized it for us. Women are not the subject or centre of their own understanding of the world when they are only considered as they relate to men in a social system designed for and by men.[14]

Women have always been identified with the function of childbearing and hence, since the development of family groupings, with the concept of "the family." This identification is crucial to an understanding of both women's actual situation and the images and symbols which define and describe it. "Women and the Family" will be the focus of a later chapter; here it is necessary to note that changes in the social organization of the family coincide with changes in emphasis with regard to popular conceptions of women's nature and role. The rise of capitalist forms of economic organization which mark the end of the Middle Ages had a major impact on the way in which women's lives were both structured and perceived. The increasing conceptual division of western society into "public" and "private" spheres of operation reflected the divorce of household from workplace and the development of "the home" as a separate realm. The concomitant image of the powerful maternal figure was invoked to elevate the status of women as pure, noble "angels of the hearth" at a time when any actual power which they may have had over the regulation of the broader society was being limited and restricted to the domestic sphere.

As the capitalist structure developed into its current corporate form, women became increasingly responsible for the private domain, and needs not met in the public world more and more fell within the task of the individual woman. Fewer people, women or men, were prepared to work as domestic servants when better working conditions and pay were available in industry. Technological advances and the mass-production of many goods previously made by women in the home relieved women of some of the physical toil of housework, but most women, from all but the most economically favoured classes, now had to perform the household tasks for their families and themselves. In addition to this, women's work in the production of middle-class status involved increasingly prescribed forms of child-rearing, companionship, display, and hostessship, in order to promote a husband's career by presenting him as a "proper" person with a "proper" family. The emotional management of strains created outside the family but experienced within the family, along with the management of those strains in the family, is all seen as the woman's job. Further, with the recognition that the workplace is insecure, alienating and, for most middle- as well as working-class men, organized in ways which are outside of their control and location, women are expected to provide the intimacy lacking outside, and to take up the emotional and economic slack in times of harship.

The so-called "sexual revolution" had its antecedents in the more liberal attitude towards sexuality of an increasingly secular society, concerned with population control and the "quality of life" and investment in the human resources necessary to run a highly complex, technologically-based system. It was part of the ideology which "eroticized the middle-class wife at the very moment when other classes of women, such as domestic servants, prostitutes, serfs and slaves were being abolished and [so] put the burden upon the wife of fulfilling all the functions that had once been carried out by a retinue of socially differentiated women."[15] This is the kind of "chef of the kitchen," "lady in the drawing room," "slut in the bedroom," image that Betty Friedan took issue with in *The Feminine Mystique*.[16] It still surfaces as the "traditional" and "correct" image of total and fascinating womanhood to which we are instructed to return in order to secure the fabric of society from destruction.[17]

The experience, rewards and costs of living under our particular form of social organization are different for each sex and each class according to the extent that their relations to the social structure are different. When evidence of the costs takes on alarming proportions, attempts are made to reform, reorganize, and shore up various elements of the system. We see the advent of programs designed to alleviate poverty, relieve human misery, curb violence and vandalism, avert suicides, remedy alcohol and drug abuse, and prevent "stress-related" illness. The scope of problems which are defined in this manner have led to a recognition that if our present system is to continue, some attention will have to be paid to those basic human needs previously considered as purely individual and private concerns. This in itself is a change in policy, although it is not often accompanied by a corresponding shift in attitude. Thus, we simultaneously recognize that people sometimes fall on hard times and have to seek social assistance from government agencies, and look down on them as "welfare bums" whose predicament is of their own making. Chronic unemployment can be temporarily alleviated by insurance payments, yet regarded as the outcome of an unwillingness to work. Ryan describes the ideology behind these programs as that of "blaming the victim," that is, providing ways to focus on society's victims rather than on the social structures which generate their problems.[18]

The contradiction which is being "rationalized" in the situation is that which indicates a more holistic view of human functioning than has been characterized under the ideology of public and private spheres. Yet, at the same time, techniques of scientific management are applied to automated work processes, dividing and partializing human input into smaller and more mechanistic components. Three strategies are employed in the rationalization of this contradiction. The first and simplest is to apportion to the state as much responsibility as possible for the destructive "social cost" of the workplace.[19] The second and most visible involves corporations in the study and implementation of measures to improve job satisfaction as a function of efficiency, and in taking on certain community activities and family concerns. The third, and for our purposes the major strategy, is also perhaps the most invidious and covert. It is ideological in the sense that it works through images and ideas which concentrate on the reality, intensity, and authenticity of experiences outside the workplace.

Despite its being obvious that the events and decisions which shape our lives take place in the political "public" arena as it is currently defined, there is a strong focus on the "private" sphere as the place where enjoyment, satisfaction, and release take place. Apart from the straightforward relation of the consumption of goods in the private world of home and leisure, which accounts for much of the stress laid on it by advertising, popular music, the media, and so on, this accomplishes a further purpose. It means that men expect all of these needs to be met outside the workplace when the work they do is exploitive, dreary, or highly pressured. Sports and leisure activities take up some of the burden, but most of it falls on women. They must shoulder, as part of their task in the private sphere which is allotted them, the satisfaction of all needs, physical, social and intimate, for men and indeed for children and for themselves, whether they work outside the home or not. Women must look to men and children to meet their needs for achievement and respect.

In the rhetoric which accomplishes the implementation of this third strategy, we find two of the age-old themes which we have been tracing: women both as destroyers and as creators of hope for the future. Women have historically been held responsible for male sexuality; for causing men to fail in their quest for celibacy, for causing impotence by witchcraft, a "crime" for which many were burned alive during the Middle Ages. After Freud it was common to read of female frigidity and inhibition as a cause of male sexual failure; now we learn that the aggressive female produced by "Women's Lib" is perceived as overpowering and threatening, and thus renders men impotent.[20] Male sexual potency and satisfaction, as well as the production of offspring, are seen as women's direct responsibility.

Women as mothers are subject to the same injunctions. They are held entirely responsible for their children's development and well-being, but if they expend all their energies to this end they are accused of smothering, emasculating, or pushing their children (and indeed their husbands) beyond endurance to satisfy their own need for achievement.[21] If they take any other route they are accused not only of neglecting, but of actually "castrating" the family.[22] The circular reasoning of this argument is that if women were to rear healthy, well-adjusted children, there would be no further problems in society. Therefore, as there are still problems in society, women must have failed in their ordained task. Therefore, like Eve, women are responsible for the ills of the world. This reasoning is supported by what Rich describes as a new archetype, "the Danger in the Home," Mom, the schizo-phrenogenic mother, the latter-day Medusa. A subtler version of this imaging, which women themselves are also inclined to find persuasive, is one which presents women's qualities as those which "the world" — that is, the "public sphere" — lacks.

Women are adjured to liberate themselves and throw the weight of their hitherto private power into the world arena. The disguise is subtle, but the view is still one which presents women as "other"; women cannot possibly need, let alone want equality or freedom for themselves, however that may be defined. The message is that the liberation of women is required to "liberate" men from their destructive activities and ultimately save the world for future generations. That women may suffer in the process is part of the archetype. Women will suffer giving birth to movements instead of to children. It is acceptable for women to suffer as long as it is altruistic, for the good of others.[23]

None of these shifts are arbitrary, mere cultural shifts, changes in fashion or ideas of a random nature. What they reflect are the changes in socio-economic organization and the fundamental needs of the system. Present trends seem to be towards another phase of glorification of the family and the woman in the home, this time couched in terms of genetic predisposition or the crucial nature of child-bearing and holding the home as a centre of emotional stability. We hear about the financial value of housework in terms of wages that would have to be paid to outside workers, and an emphasis on the home as women's valuable and demanding job. In a time of unemployment and extensive cutbacks in services outside the home, women are required to "manage" the family, that is, to create and maintain a model social structure; a stable, hard-working breadwinner, and well-behaved, high-achieving future workers. If she needs to earn a second wage to do so, she not only carries a double workload, but also may be accused of taking a man's job while neglecting her own *real* work. The family is being maintained with minimal support services to the home and a lack of services outside the home. Thus the family is forced to take back some of its previous functions, such as caring for the sick, the aged, the impaired, and all children. This must now be done in settings not designed for such functions, and, if possible, on one wage per family. Services in the community are again being organized on the basis of volunteer labour. There is little doubt at whose expense this economic coup is being accomplished.

These, then, are some of the social realities which underlie the stereotypical images of women, and which interact with these images to affect women's ability to perceive and explain their own experience. Bardwick and Douvan suggest that the stereotypes do indeed describe as well as prescribe the way most women actually are. Rich, on the other hand, sees that as human beings with "actual bodies and actual minds," we women are lost to sight under the welter of images and symbols which purport to portray us.[24]

PSYCHIATRIC THEORIES AND THEIR IMPLICATIONS FOR WOMEN

The near classic study undertaken by Broverman et al. in 1970 found that mental health professionals of various disciplines, female and male alike, endorsed as norms the cultural stereotypes of femininity and masculinity. Furthermore, they held different standards of adult mental health for females and males which were not only in line with these stereotypic views, but also reflected the different evaluation of femininity and masculinity in our society. Their definition of general adult mental health coincided with the masculine stereotype. Healthy adult women were seen to differ from healthy adults or healthy adult males by being "more submissive, less independent, less adventurous, more easily influenced, less aggressive, less competitive, more excitable in minor crises, having their feelings more easily hurt, more conceited about their appearance, less objective, and disliking math and science."[25] This constellation, as D'Arcy and Schmitz point out, goes beyond mere stereotyping — it becomes a powerful negative assessment.[26]

Although some recent studies indicate that there may have been changes in attitude in the intervening years,[27] other reports confirm that, by and large, therapists hold to many of the assessments of women laid down in cultural stereotypes which contain many of the images of women which we have been tracing.[28] Further studies indicate that these attitudes affect the perception of people's problems and their treatment.[29] In every instance the therapists were of both sexes and of different orientations ranging from psychiatrists to psychologists, social workers, marriage counsellors, and psychiatric nurses.[30] It comes as no surprise, in view of the impact of cultural images of women on other areas of scientific exploration, to find that theories of human development, personality, and behaviour are part of the stream of ideas which both embrace and transmit such images. It is impossible to examine all of the many theories and versions thereof which exist; we will consider a few of the most influential in the training of mental health professionals. To do so, we will order them on an informal continuum from those which offer a form of "psychology of women" to those in which women are invisible or their experience subsumed under the so-called generic masculine.

Psychodynamic Formulations

The theories which comprise the psychodynamic school are among the most influential to date. They are also those which contain the more fully developed formulation of "feminine" psychology. Psychoanalytic theory is the progenitor, and Freud, of course, the originator. Few theories have created more controversy or had more impact on current society, and none have received more attention from critics of sexism than Freud's. The debate on Freud's views of women and his formulation of feminine identity is complex and controversial. Here we are concerned less with the validity of his theories than with their content as it relates to the cultural imagery of our theme, and with the historical context of his ideas, which account for their influence.

Fancher clearly shows how Freud's attitudes and formulations on women developed and changed over his long career and how they contained a number of contradictions and inconsistencies.[31] Freud himself was aware of this and confessed bafflement at the end of his life, suggesting that women and women's analysts must explore for themselves the true nature of feminine development. Bearing in mind Mitchell's convincing argument that it does violence to Freud's work to abstract certain writings on women from their roots in his basic premises of the unconscious and infantile sexuality,[32] we will summarize his most pertinent formulation within this context.

Freud proposes that the female infant, entering childhood, perceives her lack of penis as something that will be remedied. When it becomes apparent that this is impossible, she recognizes her genital structure as deficient; a wound which is the result of a previous and un-remembered castration. Blaming her mother for failing to make her a boy, or for failing to protect her against the maiming which has taken place, she looks to her father to restore her lost penis. When this, too, proves impossible, she desires first her father's penis, and later his baby as a substitute. These incestuous desires are "unthinkable" and are therefore repressed at the unconscious level, recurring again after puberty as the more socially permissable desire for a baby. Thus, giving birth to a baby is the acceptable way of acquiring a substitute penis, forms a bond with the baby's father, and, if the baby is a son, provides a penis in fact as well as fantasy. This accounts for why mothers prefer male children. The female clitoris, unlike its masculine counterpart, is not a true reproductive organ, and the girl must be induced to transfer her sexual pleasure from clitoral stimulation to that received by vaginal penetration. The abandonment of the clitoris as a source of pleasure typically takes place in puberty. Freud says of this process: "The main distinction between the sexes emerges at the time of puberty, when girls are seized by a *non*-neurotic sexual repugnance, and males by libido. For at that period a further sexual zone is (wholly or in part) extinguished in females which persists in males . . . Hence, the flood of shame which overwhelms the female at this period, till the new, vaginal zone is awakened, whether spontaneously or by reflex action."[33]

Freud sees this extra "non-neurotic" repression required of women as part of the "difficult developments which lead to femininity" that renders women more frequently susceptible to hysteria, and also seems to make them less interesting.[34] The three interlocking components of femininity — masochism, narcissim, and passivity — all arise in the process of this "difficult development" at the Oedipal stage because, unlike the boy, the girl must change her love object from the same-sex mother to the opposite sex represented by the father. A further outcome of genital difference is that the girl, perceiving herself as already castrated, does not have to resolve the castration complex of the boy, who internalizes the fear of his father's retaliation to Oedipal desire in the form of a harsh and rigid superego. Women, therefore, have less superego than men.

A careful reading of Freud's work, and that of Mitchell and Fancher, reveals that he did not, in fact, make a number of controversial statements often attributed to him by followers and detractors alike. Freud did not subscribe to the form of biological determinisim of which he is often accused. He distinguished between biology and anatomy, and even his often-quoted dictum "anatomy is destiny," was stated in a specific context which emphasized the similarities between the most basic psychological processes of both men and women. Any remaining differences are accounted for by the different experiences of females and males. "Some of these different experiences" that Fancher explained, "are mere social conventions. More important, and more nearly universal, are the differences arising from anatomical conditions. The girl's mind, though innately highly similar to the boy's, must undergo certain distinctive experiences, the cost of its location in a female body: similarly for the boy. This," Fancher insists, "was the real, though often misunderstood meaning of Freud's notorious . . . comment."[35]

Similarly, the equation of feminine and masculine with passive and active was described by Freud as mere social convention, except as it applies to the active seeking of the sperm for the passive receptivity of the ovum in the act of conception. Active and passive, masculine and feminine attributes beyond this basic situation were to be found in both sexes to varying degrees. Nor did Freud categorically decree that women were biologically inferior to men, but saw their inferiority as a result of the "difficult development" towards a femininity defined by social convention and the cost of adjusting to women's situation in society.

Having said this, however, it is necessary to consider how he conceptualized the "difficult development" of femininity, and indeed the social pressures which he acknowledged as a major factor in that development. This is where some of the inconsistencies which Fancher acknowledges become most apparent. Freud's definition of the impact of culture on the individual would seem consistent with that of Lambert who sees behaviour as "itself a biological phenomenon, an interaction between the organism and environment [in which] . . . influences extrinsic to the individual affect biological events within the organism — events by which, in many cases, the structural entities and functional mechanisms within the organism develop."[36] Repression is the mental process by which those innate drives which must succumb to social pressures are internalized or rendered unconscious. By focussing on the particular repression of the libido or sexual urge during the Oedipal phase as part of normal development and as the root of neurosis, Freud proposes a process which Mitchell describes as the child's entry into the human culture. It is a universal experience, the particulars of which are prescribed by the specific culture, but which takes place regardless of the absence or presence of the actual parent. Freud's setting of these events within the intrapsychic processes of the pre-Oedical and Oedipal stages of early childhood, only echoed or re-awakened in other forms by the advent of puberty, sexual maturity, and adulthood, makes them the sole impact of "the culture" on the id, an impact which sees the creation of the ego and the superego in a closed system. This is, in fact, a much more specific and limited view of the interaction between organism and environment than that which Lambert describes. Although Freud is careful to state that his ideas are drawn from cases and are therefore "typical" rather than universal, he presents such formulations as the crucial Oedipus Complex as universal, historical and cross-cultural. This hardly supports Mitchell's contention that Freud was merely describing the actual impact of the full range of socially-determined experience on the development of femininity. The repression of sexual drives is seen as the major impact of culture; all other limitations of the individual stem from it. This is an entirely apolitical, ahistorical view which discounts or renders invisible the political realities of our society.

It has been pointed out that Freud could hardly have considered women as intellectually and morally inferior since he welcomed them into the psychoanalytic movement and treated them as colleagues with particular insights into feminine experiences. He also, however, defended himself from criticism of masculine bias, levelled by female colleagues, by suggesting that they were successful only because they had more masculine than feminine characteristics.[37] While, as Fancher suggests, his apportioning of negative qualities to women was matched by an equal share of negative characteristics in his view of men, he failed to follow through on the implications of his own theories when the result would have been an attribution of more favourable qualities to women. "The only major example of unfairness in Freud's early treatment of the two sexes was his failure to note it when his theories seemed to attribute a degree of moral superiority to women. When he altered his entire theory of moral development in 1923, it did not take him long to suggest that the opposite was true."[38]

Mitchell insists that Freud's work was descriptive, never prescriptive, yet the didactic tone of his language and his manner of presenting findings deduced from the study of adult patients as if they were observations of the child's development make it difficult to read him in this way. It is possible to recognize in Freud's writing and teaching a number of unproven, and indeed unprovable, assumptions. Not the least of these is that major formulation for feminine development — penis envy — which Caplan suggests provides an example of built-in obstacles to testability. "If a girl says she wishes she had a penis, Freud's theory is supported. If a girl says she is relieved not to have to worry about having an unprotected external genital organ, Freud's theory of reaction formation indicates that this is simply a cover-up of her 'real' penis-envy."[39] Omissions of inconvenient implications for women's superior moral force have already been noted. The overall impression one actually receives is that Freud formally holds to a different standard of what is normal and ethical for women, and presents a view which both mirrors and reinforces a number of the images of women which are already familiar. "The feminine superego," he wrote, "cannot attain the strength and independence which [in men] gives it its cultural significance." Fancher notes that Freud held that women "tend to be narcissistic, deceitful, overburdened with shame, and jealous. He also denigrated their intellectual creativity, suggesting that the only truly feminine contribution to human culture was the art of weaving, and that even that developed only as an improvement on the pubic hair as a means of hiding the defective female genitals."[40] It is exactly this type of image which has been embraced by his followers and criticized by his detractors, especially feminists.

Freud's analysand and disciple, Helene Deutsch, agreed that woman's biology made her an *"homme manqué"* (a failure as a man), and felt that the environment and culture exerted an inhibiting influence on women's aggressiveness and creativity. Penis envy alone did not account for all of women's troubles; deficient female anatomy and society seem to work together to produce femininity.[41] Despite this broader emphasis on social influence, however, Deutsch considered it against biological, psychological, and sociological laws for a woman to take any initiative. She insisted that sexual satisfaction through clitoral orgasm was a form of frigidity and a symptom of immaturity, an opinion she still holds despite the research findings of Masters and Johnson and the Hite Report.[42]

Freud had suggested that because a woman is already castrated, she does not suffer from the fear of castration, and so objectifies and sets herself up as "other." Deutsch greatly developed this as the root of narcissism, and the "fact" of castration as the root of masochism, the giving up of the idea of having a penis as the root of passivity, and all as dependent on biological, specifically genital, attributes. "Normal" femininity consisted of all these traits and "becomes active when the woman becomes a mother and renounces all active goals of her own — all her own creativity — in order to identify and fulfill herself through the activities and goals of her husband and son."[43]

Horney, Thompson, and Fromm Reichmann disputed with Freud over the central focus on penis-envy, and insisted that it was male envy of women's reporductive processes which was the root of the denigration of women, not their innate inferiority.

Erikson, himself a psychoanalyst and the author of an influential work on human development that is widely used in the training of many mental health professionals, falls within both the first and second categories of theorists. His book, *Childhood and Society,* offers a good example of a way of thinking which presents the male as prototype. In a long section on the development of the sense of identity, over 17 pages are devoted to the identity crises of adolescents. In these 17 pages, there is one paragraph only on the identity crisis of the adolescent girl, and that paragraph reads, in part: "The *sister's* crisis will come when she becomes a *mother* and when the vicissitudes of child training will perforce bring to the fore the infantile identification with her *mother*."[44] (Emphasis added.) Again, the female is referred to in relation to the male, as his sibling, and her identification as an adult is only as a mother and in relation to her own mother. Although a further section deals with the phenomenon of "momism," the overpowering and overprotective mother so dear to North American authors (males), Schwarz[45] points out that students reading *Childhood and Society* learn almost nothing about the female adolescent's search for identity, and receive a series of subtle messages indicating its lack of importance.

When Erikson does focus on women, in an essay entitled "Reflections on Womanhood," it becomes evident that he does not share Freud's view of women as inferior because of their anatomical structure. On the contrary, Erikson, like Horney, takes issue with this formulation and proposes a re-evaluation of women's reproductive organs. Women's "somatic design harbours an 'inner space' destined to bear the offspring of chosen men and, with it, a biological, psychological, and ethical commitment to take care of human infancy . . ."[46] For Erikson, women's inner space, whether she chooses to use it or not, pre-determines her personality. "Yes," he firmly says in the same essay, " . . . anatomy is destiny . . . insofar as it determines not only the range and configuration of physiological functioning and its limitation, but also, to an extent, personality configurations. The basic modalities of women's commitment and involvement naturally also reflect the ground plan of the body."[47]

Here we see a familiar and seductive use of images; the inversion of denigration to an equally stereotyped adulation based on romanticized qualities of a somewhat magical type. Women have an ethical sense and a moral commitment, anatomically based; they must now proceed from their mysterious inner sanctums where they have chosen to hide, and save the world from an excess of masculine consciousness, also anatomically determined. This is one of the approaches which Daly has attributed to "the pedestal-pushers." Both Horney and Erikson redefined the "anatomy as destiny" dictum to allow for less intrapsychic and more sociological approaches, but they remained within the biological paradigm. Indeed, Erikson unashamedly extrapolated from the work of two eminent sociobiologists in a way which they would hesitate to do themselves. He transfers the observations of baboon society to human concepts in an amazingly cavalier manner, and reveals the functionalist arguments at the core of his formulations. He sees woman's nature as defined not only by her inner space, but by her attractiveness and her ability to acquire a suitable mate with whom to have children. "For the student of development and practitioner of psychoanalysis knows that the stage in life crucial for the emergence of an integrated female identity is the step from youth to maturity, the state when the young woman . . . relinquishes the care received from the parental family and the extended care of institutions of education, in order to commit herself to the love of a stranger and to the care to be given to his or her offspring . . ."[48] "Young women often ask whether they can 'have an identity' before they know whom they will marry and for whom they will make a home. Granted that something in the young woman's identity must keep itself open for the peculiarities of the man to be joined and of the children to be brought up, I think that much of a young woman's identity is already defined in her kind of attractiveness and in the selectivity of her search for the man (or men) by whom she wishes to be sought."[49] Women may choose not to fulfill their destiny in this way, particularly, by implication, if they are not attractive enough to acquire a mate, but it would violate their natural capacities to engage in work that was not nurturing, caring, and serving humanity.

A recent replication of Erikson's original research on "inner space," which provided the foundation for his theory of feminine identity, reveals methodological flaws and interpretive leaps in his work. Caplan's[50] study indicates the extent to which Erikson's findings were coloured by his acceptance of prevailing images of women. The extent of the acceptance of Erikson's views in the field of human development in itself indicates the prevalence of those images in what we have assumed to be "scientific" knowledge.

Interactional and Humanistic Formulations

The work of Sullivan is also extensively used in the training of mental health professionals, particularly because of his focus on learning and interaction in the development of self-identity. Although the constant use of "he" in reference to the person or "self" seems at first glance a matter of semantics, perusal of his idiosyncratic writings does not bear this out. The interactive and interpersonal components of identity appear to be conceptualized soley from the perspective of the male. In such formulations as "undifferentiated anxiety," we learn that the baby boy, with a convenient bend of the elbow, finds a tempting protuberance, the manipulation of which brings great pleasure. When his overanxious and puritanical mother frequently dissuades him from the practice, her anxiety is conveyed to the child, and from this inter-action stems the dissociative "not me" position and possibly an ensuing genital phobia. Sullivan's charming descriptions of growing up are couched in terms of chums, team sports, and lusty heterosexual en-counters, but females seem to appear magically, to be related to at appropriate times as wives and mothers. Among his formulations of infant interaction we find the symbolic representation of the Good Breast mother and the Bad Breast mother, archetypes of all-giving or withholding female power.[51]

Before moving on to a brief consideration of the theories which do not distinguish between the sexes in offering explanations of human be-haviour, there is a final and perhaps surprising addition to be made to the psychodynamic school. Maslow has exerted a profound influence on the experiential school of psychotherapy and on humanistic psy-chology which contain many elements of the psychodynamic model against which they purport to revolt. The free and full development of human potential would seem an encouraging goal for women and men alike. Maslow posits a hierarchy of needs which must be satisfied in order for the individual to attain the goal of self-actualization for maxi-mum human potential. Basic needs for food, shelter, safety, love and esteem must be met before those associated with actualization become salient. Maslow fails to recognize the social organization which appor-tions the maintenance of basic needs to women and other subordinate groups. He regards this as a matter of individual good or bad fortune, an accident of birth. A reading of his description of the two basic life stances in his schema reveals how closely they conform to the feminine and masculine stereotypes held by society in general, and to the charac-teristics of those in dominant and subordinate relationships. To make this point more emphatic, the pronoun in the first quotation, Maslow's description of the Deficiency-Motivated person (driven by survival needs) has been changed to "she." The second paragraph stands as written.

"The need for safety, belongingness, love relations, and full respect can be satisfied only by other people, i.e., only from outside the person. This means considerable dependence on the environment. A person in this dependent position cannot really be said to be governing [her] self, or in control of [her] own fate. [S]he *must* be beholden to the sources of supply of needed gratification. Their wishes, their whims, their rules and laws govern [her] and must be appeased lest [s]he jeopardize [her] sources of supply. [S]he must be to an extent 'other-directed' and *must* be sensitive to other people's approval, affection, and good will. This is the same as saying that [s]he must adapt and adjust by being flexible and responsive, and by changing [her] self to fit the external situation. Because of this, the Deficiency-Motivated person must be more afraid of the environment, since there is always the possibility that it may fail or disappoint [her]. We know now that this kind of anxious dependence breeds hostility as well. All of which adds up to a lack of freedom, more or less, depending on the good fortune or bad fortune of the individual.

"In contrast, the self-actualizing individual by definition gratified in his basic needs, is far less dependent, far less beholden, far more autonomous and self-directed. Far from needing other people, Growth-Motivated people may actually be hampered by them. I have already reported their liking for privacy, or detachment, and for meditativeness. Such people become far more self-sufficient and self-contained. The determinants which govern them are now primarily inner ones, rather than social or environmental. They are the laws of their own inner nature, their potentialities and capacities, their talents, their latent resources, their creative impulses, their need to know themselves and to become more and more integrated and unified, more and more aware of what they really are, of what they really want, of what their call or vocation or fate is to be."[52] (Emphasis in original.)

Elsewhere among Maslow's postulates on human development we find a discussion of individual capacities which "like organs must be used or they will atrophy or become a disease centre, thus diminishing the person." These attributes include: "intelligence, the uterus, the eyes, and the capacity for love."[53] Further, we learn that: "self-actualization is not altogether general. It takes place via femaleness *or* maleness, which are prepotent to general humanness. That is, one must first be a healthy, femaleness-fulfilled woman before general-human self-actualization becomes possible."[54] (Note Maslow's use of the female as an example.)

In a later work, Maslow discusses such concepts as bisexuality and the dangers of rigid sexual dichotomies.[55] An earlier article deals with the correlates of self-esteem (dominance-feeling!) and sexuality in women.[56] His major and most influential writings, however, indicate a grave lack of appreciation of the realities of women's lives, and of the implication of his Deficiency- and Growth-Motivated characterization.[57] By insisting that realization of the capacity of the uterus is a requirement for self-actualization, he sets up a situation which disqualifies childless women from that potential. Women must become wives or at least mothers, thereby rendering many of the qualities of Growth-Motivation unattainable for most women in this society, and even, in Deutsch's term, pathological. It would seem that Maslow, like Deutsch, is proposing that women must fulfill themselves by providing for the basic needs of others, namely, children. Such a prescription can only be called vicarious self-actualization.

Behavioral Formulations

Behaviour modification, based on learning theory, is the main position which illustrates the second grouping of theories — those which deal with human behaviour in general terms. In a sense, what we are considering here is "psychological technology" which is not in itself biased against women. By its very neutrality in a far from natural setting, however, it provides for abuses of authority and reinforcement of biases and cultural stereotypes. The lack of control of the nature or content of the behaviour to be modified by the often highly effective methods employed is a matter for concern. Here is an example of a common usage with regard to women, particularly in institutional settings. Token economy programs are frequently set up to "modify" behaviour in hospitals and prisons. Patients or prisoners earn tokens for appropriate behaviour in order to obtain meals, attend occupational therapy, walk in the grounds, and even in order to obtain mattresses and bedding. When the patients are women, the appropriate behaviour thus enforced usually includes such things as applying lipstick, attending the beauty parlour, dressing neatly, smiling, and saying "please" and "thank you" in a pleasant manner. This form of adjustment can be very effective. Women soon learn to "play the game" and "be good." In fact, they learn that in order to survive in any form of comfort they must be docile, submissive, passive, pleasing; in other words, "feminine."

Any hostility or even assertive objection to the regime can immediately be labelled as a symptom of their "sickness," a criminal disposition, inappropriate, and therefore bad. This message is seen to apply to behaviour outside the institution; the training is meant to teach them how to behave in the outside world. In this way the very tenets of behaviour modification, which on the surface take into account the contextual implications of behaviour, can be used in a manner so limited in analysis as to enforce conformity to a socially acceptable, but drastically devalued feminine stereotype. An additional trap in this situation is that patients who prove to be good and willing workers may be kept in the hospital setting as a marginal labour force.[58] This, of course, is not a function of the techniques themselves, but an illustration of how they allow ample room for the manipulation of one group by another in accordance with social demands.

EFFECTS AND CONCLUSIONS

Tracing the images of women through various historical forms and periods to the present time has involved us in evaluating the part these images play in a variety of psychiatric theories, and in turn, what part these theories play in maintaining, establishing, or legitimizing these images as the true "nature of women." Again and again we find an affirmation of women as existing only in relation to men and to the views of them held by men. Aristotle claimed that: "The female is a female by virtue of certain lack of qualities. We should regard the female as afflicted with a natural defectiveness." Freud defines that defectiveness in anatomical terms as the lack of a penis, and from this lack stems woman's deficient "superego," which is interpreted to mean that "she is largely without moral sense, inclined to be less ethically rigorous, have less perception of justice, is more subject to emotional bias, and unable to contribute to culture."[59]

The Judeo-Christian tradition sees woman as Adam's rib, responsible for the fall of mankind from perfect innocence, destined to suffer, but able to produce the male redeemer, and influence the world through purity, sacrifice, and motherhood. Erikson, and to some extent, Horney and other post-Freudians, see women's biological function in reproduction as generating a psychological and ethical commitment to rescue the world from strife and disaster. A socio-biologist, Barash, concluding there there is a biological basis for human behaviour, particularly the relegation of women to the nursery, suggests that ". . . there should be a sweetness to life when it accords with the adaptive wisdom of evolution."[60] Weisstein points out that most post-Freudians regard women's life task as that of "joyful altruism and nurturance; her true nature is that of a happy servant."[61] Rheingold, a Freudian psychologist, also insists that "anatomy decrees the life of a woman . . . when women grow up without dread of their biological functioning and without subversion by feminist doctrines, and therefore enter upon motherhood with a sense of fulfillment and altruistic sentiment, we shall attain the goal of a good life and a secure world in which to live it."[62]

A number of feminist critics have pointed out the contradictions contained in these views; namely, how it is that such maimed and inferior beings can actually wield power over the security of the entire world, and why, if this is their natural, innate, given, and moral function, they so consistently required education, enforcement and control by men to keep them in their place. Some psychoanalysts, such as Farnham, resolved the contradiction by seeing women's discontent as a projection of their personal inadequacies, and as a proof of illness. Feminism, according to Lundberg and Farnham, is a deep illness, and any discontented woman, feminist or not, now shares in causing disastrous consequences for the world.[63]

Since the images from mythology, folklore and religion are carried over as assumptions into theories which underlie psychiatric treatment, it is obvious that these theories and areas are not neutral, objective, and independent of the context in which they operate. "The biosocial sciences," Haraway suggests, "have not simply been sexist mirrors of our own social world. They have also been tools in the reproduction of that world, both in supplying legitimating ideologies and in enhancing material power."[64] By seeking to explain this social world in terms of the individual differences between the sexes (or even between different people of differing social locations) based on the western ideology of the individual as the basic unit of study, a form of scientific practice has developed which takes already socially organized factors, such as concepts of femininity and masculinity or even "sex differences" as explanations in themselves rather than that which requires explanation.

This, in turn, takes for granted a view of women as "other," as objects defined only in relation to man as the prototype of human existence. It sets up the framework of study in the form of questions which arise out of this perception, rather than one which questions and challenges the view itself. The result of this procedure is findings which purport to give scientific validity to the discovery of the world as it has already been constructed; a scientific rationale for the way things are, rather than an explanation or an understanding of how they came to be so. Thus we can see that the "scientific" approaches to human behaviour which we have used to illustrate our contention take their place in a history of ideas, and have a distinct function in the organizing and ruling of society. The ideas of Darwin and Spencer were most influential at a time when women were being idolized in an invalid-like state of enforced passivity. Taking the "natural" passivity of women, as opposed to the corresponding active nature of men, as a starting point (a procedure which involves ignoring the work of women in the home, labour force, and as servants and slaves), suppositional theories of evolution could be developed in which women were mere bystanders to the drives and achievements of men. The "sexual reciprocity" of female primates, so defined, is seen to confirm the natural subordination of all females of all species.[65] Allen declared in 1889 that women were not even half the human race, since biological science had proved them to be but incubators, necessary for the continuance of the race, but with no part in the mechanisms of human inheritance.[66] Such a statement could certainly not have been based on verified genetic information, but it does bear a striking similarity to the medieval theory of the "*homonculus,*" or "tiny-man" with which the female was thought to be impregnated, and which contained the complete characteristics of the new adult human being, ready to be incubated.

Zucherman, among other natural scientists, subscribed to a similar theory of evolutionary motivation to that proposed by Freud in "Civilization and its Discontents."[67] His "mode of blending covert Freudianism, bio-chemical mechanism, and studies of social behaviour has had a long and influential life."[68] What he proposed was a theory of evolution based on the motivational drive of reproduction. In this formulation "dominance was closely linked to male competition for control of resources (females). Females then emerged as natural, raw material for the imposition of male order — through the consequences of reproductive physiology."[69] Freud, while patently less misogynistic than a number of his contemporaries,[70] and while proposing that civilization was considerably more sexually repressive for females, held that civilization came about through the sublimation of reproductive urges into creative and intellectual tasks, which are the domain of men. Oppression and unequal power relations are thus dissolved or reduced to "repression" and justified as evolutionary.

These speculative theories have much in common with the traditional and influential metaphor of the "body politic" which equates the organic structure of the human or animal body with the structure and function of the state and, indeed, the cosmos. Haraway points out that this union of the political with the physiological "has been a major source of ancient and modern justification for domination based on differences seen as natural, given, inescapable, and therefore moral."[71] The head (reason) rules the body as the king rules the state, and so on. Contained in the tradition is the familiar equation of women with nature and men with reason, civilization, and the head or ruling position.

Medicine in general embraced certain of the functions of moral control which were previously the province of religion. Ehrenreich and English suggest that psychiatry, as it developed, took over certain of these moral functions from medicine and became a further instrument for controlling the lives of women.[72] The ideas and practices involved in this function are not merely general and cultural, but quite specific.

Freud's formulations concerning women define their mental processes and anatomical structures only in relation to men. Women's reproductive functions become a substitute for the desired penis. Although female sexuality is re-admitted into the realm of experience from whence it had been banished by mid- to late-Victorian mores, it can only be attained in mature form through the vaginal orgasm, which by definition depends on the introduction of the penis. Any other form of sexual expression is pathological; an indication of frigidity. Freud's Oedipal formulations trace the power of "the Fathers," that is, of a patriarchal culture, with the male as prototype. There is no symmetrical power for "the Mothers," and no definition of men as incomplete without the complementary presence of women. Once again, the male is identified with culture, and the female with nature or primitivism. Later theorists, like Erikson, Horney, and Thompson, attempt to introduce symmetry by suggesting a projected male envy of the womb as more likely than penis envy. More recently, emphasis on the power of the mother has been developed, and with an entirely different focus. This perspective admits the influence of early childhood experience in a way which ties women to child-rearing as well as to childbearing.

It characterizes the influence of the mother as paramount for the development of the child and as a potentially destructive force.

There is a further aspect to the specificity of these formulations, and this is concerned with their use to influence and treat women. Psychodynamic formulations originally grew out of and applied to the upper middle classes. Jean Baker Miller[73] suggests that psychoanalysis in particular, growing as it did from Freud's conviction that society had become overly repressive (especially of the basic sexual drives), was developed in order to re-introduce a balance of feeling and emotion which had been excluded by over-emphasis on rational, intellectual modes of living and ruling. If this is indeed its main focus, then psychoanalytic theory and treatment with regard to women raises some troublesome questions. Miller thinks that: "We came to 'need' psychoanalysis precisely because certain essential parts of man's experience have been very problematic and therefore unacknowledged, unexplored, and denied . . . without realizing that these areas of experience may have been kept out of people's conscious awareness by virtue of their being so heavily dissociated from men, and so heavily associated with women."[74]

Psychoanalysis, then, could be described as a means of helping men of the dominant class come to terms with these unacknowledged or denied "nonrational" areas of experience; to consciously accept, control and understand in positive terms those areas which society has demanded be repressed, particularly those concerned with sexuality. And indeed it may. Since women have been designated those nonrational areas associated with emotions and with interpersonal relationships, psychoanalysis would logically provide a way for women of the ruling class to come to terms with the rational areas from which they have been excluded, as well as the sexual aspects of human experience denied to them. And indeed it does; but not in a way which introduces symmetry between the sexes. Where men are potentially enabled to see as "natural" those thoughts and feelings brought to consciousness through the therapeutic process, women are instructed to see their limitations as natural and their discontent, anger, or resistance as "unnatural," as a rejection of true femininity. "Penis envy" is the specific term used to describe any attempt by women to reappropriate both the rational mode from which they are excluded, and the power which membership in it bestows. Traditional psychoanalysis brands as pathological the very factors which would manifest such symmetry for the understanding and treatment of women.

Far from engendering in women a sense of how their position as the emotional and relational repositories of internal conflicts has maimed and disqualified them for participation in the "public" world of rational and intellectual production, psychoanalytic formulations have been used as the tools which present and teach the conformity of feeling as to the proper, healthy way for women to be. Women have been expected, through therapy, to learn or relearn how to derive their emotional well-being from the achievement of others, namely men and male children. They have been taught how to accept as natural their lot as "other," how to be happy servants, and how to live the vicarious and second-hand life of the "private sphere." Women had to be given a way to be "rationally" altruistic, and to see this as the only way in which to understand their experience. Although Freud eschewed the notion of adjustment as the aim of therapy, it is to this end that his theories have come to be used — as a complex and intricate method of enforcing adjustment to the position which women are required to fulfill regardless of their personal inclinations or attributes. As such, his work takes its place alongside other forms of "prescriptive" literature which instruct women in subordination, and how to make the most of the rewards which adherence to such a position may bring.

The rationale used by men in the struggle against the admission of women to the professions, in labours laws and regulations, and in the legal battles over the consideration of women as persons, is couched in arguments concerning women's frailty and need for protection from the public world. Women are not fit to inhabit a man's world because they lack "sterner qualities." Freud supports the same rationale by postulating women's weaker superego and the exhaustion of intellectual and creative abilities in "the difficult development which leads to femininity." Women, therefore, need a man to protect and provide for them. In spite of the emphasis on the private sphere in the late nineteenth century, it was not domestic virtue which confined women there so much as a frail and delicate nature. This despite the reality that childbirth was both more frequent and more dangerous than it is now. Freud was not much interested in motherhood or the experience of women as mothers. The exploration of the influence of the mother on the early years of childhood he left to his disciples, particularly the women. They did not fail him.

The ideology of early childhood experience, bonding, the essential presence of the mother, and only the mother, in the lives of children, is a more recent phenomenon in psychiatry, social policy, and legislative arguments. It has gained momentum since the 1920s and 30s and has truly come into its own since the Second World War. Only since that time have middle-class women been required or expected to look after their children without the help of domestic servants or other family members. The decline of the nursemaid and the ascendance of theories of maternal instinct would seem to go hand in hand. Ideology is created by and for the dominant class, and filters down to the working class as it takes hold. The emphasis on maternity as the sole occupation has never been as intrinsic to the working-class woman, although, indeed, maternity and child-rearing are seen as her responsibility and her's alone. Theories evolved by psychologists and psychiatrists reinforced this view of woman's destiny and applied it in its most coherent and persuasive form to the more educated woman, who is more apt to be influenced by it. The YAVIS syndrome, which Schofield identifies as the preference of psychotherapists for patients who are Youthful, Attractive, Verbal, Intelligent and Successful, would be more accurate if F for Female replaced the S to complete the description.[75] The choice patient for therapists of the psychodynamic school is female and of childbearing years. Older women, adolescents, working-class and minority-group women are seldom treated with "talking" therapy.[76] Where official statistics for private and outpatient treatment (usually psychodynamic in orientation) are kept, it is found that far more women than men receive such treatment. Chesler proposes that the therapeutic relationship which most resembles the relationship of marriage is seen as the most satisfying to middle-class women patients and therapists alike. The function of reproducing this unequal power relationship is to educate women in therapy to be better wives and mothers.[77]

Rawlings and Carter suggest that the insidious result of an ideology which labels women's misery and revolt as mental illness "is to lay blame for society's ills on women's shoulders. Women thus become societal scapegoats; this allows the roots of their oppression and social disorganization to remain unexamined."[78] The image of women as societal scapegoats, however, stretches back far beyond this definition of mental illness and the concomitant pressure to internalize guilt and shame; the definition itself is merely a most recent and influential manifestation of this theme.

We are not in any way suggesting that psychologists, other social scientists, psychiatrist, lawyers, or politicans conspire to devise theories and laws which will keep women in their place. It is clear, however, that the ideological way of proceeding by taking as an explanation the very thing that needs to be explained, allows for age-old beliefs about women to be incorporated into each facet of society without any evident need for empirical support. These shared beliefs, in the words of Zachs and Wilson, "shape reality and explain phenomena, and depend for their credibility not on empirical verification, but on antiquity and reiteration. Their tenacity is attributable to the manner in which they serve social needs, and not to their capacity to reveal social truths."[79]

≡   ≡   ≡

CHAPTER V

SEX ROLES AND SEX-ROLE STEREOTYPES

"WHEN A SUBJECT IS HIGHLY CONTROVERSIAL, AND ANY question about sex is that, one cannot hope to tell the truth. One can only show how one came to hold whatever opinion one does hold."
— Virginia Woolf[1]

Sex-role stereotypes reflect descriptions, prescriptions, and proscriptions based on archetypal images of women and men, and long-standing beliefs in male superiority. They provide both a framework and a justification for the socialization of males to be dominant, aggressive, competitive, controlling, insensitive and rational, and of females to be subordinate, passive, non-competitive, compliant, caring, and emotional.

DIVERGENT OPINIONS

A review of the literature opens up a veritable Pandora's box of theories, opinions, beliefs and dire warnings. One is soon lost in the maze of contradictions. Traditionally, three basic components of sexual identity are envisaged for the healthy personality. There should be a preference for members of the opposite sex; a clear-cut sex-role identity as either masculine or feminine, depending on one's sex; a gender identity, a secure sense of femaleness or maleness. Women and men must be as different in psychological makeup as they appear physically. Parents must instill these dichotomous concepts in their children if they are to develop normal gender identity.[2] [3] Otherwise they are laying themselves open to the perils of sex-role diffusion and the production

92

of gray, affectless, neuter children.[4] Some writers are very strident in their predictions. Rheingold[5] warns that a good life and a stable world can only be attained if women accept their reproductive functions, avoid contamination by feminist doctrines, and become fulfilled and altruistic mothers. In the concluding chapter of his influential book, *The First Year of Life,* Spitz[6] contends that the rapid disintegration of the family in western society is due both to the decrease of patriarchal authority and to the mother's absence from the home. In a recently published book, Voth,[7] a psychoanalyst at the Menninger Clinic, states that all responsible people should oppose the blurring of values which distinguish men from women. He feels that "the family is in danger because the personalities of men and women are increasingly less mature, the distinction between male and female is less clear, and because social values which maintain or support sex role differences and the family are changing." Voth calls for women to return home as mature wives, and men to resume their proper role of authority in the family.

On the other hand, Bernard[8] has outlined "the bitter fruits of extreme sex role specialization," accenting the extreme specialization of women in the maternal role, the institutionalization of motherhood, and the work-intoxicated father. Havoc, she contends, has been wreaked on us all. Similarly, Favazza and Oman[9] stress that the psychiatrist must recognize the crippling effect of assumed sex-linked behaviours on human potential. They endorse Meads's[10] contention that a society can create deviants by disregarding the totality of human potential and artificially connecting sex with specific approved behaviours. Many studies have indicated the undesirable effects of a high level of sex typing. High femininity in females has consistently been correlated with low self-esteem, low self-acceptance and high anxiety.[11] Similarly, extreme masculinity is accompanied by high anxiety, high neuroticism and low self-acceptance.[12]

Rigid sex-role expectations constrict and inhibit a child's development.[13] Lerner[14] stresses a growing appreciation of the deep guilt, anxiety, and inhibition that result when a child is told that his or her skills, interests or behaviours are gender-inappropriate. She links the little girl's anxiety and guilt about non-domestic strivings with "numerous publications in the psychoanalytic literature which suggest that many women who seemingly 'choose' to relinquish self seeking ambitious strivings do so because they cannot freely and without guilt fulfill themselves through personal achievement." She notes that there is equal, or even more intense, pressure on men to relinquish so-called feminine aspects of themselves.

Before 1974 a few writers, such as Jung and Bakan, espoused dualistic models of femininity and masculinity and rejected the traditional bipolar model.[15] During the last few years, however, the concept of androgyny has been proposed as an alternative to rigid sex roles.[16] This concept has generated much literature, with staunch proponents and a growing number of critics. Proponents of androgyny equate it with mental health, and depict the androgynous person as having the best of both worlds, a combination of masculine and feminine traits, and an ability to use these constructively and flexibly.[17] The concept has been extensively challenged on methodological grounds by authors point to the lack of agreement on conceptualizations and definitions of androgyny and how it should be measured.[18] More important, however, is the realization that adherents of the androgyny construct face the same pitfalls as those who espouse traditional bipolar models. The equation of androgyny with mental health perpetuates the deep-seated and illogical assumption that there is a direct link between sex roles and personal adjustment. Moreoever, "The androgyny concept and the androgyny model of mental health appear to exist in a theoretical psychological vacuum as no thorough discussion of the physiological, developmental, social or historical factors involved has been presented."[19]

There are differing opinions about the direction of societal changes. Some think that old patterns are changing and thus highlight trends in education, labour patterns, decreasing birth rates, alternate family forms, feminist influences, and legal and technological changes.[20] Others have a more pessimistic view. Nadelson[21] contends that attitudes and values related to sex roles have persisted or become even more tenacious and rigid. She comments that a decreasing tolerance for deviance or "boundary violation" is perhaps an attempt to maintain a stable foothold when surrounded by unpredictability and change. Acker[22] asks whether the changes "portend a fundamental re-ordering of relationships between women and men? Or are they adaptations to changes in labor market demands for more female workers and alterations in some areas of social life (e.g., legalization of abortion) which leave fundamentally unchanged an underlying structure?" From the view point of a person who has experienced life in both roles, Jan Morris, who underwent a sex-change operation, writes that: "There seems to me no aspect of existence, no moment of the day, no contact, no arrangement, no response, which is not different for men and women. The very tone of voice in which I was now addressed, the very posture of the person next in queue, the very feel in the air when I entered a room or sat at a restaurant table, constantly emphasized my change of status."[23]

It is against this backdrop of opposing and contradictory opinions that we must further examine definitions, theories, thoughts and beliefs about sex roles.

DEFINITIONS

Here the lack of clarity is marked, with the terms "sex role," "gender role" and "gender-identity role" being used apparently interchangeably in many papers.[24] "Femininity" and "masculinity" are terms invested with a great deal of conceptual confusion. The Group for the Advancement of Psychiatry emphasizes that "terms like *male* and *female* or *masculine* and *feminine* are used loosely without specification as to whether one is referring to a biological attribute, cultural stereotype, physiological characteristic or some second-order association of trait with sex — for example, the trait of aggressiveness with the male."[25] Psychology likewise has been retarded by "psychometric insistence that that which is male is masculine and that which is female is feminine."[26]

Stoller[27] attempts to define masculinity and femininity as "What a person and that person's parents, peers and society agree is femininity (masculinity); the criteria change from place to place and time to time. Such usage frees us from the impasse produced by biologizing, e.g., that masculinity equals activity and femininity passivity."

Stoller appears to be taking cultural factors into account and viewing definitions of sex roles as evolutionary. This overlaps with sociological viewpoints. Stoller[28] emphasizes: "Strictly speaking, there are no such things as 'sex roles' though the term is often referred to in the social sciences. It concerns the complicated process in society whereby children separated by gender at birth become boy-girl, woman-man, feminine-masculine. It concerns the distribution of rewards and opportunities by gender, as well as the expectations placed on each. It means to examine the differences between men and women as well as the consequences of these differences for individuals. This is very different from what 'sex role,' strictly speaking, implied. A role is the pattern of behavior associated with a position (or status) in society. Statuses provide a basis for social identity. Gender (not sex) is one basis for identity. To speak of a sex role is to miss the complexity of how gender identity systems operate in real life." Block[29] says: "By sex roles, I mean the constellation of qualities an individual understands to characterize males and females in his culture. By direct implication, an individual's conception of sex roles will influence in important ways both his behavior and his self evaluation."

Much recent writing does appear to reflect the idea that sex roles are not biological givens, and that the term "sex role" is fraught with subjectivity and ambiguity. An attempt to move away from relative and culture-bound concepts has produced the term "core gender identity." Stoller[30] emphasizes that the feeling "I am a male" is basic and different from the sense "I am manly" or masculine. Money[31] thinks that the use of the new terms relieves the terrific strain on the etymological stem, "sex," and defines gender identity as "the sameness, unity and persistence of one's individuality as male or female as experienced in self awareness and behavior. Gender identity is the private experience of gender role, and gender role is the public expression of gender identity."

While these definitions seem to add clarity, we should keep in mind Bradley's[32] caution that gender identity is a hypothetical construct, and should guard against reifying it.

THEORIES

There are numerous theories about the development of sexual identity or gender identity and related sex or gender role. Although Freud's theories still underly much psychiatric thinking, contradictions can be seen in his work. At one point he cautioned that masculine behaviour should not be equated with activity and feminine behaviour with passivity.[33] Neither he nor his followers heeded this warning, however. In other works he views masculinity and femininity as biologically endowed, and defines femininity as consisting of three characteristics: passivity, masochism and narcissism. He relates masochism to women's "thralldom" in marriage.[34] Freud envisaged so many hurdles to female sexual development[35] that he perceived her as having no energy for intellectual pursuits and only enough to devote herself to motherhood. The female, he contended, has a weak superego as she has not had to suffer through castration anxiety. Thus she is less moral, has little sense of justice, is submissive, emotional and makes no cultural contributions.[36] Freud's portrayal of feminine masochism, passivity and narcissism has been reinforced and glorified by Deutsch[37] and by Bonaparte,[38] who went so far as to attribute her female patients' sexual frigidity to an anatomical defect in the placement of the clitoris. She worked closely with an eminent Viennese surgeon who, adopting her theories, assisted in her therapeutic endeavors by performing a surgical procedure described as a "clitoral-vaginal reconciliation," in which the clitoris was repositioned in order to be available for more direct stimulation by the penis during intercourse. Robinson's[39] widely read book, *The Power of Sexual Surrender*, stated that "in sexual intercourse, as in life, the man is the actor, woman the passive one, the receiver, the acted upon. There is a tremendous surging physical ecstasy in the yielding itself, in the feeling of being the passive instrument of another person, of being stretched out supinely beneath him, taken up will-lessly by his passion as leaves are swept before a wind." Freud's activity-passivity dimensions are also clearly seen in Erikson's[40] depiction of the male's intrusiveness and the woman's inner space.

We should note that psychoanalytic libidinal stage theory postulates that the question of sexual identity does not arise until the child is two or three years old. At that time, the discovery of the genitalia coincides with the maturation of sexual drive. Thus the biological origin of sexual identity — the sense of maleness or femaleness originates in the child's sexual drive and genitalia.

There is a growing realization that Freud's notions of masculinity and femininity reflect what he saw in a restrictive and patriarchal society. Zilboorg[41] stresses that androcentric bias "led to the construction in psychoanalysis of a hypothesis according to which the woman achieves her birthright in a circuitous and highly complex series of psychobiological gyrations." Marmor[42] emphasizes that "There is probably no area in Freud's writings more fraught with theoretical and clinical contradictions than his pronouncements concerning feminine psychophysiology." In dismissing as myth the assumption that normal women are submissive and masochistic while normal men are dominant and aggressive, he states: "Nowhere does the cultural bias inherent in Freud's views about the nature of women become more apparent than in his bland assumption that women have less adequate superegos than men. . . . The record of women in England and America in the past four decades on behalf of social justice and human brotherhood compares more than favorably with that of men.'' Discussing Erikson's famous experiment where children were asked to construct a scene, he points out the massive number of acculturation factors affecting the children, and criticizes Erikson's assumption that the differences in their constructions derived only from anatomical differences between the sexes. Tooley[43] accents the need for revision of the theory of male psychosexual development, pointing out that "Male theorists and practitioners have made virtues of the harsh facts of male socialization."

Many studies have shown that, contrary to Freud's formulation, sex-typing begins at birth, and gender identity is firmly established in the first two to two-and-a-half years of life. Although an occasional author stresses inherent factors alone,[44] and others agree that biologic and genetic factors play a part,[45] there is more and more agreement that the sex of assingment is the most important and overriding variable determining gender identity.[46] This has been convincingly demonstrated in cases where the biological sex and the assigned sex of the child are different. Money and Erhardt[47] hypothesize that gonadal hormones exert a prenatal influence on the developing brain, and that this brain dimorphism becomes the biological determinant of a separate male or female gender identity. This biological component, however, is overshadowed by postnatal influences.[48] Bradley[49] has stressed the importance of temperamental factors, noting that the passive, sensitive boy is more vulnerable to difficulties with gender identity.

If we accept the overriding importance of assigned sex, how do children develop gender identity and related gender role?[50] Learning theorists stress modelling.[51] Cognitive theoriests[52] emphasize the child's early self-classification, which parallels language development. Developmental theories appear to be of distinct relevance, as we can set them alongside Piagetian theories of cognitive development (and wonder how children are best given a specific sense of gender identity before they can proceed, as they get older, to a more abstract examination of the vicissitudes of gender role). Studying children between the ages of six and eighteen, Ullian[53] postulated six sequential age-related levels of gender role conceptualizations. Initially, there is a biological orientation which explains masculine and feminine traits in terms of external, bodily differences, and finally, a psychological orientation develops with an awareness that masculinity and femininity need not be dependent on traditional standards, roles, and behaviours. Rebecca, Hefner and Oleshansky[54] have proposed a similar model, that of "sex-role transcendence." They postulate that sex-role development progresses from the undifferentiated to the polarized, and then to the transcendent. They emphasize that the expression of polarity is a crucial developmental task for the child.

If we accept that the child needs a concerete sense of femaleness or maleness in order to gain a stable gender identity, we should next examine how this is given in our society and in other cultures, while asking ourselves if the present way is necessary and right, or restricting and overstated (or somewhere in between?). To what extent is sex role a relative and culture-bound phenomenon? Do parents need to present clear-cut sex-role differences to the child, as suggested by Talcott Parsons' model[55] for the functional family, where mother's role is to be expressive, father's instrumental? The mother is to be sensitive and nurturant, her care for the children including socializing them for appropriate sex and occupational roles, and to support father's provider role. The father is to give adequate economic support and generally oversee the household. This view is also presented by Westley and Epstein in their book, *The Silent Majority*.[56] They claim that the most mentally healthy children are produced by homes with dominant fathers and traditionally feminine mothers — which takes us back to Voth's extravagant claims that the future of society depends on a reversal of the present trends towards blurring of sex roles.[57]

Evidence from biology is often used by proponents of the view that our present sex roles — masculinity equated with power, leadership, aggression, competitiveness, and femininity with submission, compliance, nurturance, sensitivity — are right, natural, fixed and immutable. On the other hand, findings from cross-cultural and historical studies may be used by those who are trying to point out that the sex roles that we may consider to be the natural order of things are actually peculiar to western industrial society of the nineteenth and twentieth centuries.

Theories derived from animal behaviour have been drawn on to "prove" that males should be dominant, aggressive, keep females in subjugation, and form elite male kinship bonds. Seidenberg[58] has called this "male self-serving mythopoeism," and Morgan,[59] naming writers such as Tiger,[60] Morris,[61] and Ardrey,[62] "Tarzanists," points out some major contradictions in the way in which their theories have been evolved. In an evolutionary sense, humans are closest to gorillas and chimpanzees, who are relatively peaceloving and unaggressive. Various species show every imaginable mode of relationship between the sexes, from gibbons who demonstrate little, if any, personality differences between the sexes,[63] to male marmosets who perform a large proportion of the child care,[64] to female lions who do most of the hunting and killing.[65] Some ethologists, however, choose to derive paradigms for human behaviour from the study of species where the male is dominant and aggressive.[66] In describing baboons, Ardrey states that "the student of man may find the baboon the most instructive of species. Among primates his aggressiveness is second only to man's. He is born a bully, a born criminal, a born candidate for the hangman's noose. He is as submissive as a truck, as inoffensive as a bulldozer, as gentle as a power driven lawnmower." Ardrey goes on to stress that the male baboon, twice the size of the female, keeps a harem of them in terrified subjection. He imposes his will brutally on weaker males, demanding instant and unquestioning obedience. Using such tautological arguments, ethologists attempt to justify male aggressiveness and the oppression of females.

Through attempting to explain all social behaviour by evolutionary principles, sociobiology[67] has rapidly become the most prominent and influential theory of those which postulate a biological basis for sex differences in behaviour. Relying on Darwin's theory of natural selection, sociobiology assumes that behaviour which has a genetic component must be adaptive, and therefore natural and right: "There should be a sweetness to life when it accords with the adaptive wisdom of evolution."[68] Attempting to identify biologically-determined traits, sociobiologists look for universals in human behaviour, which they then link with similar non-human primate behaviour in order to strengthen the argument that human behaviour has evolved through natural selection. Although no behavioural traits have been found that are common to all cultures,[69] sociobiologists claim to have found universals almost entirely related to sex differences and state that, "ironically, mother nature appears to be a sexist."[70] Thus aggressive dominance systems, hierarchy, competition, territoriality, subordination of females, and intensive and prolonged maternal care, are deemed natural and necessary. Sociobiologists emphasize that "it's time we started viewing ourselves as having biological, genetic and natural components to our behavior, and that we start setting up a physical and social world to match those tendencies."[71]

Many arguments for the biological basis of sex differences have centred around androgens, male sex hormones which are crucial to the pre-natal development of a male mammal.[72] It is often assumed that androgens are central to post-natal male behaviour. Experiments on rats have demonstrated that injections of androgen "cause" aggression. Androcentric hypotheses, developed from these studies, assert that men are aggressive, dominant and superior because of inborn hormonal differences. These blithe assumptions about the unique effect of androgens on rodent and, by extrapolation, human behaviour, have been called into question by recent research which indicates that oestrogens may actually be causing so-called androgen effects. Androgens, when administered, are converted within the cells to oestrogens, thus the "androgen" effects can be blocked by anti-oestrogen drugs but not by anti-androgen drugs.[73]

While neuroethology, biology and genetics may contribute to our understanding of human functioning, caution needs to be exercised when it comes to drawing conclusions based solely on animal studies. The link between animal and human behavior has yet to be established and the causal nature of the relationship between hormones such as androgens and sex-linked characteristics, such as dominance and superiority is a tenuous one. In a recent consideration of the subject of aggression by men toward women, Stark-Adamec and Adamec[74] point to the complexity of the issue of aggression and its biological components. They cite evidence which supports the striking impact of environmental features, the "social history," and existing dominance relationships on primates subjected to particular neural activation and hormonal manipulation to provoke socially aggressive behaviour.[75] This kind of careful consideration draws attention to the necessity for a rigorous critique of the sometimes simplistic connections and suppositions made by those who seek to explain and justify human activity, sex-linked characteristics and social structures as being solely a function of hormonal or genetic factors.

Traditional ideas about sex-linked behaviour were first rocked by Margaret Mead in 1935.[76] Studying three tribes in New Guinea, she found that Arapesh women and men were (in western terms) maternal as parents, feminine and unaggressive. By contrast, Mundagugamor women and men were aggressive, ruthless and highly sexed. A third tribe, the Tchambuli, provided another contrast with western culture. Here, women were the dominant, impersonal, managing partners and men were less responsible and emotionally dependent. Since then many cross-cultural studies have shown a variability of patterns across the world, and have demonstrated that in virtually every society, women and men are expected to act in sex-specific ways. Henshel[77] comments that "comparative anthropology has shown that a man may be socialized to be peace loving or aggressive, passive or hyperactive, monogamous or polygamous." Gould[78] notes that "comparative studies of men and women at different periods in history and others conducted during the same period but in different cultures support the thesis that there are no patterns of behavior peculiar to one sex — which cannot be observed in the opposite sex."

Recently, beliefs in the fixed, immutable character of gender identity by the age of one-and-a-half, with dire emotional consequences if a change is attempted, have been called into question by reports from the Dominican Republic[79] of children with a hormonal abnormality who appear female at birth and are socialized as such. At puberty they become unmistakably male, and most children change their gender role at that point and readily accept their new identity. Most reports fail to emphasize, or even mention, the most likely cause of their easy acceptance of their new sex: males in that culture have a high degree of freedom and independence, while females lead a very sheltered, restricted life.

Writers of women's history have uncovered similar dimensions. They focus on the delineation of sex roles, investigating their sources, their disparity or similarity, and their rigidity or fluidity. This examination illustrates how sex roles serve to shape the careers, consciousness and activity of women and men.[80] Surveying four centuries and "untangling the roots of modern sex roles," Block[81] describes fewer innate sexual distinctions in the sexteenth and seventeenth centuries. Literature tended to extoll the same qualities in women that were most admired in men. For both sexes the chief virtues were piety, courage, wisdom, and sexual constancy. In addition, women were more modest and submissive to virtuous men. Thus, women "were measured against essentially the same standard as men and were judged worthy of a position one rung beneath." Sex roles in the eighteenth and nineteenth centuries diverged widely once again, related to changes in culture and economy.

These findings do not support the concept of some kind of ideal norm for sex-linked behaviour. Nor do they support the belief, held by many, that because it happens in a particular way in our society, it is therefore right. The Rappaports[82] emphasize that "in the human sciences the argument that a given pattern is the statistical norm, that all through history the pattern has been modal, that primitive tribes show it, and that animals show it, are used daily to support assertions about the limitations of human nature. Because men have tended to be economic providers and women have cared for infants, it is argued that babies need their mothers and that men need to be breadwinners. Because the nuclear family has been, in recent times, the basic form of social organization, it is assumed that it is the form best adapted to modern society. Because men are more ambitious and committed to work in contemporary society than women, it is argued that this is the way that men and women basically are . . ."

It can be argued, then, that sex role or gender role is an ethnocentric or culture-bound phenomenon, and that sex roles and the ideologies supporting them are one of the sets of principles that regulate and order a society (other sets of principles are developed around class, age, race, religion, etc.).

Let us now look at how female and male children are socialized in our culture.

THE SOCIALIZATION OF FEMALE AND MALE CHILDREN

Socialization begins at birth. Parents behave differently towards female and male infants. Rubin, Provenzano and Luria[83] found that mothers consistently reported that their one-day-old female infants were softer, finer, smaller, and more inattentive than male infants. The researchers did not find these differences. Studies of older infants demonstrated ongoing mother-child interactional differences depending on the child's sex. Moss[84] found that mothers tend to leave boys crying, and pick up the girls. Boys are held, stimulated and aroused; while mothers smile, talk, and vocalize more to girls. In another study, the same six-month-old infant was presented to eleven mothers who were not aware of its sex. If the mother was told that the baby was a "girl" she attempted to interest "her" in a doll; if she thought it was a "boy" she would hand "him" a train. The mothers thought that the "girl" was softer, more delicate, etc., even though the same infant was presented to all mothers. Strikingly, these mothers had no awareness that their behaviour and perceptions varied with the sex of the child.

Parents emphasize achievement,[85] competition, control of affect and the assumption of personal responsibility for their sons, and expect "lady-like" behaviour of their daughters.

Two subcultures develop in a family. Females are involved with house, babies, kitchen and food, and males with cars, garages, sports and teams.[86] Boys are encouraged to be assertive, to stand up for their rights, and defend themselves. They are directed towards activities, ideas and things rather than towards feelings, people and contemplation. The directives for girls are more or less the reverse. Parents often create guilt and anxiety in their children by emphasizing to them what they should *not* do if they want to be considered masculine or feminine. Boys, especially, are discouraged from what is viewed as opposite sex behaviour. The need to be masculine or feminine becomes an emotionally loaded and vulnerable situation about which the individual is prone to feel anxious. Similarly, nursery-school teachers were found to encourage differential patterns of passivity, assertion, aggressiveness in girls and boys.[87] They also reinforced sex-typed tactics for getting adult attention. Boys received more instruction and more reward for academic tasks; over all, little girls received considerably less adult response and attention, an effect that has also been demonstrated in families.[88] As a consequence of these stereotypes, little girls who, at three-and-a-half, display problem-solving skills and are confident, active and expressive are, by five-and-a-half, "inhibited, less attractive, less vital, more isolated" and "were frequently scapegoated and victimised by their peers." The same skills and attributes, however, persist in boys, who retained their three-and-a-half-year-old characteristics at age five-and-a-half.[89]

Thus, a girl is programmed to think that her primary achievement is to be a wife and mother. She is led to believe that she will be happy and fulfilled if she serves others, devoting herself to meeting the needs of her husband and children. In addition to providing for the physical needs of her family, she is the emotional organizer, the mediator of feelings, whose responsibility it is to dampen or absorb tensions, avoid confrontations, divert energies, and generally keep the family running smoothly. Her commitment and assignment to this role is so all-encompassing that she retains it and all its responsibilities even if she has a second job in the workplace.[90] The enormity of her task, however, goes largely unrecognized and unrewarded. Women's responsibility for emotional relationships in the family, for child care, and for household tasks, is seen as far less valuable than the breadwinner and father role. Women's tasks are essential, but outside of the "real world," and so "women work with the pervasive sense that what they do does not matter as much as what men do."[91]

Low in self-esteem, accepting society's view that she is less important, less worthy and less competent than a man, and that she needs a man to protect her and allow her to find fulfillment in meeting his needs, a woman spends many hours on her physical appearance. She takes tremendous pains to achieve the faddish and evanescent ideals of feminine beauty. She may starve herself to the point of emaciation, deform her feet with high heels and pointed-toe shoes, corset herself until she can scarcely breathe, hobble herself in a tight skirt, or bleach the life out of her hair. Devaluing herself and the rest of her sex, she distrusts other women, and views them as competitors for male attention.[92]

Lacking confidence in herself and her own opinions, she relies on others, paricularly males, for affirmation and direction. She feels that is dangerous to openly pursue her own interests and needs, as she may threaten or lose her relationship with a man. She tries to get her needs satisfied by "feminine wiles" – flattery, cajoling, manipulation. She cannot openly express her resentment, conflict is usually covert, and may express itself in subtle ways such as a slow and invidious deprecation, by the wife, of the husband's abilities as a husband, father and breadwinner.

A boy grows up to be a man whose identity is bound up with his ability to be a success – a good provider, and with the need for dominance, compettitiveness, control, rational structuring and toughness. Emotionality, sensitivity and feeling are viewed as sissy, soft, effeminate, unmanly, appropriate for women but not for men. Henshel[93] comments: "Inasmuch as warmth, tenderness and capacity to express one's feelings are *human* traits, boys are cheated out of their very nature by being prevented from developing these characteristics. Through the education (or lack thereof) they receive, males are alienated from the interpersonal aspects of their roles as husbands, lovers and fathers. Consequently their own girlfriends, wives and children will also be deprived later as these men will be unable to satisfactorily provide the emotional requisites of a truly human relationship." Making similar points, Nichols[94] contends: "Tomorrow men will look back on the 1970's and remark on the constriction affecting their sex. In future decades today's male role will be remembered as a strait jacket." Leonard Schein[95] thinks that sex-role conditioning hurts men in five fundamental ways: men are prevented from becoming whole, autonomous, emotional, loving human beings; they are turned into "success objects"; they are out of touch with their bodies and sexuality; they are harmed by being socialized to view women as inferior human beings, and to hate them; and they are not allowed to spend meaningful time growing with and caring for children. In a similar vein, Seidenberg[96] hypothesizes that men become the victims of their own advantages. Men have to prove their "unearned superiority," and may have to "resort to pseudo self-enhancement such as uncalled-for bravery, bravado, cunning, tricks, and outmoded feats of courage. On the other hand, he must assume an often unneeded executive role with his wife. This entails both a dictatorial attitude and at the same time a subtle campaign of depreciation of her talents, ability, and intelligence. Authority must often be exerted, as upon children, to prove and maintain dominance."

FUTURE DIRECTIONS?

We may argue that there have been some changes; people are more flexible, parents are asking questions, men are tired of their tough role. But the obstacles to change are massive, the tide still flows strongly in the other direction.[97] This can be clearly seen if we look at what is being presented to parents in parenting manuals, and what is being presented to their children via educational materials.[98]

Analyzing the "three superstars of popular child rearing books" (Spock, Ginott, and Dodson), Callahan[99] comments: "From reading these parental guidebooks you could get the idea that nineteenth-century sex roles were still in force in society. Anatomy is Destiny and Nature rules; the women's liberation movement never happened . . . it's no surprise, given this patriarchal world view, that penis envy is seen as a problem for little girls." She stresses: ". . . all the parental guidebooks reflect the individualism, privatism and sexism of American society. There is little recognition of alternate lifestyles, no consciousness of cross-cultural variations or even any class or ethnic differences in

America. These are mainstream, middle-class white oriented books. . . . Any idea of the social and political context in which parents raise their children is totally absent. . . . How to get children involved in the community, and instill a sense of larger social and cultural purposes, is ignored."

Educational materials present similarly stereotyped perspectives. Elementary school readers portray rigid sex roles.[100] Boys are depicted when the following activities or traits occur: problem-solving success, strength, bravery, cleverness and ingenuity, acquisition of skills, elective helpfulness, adventurous or imaginative play, gaining rewards, and altruism. By contrast, girls display: passivity, dependency, routine helpfulness, victimization, humiliation, goal constriction, and rehearsal for domesticity. The authors of this study also noted that boy, man or male animal stories or biographies predominated by a ratio ranging from 2:1 to 6:1 over girl, woman and female animal stories. Studying prize-winning picture books for young children, Weitzman et al.[101] discovered similar emphases on male and female activities, and an even greater discrepancy as to major themes. Females were under-represented by 11:1 in the illustrations. Counting animals, the ratio increased to 95 male animals to every one female animal! How could little girls fail to learn which sex is important and primary? Various commissions, committees and reports have suggested that schoolbooks need to be purged of this sexist material. However, these suggestions go largely unheeded, presumably because the majority would agree with Voth,[102] who pontificates: "I am appalled by the trend of some teachers to adopt teaching styles and classroom attitudes that minimize the differences between the sexes. This is *wrong*. Children should leave school as educated *boys* and *girls*, not as educated sexless beings or confused about sex role differences. Take a close look at educators who advocate these new trends in blurring sex role differences between boys and girls in the nursery and classroom and you will see women who are not fully feminine and men who are not fully masculine." (Emphasis in the original.)

Dogmatic statements of these kinds reflect the major obstacle to change or to acceptance of a variety of ways of socializing children. Such statements reflect most people's unquestioning acceptance that what appears to be the "natural order" of things is right, as pointed out both by John Stuart Mill in *The Subjection of Women*, written in 1869,[103] and by the Rappaports.[104] Prevalent, too, is the assumption that a return to the old order of things is the only way to save the world.[105]

Henshel[106] contends: "Both men and women are slowly induced into believing that the differential outcome of this socialization process is natural, meaning that women are what they are, rather than what they, just like men, have been forced to internalize." Analyzing male-female relationships in terms of dominant-subordinate interactions, Miller[107] places emphasis on the inability of the dominant group to see this situation as other than "normal." Stephenson[108] has noted that the literature on oppression has great relevance for the study of female-male relationships in our society. There is a striking parallel between the use of sex-role stereotypes to deny rights to women and to blacks. The oppression of blacks was rationalized by a stereotype which described them as dependent, emotional, amoral, childlike, and unintellectual.[109] Even arguments about the biological underpinnings show a clear resemblance. Woman's lesser intellectual capacity was attributed to the small size of her skull and brain,[110] and the black's low intelligence to their large skulls which were felt to indicate evolutionary primitivism.[111]

Rigid beliefs about sex roles, about how girls and boys, women and men, mothers and fathers should behave, make it impossible for us to understand what the world is really like for people. These stereotypes, reflected in theory and practice, and seen in therapists' attitudes, can make a family's experience unhelpful or even destructive.

IMPLICATIONS

(These implications will be illustrated with case histories from the practice of P.S. Penfold.)

The pervasive effect of these sex-role stereotypes impinges constantly on my work as a child and family psychiatrist. Biases emerge in the concerns of parents and the reports of other professionasls.

Common parental perceptions of what is "right" and "normal" are illustrated by the following case histories of four children. To illustrate points more clearly, they are presented in pairs.

■ John A. and Jane B. were both referred because of underachievement in school. Both were quiet, low-energy, sensitive children, and both were overshadowed by a noisy, rambunctious, assertive, sociable, popular and athletic older brother. Both needed acceptance, to be seen as individuals in their own right, to have their temperament understood by their parents, and to be helped to make their needs known. Ways of helping John and Jane become more assertive were discussed with both sets of parents. The A.'s agreed that John's compliant and unassertive behaviour was a major problem and said, "How is he going to get on in the world if he lets people trample on him like that?" They were eager for direction. The B.'s, on the other hand, were reluctant. Mr. B. stressed his feeling that Jane was "a delightfully compliant little girl — why change that?"

■   Concerns about cross-sex behaviour came up during the assessments of Tom C. and Tessa D., both seven. The C.'s were extremely worried about Tom's effeminate behaviour, and that his peers were teasing him and calling him "sissy." He liked to dress up in his mother's clothes and high heels, and was interested in jewelry and perfume. He did not like rough sports and, to his father's chagrin, refused to take part in soccer or ice hockey. He liked to draw and paint. The D.'s had little concern about Tessa's tomboyish behaviour. They presumed that she would grow out of it, as had her elder sister. Tessa was energetic, rough, and played "Army" and soccer with a group of boys. She wore jeans and T-shirts, donning dresses occasionally with extreme reluctance and vociferous protest. She dressed up in her father's clothes, particularly enjoying wearing his old Army hat and belt. She liked helping her father work on the car, and wanted a collection of tools of her own. Her burning ambition was to join an ice hockey team.

This second pair of case histories illustrates a common experience in child psychiatry — that parents are very concerned about cross-sex behaviour in boys. As described earlier, more pressure is exerted on boys, for whom more rigid sex-role expectations are prescribed. It also illustrates the greater value attributed to males and "masculine" behaviour in our society, so that parents can tolerate or even welcome some "masculine" behaviour in a girl, but become extremely distressed when "feminine" behaviour is exhibited by a boy. This anxiety is, of course, reflected in the professional literature, where there are a number of articles about the treatment of effeminate boys.[112]

Beliefs about the importance of traditional sex-role socialization appear very strongly in judgements about parenting.

■ Wayne was the third child of a single-parent mother. Both of his older sisters were doing well. Wayne's teacher described his poor academic work, daydreaming, lack of attention, low motivation, problems with concentration, disruptive behaviour in class, and problems with other children. Reports from the family doctor and the school counsellor suggested that Wayne's behaviour was due to the lack of a male model at home. His teacher was even more explicit: "The only thing wrong with Wayne is his mother." Wayne was eventually found to have a severe learning disability, which accounted for his academic difficulties and related behaviour problems.

■ Debbie was originally referred to me because of severe post-partum anxiety. At that time she was living with a man twenty years her senior, with whom she had a difficult and unrewarding relationship. She subsequently left him and lived alone with her son, Pete. Two years later, she "came out" as a lesbian, and began to live with Joan, who shared the care of Pete. Debbie and Joan came in on several occasions to talk about their anxieties about bringing up a boy. Although committed to a homosexual lifestyle herself, Debbie expressed many fears about the teasing Pete would get in school, and that he would not have any friends. We discussed how compromises may need to be made between personal beliefs and practicalities, and that Pete did need to learn how to get on in the outside world. He did need friends, a feeling of belonging and of being like other children. We talked about this in the light of children's intellectual development, how a child's black-and-white view of the world is gradually replaced by the capacity for some abstract thought. Later on, Pete would be able to appreciate ambiguities, gray areas, and Debbie's dilemmas. Pete did well. He had much contact with his grandparents, and a male friend of Joan's took him out. While both women worked, he was with a day-care mother and got on well with children of both sexes. When Pete was four, and when I was on holiday, he developed pneumonia and was admitted to hospital. The pediatrician, perturbed by Pete's description of his "two Moms," asked for a psychiatric consultation. The psychiatrist said that there was "nothing wrong yet," but told Debbie that he felt that Pete was at risk because "lesbians hate men." He warned her to guard against "irrational, hostile feelings" towards Pete, and suggested that she should enter therapy.

■ Tom, age eleven, lived with his mother, Monica, and his step-father, John. His homosexual father, Les, saw him most weekends and Tom often stayed overnight at Les' apartment. Monica and John were convinced that he was being a bad influence on Tom and would push him into a life of homosexuality. They wanted me to recommend that Tom's visits with Les be either terminated or allowed only in a super-vised situation. Assessment demonstrated that Tom was a well-adjusted youngster, who felt torn between his parents and wished to continue visiting with his father, with whom he shared interests in music and astronomy. There appeared to be no reason why Tom should not freely visit his father.

Professionals who espouse traditional beliefs may exert an enor-mous pressure and change the course of an individual's life.

■ Mrs. W., recently separated from her husband, described multiple problems with her two children. She felt desperate, unable to cope, and had made two suicide attempts. Mrs. W. stated that she had been in a secure and loving lesbian relationship for four years, from age 21 to 25. She then developed a gastrointestinal problem for which no physical cause could be found. She was sent to a psychiatrist, who formulated her problem to be the result of an ambivalent relationship with her mother and her consequent "deviant sex-role preference." He persuad-ed her to terminate the lesbian relationship and urged her: "You'd better marry the first man who comes along — the way you look." She did, with disastrous results.

To move beyond sex-role stereotypes and to develop a useful set of principles which are value-free, yet aid parents in understanding and meeting thier children's needs, we have made some working assump-tions. The first is that children need a basic sense of maleness or female-ness. Even if one's goal is psychological androgyny, there are still two sexes, two biological givens. A little girl needs to be comfortable with, and proud of, her female body build, her breasts, genitalia, uterus, her ability to become pregnant, bear a child and lactate. Similarly, a little boy should have pride in his male body build, genitalia, and his capacity to have erections, ejaculate and father a child. Children can gain these feelings from their parents or parent, not necessarily of the same sex. To gain a secure sense of their gender, however, children do not need to be surrounded by all the superficial sex-role characteristics to do with dress, division of tasks, and so on, which are typical of our culture. Grappling with the same issue, the Group for the Advancement of Psychiatry asked: "If mother and father divide all tasks equally, will the child have a clear-cut sense of the two sexes simply from their anatomical differences? And if not, does it matter?"[113]

The second assumption is that the difficulties, progress and future needs of any child in any lifestyle can be clarified by focussing on the child's needs for affection, stimulation, continuity, and guidance. The first three needs are those cited by Anna Freud; the fourth has evolved out of our own experience both as parents and professionals, which has highlighted children's need for clear boundaries and a gradual, step-wise increase of responsibility and independence at a rate that they can handle.

CONCLUSION

Sex roles or gender roles are culture-bound or ethnocentric concepts, and the large volume of research on sex differences that supports sex-role stereotypes is the handmaiden of social myth.[114] "We polish animal mirrors to look for ourselves."[115] The biosocial sciences, however, "have not simply been sexist mirrors of our social world. They have also been tools in the reproduction of that world, both in supplying legitimating ideologies and enhancing material power."[116] Sex roles and the ideologies supporting them are one of the sets of principles that regulate and order a society. Sex-role stereotypes function to ensure that the work and reproduction necessary for the continuance of that culture are accomplished. Historical research has shown that times of social unrest and questioning coincide with widespread interest in biological determinism which provides a rationale for the status quo.[117] These beliefs presently influence public opinion and the direction of scientific research. This explains why sociobiology, a collection of flawed hypotheses and distorted premises, has immediate appeal and has become very influential.

Sex-role stereotypes conceal women's oppression and legitimate male dominance. Zilboorg[118] comments: "It does seem that androcentric bias interferes with recognising some fundamental error. Should one admit that he has been in error, he will be confronted with the necessity of recognising woman's biopsychological independence, so to speak — the equality of the sexes in the scheme of things." Although there have been many questions about, and challenges to, sex-role stereotypes, they are pervasive, powerful, and are presently being re-stated as the answer to the world's problems. Theories and opinion state that women should stay at home, should care for their children without abandoning them to the damaging influence of daycare, should socialize them properly as boys and girls, should be subordinate to men, and should accept their own femininity.

The function of sex-role stereotypes and their pervasiveness is being studied in several ways, yet much more work remains to be done. There is a lively debate in history and anthropology about whether there has always been universal sexual asymmetry and subordination of women.[119] For instance, there is vehement controversy about whether the process of industrialization and urbanization has led to the im-provement or deterioration of women's status.[120] A Study that used factor analysis on data about women from a number of countries found that women's socio-educational status is correlated with high overall levels of education, socialism, Christianity, and a high child/woman ratio. Women's economic status is related to high overall levels of educa-tion, socialism, and a high proportion of women in the population.[121]

While there is much to unravel, "The most telling experiment that could be done at this time in history is to thoroughly equalise oppor-tunities, from childhood on, and then see if women are still passive, nurturant, dependent housewives and secretaries and maids who don't become doctors, lawyers or presidents."[122]

≡　　　　　≡　　　　　≡

CHAPTER VI

WOMAN AND THE FAMILY

CRUCIAL TO OUR UNDERSTANDING of how psychiatric theories present the family and reinforce women's oppressed position within families, is the recognition that the family is not what it seems. Beliefs about the family, and the institution of motherhood as set forth as a sacred calling, do not fit with what is actually going on in families, with women's experience, or with women's devalued and subordinate role. The family is visualized as a private setting where individual emotional needs are met. In fact, experiences, patterns, and attitudes within families evolve in a direction that best meets the needs of society. Families are forced to absorb tensions that arise in the public realm. Psychiatric theories, however, function to locate and contain within the individual or within the individual family unit the stress, damage, and dysfunctional aspects of the system in which we live. Psychiatric theories that present biology as destiny, motherhood as the norm, and which assign responsibility to mothers for their children's problems, become popularized in child-rearing literature and in the media, exert an enormous influence, and obscure the role of social structures in the production of family distress.

Similarly, beliefs and theories continue to support the notion that the ideal family consists of two parents, male and female, with clearly defined sex roles. The mother should stay at home and have primary responsibility for the children, preferably being available to them 24 hours a day, seven days a week, particularly in the first five years of their lives. The father should be the senior partner and the breadwinner. If the mother works outside the home, her job should not impinge on her childcare responsibilities, or on her husband's status as primary wage earner. This family is envisaged as self-sufficient and needs no help from outside resources. Although this nuclear family is specific to advanced, industrial society, and is unusual both cross-culturally and historically, it is nonethless held as the ideal unit for rearing children. All other arrangements are thought to be, if not actually deviant and productive of pathology, definitely second-class and risky. This "second-class" grouping includes a vast array of alternative family forms such as one-parent families, childless couples, communes, loose, extended family forms such as those of native Indians, divorced and separated patents attempting joint custody, group homes and institutional settings for children, two parent families where the father assumes major responsibility for childcare, and families where the mother has a serious commitment to working outside the home.

These "second-class" forms greatly outnumber traditional nuclear families. How and why does the traditional nuclear family, conceived of as a potentially harmonious haven of domestic bliss, retain its pervasive appeal as an ideal for which we must always strive? While clear understandings of the contradictions inherent in the concept of family are only slowly emerging to awe us with their complexity, we have found three main dimensions that are crucial to our comprehension. These are: historical and cross-cultural perspectives which relate the family form and changes to the structuring of society, with economic structuring assuming particular importance; a recognition of the ways in which present day families are shaped, intruded upon, and buffeted by stresses from social structures; and a grasp of how psychiatic theories both reflect and shape current opinion about the family.

HISTORICAL PERSPECTIVES

An examination of the evolution of the family shows that the family changes in form according to its relation to the economic structuring of the society of which it is an integral part.

For our purposes we shall focus on the family in western society during the process of industrialization, and on women's role within the family. In the feudal system there were two classes. The upper-class family was a household with ties of kinship and fealty in which the main function of women was the transference of property through marriage alliances, the bearing of heirs, and the administration of certain parts of the household enterprise. Women of this ruling class were chatelaines and managers of large, relatively self-sufficient units that included retainers, followers, servants, children and, in times of war, people from the surrounding areas. Members of lower-class families lived mainly within this upper-class household or in tiny hovels that were merely shelter to be used after working in the fields.

With the social changes of the late Middle Ages and the development of a middle class, other forms of household emerged. Many took the form of craft and merchant enterprises in which women participated in a variety of ways. The labouring and peasant classes were increasingly absorbed into urban centres. Women who had worked in the fields and in cottage industries alongside their husbands, menfolk and children, now often worked in factories and mines. For most women, of all classes, the household was their workplace for at least part of their lives. Their labour was essential to the maintenance of the household through provision of basic requirements for survival. This gradually changed with the increasing industrial manufacture of essentials such as clothing, soap, candles, and food. The relation of the household changed to one that depended more and more on a cash wage with which to purchase commodities, and women's role became more and more that of a manager of consumption rather than a producer of essential materials.

Western society was increasingly characterized as being composed of two separate spheres. The public sphere was the world of the workplace and the economy. Its values were those of materialism, competition, aggrandizement, power and action, to be achieved through rational methods, colonialism, imperialism, and scientific management. It was almost entirely composed of, and controlled by men. The private sphere came to be defined as that which was excluded from the public sphere. The decline of the power of institutionalized religion and spiritual values as guiding forces meant that religion was seen as a matter of private conscience, charity as a matter of personal choice. Morality, culture and, above all, "the family," were seen as private domains beyond the concern of the "real" work world of men, although, of course, regulated by them. Emotional, spiritual or artistic activities were associated with the private sphere and with womanly things: necessary perhaps, but trivial beside the real work of the public sector. Women, although appearing to gain respect and security from their elevated status as "queens" or "angels of the hearth,"[1] actually had any power and participation they had had in the regulation of broader society even more severely limited and restricted to the domestic domain. They were to be the conscience of the family, the soothing substitute for, or representative of the spiritual power of the church, the refuge from the savage world of capitalist expansion. The status of women without family affiliation was more desperate than ever, especially if they were of the lower class. In the early days of industrialization, they could seldom earn a living alone, and had little option but to become "the other kind of women" in the seamy underside of Victorian prudery. These women were responsible for meeting the sexual and sensual needs that were denied by "angels" and "good" women. In Europe, this situation was mostly related to class factors, but in the United States it had the added dimension and symbolism of race, with good, pure, white women characterized as one side of the moral dichotomy and bad, seductive, black women as the other.

The idealization and glorification of woman's role in the family was accompanied by a devaluation of her worth, so that she was no longer viewed as a productive member of the family. The "angel of the hearth" image hid the change in the relation of women to the productive public sphere. As a private, unpaid service to the male wage-earner, her work became invisible. As she had to manage the domestic sphere on money given to her by her husband, she was placed in a private and subordinate relation to him, performing her services in order to enable him to fulfill his role in the public sphere to which he was her indirect access. Her economic contribution was obscured by its private nature. The limiting of women's sphere of influence to the home and her enforced dependence on man and his wage, can be seen as a partial solution to unemployment, which began to be a persistent problem at the end of the nineteenth century. Women's place in the home at the centre of the family was promoted by unions, the state, and the media.

Galbraith[2] describes the conversion of women into a class of "crypto-servants." He emphasizes that the concept of "convenient social virtue" is used extensively to get people to perform unpleasant tasks, and states that the ultimate success of this concept has been to induce women to happily take on menial personal service and view this as virtuous and necessary. "The sentimental cult of domestic virtues is the cheapest method at society's disposal of keeping women quiet without seriously considering their grievances or improving their position."[3] Successfully used to this day, the concept tells homemaking women that they are performing the most sacred duty while keeping them at the level of unpaid drudgery.

Research in the past century shows that while some women continued to work outside the home, they were considered marginal and temporary in the workplace, and were therefore confined to segregated, low-paying, and non-organized sectors of the economy. During the Second World War, traditional ideas about women's place and abilities were temporarily suspended, as women were needed to maintain the labour force. Women of all classes worked in jobs previously restricted to men. At the end of the war, many measures were employed to ensure that they would vacate the jobs in favour of returning veterans. Support systems such as nurseries, home helps, subsidized canteens, and after-school care were withdrawn. Advertising in women's magazines, films, television commercials and every other possible sphere, presented marriage and domesticity as women's natural destiny, with housework, childbearing and child-rearing as a joyous, fulfilling, and uplifting vocation. This, combined with the attitudes of business and labour, present since the 1920s and 30s in such measures as protective lesgislation to restrict women's participation, reinforced an exodus of women from the work force and a return to the private sphere of the family.

Today's family continues to demonstrate the dimensions described above. The working-class home, whose members have incorporated middle-class values, is now more than a mere shelter. It is a place where the woman provides care, maintenance and subsistence for the workers, and safety for the children in a way that ideally provides a unified defence or refuge from the exploitation of the workplace. This is, in itself, her "job." Because she is dependent on the man's wage to do her work in the home, her "job" is dependent on his continued employment. Women often appear to be a conservative force, or politically backward because they are a pressure on the wage-earners to keep earning so that they can provide for the needs of the family. Thus the wage-earner's identity and place in the family is determined by his employment. With the rise of corporate forms of organization this is, in turn, determined outside his own workplace or locality by corporate structures beyond his comprehension. These strictures generate many of the pressures and tensions that arise in the family, although they are determined outside of it. Not only does the woman experience these tensions, but she must also, as one of her jobs, handle and defuse them.

The middle-class woman must not only provide care, shelter and security for her family, but must also produce the correct image of the family and its home. It is part of a woman's work in the middle-class family to provide the setting, educational pursuits and displays that mark the family as members of that class. In this sense, the style of the home and, in particular, the accomplishments of the children, are the products of the wife's work, and it is through them that her worth and skill are judged. In an age where the actual features of that work are more and more mass-produced and externally determined by the demands of society as represented in women's magazines, films and commercials, this work lacks much of the individual stamp of the women's personal style and skill, except as an efficient consumer and ingenious manager. The middle-class wife is not allowed to achieve in her own right, but can only seek vicarious achievement through the display of her home, the talents and achievements of her children, and the career success of her husband.

In families where the wife works outside the home, she remains responsible for the physical and emotional organization of the household, and amost inevitably finds herself doing two jobs.[4]

CROSS-CULTURAL PERSPECTIVES

While the preceding section related changes in the family to economic changes, particularly industrialization, and pointed out that hallowed beliefs about women's role and place were temporarily suspended during World War II, more specific examples may give the reader a clearer sense of our point — the essential contradiction inherent in the concept of the family as a private entity shaped by the individual family members. The relationship beween family and state is more readily recognized in socialist countries, and difficult to see in capitalist societies which are wedded to principles of democracy, individual rights, voluntary choice, and bound up in the myths of the domestic, ideal family, with the underlying separation between public and private spheres.

Following the Russian Revolution in 1917, Lenin called for the political and economic equality of women. In 1924, the Comintern proclaimed that the Revolution would be impotent as long as the notion of family and family relationships continued to exist. De-emphasis on marriage, easy divorce, legalized abortions, maternity leave and the opening up of all trades and professions to women greatly changed the shape of family life and led to a greatly decreased birth rate. Concern about repopulating the country, however, led to a complete departure from those principles that had earlier been espoused as an essential part of the revolution. Sexual morality has become strict, divorce and abortion are not readily available, and the family is once more enthroned as an essential element of Russian society. Thus women are supposed to be both workers and housekeepers. More recently, purportedly because of the falling birthrate, women have been barred from jobs involving heavy labour.

Changes in the family may be prescribed by political leaders to meet the needs of the state. In Nazi Germany, all women, married or otherwise, were urged to have as many children as possible. Hitler promised that he would personally become the godfather of any woman's seventh son. Similar pleas for more children were contained in Winston Churchill's stirring speeches to war-time England. In Japan, in 1974, birth-control pills became virtually unavailable, and a liberal abortion law was rescinded when the birth rate began to decline and the supply of cheap labour was threatened.

In non-industrialized societies, families have a different form. In most cultures around the world mothers share infant and childcare responsibilities with others and are not the principal companions and caretakers of young children. In horticultural and pastoral societies, the structure of the family is shaped by economic demands.[5] Subsistence pressures may necessitate mothers being away from home at times, so the early and responsible involvement of children in domestic tasks and childcare is essential to the domestic economy. Children, particularly girls, may have day-long chores by the time they are six or seven years old.[6] Large or extended families are common in these cultures, and it is rare for a family to live separately from both husband and wife's kin. The children's experience of having multiple caretakers, and having charge of younger children themselves, is thought to lead to more intense sex-role differentiation, and to the development of nurturant, responsible, prosocial behaviour.[7]

THE SHAPING OF A FAMILY IN WESTERN SOCIETY

Far from being the private haven of respite where the weary worker can have a fulfilling personal life that is totally separate from the outside world, families are shaped, intruded upon and buffeted by stresses from external social structures. Families are affected by the workplace, by family law, by the health, education and welfare systems, by tax policies and rental regulations. These structures, in turn, contain many of our society's basic sentiments about family life. For instance, the negligible constraints on marriage and many strictures on divorce make evident which one is being encouraged. For some families, racism and sexism compound the stresses.

The workplace, where at least one family member spends half of her or his working life, is almost invariably the major influence. Families are affected by death and injury on the job, by shift work, the increasingly sedentary and routine nature of many jobs, and by job insecurity, redundancy and unemployment. In Canada, 1,036,00 workers were injured on the job in 1977, and more than 900 died.[8] Berman[9] states that in North America more people on the job are killed or injured each year by accidents or industrial contaminants than the total number of Americans killed or wounded during the entire Vietnam War. Shift work, particularly "afternoons," has a vast impact on family life, and can limit or even eliminate parent-child involvement. Low-echelon, low-income families are especially vulnerable to fear of unemployment,[10] lack of pension security, and encroaching mechanisation. These same families are also more susceptible to experiencing feelings of alienation, boredom and apathy in jobs that have little or no room for personal input, initiative and creativity. Flying in the face of the myths about stressed executives and their susceptibility to coronary heart disease, and perhaps serving as an indicator of the amount of stress experienced by lower-class workers, is the finding that the incidence of coronary heart disease increases, in both men and women, as one goes *down* the rungs of the "corporate ladder." "Workmen," compared to "executives" are almost four times more likely to have coronary heart disease.[11] The amount of family income derived from the workplace is often a greater source of stress than the job itself. Income limits a family's choice of housing, schools, recreation, diet, clothing and transport.[12] The neighborhood within which they can afford accomodation will further affect the family by the extent and quality of services available, and through peer group influences on their children. For instance, studies of lower-class areas of cities demonstrate fewer parks and recreational facilities, schools that are more crowded, that doctors rarely locate in these areas, and that grocery stores there charge more for food than in middle-class areas. It is not surprising, then, that unemployment is the major determining factor of divorce and problems in relationships.[13]

The education system, with which a family's children may be involved for almost a half (or more, when homework is included) of their waking hours, shapes both the children and their parents. Families who are out of tune with the goals, explicit and implicit, of the education system may experience devastating feedback from schools and be labelled as inadequate or deviant. This feedback, in turn, produces stresses and strains within the family. Schools are hierarchical, success-oriented, and imbued with middle-class principles. They reinforce both sex-roles and class structures, the latter being shown by a number of studies which demonstrate that high school graduation, college entrance and achievement are more closely related to family income than to any other variable — including intelligence.[14]

Once involved with the welfare system, a family may experience many stresses and indignities. Social assistance is handed out grudgingly, in amounts that maintain a family at or below the poverty line. Poor housing, inadequate diet, ill-fitting clothing, little or no funds for transport, recreation or holidays may indeed produce the apathy, alienation and "lack of motivation" with which the poor are often described. But this lifestyle is maintained and reinforced by welfare policies that stringently require that any extra income be reported and deducted from social assistance cheques, and which intrusively and stereotypically assume that if a mother on social assistance has a man living with her, he should immediately assume all financial responsibility for her and her family. Beset by all these obstacles, families living in poverty are more likely to erupt into violence; and poor parents are more likely to be labelled as neglecting and inadequate. The social conditions underlying these problems are rarely addressed, however, and families are likely to be given counselling or sent to parent-education classes.[15] Their children may be placed in foster homes where the foster parents receive much more funding and assistance than is available to the children in their own homes. Despite findings such as those reported by the Nation Council on Welfare, which estimates that 1,657,017 Canadian children are now living in economic situations sufficiently impoverished to cause health problems, many stemming from nutritional deficiencies, [16] the impact of poverty on families continues to be ignored and families are variously blamed, counselled or split asunder.

Western society's racial prejudices and sexual asymmetry are cloaked by the pervasive belief in equality of opportunity; that any person who works hard can achieve and be successful. Minority group parents, families with single-parent mothers, and families where the mother's income is vital, are subject to discrimination in employment and residential patterns and to the lack of needed support services. Few of Canada's native Indians finish high school, only 30% of the adults are employed, and families are beset by poverty and alcoholism. A shockingly high proportion of foster children are native Indian, as is almost half of Canada's prison population. Again, while these statistics are often accounted for by the natives' character and inadequacy as parents, these prejudicial beliefs are belied by historical studies of native races before they suffered the exploitation and discrimination that accompanied the arrival of white society.[17]

Present in all social structures, pervasive in all areas of family life, the sexual asymmetry of our society affects women and their families. Sexism in employment has a devastating effect on some families, along with public policies that endorse the old adage that "Woman's place is in the home," and fail to promote adequate support for working mothers, such as readily available daycare and after-school care. Women's work inside the home is trivialized and not taken seriously, and in the same way "Women's work" in the work place is usually underpaid and often non-unionized. Canadian women form a vast legion of secretaries, domestic staff, waitresses, childcare workers, teachers, social workers, nurses, and others in the lower rungs of the health care system who are, on average, paid 50% of the wages that men earn. A recent survey of 19 nations by the Organisation for Economic Cooperation and Development showed that not only does Canada pay women, relative to men, less that any other industrial country, but that Canada is the only country where women lost ground to men, with regard to earnings, between 1968 and 1977. In Sweden, where concerted attempts have been made to reduce sexual stereotyping of jobs and wage differentials, and to provide more adequate supports to working mothers, women's wages average 87% of men's.

Of the more than 600,000 single-parent families in Canada, about 90% are headed by mothers and most live in poverty.[18] Single-parent mothers and their families can be seen to bear the brunt of pressures from, and face obstacles provided by, outside social structures. Child support payments awarded by courts are usually inadequate, and often fail to materialize as there is no way that payments can be enforced. Mothers are often penalized for their ex-husbands' failure to support their children; they are forced to pursue the husbands through court action and are not considered to be eligible for social assistance until they are practically destitute. In the job market, single mothers earn low wages, and thus are unable to afford, let alone find, adequate childcare. Added to this are the common beliefs that single-parent mothers are undesireable or unreliable tenants, that they will inevitably have problem children, and that they are generally irresponsible and inadequate mothers or even sexually profligate.

THEORIES, THE FAMILY AND SOCIAL CHANGES

The institution of the family and the child-rearing function ascribed to the parents are believed to be fundamental to the survival of society. The family, like other societal institutions — economic, political, religious, legal, educational, medical — has received the attention of critical commentators of the social order in every historical period. Scientific, medical and psychiatric theories about the family have developed in the same mold and both reflect and reinforce changes in social structures. The popularity and ascendancy of some theories, compared to the short life and rapid disappearance of others, relate to how the theories fit with predominant social, political and economic trends. Theories flourish if they are useful as tools to conserve the traditional functions of the family: to maintain men in the work force, to preserve the subordinate status of women, and to socialize children both as future workers and in the values of western society.

An examination of some of the changing concerns about the family over the past 100 years, and the theories which reflected and reinforced these concerns, will illustrate our point. At the end of the nineteenth century, children were clearly perceived as a national asset. The declining birthrate and high infant mortality were of crucial importance. Focussing on British history, Davin[19] states that immediate clues to the interest in birthrate were evident in debates in the national and medical press and in the journals of learned societies. Discussions of the birth-rate were replete with constant references to national and imperial interests. The debate, she thinks, was galvanised by Britain's poor performance in the Boer war, the course of which had exposed the poor health of the British working class. Furthermore, she adds, competition from recently industrialized Germany, the United States and Japan highlighted the need for healthy and productive workers.

At the beginning of this century the family was pinpointed as the proper context for this surge of concern about the bearing and rearing of children; the next generation of workers and soldiers, the Imperial or Colonial race. The political, economic and public health roots of the problems of high infant mortality, poor physique, chronic illness, pervasive fatigue and apathy were ignored, and the problem was seen as a matter of poor genetic stock and/or inadequate mothering. Davin notes that Rowntree's survey of York suggested that more than one quarter of the population was living at a standard insufficient to maintain mere physical efficiency. A Parliamentary Committee of 1904 described overcrowding, unsanitary conditions, pollution and smoke. Recommendations about these environmental problems were ignored, and those suggesting the education of mothers were endorsed.

Marriage and breeding of those of healthy stock was felt to be a vital necessity. Eugenic sterilization laws were enacted in some countries, some Canadian provinces and some of the American states. Those thought to be poor genetic risks were refused marriage licences or even sterilized. Medical theories reflected these beliefs. Lombroso wrote convincingly on the identifiable physical attributes of the criminal personality. The famous family histories of the Jukes and Kallikaks purported to trace the descent of several hundred criminals, vagrants, and prostitutes to the mating of a retarded couple.[20] Doctors, in addition to sterilizing unsuitable parents, were given the responsibility of discouraging their upper- and middle-class patients from restricting their families. In a speech, the President of the British Gynaecological Society[21] warned that marriages among the better classes were so sterile that "a quite undue and dangerous proportion of the rising generation is recruited from the lower, the more ignorant, the more vicious and semi-criminal population." Instilling shame and duty into the audience the President emphasized that "ours will be to a very large sense the blame if in after years the lamp of the Anglo-Saxons is found to be burning dimly."

At the same time, a powerful ideology of motherhood was emerging that emphasized women's duty to bear and rear healthy children, one which blamed infant deaths and sick children on maternal ignorance or neglect. Mothers were given an overwhelming responsibility as "the transformation of society begins with the unborn child. . . This transformation requires an entirely new conception of the vocation of mother, a tremendous effort of will, continuous inspiration."[22] During the first decade of the twentieth century, societies concerned with child welfare, child health and the education of mothers were formed throughout Britain and North America. Legions of "health visitors" went to lower-class homes, supposedly to promote family health. Children were medically inspected in school, and school girls taught hygiene and cookery. The invasion of lower-class families by Children's Aid Societies, nurses, health visitors and others, while clearly related to health concerns, has other roots. As we have already documented, the increasing industrialization of the early twentieth century led to the movement of traditional home crafts into the factories. A focus was needed for women's energies. This void was filled by domestic science theories which advocated a precise, structured and time-consuming approach to housework and a war against germs.[23] Many middle- and upper-class women volunteered to help the poor, not with money, but by imposing on them the same obsessively structured approach to housework, cleanliness and diet. Alternatively, they served on boards of directors and committees of voluntary agencies, such as the Children's Aid Societies.

World War I, with its immense loss of life, provided another stimulus for child welfare and child health policies as it became evident that modern warfare consumed a vast number of soldiers and that victory would ultimately depend on a nation's production of large numbers of healthy children. Between the World Wars the spread of contraception was accompanied by a decreased family size and a higher standard of living. In the context of an intense and home-based family life, motherhood was accorded the utmost importance. The lay "Mother's Movement," which sought to respond by reinterpreting motherhood as a profession, was quickly superseded by experts who advocated "Scientific Motherhood." The goal of scientific motherhood was to bring the home into harmony with industrial conditions. The major experts,

Hall[24] and Watson,[25] prescribed routines that would train children to be neat, polite, clean, well-disciplined, precise and efficient. Behaviourist Watson claimed that he could guarantee to take one baby at random from a selection of a dozen healthy infants, create its own specified environment, and train it to perform in any kind of profession or job "regardless of his talents, penchants, abilities, vocation and race of his ancestors." Child-rearing books based on Watson's work instructed mothers to keep their babies on very strict schedules,[26] and to avoid spoiling them by picking them up or giving them too much affection. The infant was viewed as a lump of clay to be molded by the parents, primarily by the mother. Davin thinks that this new incarnation of motherhood, accompanied by a focus on the need for a comfortable home and the importance of family life, fitted well with industry's new orientation towards production for a mass market and laid the foundation for the postwar consumer housewife.

During World War II, as we have already noted, much of the ideology surrounding motherhood was temporarily suspended so that women could maintain the labour force. Mitchell[27] highlights the contribution of child psychoanalysis to the restructuring of the British family following World War II. Women were forced to return home by regulations that barred married women from many jobs and most professions. This was reinforced by appeals to maternal guilt. The work of Bowlby, Winnicott, Klein, and Isaacs was, she thinks, used for ideological purposes. Popularized on radio and in women's magazines, their work was used to focus on mother-care, the importance of the relationship between mother and baby, the need for mothers to stay at home, and the dangers of "maternal deprivation" if they didn't. The invidious effects of absent fathers, bombs and poverty were ignored. The responsibility was given to the mother.

The end of World War II, during which labour and military requirements reasserted the need for population growth, ushered in an era which included the "Baby Boom" and the "Feminine Mystique," with accompanying emphasis on consumerism and private fulfillment. Experts denounced rigid child-rearing regimes, permissiveness became the order of the day, and "libidinal motherhood" the ideal. Mothers were urged to adapt to the instinctual needs of their children and to provide a perfectly nourishing environment.[28] Passionate fulfillment, mothers were told, was to be found in the joys of childcare, pregnancy and breast-feeding. As in the nineteenth century, education was once again viewed as a threat to femininity and motherliness. The mother's regression to a childlike state was thought to be the prerequisite for an ideal mother-infant bond.[29] Working mothers in the 1940s and 1950s were urged to stop working and give in to their natural instincts. In droves, mothers stayed home, had large families and committed themselves to the creation of a perfect environment for husband and children.

While mothers were being idealized, an undercurrent of blame was developing, and mothers again became convenient scapegoats for a wide range of problems, many of which had political and economic roots. Mothers were, and often still are, held responsible for juvenile delinquency, adult criminality, and all mental illness and emotional and behavioural problems in their children and adult offspring. Wylie's famous book, *Generation of Vipers,*[30] accused the American "Mom," nonworking wives and mothers, of ruining their menfolk. The accusative "Mom" quickly gained credence in professional literature, and "Momism" gained the status of a diagnostic term. Erikson stated: " 'Mom' is a woman in whose life cycle remnants of infantility join advanced senility to crowd out the middle range of mature womanhood, which thus becomes self-absorbed and stagnant."[31] Theories about "bad mothers" held sway from the 1940s to the 1960s and are still pervasive today. Each childhood disorder was traced to pathology in the mother, according to a legion of experts. Theories and child-rearing texts based on Freud's work present behaviour and personality development as entirely dependent on the quality of the mother-child relationship during the first few years of life. The very influential work of Bowlby[32] and Spitz[33] on the effects of mother-child separation reinforced beliefs that infants require the undivided attention of their mothers for the first two or three years of their life. Drawing on his work with war orphans and children who had been hospitalized for long periods, Bowlby postulated that "maternal deprivation" caused delinquency, mental retardation, dwarfism, depression, and affectionless psychopathy. Furthermore, Bowlby[34] charged that a state of "partial deprivation" and consequent destructive effects on the child could occur when a child lacked full-time constant attention from his mother. In his widely-read book, *The First Year of Life,* Spitz[35] depicted the mother-child relationship as a closed dyad. A variety of "psychotoxic" maternal attitudes were related to conditions such as infantile eczema, colic, rocking, and fecal play. In his concluding chapter, Spitz contended that the rapid disintegration of the traditional forms of the family in western society was due to a decrease in patriarchal authority and to the mother's absence from the home. We should note that fathers are accorded one paragraph in Spitz's book! These writings have had profound effects on mothers, families, professionals, child-rearing practices, and on legislators who can, for instance, use the findings as an argument against readily available daycare, especially for children under three, against all kinds of group residential care,[36] and as a reason for keeping mothers out of the work force. If mothers are not guilty of rejecting or depriving their children they could be accused of "overprotection."[37] Overprotection and rejection were felt to represent two sides of a coin, alternate ways in which a woman might express unconscious hostilities – a perfect "Catch-22."

The mother's primary responsibility for the child's adjustment appeared repeatedly in theories about families and children. For instance, the "bad mother" has a pervasive role in the literature about childhood asthma. Mothers of asthmatic children have been accused of unconscious hostility and accompanying rejection or over-protection.[38] Asthmatic attacks were depicted as the child's plea to the mother, asking her not to desert him.[39] Mothers were characterized as both seductive and prohibitive, binding their children to them, and at the same time rejecting any signs of sexual interest.[40] The "repressed cry for help"[41] still appears with startling regularity in hospital consultations done by psychiatrists about asthmatic children.

Delinquency was often attributed to defects in the mother-child relationship. The lack of a meaningful primary relationship with the mother was felt to be a precursor of psychopathic development.[42] Lack of parental response, especially maternal,[43] and separations from the mother were stressed.[44] A chronically hostile mother was felt to produce an intense anxiety in her child, who perceived himself as "bad me" and might later undergo a "malevolent transformation" of personality.[45] The assumption that all delinquents are emotionally disturbed is still prevalent[46] and delinquency is often considered to be synonymous with antisocial personality disorders.

Many theories about schizophrenia assigned culpability to the mother. The "schizophrenogenic mother" was portrayed as cold, aloof and dominating,[47] nagging and hostile,[48] destructive and engulfing,[49] morally sadistic, critical and demanding.[50] Families demonstrated marital "schism" where there was open conflict, and "skew" where there was a subtle battle for dominance.[51] The mother was depicted as putting her child in a "double bind" by demanding affection and simultaneously rejecting it. The child's only escape from this impossible situation was into the fantasy world of mental illness.[52]

A review of family therapy and schizophrenia stresses that family therapists continue to use these concepts in their work.[53] Once constructed this way by a therapist, all family behaviour tends to be fitted into a pathological framework. A clear example of this is given by Wilson[54] in her book, *This Stranger, My Son*. Talking to the psychiatrist, she becomes increasingly embarrassed and defensive as she tries to explain that she and her husband have a good home and marriage, and that she is baffled by her son's illness. The psychiatrist tells her that although she may not be aware of it, the cause lies within the family. He stresses that no child is born with problems, and that her son has been damaged in their home.

Parents of autistic children, particularly mothers, were viewed as causing their child's terrible affliction. Mothers were described as self-centered and cold,[55] annihilating,[56] and totally uncaring.[57] A telling example of the destructive impact, yet seductive appeal, of the psychological view of autism is given by the report of a psychiatrist father of an autistic and retarded child.[58] Initially, his son Tom was assessed by an eclectic child psychiatrist and a multidisciplinary team and diagnosed as brain-damaged with mental retardation and autism. As a prerequisite for school placement, a cursory assessment was done by a special education team including a child psychiatrist. Tom was rediagnosed as schizophrenic, and his illness attributed to the family environment. Propelled by her guilt about Tom's condition and her reluctance to accept the diagnosis of brain damage and mental retardation, Tom's mother eagerly collaborated with a social worker in an exploration of the "sickness" in the family. Tom's condition persisted unchanged, so play therapy was added to the management plan. When this also failed, placement in a residential treatment centre was recommended. Despite Tom's failure to improve with psychological methods, and despite the clear signs of underlying brain damage, the "powerful current of opinion that we were schizophrenogenic parents" continued through several more assessments and a period of hospitalization. Gradually, Tom's mother became more skeptical about the insinuations that Tom's disorder was family-induced, became disenchanted and severed connections with all the authorities who insisted that Tom's illness was functional rather than organic in origin. She was then able to recognize and accept Tom's limitations without giving up all hope.

Massive social changes over the last 15 years have been accompanied by the knowledge explosion, including a proliferation of psychiatric theories and therapeutic modalities. A predominant climate of liberal humanism from the late 1960s to the mid-1970s, during which various rights movements grew, has been partially superseded by a conservative backlash. Similarly, social and community mental health models of psychiatry have almost vanished, and a strong emphasis on the medical model of psychiatry has emerged.

During this time many problems and stresses, barely discernible in earlier periods, have become increasingly evident. Rapid urbanization has given rise to overcrowding and the formation of ghettos has provided an environment conducive to the eruption of violence. Technological progress and automation have led to alienation on the job, redundancy and unemployment. Electronic wizardry allows the media to present a worldwide picture of wars, terrorism, starvation, threats, kidnapping, violent deaths and disasters. World economics no longer follow Keynesian logic, and inflation and recession combine to erode incomes and savings and sabotage the plans of individuals and corporations alike. Dwindling resources and increased pollution are acknowledged, but at the same time encouraged by rampant consumerism and massive advertising. Families are increasingly isolated from support systems, and the growing statistics of divorce, child abuse, wife abuse, working mothers, childless couples, alcoholism and stress diseases lead some to believe that the emotional basis of family life is dissolving.

People with minority group status tend to be more sensitive to the oppression inherent in our social structures: women, blacks, native Indians, other ethnic groups, students, and lower-class persons. As individuals and members of groups they may question established institutions, be suspicious of professionals, expect solutions, believe in support and self-help groups, challenge our materialistic society and its pervasive consumerism, work to conserve natural resources, decry discrimination and sexual asymmetry, and push for a more equal distribution of income and other resources. Social and community mental health models of psychiatry relate to these beliefs, as do, for instance, feminist therapy and work that has pointed out how psychiatry has perpetuated myths and biases about black families.[59] Some social and community psychiatrists with a critical perspective give much weight to the environmental roots of mental health. They downplay their role as experts, see themselves as equal members of a multidisciplinary team, and promote the use of lay therapists and the formation of self-help groups. Their virtual demise can be related to the present ascendency of conservative ideology, and to their own tendency to oversell community mental health and to create and reflect the public's hope that community mental health centres would eliminate criminality, juvenile delinquency and mental illness.

Despite the current vogue for traditional models, there is a growing body of literature which fails to support traditional concepts, accents the contradictions within psychiatric and child development theory, and supports a critical position. Questions about the importance of early experiences, the concept of "maternal deprivation," the need for an intense, exclusive mother-infant bond, and the supposedly detrimental effect of father's absence have been asked. For instance, studies that attempt to predict later psychological development from data collected during infancy and early childhood fail to support the view that adult mental health is determined by events in the first few years of life.[60] One writer observes: "I see our apparent inability to make empirical predictions about later personality from the early years as so much against good sense, common observations, and the thrust of all the developmental theories that I can take it only as an indictment of established paradigms and methods."[61] This is illustrated by studies of Korean and Greek war orphans who lived uncertain lives during the war years and were subsequently adopted into North American homes between the ages of five months and ten years. The study showed that the majority made a good adjustment and developed affectionate relationships with their adopting families.[62] These findings do not support beliefs about the primacy of early experiences, continuity, and the need for an intense one-to-one relationship with only one mothering figure. Careful examination of studies of "maternal deprivation"[63] and mother-child separation shows that they were often based on institutionalized children who were suffering from a devastating lack of both environmental and human stimulation. "Stimulus deprivation" was the problem, not "maternal deprivation." Reviews of research on fatherless homes have failed to substantiate commonly held beliefs that the lack of a father is universally detrimental to children.[64] Belatedly, accounts of how a father' presence affects children have begun to appear. Attention is drawn to the sparseness of this literature by one title: "The

Fathers (Not the Mothers): Their Importance and Influence With
Infants and Young Children."[65]

As yet, few writers have attempted to analyse these contradictions
and to delinate links between theories of child development and family
relationships and underlying social, political and economic beliefs and
trends. As a prelude to their study of the effect of daycare on infants,
Kagan et al. examine the ideological foundations of modern developmental psychology, and demonstrate their roots in societal beliefs,
arguing that "it is likely that contemporary Western scientists, living in
a human society that is intensely competitive, individualistic, and
friendly to the view that maximal accumulation of status, power and
wealth defines adaptation, have projected that mental attitude onto
nature."[66] The most comprehensive attempt to date to examine the
effect of theories on women and their families is Ehrenreich and
English's book, *For Her Own Good: 150 Years of Experts' Advice to
Women.*[67]

Those less sensitive or insensitive to the oppression inherent in our
social structures are more likely to be middle- or upper-class, white
males, working in business, industry or professions. Their actual job
situation may require and reinforce their blindness. For instance, an
industrial physician who works in an asbestos plant, alluded to the
problem of asbestososis but stated that the measure to be promoted
was to insist that workers refrain from smoking as they were making
themselves more vulnerable to the harmful effects of asbestos. Toffler[68]
categorizes future shock victims into four groups: Deniers, Specialists,
Reversionists, and Supersimplifiers. We venture to add a fifth: Victim
Blamers. The categories are, of course, not mutually exclusive, but the
will provide a focus to our argument.

"Deniers" block out unwelcome reality, perhaps with alcohol,
drugs, or mindless T.V. Although "Specialists" attempt to keep pace
with change, this applies only to a single, narrow sector of their lives.
While making use of all the latest innovations in their profession, they
continue to be firmly closed to any suggestions about the need for innovative changes in the social, political or economic arena. Toffler
offers physicians and financiers as examples of "Specialists." Psychiatrists, who identify themselves first and foremost as physicians, espouse
the medical model and view, for instance, new discoveries in brain
biochemistry as heralding a new era for psychiatry. Psychiatrists, reeling
under the constant criticism that psychiatry receives, are escaping from

134 —

the maligned community mental health model with its threats to the medical status of psychiatry, and are flocking back to the rigid, medical "Specialist" model of psychiatry. This model attributes problems to an individual's biologic makeup, hence treatment (usually medication) is aimed towards the presumed underlying biochemical or hormonal imbalance. Mothers in families are not explicitly scapegoated and blamed, but this model can lead to the assumption that a mother who complains of symptoms such as fatigue, insomnia, confusion, irritability or feeling miserable, is actually sick. Mothers, who are frequently the recipients of stress from other areas such as their husband's workplace or their children's schools, may be diagnosed as depressed or neurotic and placed in a sick role, to the detriment of themselves and their families.

"Reversionists" obsessively seek out previously successful routines and lifestyles that are now irrelevant and inappropriate. Toffler points out similarities between both ends of the political spectrum. The right-wing Reversionist focuses on a small town past where law, order and predictability prevail. The left-wing Reversionist, imbued with images of a bucolic idyll, dreams of reviving an even older social system and may attempt to realize this dream in a rural commune or a small plot in the wilderness. A great deal of present day conservative ideology can be subsumed under "Reversionism," e.g., the "Back to the Family" themes, anti-ERA forces, and the anti-abortion movement. Much psychiatric theory meshes well with "Reversionist" expectations, including the "bad mother" theories, the notion that mothers must be constantly available to their young children, and the sex-role stereotypes within theories which were described in the previous chapter. Family therapy, a comparatively recent development, is still wedded to individualistic explanations and promotes the belief that all emotional disorder arises and can be treated within the family.

Three main schools of family therapy have emerged: the psychoanalytic model, the behavioural model, and the systems model. Derived from the individual psychoanalytic model, psychoanalytic family therapy assumes that unconscious needs and conflicts are transferred from the family of origin to the marital relationship, thus causing marital dysfunction and family problems. Treatment relies on "intensive processes of working through and restructuring the family."[69] Sonne and Lincoln[70] state that in the early phases of treatment it is essential "for the female co-therapist to support the male therapist's aggressiveness," and in the later stages "for the male therapist to support the female therapist's femininity." Thus, restructuring is often based on a heterosexual co-therapy team which accentuates traditional sex roles.

The behavioural model of family therapy views the family as a system of interlocking reciprocal behaviours. Behavioural family therapy seeks to "change the family's usual provision of consequences of behaviour or contingencies of reinforcement."[71] For instance, a "sample contract" states that "If Mary has dinner ready at 6:00 each weeknight, Bill will take her out to dinner on Saturday." "If Bill spends half an hour playing with the children each weeknight, Mary will not object to his having one night out with the boys."[72] Various strategies for change are described, and can often be seen to rest on and reinforce the same traditional assumptions about family structure and sex roles that are seen in other theories.

Similarly, the systems orientation emphasizes behaviour, accountability and specific behavioural goals. Deviant behaviour is assumed to be maintained and constantly reinforced by the family system. Bowen,[73] a major proponent, states that families consist of sets of interlocking triads. Systems therapists use a variety of strategies in an attempt to alter mutually destructive and self-reinforcing patterns in the family, often without trying to produce insight into the origin of the difficulties.

Behavioural and systems models of family therapy are potentially more able to accomodate families which do not adhere to culturally prescribed patterns, but they do not seek to impart any understanding of the role of social structures in family distress. All three types of therapy, in fact, function to locate and contain within the family difficulties and distress which are freqently derived from stresses outside the family. Thus, family therapy supports, or at least does not challenge "Reversionist" ideology. This ideology, however, is greatly promoted by books such as *The Castrated Family*,[74] by the psychoanalyst Voth. He assumes that the "liberated" mother has castrated her family, and in so doing he echoes the earlier sentiments of Rheingold,[75] who warns that a good life and a stable world can be attained only if women accept their reproductive functions, avoid contamination by feminist doctrines, and become fulfilled and altruistic mothers. He contends that "the syndrome of decay, and evil tendency in man is basically rooted in the mother-child relationship."[76]

The "Back to the Family" theme is convenient for politicians and for a time of economic recession. It can be used to rationalize the closing of institutions and the cutbacks of services to the mentally ill, handicapped, chronically ill, elderly, and abused and neglected children. According to current policies, all of these people can and should be maintained at home.[77] Of course, this assumes that there is a mother at home who is willing and able to be a full-time servant and nurturer.

"Supersimplifiers" seek a simple, neat equation to explain the rich complexities that threaten to engulf them. For some, this is provided by a lifelong religious framework. Others seek a similar framework, purpose and answer in new religious cults, political groups, the Human Potential Movement, EST, Lifespring, and various special lifestyles. A single event may be accorded enormous significance, such as the belief that the proper bonding at birth will innoculate babies against a lifetime of ills and be a major force in producing a better world. "Supersimplification," as well as "Reversionism," can also be seen to embrace the tremendous current emphasis on the family. Simplistic expectations that the family alone will be able to provide for intimacy and personal growth are frequently dashed, and the disharmony, divorce, child abuse or whatever, viewed as a failure of the participants rather than an indictment of the concept. Medical and psychiatric theories, with their rituals of diagnosis and detection of a disease, provide a ready vehicle for "supersimplification" and the attribution of family difficulties to the genetically inherited personality or illness of family members, their individual biochemical or hormonal patterns, or to pathological interaction based on the parent's unconscious conflicts derived from their families of origin. Most psychiatric theories, in fact, could be subsumed under the rubric of "Supersimplification." Their staunch proponents insist that their method or theory is right, sometimes using an unassailable system of "logic" to support their argument. For instance, one author, during training, tried to argue with a psychoanalyst supervisor and point out different possible explanations for the family's difficulties. The supervisor's analysis of the mother's contribution to the child's Oedipal conflict was persuasive and erudite, and any attempts at alternate formulations were dismissed as "repression" and "denial" on the supervisee's part. "Supersimplificiation" allows family distress to be constructed as a problem of the individuals within the family, or of the family itself. It precludes recognition of the complex, interwoven forces that impinge on, and in turn create stresses within the family.

As described by Ryan,[78] "Victim Blamers" hold the victim of a social problem responsible for causing it. "Welfare bums" are blamed for being lazy, native Indians for being drunken and irresponsible, delinquent youth for being incorrigible, alcoholics for lacking willpower, and women who are addicted to psychotropic drugs for being neurotic or ungrateful for all their "privileges." "Victim Blaming" in psychiatric theory is particularly rife in theories concerning violence towards women. "Victim Blaming" plays a major role in Health Promotion, a new ideology that has appeared simultaneously in Canada, Britain and the United States over the past five years. If examined superficially, Health Promotion appears to be progressive and responsible thinking. Currently, Health Promotion calls to mind exhortations towards a healthy lifestyle including a sensible diet, exercise, awareness of stress-reduction techniques, complete avoidance of smoking and minimal use of alcohol. The formation of self-help groups, and demands for the deprofessionalization and demystification of medicine can also be subsumed under the umbrella of Health Promotion. These principles can be traced back to the rights movements of the 60's, with their suspicion of professionals and institutions.[79] Health Promotion ideology also meshes with, and is co-opted by a conservative ideology which blames individuals for their health problems, allows cutbacks of medical and other services which may be vital rather than superfluous, and permits the vested interests of government and industry to continue unchecked. Health Promotion ideology can lend itself neatly to furthering the discrimination against and oppression of many groups of people in Canadian society, depriving them of needed services and obscuring the role of invidious forces in our society that are detrimental to health.[80] Health Promotion puts the onus on the individual and the family, particularly the mother, to provide the right diet, forbid alcohol and smoking, insist on exercise, recreation, and stress-reduction. Even if the family had the financial resources, it would take nothing short of a miracle to expect these measures to counteract all the stresses of the workplace, effects of food additives, environmenal carcinogens, industrial pollution, occupational hazards, to say nothing of the constant bombardment of persuasive advertising and encouragement to consume.

In general, the emphasis on the mother-child dyad alone, and the consequent blaming of the mother for all difficulties, has decreased over the last 15 years, giving way to a plethora of theories. Almost all of these locate the difficulty within the family, and most treatment calls for the family to return to or even accentuate a traditional way of functioning, with mothers still being expected to be self-sacrificing nurturers, or "superwomen" if they are also working outside the home.

CONCLUSIONS

Janeway[81] describes how the myth that "woman's place is in the home," is used by society to avoid helping women who work outside the home by providing daycare centres and nursery schools, by facilitating steady part-time jobs in industry, and part-time training in universities. Similarly, psychiatric theories that blame mothers and their families allow society to avoid looking at and trying to alleviate the numerous pressures that families face today, including poverty, unemployment, discrimination, poor housing, lack of stable support systems, unsuitable educational programmes, and a variety of emotional stresses.

Psychiatric theories have reassured the public that the stress, distress, devastation, crime and violence that they perceive around them are a result of individual or family pathology that could be treated on a case-by-case basis. For instance, the confusion about delinquency and the frequent underlying assumption that the cause lies within the family (probably a mother-child relationship that has produced an emotionally disturbed child), leads to outcries for more psychiatric services following outbreaks of juvenile crime or a particularly sensational crime. It also leads to a media focus on the mother of the criminal or delinquent, to delinquency-prevention programmes centred on family counselling, and to the expectation that boys growing up with a single-parent mother will become delinquent. These beliefs persist despite studies that show that a mental-health approach to delinquency is useless or even damaging. As we have illustrated, popular beliefs are contained within psychiatric theories which, in turn, can give "scientific validity" to the same popular assumptions. So we have a self-perpetuating process which, as we have also tried to show, can snowball and gain rapid ascendancy when society's needs dovetail with the ideology presented by the theory.

A closer look at the family reveals the present-day isolation in which women work, and the conflicts inherent in their role and in the dominant-subordinate male-female relationships that are part of the organization of our society. Women are led to believe that they will be happy and fulfilled if they serve others, yet their role in the family has become progressively devalued, so that childcare, housework, and the organization of emotional relationships in the family are seen to be less important that what goes on in the "real world." The institution of motherhood glorifies and extolls motherhood as a sacred calling — in actuality, women in the family are subordinates and face many obstacles and inequities. Women are caught in these paradoxes, in a situation that can become stifling, stagnating, or an emotional pressure-cooker. Our contention that there are stresses and strains within all families, whether "normal" or "abormal," are confirmed by various research findings. Researchers studying visually impaired children and their families, and using a control group of normal children, hypothesized that parents of the visually impaired children would be more likely to seek counselling and/or take tranquillizers. They were surprised to find the same incidence in families with visually impaired children and ones with normal children.[82] Studying autistic children and their families, and a control group of normal children and their families, de Myer had similar findings, and comments: "One hesitates whether to conclude that autistic parents are exceptionally resilient or that raising a normal family is almost as stressful as raising one containing an autistic child."[83]

Thus the actuality of women's experience in the family is hidden both from us and from them by societal beliefs about women's place and role, and by the fact that all the theories, values and symbols that are available to them are provided by men. New frameworks will have to consider both women's experience and the function of the family as an ideological structure of the state. New understanding and new theory must recognize that the origins of stress, relationships and expectations within the supposed privacy of the family lie in institutions outside the family. Families are affected by: the education system; stresses in the workplace; the legal structures of marriage, divorce, child custody, abortion and sexuality; models of behaviour for women and men, parents and children; the advice of professionals; class inequalities; and the sexual asymmetry that is embedded in all areas of society.

At the same time, we have to take a new look at whether our theories about mother-infant attachment, child development, and family relationships are valid and scientific or whether they merely reflect cultural beliefs and thus serve both to perpetuate the status quo in our society and to hide the fact that the social structures themselves may be at fault. If early mother-child relationships are seen as shapers of destiny, then mothers become easy scapegoats and provide a convenient reason to avoid a critical examination of our social structures. This belief also stands in the way of attempts to delineate children's basic needs and to explore alternate methods of child-rearing.

To re-emphasize the contention made at the beginning of this chapter: the understanding of the family as an institution, and the psychiatric construction of the family are complex topics. Much work remains to be done.

$$\equiv \qquad \equiv \qquad \equiv$$

CHAPTER VII

VIOLENCE TOWARDS WOMEN

VIOLENCE TOWARDS WOMEN IS VERY COMMON, but most often ignored and vastly underreported. As part of the natural order" of things, it is largely invisible. Reflecting and reinforcing stereotypes of masculinity and feminity, psychiatric theories and attitudes, the criminal justice system and other institutions of society serve to condone and minimize violence towards women. Men are protected and their actions viewed as understandable. The abuse may be rationalized by assuming that the man was out of control because he was provoked, drunk or disturbed. Commonly, all or most of the responsibility is assigned to the woman victim. Rape will be the major focus for this chapter and will serve as a paradigm for examining other forms of violence towards women.

RAPE

Many rapes go unreported. Women fear reprisal or ridicule and, filled with shame and humiliation, may decide that they can tell no one. Or they tell a few friends, relatives or a rape relief service but do not make a report to the police. In 1976, 2,915 rapes were reported to Canadian police. Of these, 1,087 were considered to be "unfounded," so that the "actual number" is 1,828. This was an increase of 48% over 1972, when 1,235 rapes were reported. Thus the rape report rate in 1976 was 15.8 per 100,000 female population, compared to 11.8 per 100,000 in 1972.[1] Based on their studies of rape in Vancouver and Toronto, Clark and Lewis[2] estimate that between 1.8 and 7% of rapists are convicted, the rest are unreported or lack sufficient credible evidence to proceed through the criminal justice system. Making a conservative estimate derived from U.S. statistics, Johnson[3] states that if current conditions prevail, between 20 and 30% of girls now 12 years old will suffer a violent sexual attack sometime during their lives.

Common Beliefs

Assumptions about rape contradict each other and illustrate the confusion about the subject. Most people believe that it is a spontaneous and purely sexual act engaged in to satisfy sexual urges. Stereotypical rapists are thought to be men with sexual problems who are unable to control their sexual impulses. They are thought to be different from normal men in that they have no legitimate or alternative sexual outlet, and because they sometimes subject their victims to humiliating experiences. The extreme view of rape as a moral outrage committed by a sexual psychopath against an unsuspecting, pure, virgin victim is promulgated by the media, and underlies the opinion that all other occurrences are not *really* rape. When rapists are not viewed as sexual psychopaths, they are often seen as men whose natural sexual impulse is triggered by provocative, teasing women. Responsibility for the rape can then be totally or partially assigned to the victims. They should not have been hitch-hiking, should not have gone for a drink, should not have displayed their bodies in any way which could be construed as inviting sexual advances, and so on. The shifting of responsibility to the victims is also made possible by distorted perceptions of women's sexuality: rape may be though to be potentially very exciting and satisfying for women as they are taken by force, absolved of responsibility and guilt and can relax and enjoy a purely sensual experience. Women, they believe, frequently say "No" when they mean "Yes."

Another belief is that women fabricate. It is thought that many women consent to sexual intercourse and cry rape after the event, when they are overcome by remorse. This is often applied to adolescent girls who are assumed to tell their parents they have been raped to cover up their sexual misdemeanours. A vengeful woman, it is thought, may accuse a man of rape to get back at him, and thus attempt to get an innocent male imprisoned.[4]

Smart[5] comments that stereotypes of rapist and victim make it difficult for "normal" men and women to view themselves as either. Acts which could be defined as rape are viewed merely as overly energetic sexual intercourse. She feels that after a rape, both rapist and victim may rethink the situation and reinterpret the event and the circumstances leading up to it according to their respective understandings of rape.

Historical Background

Over the centuries, attitudes towards rape appear to range from strict prohibition and punishment (when the victim was a betrothed or propertied virgin) to acceptance or promotion (when victims were perceived as unavoidable casualties or spoils of war). The ancient Babylonian Code of Hammurabi instructed that the man who raped a betrothed virgin should be killed. If a married woman was raped, however, both participants were bound and thrown in the river. Husbands could rescue their wives if they wished.

Biblical stories, such as the Genesis account of Dinah, the virgin daughter of Jacob, tell of the capture of women from other tribes to be used as field hands, slaves, concubines and breeders of more slaves. Brownmiller points out that these biblical portrayals were often used as justification for the manner in which eighteenth-century slave holders used their slaves. Another famous example of capturing women during war is the rape of the Sabine women, which purportedly led to the founding of Rome. This event was portrayed by a number of artists in later centuries. The Sabine women were invariably depicted as buxom, luscious, and apparently enjoying themselves. Brownmiller remarks that this and other portrayals of captured women in art and literature cannot be accidental and represents "the universal promulgation of a parable of rape that places the full burden of blame squarely on a lascivious female of another race or nation."[6]

Before the Norman conquest of England in 1066, the penalty there for rape of a high-born, propertied virgin was death and dismemberment. William the Conqueror reduced this punishment to the loss of both eyes and castration. Victims could, however, decide to marry their rapists and save them from death or mutilation. As far as we can gather from early accounts, rapists of women who were not propertied virgins received little or no punishment. At the end of the fourteeenth century, the Statutes of Westminster, formulated by Henry I, included the rape of married women in the concept of forcible rape. A definition of "lesser ravishment" was applied to the wife who did not object strenuously enough, and the husband, considered to be the aggrieved party, could appropriate the wife's dowery. In principle, the legal concept of criminal rape was extended to include widows, nuns, prostitutes and concubines. However, the complaints of women, apart from the well-substantiated case of the propertied virgin or the upper-class married woman, have continued to be treated with disbelief or suspicion. In the seventeenth century, Lord Chief Justice Matthew Hale wrote, "Rape is an accusation easily to be made and hard to be proved, and harder to be defended by the party accused, tho never so innocent." This is "an old saw that has been quoted by virtually every legal writer who has discussed rape."[7] As late as 1973, it was included in California's standard set of jury instructions for cases of rape. It was followed by the admonition "therefore the law requires that you examine the testimony of the female person named in the information with caution."

Brownmiller[8] emphasizes that the two centuries of slavery in the American South ". . . is a perfect study of rape in all its complexities, for the black woman's sexual integrity was deliberately crushed in order that slavery might profitably endure." They were expected to produce a steady stream of slave babies, future workers for their owners. The father of the babies might be an arbitrarily assigned mate, or the plantation owner or overseer who viewed slave women as objects to be used for their sexual pleasure. The concept of raping a slave was nonexistent. Master-slave sexual relationships were not considered as rape; one could not rape one's own property. Plantation law considered rape of one man's slave by another white man as merely a "trespass." She goes on to point out that: "The examples we find in abolitionist literature that express concern over the sexual abuse of female slaves are frequently couched in terms of sympathy for the abused women's *husbands*."

It appears that the definition of the raped woman as property of a man — father, husband, husband-to-be, or owner, is the major dimension in societal attitudes towards rape. This comes into focus even more clearly when we study rape and war.

RAPE AND WAR

Brownmiller[9] argues that down through the ages rape has been the prerogative of the conquering army, a measure of the victory, and part of the soldiers' proof of masculinity and success. Beyond the triumph is the rapists' part of the pattern of national terror and subjugation imposed by the conquering army. She points out that ". . . men appropriate rape of 'their women' as part of their own male anguish of defeat." This egocentric view, she stresses, does have some validity as ". . . rape by a conqueror is compelling evidence of the conquered's status of masculine impotence . . . Rape by a conquering soldier destroys all remaining illusions of power and property for men of the defeated side."

Events in Bangla-Desh in 1971 illustrate the rejection of the raped woman as damaged property. Hundreds of thousands of Bengali women were raped by Pakistani soldiers. Bengali women traditionally led cloistered lives and rape victims were ostracized. Also by tradition, no Moslem husbands would take back wives who had been touched by other men, even if the women were taken by force. The government of Bangla-Desh attempted to cope with the situation by telling the husbands that the women were victims and should be considered as national heroines. Very few were taken back, however, and many thousands of women were left homeless, some to find their way into brothels, though others were more fortunate and entered shelters for rape victims and rehabilitation programs.

Brownmiller comments that the number of rapes per capita during the nine-month occupation of Bangla-Desh was no greater than the incidence in other wars — such as in Belgium and France during the first few months of World War I, or in Soviet Russia during World War II. However, for the first time in the history of rape of women during war, the Bangla-Desh situation received serious national attention because of a growing feminist consciousness that viewed rape as a political issue.

THEORIES

Little is written about rape in traditional psychiatric textbooks. In the index of Freedman, Kaplan and Sadock's *Comprehensive Textbook of Psychiatry*, there are five citations on rape and in this 2,571 page textbook only three-quarters of one page is devoted to rape, focussing mostly on legal aspects. It is interesting to note than an equivalent amount of space (half a page and six references) is accorded to Koro, a disease found among men of the Malay archipelago and South China. Men afflicted with Koro fear that their penises are shrinking and may disappear into their abdomens, resulting in death. This gives us some idea about priorities for psychiatry, as the fantasized disappearance of Malay penises seems to be accorded the same importance as rape, an extreme trauma suffered by hundreds of thousands of women.

There are three major types of theory. One set views rape as an irresistible impulse that can occur in a normal man and, under special circumstances, leads to rape. Another set of theories assigns responsibility for rape to males, but argues that they are psychotic, neurotic or suffering from a personality disorder. The third variety places the blame on the victims, and/or mothers and wives of the sexual offenders.

Glueck[10] argued, in 1925, that irresistible impulse and insanity affect individuals in similar ways. Both are involuntary and the person is not accountable for his or her actions. Many psychiatric formulations since then have depicted rapists as victims of an "uncontrollable urge, committed without logic or rationale, under the influence of a strong overpowering drive"[11] and "driven by uncontrollable impulsions."[12]

The disease theory states that rapists are sick, perverted, sadistic individuals who had abnormal childhoods and who often have latent homosexual tendencies. Early writers thought that rape resulted from a disease of the brain.[13] Karpman,[14] writing in the 1950s, argued that rapists suffered from "paraphiliac neurosis" and stated that rapists are "victims of a disease from which many of them suffer more than their victims."[15] Other theorists described rape as a means of compensating for sexual inadequacy[16] or as an expression of latent homosexuality.[17] More recently, a widely read article by psychoanalyst Littner[18] re-emphasized that rape is a symptom of mental disease and stated, "The single most important item we need to know about the sex offender is how sick he is emotionally. This is far more important than the crime he has committed." Other studies, however, failed to support the notion that the rapist is mentally ill[19] and over the last decade, studies of the pathology of the rapist have given way to studies which examine the interaction between the rapist and his victim.

Studies of rape victims, and the growing interests in victimology (the study of the characteristics of victims of crime and disaster), were predated by the writings of Helene Deutsch[20] and of Hollander, who concluded that "rape of women is very rare indeed."[21] Describing rape victims as hysterical and masochistic women who, influenced by their colourful rape fantasties, were unable to separate reality from fantasy, Deutsch wrote, "Rape fantasies often have such irresistible verisimilitude that even the most experienced judges are misled in trials of innocent men accused of rape by hysterical women."

Victimology dates back to 1940, to the writings of Von Hentig[22] who argued that there are born victims who are self-destructive, self-harming, and seductive. Amir's study of rape in Philadelphia[23] is a more recent example of the application of victimology theory to rape. Stating that 19% of the rapes in the study were victim precipitated, Amir contends that the victim-offender relationship, the moral character of the victim, and the "victim's personality make-up that may orient her towards the offender and the offense" should be examined. For instance, hitch-hike rape is designated a victim-precipitated offence. Similarly, MacDonald[24] attributes rape to the victims' temperament and their "libertine social surroundings." "True victims," according to Littner,[25] do not have a conscious or unconscious wish to be raped. "Professional victims," on the other hand, do have an unconscious desire to be sexually molested and "unwittingly cooperate with the rapist." This sentiment is echoed by Abrahamsen[26] whose case study of a single victim emphasizes "unconscious complicity." Other writers focus on a conscious wish to be raped, emphasizing flirtatious and provocative behaviour.[27]

A study of the wives of eight convicted rapists concluded "there can be no doubt that sexual frustration that the wives caused is one of the factors motivating rape, which might tentatively be an attempt to force a seductive but rejecting mother into submission."[28] The wives were described as competing with men, negating their femininity, sleeping in their underwear, and being generally frigid. The assignment of responsibility to wives is also illustrated by Roberts and Pacht's[29] suggestion that assessment of the wife's personality should play an important part in parole decisions: "For the married offender, his wife's attitude to him, her personality, her emotional or other problems, and the degree to which she contributes to his sexual difficulty make a substantial difference in his impulse control."

Rage towards a rejecting mother-figure often plays a central part in the formulation of the dynamics of the rapist, and the rape is perceived as "an outpouring of pent-up aggression and sexuality; the victim represents mother, sister, and all women who have tantalized him with their warmth and sexuality but who have also deprived him." Rape is said to have "its roots in maternal frustration commencing at the pre-Oedipal stage"[30] and "the mother who forces her children to eat or demands bowel regularity by imposed enemas may be raping the child orally or anally."[31] Rape by expectant fathers is attributed to their sexual deprivation, and to their lashing out against their pregnant wives who are perceived as withholding mother-figures.[32]

Many writers report an association between rape and alcohol consumption by the rapist.[33] Most of these reports maintain that the alcohol, by removing social restraints and inhibitions, leaves men at the mercy of their sexual drives.

ATTITUDES OF COURTS, POLICE, HOSPITALS, AND PROFESSIONALS

(These will be illustrated with some case histories from the practice of P.S. Penfold.)

Clark and Lewis[34] stress that "the progress of a rape case through the criminal justice system reflects a highly selective process of elimination. Only a fraction of all rapes are reported; only a fraction of reported rapes are classified as founded; only a fraction of founded cases lead to an arrest; only a fraction of the suspects arrested are convicted." They feel that this is "something of a monument of injustice, and a serious indictment of our criminal justice system." While describing the biased views of some police officers, they emphasize that the major reason for considering a rape case as founded is based on practical decisions about how well such a case would fare during a trial. They state that "the police are unwilling to push a case to prosecution if they know an acquittal is likely, because a great deal of time, energy, and public money goes into the preparation of each case. Also, the police know just how difficult it is to achieve conviction in a rape case and how reluctant crown attorneys are to prosecute problematical cases." Clark and Lewis go on to describe the empathy the police often have for rape victims, and their anger about the treatment of victims during a trial and the low conviction rates.

■ Martha, a 35-year-old divorced woman, went on a pre-arranged blind date, meeting John at a downtown hotel. After dinner and drinks, they went to John's apartment where, after two more drinks, John demanded sex. On being rebuffed, John became loud and threatening, eventually forcing Martha to undress at knifepoint and then subjecting her to a variety of indignities. After several hours, Martha was allowed to get dressed and leave. Apparently oblivious to the situation, John asked for another "date." Martha was examined at a hospital; no signs of physical abuse were found. The police, who listened sympathetically, advised that the allegations of rape would be very difficult to substantiate. Martha decided not to pursue the charge.

Despite amendments to the Canadian Criminal Code in 1976, which abolished the judge's instruction to the jury about the need for corroborative evidence to substantiate the women's testimony, and which placed stricter controls on the defence lawyer's examination of the victim's sexual history, the complainant's progress through the various phases of the criminal justice system is still an ordeal. The courtroom "becomes the microcosm of society in which every stereotyped assumption about women is enacted . . ."[35] Defence counsels play on all of these assumptions in their attempts to get rapists acquitted. They do everything they can to undermine the victims' credibility and persuade the jury that they are lying, or merely got what they deserved.

■ Judy, aged 19, brought a rape charge against her father's business acquaintance, Mr. L. During the trial, the defence lawyer emphasized that Judy had accepted a ride with Mr. L., gone for several drinks, and then gone to Mr. L.'s apartment. Describing Judy's "seductive behaviour," tight jeans and scanty T-shirt, the lawyer made a telling case for Mr. L.'s belief that Judy was saying "No" but really meaning "Yes." Matters were clinched when Judy's psychiatric history and previous sexual involvement with an older man were brought to light. Judy was depicted as unstable, seductive, unpredictable, promiscuous, and a liar. Mr. L. was acquitted.

Clark and Lewis point out that: "The emphasis on the victim's character, the demand for corroboration, the way in which the need for proof beyond a reasonable doubt casts the onus on the victim, all work together in a rape trial to weaken the prosecution's case and make conviction very unlikely." In many cases, a young and inexperienced crown counsel opposes a very experienced defence counsel who has a large repertoire of tactics designed to cast doubt on the victim's account. The defence counsel may have an array of "expert witnesses" such as psychiatrists who can be used to destroy the credibility of the victim or provide rationalizations for the rapist's behaviour.

Prior to entering the criminal justice system, the rape victim is likely to have gone to a hospital. There, unless the hospital has a clear policy about the management of rape and has both designated and trained staff to work with the victims, staff are likely to have both biased personal attitudes and fears of legal involvement. Vancouver women felt that their treatment by medical personnel was impersonal, biased, and unsympathetic. One woman commented that the medical examination felt like "another rape."[36]

THE MYTHOLOGY OF RAPE

Both lay beliefs and psychiatric theories view rape as a spontaneous sexual act resulting from the underlying, extremely strong, biological imperative to which men are subject. Freud[37] described the natural aggressiveness of the male as follows: "Nature has paid less careful attention to the demands of the female function than to those of masculinity . . . . The achievement of the biological aim is entrusted to the aggressiveness of the male, and is to some extent independent of the co-operation of the female." Male sexual aggression is thus deemed necessary for the continuation of the species. Marie Bonaparte[38] carried this even further, depicting the small boy's sexual aggression as murderous. "What the small boy apparently yearns to accomplish is an anal, cloacal, intestinal penetration of the mother; a bloody disemboweling event. The child of two, three or four, despite, or rather because of, infancy, is really a potential Jack the Ripper." Aggressive sexuality is condoned and reinforced by the Freudian point of view, which dismisses anything else as "tepid, epicene and prissy."[39] Societal beliefs about masculinity parallel psychiatric thought. Masculinity is equated with power, domination, and sexual prowess. Sex and violence are closely linked and idealized in art, literature, advertising and other media. Cultural heroes, such as James Bond, are totally ruthless, powerful and sexually attractive.

Men are expected to apply a certain amount of pressure. Within these belief systems rape can readily be dismissed as an energetic seduction, or explained as the result of an irresistible impulse.

The logic of the irresistible impulse theory was questioned by Sutherland,[40] who noted that most convicted rapists were between the ages of 20 and 29, and asked why the impulse rarely occurred before or after that point. In describing very low recidivism rates, Sutherland questioned whether an irresistible impulse could come but once per lifetime? More doubt is cast by the studies that show that most rapes are planned, that up to 50% have more than one perpetrator, and that force is used in a large proportion of cases.[41] Clark and Lewis's findings about the sexual performance of the rapist do not support the notion of the excessive sexual powers or extreme sexual urges of the rapist. Many of the police reports that they studied suggested problems with erection and orgasm.[42]

Brownmiller's[43] account of the imaginative profile of the Boston strangler, constructed by a medical-psychiatric committee, shows without doubt the influence of traditional beliefs about rape. The committee, noting that one of the victims was a seventy-five-year-old woman, postulated that the killer was a conservative, tidy, orderly fellow who was quite likely to be middle-aged, impotent and homosexual. They felt that , consumed by hatred for an overwhelming, seductive, punitive, sweet, orderly, neat and compulsive mother, the strangler was driven to mutilate and murder old women in a manner that revealed both love and hate. Upon his capture the strangler "single-handedly smashed every cherished psychiatric concept of a sex murderer. . . . He proved to be genuinely attached to his mother, who was still alive, and not particularly sweet, neat or overwhelming."

While mythology may suggest that most rapists are sexual perverts who hide in the bushes and hate their mothers, the rapists in Amir's series, and in the Toronto and Vancouver studies were mostly young, lower-class men. Amir noted that they appeared to by psychiatrically normal but tended to have past records of a variety of assaults, including rape. He argued that men learn to view aggressive conquest as an appropriate substitute for failures in the economic and social spheres. Thus, exploitive and aggressive behaviour towards women is viewed as normal and understandable, and not conceived of as wrong. Similarly, Russel[44] describes rape as an overconforming rather than a deviant act. It can be understood as "an extreme acting out of qualities that are regarded as super-masculine in this and many other societies: aggression, force, power, strength, toughness, dominance, competitiveness." These notions of masculinity may be acted out in the sexual arena by "men who feel powerless in the rest of their lives, and men whose masculinity is threatened by their sense of powerlessness."

Clark and Lewis, who view rape as a function of our sexually co-ercive society, state that men who are unable to find sexual gratifica-tion through legitimate means (which often include elements of coer-cion) have to resort to the use or the threat of violence. The power of cultural sanctions for rape and of beliefs about man's natural aggressive-ness are illustrated by Clark and Lewis's finding that few rapists thought they had done anything wrong: "Some of them went to incredible lengths to see their behaviour as 'normal' and acceptable." The rapists' attitudes and explanations of their behaviour were on a continuum. At one end were men who made no attempt to disguise their behaviour, attributing no importance to their victim's wishes and feelings. As they did not view women as self-determining individuals, rape was a mean-ingless concept. At the other end of the continuum were men who rationalized their actions and avoided viewing them as rape. They at-tempted to deny the coerciveness of the act and characterized it as a "date" or "seduction."[45]

Psychiatric theories and lay beliefs intertwine and embody the notions that the rape victim "asked for it" or "She said 'No,' but meant 'Yes'." The idea that a woman provokes and actually enjoys rape is both reflected and reinforced by the concept of female masochism. In psychoanalytic theory this concept is described as part of the biologi-cally determined triad of feminine characteristics: passivity, narcissism and masochism. Women's occasional rape fantasies are used to support this position and can lead to the notion that rape is a virtually victim-less crime. While some people indulge in masochistic fantasies which may include a fantasy rapist, this bears no relation to an unchosen assault by a rapist in real life. When the victim-precipitation theories of rape, which reinforce and reflect the assumption that the women de-served it, are examined, circular thinking becomes obvious and it ap-pears that the concept of victim precipitation can serve to blame the victims for their fate. Amir[46] states "A woman's behaviour, if passive, may be seen as worthy to suit action, and if active, may be taken as an actual promise of success to one's sexual intentions." Despite this,

Amir goes on to argue "If the victim is not solely responsible for what becomes the unfortunate event, at least she is often the complementary partner."

The "She asked for it" hypothesis was examined by Geller[47] in 1974 in a study of female hitchhikers during the 23-day Toronto Transit strike. During the strike, the number of sexual offenses against female hitchhikers was eight times that of the pre- and post-strike periods. Geller concluded that the opportunity to commit a sexual offense and the availability of a female victim are the variables that determine the occurrence of such an offense and that the results disprove the theory that conscious or unconscious motivation on the part of the female victim contributes to the offense. A U.S. study of victim-precipitating behaviour showed that in only 4% of the offenses was there any behaviour that could possibly be seen as encouragement.[48] The inescapable conclusion that any behaviour on the victim's part can be construed as encouragement is confirmed by a study of imprisoned rapists which demonstrated that they often look on grudging and reluctant victim cooperation as evidence of enthusiasm.[49]

The no-win situation for victims is further illustrated by beliefs about the role of alcohol. While alcohol intake may be viewed as an extenuating circumstance for rapitsts, it is an incriminating one for victims and is used to discredit their reports and their characters. An extensive review of the literature failed to establish a relationship between alcohol and sexual desire, and suggested only tenuous links between alcohol intake and aggression.[50] Rada[51] has presented a more cogent explanaton, suggesting that rapists, relying on the widespread belief that alcohol causes disinhibition, use alcohol as an excuse for their behaviour.

Despite a lack of evidence, beliefs about the victims' duplicity are so powerful that the rape victims often become the offenders in rape cases. They are interrogated with the suspicion that they are lying, that they really consented at the time, that they said "No" and meant "Yes," and that they were provocative and thus deserved what they got. Thus, women are readily blamed, except in circumstances of extreme violence or where their status, character and background give them high credibility. Laws, the criminal justice system, psychiatric theories and attitudes all contain this "blame the victim" ideology and function to protect rapists, of whom only a small percentage are convicted.

Clark and Lewis's studies demonstrate that the primary determinant of how the victim's report is dealt with by the police is her background and character. The emphasis is not on the rapist or the offense, but on the victims' emotional and physical conditions when they report the crime, their age, and their marital and occupational status. There are some women, they postulate, who "can't be raped" and who are "open territory" for rapists. Women who are teenagers, have a history of mental illness, who are unemployed or on welfare, who are separated, divorced or common-law, are likely to fall into this group. Other indicators that the situation probably was not rape are the perception of the victim as "drunk," the fact that she was not hysterical when she reported the rape, that she knew the offender, or that she voluntarily accepted a ride in the car or visit to the apartment of the offender.

These common beliefs about rape and their reflection in psychiatric theories and attitudes, in laws and the processes of the criminal justice system, do not fit with what actually happens when a woman is raped. Studies of rape victims,[52] first-hand accounts of the experience of being raped,[53] and the information collected by rape crisis and counselling centres[54] all serve to identify rape as an assault, a ritual of power and hostility and "a gross and extreme form of social regulation by which woman is brutally stripped of her humanity and confronted with her definition as a non-person, a function."[55] Case studies of rapists have suggested that for about two-thirds of them power motives are uppermost, while rage, contempt and hatred for women are primary motives for the other third. Rapists see women as ungiving, unloving whores and bitches. They seek revenge and their aim is degradation and humiliation.[56]

Stereotyped beliefs about rape denigrate women's experience of rape as a life-threatening assault and serve to prevent women from obtaining the treatment, support and ongoing management that they need and deserve at the time of the rape and during the subsequent months.[57]

What factors are operating to allow the continued existence of this extremely skewed view of rape? Major determinants include woman's subordinate status as male property, sex-role stereotypes of masculinity and femininity, and archetypal images of women. Historical attitudes towards rape and the evolution of rape laws show very clearly that this is an offense against the man to whom the woman belongs. Propertied virgins were of value to both their fathers and husbands-to-be, thus their rape carried severe punishments. While abolitionist literature did recognize the rape of black women as a problem, the concern was couched in terms of sympathy for the women's husbands. Raped Bangla-Desh women were rejected by their husbands who saw them as damaged property.

In studies of rape ". . . the subordinate position of women in contemporary, industrial society is rarely addressed and never satisfactorily analyzed . . . it being assumed that sexual stratification is a reflection of the natural order of things."[58] The status of woman as man's property has wide ramifications. Rape is not viewed as a violation of women's rights and is only treated as an offense against the person if the victim is severely injured. The Virgin-Whore dichotomy can be clearly seen in attitudes towards rape victims: "Only nice girls get raped." Fear and loathing of women can be seen in many portrayals of sexuality, including the writings of Miller, Mailer, and Hemingway.

INCEST AND SEXUAL ABUSE
OF CHILDREN AND ADOLESCENTS

(Illustrations will be drawn from the practice of P.S. Penfold).

A Vancouver study of rape showed that 41.9% of the victims were aged 14 to 19.[59] It is estimated that 80,000 to 100,000 U.S. children are sexually molested each year. In about 25% of the cases, the abuser is a relative. Incest appears to follow the general pattern of child sexual abuse in which 97% of the offenders are male and 92% of the victims are female. In sexually abusive families, father-daughter incest is overwhelmingly predominant.[60] In a study of 200 court cases in the Chicago area, there were 164 cases of father-daughter incest as compared with two cases of mother-son incest.[61]

Incest and child sexual abuse are vastly underreported. The present epidemic of paediatric gonorrhea may be grim evidence of the incidence of sexual abuse; it is almost always an indicator that the child has been sexually assaulted.[62] In one study where children and families were carefully interviewed and observed, sexual contact was proven in 44 out of 45 cases in the 1 to 9 age group.[63] This serves "as a lesson and a challenge to all who would postulate non-venereal transmitting of this disease to young children when a history of sexual contact has not been elicited."[64]

Child victims of sexual abuse are surrounded by myths, beliefs, and attitudes which are similar to those concerning the rape victim. Children, it is thought, can be so nubile, sexually provocative and seductive that the adult is unable to resist their advances. They may fabricate a story of sexual abuse to get revenge. Many believe that father-daughter incest occurs because mothers do not watch their daughters carefully enough, or because they have sexually frustrated their husbands. Long-standing beliefs about incest are embodied by the biblicial story of Lot, whose wife turned into a pillar of salt. Lot is depicted as helpless in the hands of several daughters who seduced him with the help of alcohol. Psychiatric theories contain similar beliefs. Freud's theory of infantile sexuality both reflects and reinforces the assumption that incestuous feelings arise within the child and influence adults. The little girl incest victim is portrayed as seductive, aggressive,[65] manipulative,[66] and lying.[67]

■   Fourteen-year-old Sonya confided to her school counsellor that her father was sexually abusing her. The social worker who investigated the family believed Sonya's report, but the social worker's supervisor felt that Sonya was lying, making false accusations so that she could leave home and live with her sister, Diana. Eventually, Sonya was placed with her sister and entered assessment and then treatment with me. Diana, who had also been sexually abused and who was very distraught about her failure to report the abuse and thus protect her younger sister, was immediately ostracized by the parents and the rest of the family who maintained that Diana and Sonya were "trying to stir up trouble."

Another set of theories depicts the mother as sick,[68] childish,[69] self-centered and cold,[70] failing to protect the child,[71] and sexually frigid.[72]

■   Mr. A., a stepfather, repeatedly sexually abused 8-year-old Nancy while Mrs. A. was working on evening shifts, threatening the child with dire consequences if she told her mother. A psychiatric report on this family dwelt mainly on Mrs. A.'s childhood background and her poor relationship with her mother, and her lack of responsiveness to her husband's sexual needs. It was concluded that Mrs. A. had failed to protect

Nancy because she worked afternoons, that she had not created a trusting relationship which would enable Nancy to confide in her, and that her lack of sexual responsiveness played a major causative role. Mr. A.'s responsibility was barely mentioned.

Some investigators allege that incest is not harmful for some children,[73] or that it is a relatively insignificant cultural phenomenon produced by social isolation or crowding.[74] Other researchers, however, have documented the destructive effect of incest on the child.[75] A strong association between incest and later promiscuity or prostitution has been demonstrated.[76]

■ Loretta, a 17-year-old prostitute, was brought into a general hospital emergency department suffering from an overdose. As she recovered she expressed many thoughts of suicide, claiming "I don't give a shit what happens to me." Loretta described long-standing sexual abuse from her father, including several years of regular intercourse. At 14 she was angered by her father's extreme jealousy of her boyfriend and told a friend of the abuse. Her friend's mother reported it to the police and in the ensuing few weeks, Loretta was removed from her home, and placed in a foster home far from her friends and familiar school. Her father was sent to jail, the family had to go on welfare and lost possession of their house. Loretta's mother accused her of breaking up the family. Loretta felt she had lost everything, and that the family misfortunes were all her fault. Depressed, angry, bitter, resentful and self-blaming, she dropped out of school, started using drugs and became promiscuous. After going through several foster homes in quick succession, Loretta joined several girls who shared and apartment and were prostituting. Although prostitution brought ready money, it served only to confirm Loretta's image of herself as bad, seductive and destructive.

As adults, incest victims have a sense of distance and isolation from others and do not feel entitled to care and respect. They feel responsible for the incest situation and experience themselves as powerful and dangerous to men. They depict themselves as "witches," "bitches," or "whores," and see themselves as socially stigmatized. The victims tend to idealize their fathers and have a sense of estrangement from and betrayal by their mothers. Daughters view their mothers as ". . . helpless, frail, downtrodden victims, who are unable to take care of themselves, much less to protect their children."[77]

■   Jean, a 29-year-old preschool teacher, consulted me about her ten-year-old son, Mark, who was defiant and difficult. After several sessions, Jean told me that Mark, unbeknownst to all of her relatives, was her father's son. With disgust she described how she had shielded and protected her father and allowed him to direct and influence her during the first few years of Mark's life. She had tended to idealize her father and feel betrayed by her mother whom she also perceived as passive, helpless and downtrodden. Unable to tell anyone the truth about Mark's paternity, she felt weighed down by the caretaking responsibility and by feelings of ambivalence towards Mark as her father's child and the product of a guilt-ridden relationship. In addition, she perceived herself as a bad and seductive person, the bearer of a guilty secret and thus tended to keep herself isolated and aloof from others. Jean told me that it had taken her ten years to begin to get the experience in perspective and to see Mark as a person, not the reincarnation of her father. She attributed much of her growth to attending a woman's group, sharing her secret, getting much positive feedback and realizing that there were many good things in the life she had built for Mark and herself.

BATTERED WOMEN

Data on the frequency of violence among family members is not readily available. Agencies misidentify the problem to the point where statistics are not valid. Other cases are buried in divorce and homicide statistics. Its frequency, however, is suggested by Gelles's experiences in seeking a non-violent control group for the violent families studied in *The Violent Home*.[78] Of the supposedly non-violent neighbouring families, 37% had experienced at least one incident of violence and for 12% violence was a regular occurrence. Of 499 murders committed in Canada in 1974, 158 (31.6%) were within the family. Between 1968 and 1974, 37.3% of all murders in Canada were described as domestic.[79]

Police statistics show a high incidence of "domestic disputes." Vancouver police receive about forty of these calls per day.[80] A pilot study[81] of 105 agencies in the Greater Vancouver area (population approximately 1.3 million) which attempted to ascertain the incidence of the battered wife problem, demonstrated that most agencies do not record the incidence of wife beating. A total of 1,361 abused wives were reported for a six-month period ending May 1976. Increased recognition and reporting of the problem was demonstrated towards the end of this period. A "conservative estimate" suggests that over one million American women get punched, slapped, shoved, or brutally beaten each year by the men in their lives.[82] Wife battering is probably the most unreported crime today. Women are very reluctant to communicate their plight, convinced that they represent an isolated and unique situation. Hiberman and Munson,[83] who identified wife beating in half of the women referred to them for psychiatric assessment, found that this pattern had been previously recognized by health clinic staff in only *four* of the *sixty* women.

Increased violence towards the pregnant woman is noted by some authors who believe that, for some couples, violence that brings about a miscarriage is more acceptable than an abortion.[84]

Common Beliefs

Most men share the belief that "a woman will behave better and may even enjoy the feeling of being put in her 'rightful' (subservient) place by physical punishment. Part of male folklore has it that women really enjoy the male domination-female submissive relationship."[85] This sentiment is expressed in the old saying "a woman, a dog, and a walnut tree, the more they are beaten, the better they be." In a tough-guy movie role, Humphrey Bogart says "Dames are simple. I never did see one that didn't understand a slap in the mouth." Women who are beaten, it is often felt, deserved it or brought it on themselves. Many imagine that wife beating is sexually titillating or is a form of sexual perversion.[86] Some believe that alcohol is a cause of wife beating, and others think that wife beaters must be mentally ill. Beaten wives may have the opinion that "that's the way men are, you just have to take it."

Historical Aspects

Women have always been viewed as men's property, subordinate to them and subject to their wishes. The biblical woman was made from man's rib, and Tennyson echoed this with the phrase "God made the woman for the man." As shadows, subordinates, subjects, women often got short shrift if they failed to obey their lord and master. During the Middle Ages, European squires and noblemen beat their wives as readily as they beat their serfs. Women were burned alive in medieval times "for threatening their husbands, for talking back to a priest, for stealing, for prostitution, for adultery, for bearing a child out of wedlock, for committing sodomy, even though the priest or husband that committed it was forgiven, for masturbating, for lesbianism, for child neglect, for scolding or nagging, and even for miscarrying, even though the miscarriage was caused by a kick or a blow from the husband."[8][7] In the sixteenth century, during the reign of Ivan the Terrible, the Russian Church legitimized the oppression of women by issuing a Household Ordinance which described the most effective ways for men to beat their wives!

There has been gradual reform, though unfortunately, it is often only a token one. An 1824 legal decision in Mississippi allowed husbands to administer only "moderate chastisement in cases of emergency." In 1885 a law was passed that prohibited British husbands from selling their wives or daughters into prostitution — if they were under sixteen. Again in England, in 1891, special legislation was passed to prevent husbands from keeping their wives under lock and key. A French court, in 1924, ruled that husbands did not have the right to beat their wives. In the early 1970s, several countries made wife beating illegal — including Scotland and Iran. In late 1972, a new penal code was introduced in Brazil which prohibited husbands from selling, renting, or gambling their wives away.

Theories

Battered women are seldom mentioned in traditional textbooks. *The Comprehensive Textbook of Psychiatry* contains two sentences about domestic violence. Among a number of references to aggression there is no reference to aggression towards women or wives.

Studies of family violence examine social, cultural and psychological dimensions.[88] Social factors include the learning of aggressive behaviour from a parent figure, and debilitating or demeaning conditions such as poverty or unemployment. Cultural factors mentioned include the norms of our society which condone and sometimes promote violent behaviour.[89] Psychological theories include views about wife beaters, their wives, and the nature of the interaction between them. As with studies of rapists, few wife beaters have been found to be overtly mentally ill.[90] Role reversal is throught to be the crux of the problem by some writers who describe the husbands as passive, submissive, indecisive and sexually inadequate, while the wives are aggressive, domineering, masculine and masochistic.[91] The assumption of the women's masochism permeates many theories. Wives are sometimes depicted as nagging or bickering, and ultimately provoking their husbands to violence.[92]

Otherwise, there is a focus on the intimate relationship between partners. Long-term intimate relationships are believed to be conducive to anger and possibly to violence.[93] Storr,[94] appearing to espouse the Freudian model of the submissive, masochistic female and the dominant, aggressive male, maintains that "it is only when intense aggressiveness exists between two individuals that love can arise." Storr relates family stability and the sexual adjustment of the partners to male dominance and the touch of ruthlessness which, Storr thinks, is admired in men: "The idea of being seized and borne off by a ruthless male who will wreak his sexual will on his helpless victim has universal appeal to the female sex." Such theoretical material as there is, then, seems to serve to normalize or excuse men's violent behaviour and to focus any blame on the victim of abuse.

ATTITUDES OF POLICE, HOSPITALS, AGENCIES, AND PROFESSIONALS

(Illustrations will be drawn from the practice of P.S. Penfold.)

Police are reluctant to intervene in "domestic disputes" and loath to arrest a man in his own home. They know, too, that women who charge their husbands frequently drop those charges later. Sentences for men who assault their wives are usually much lighter than those they would get for assaulting a neighbour.[95] Assault charges brought by a wife are usually heard in family court rather than in a criminal court where assault charges are routinely heard. Family court recommendations often include counselling and they focus on trying to keep the family together. Women who seek protection from a battering husband may find the police unwilling to make repeated interventions, and that peace bonds or restraining orders are virtually meaningless pieces of paper. They are often afraid of court procedures, ignorant of the processes of separation and divorce, unaware of their rights and frightened of losing the custody of their children. Lawyers are rarely helpful to them.[96]

Women who decide to leave battering husbands receive little support from social agencies.[97] Social workers may minimize problems and attempt to keep families together.[98] Women may receive assistance for a few nights' stay away from home, or be caught between the social welfare department and landlords. They are told that they cannot receive social assistance until they have a place to stay and at the same time they cannot rent an apartment because they have no money for a deposit! In any event, women may not relish the prospect of trying to raise their families on welfare payments (which are frequently well below the poverty line).

■ A battered wife from Surrey, the mother of a 13-year-old girl who was referred for refusing to go to school, anxiety, fearfulness, and multiple aches and pains, called me up to say that she had decided to leave her husband. It was, however, impossible. She had no job skills, nowhere to go, and no relatives. The welfare office, after much persistence on her part, told her that they would support her once she had left home and filed for divorce. Every landlord she approached wanted a downpayment. She had no money. Her husband never gave her money, he even took her grocery shopping. Over the 14 years of their marriage she had suffered, she told me, numerous black eyes and cigarette burns, six cracked ribs, a fractured jaw, a broken nose, a cracked skull and a broken arm. Amazingly, none of these injuries had been identified as wife abuse by the various doctors and hospitals who believed her husband's tale that she slipped and fell, had fallen down stairs, tripped, etc. She had been to a psychiatrist for a couple of years for the treatment of depression. The psychiatrist, too, never found out about the abuse she was receiving, and treated her with medication.

Hospitals, clinics and physicians frequently fail to identify battered women. Pizzey[99] charges that doctors neglect or ignore evidence that women are being battered, perhaps to avoid the possibility of going to court. She emphasizes that psychiatrists, who are mostly men, are "incredibly remote from the problems of a battered woman in a working class home." Hospitals, she insists, have "their heads firmly buried in the sand."

■   Six-year-old Tommy B. was referred to the Child Psychiatry Clinic for assessment of hyperactivity and aggressive behaviour. Tommy had been seen by several other doctors and mental health clinic personnel. Ritalin had been tried and Mrs. B. had been counselled about how to handle Tommy's behaviour. Neither had any effect.

When interviewed by myself and a male medical student, Tommy was tense, controlled, suspicious and initially refused to participate in any play, eyeing the medical student apprehensively. In a second interview, Tommy initiated some aggressive puppet play.

Mrs. B. complained at length about Tommy's provocative, negative, hostile and difficult behaviour. She was sure that some kind of disease must be causing such extreme behaviour. Tommy had been even more difficult, she emphasized, since she and her husband split up. She stressed that her husband was "hard on the kids," and didn't have much patience. At this point I asked her if her husband had abused her and, to the astonishment and horror of the medical student, she gave a long and gruesome account of repeated, severe beatings, usually witnessed by the children. Tommy, she admitted, looked just like her husband and she was sure that Tommy would "go the same way."

It was clear that Tommy had a violent model and that the increase in aggressive behaviour after Mr. B.'s departure was related to separation anxiety and identification with an absent father. Tommy's agression was also being reinforced by Mrs. B.'s expectations.

An investigation of the basic causes for lack of awareness and understanding of woman-abuse found little or no teaching about family violence in schools of medicine, law, and social work in Canada. Many police colleges in North America, on the other hand, offer training in "domestic crisis intervention."[100] As first resources in cases of domestic violence, as in rape, police generally have more understanding and sympathy than agencies and professionals who are more distant from the scene.

It seems that the physical abuse of women is frequent, viewed as "normal" or not very serious, and attributed to the women's masochism.

Services focus on keeping families together, and women who decide to leave their husbands face innumerable obstacles and biases. What actually does happen in the families of battered women? Some recent studies and books, and discussions with battered women, afford a closer look.

RECENT PERSPECTIVES

Why do women stay in situations where they are being battered? Do they really enjoy being beaten, find it sexually titillating, or necessary to feed their innate masochism? Do they deny or fail to complain about being beaten because they wish to continue with an essentially sexual sport?

A study of 100 English wives who had received severe physical injury as a result of deliberate and repeated beatings, showed that they were inescapably trapped in violent marriages, had little education and no prospect of economic independence. They had a total of 315 children. The women, wanting to leave the parental home, had hurriedly entered subsequently disastrous marriages, attracted by the apparent protectiveness of their mate. Seventy-one of the 100 women were taking anti-depressants or tranquilizers at the time of the survey.[101]

Women give many rationalizations for staying "but fear is the common denominator."[102] When wives leave home, their husbands often continue to harass and threaten them. Women whose primary source of identity is their marriage will feel at fault when it fails, and too ashamed and humiliated to tell relatives and friends about the abuse. Women who take their nurturing role very seriously can readily rationalize, "Oh, but my husband needs me." The more violent the husbands are, the more they are perceived to be "sick" and thus needful of their wives. Women hanging on to the mythical ideal of the happy marriage may tell themselves that they still love their husbands, that they will change some day, that they cannot do without their men, and that they should stay with them for the sake of the children.

In addition to factors arising from women's socialization and their emotional paralysis arising from fear or depression, economic dependency is a major practical reason why many women cannot leave. Many violent husbands insist on handling all the money themselves, including personally supervising and paying for the grocery shopping. Even women in middle-class homes may have no access to money which could finance plans for leaving.

Many studies tend to paint a picture of the beaten wife as apathetic, uneducated, unskilled in the workplace, and thoroughly trapped. Wife beating, however, is found in all classes. It seems probable that the impression that domestic violence is a lower-class phenomenon reflects the greater visibility of lower-class families to police and hospitals, while middle-class women have more opportunities to hide and explain away injuries.[103] Some studies emphasize women's vulnerability if they are better educated, better paid, or hold higher status jobs than their husbands.[104] Gelles argues that "the husband's inferior achieved status is a source of frustration for both himself and his wife," and feels that this can give rise to conflicts which may lead to violence.[105] Again, as with rape, most theories about wife beating tend to normalize or excuse male violence. They suggest, sometimes subtly, sometimes blatantly, that the causes of the problem are to be found in the characteristics or behaviour of the women who are beaten.

PROSTITUTION

Prostitution affords a clear example of exploitation, coercion and violence towards women. Pimps coerce women who are actual or potential prostitutes. Prostitutes are sometimes beaten by pimps, and the chance of encountering violence from customers is always present. The prostitute who is raped has little or no legal recourse; the police will rarely lay a charge.

Common beliefs hold that some prostitutes are degenerate women who crave sex and enjoy indiscriminate sexual intercourse, while others are lesbians and hate men. Their involvement in prostitution is attributed to their sickness, weakness, inadequacy or other personal problems. The male side of the equation receives little attention; it is assumed that prostitution takes care of unmet, urgent male sexual needs.

Theories about prostitution reflect these common beliefs. Both classical and recent theorists have stated that prostitutes are degenerate, primitive, and uncivilized.[106] Freudian explanations of promiscuity depict an unresolved Oedipal conflict so that the woman's sexual partners are merely surrogates for a beloved father. Satisfaction is unobtainable; therefore, the woman perpetually searches for new partners.

Thus, prostitution can be viewed as the outcome of a craving for sex which has either biological or psychological roots. Several theorists believe that the prostitute has a need to debase the male or the father figure.[107] This is sometimes called the Circe complex; the wish to turn men into swine.[108] An unresolved Oedipal conflict is also viewed as the basis for overt or latent homsexuality in prostitutes.[109] The common feature of their background is thought to be "a strong attachment to a father who was inadequate or unable to support such attachment."[110] Their hatred and contempt of men is emphasized and attributed to their fear of being contaminated by men and their desire to be the more powerful partner in an interaction. As already outlined in the description of rape theories, male sexuality is viewed as urgent, uncontrollable, and a biological necessity. Thus, prostitution is seen as existing to cater to normal "male incontinence."[111]

The evidence on which some of these theories are based is very shaky. In a study where the major focus was the homosexuality or latent homosexuality of adolescent prostitutes, only four out of 400 were overtly homosexual and the reader is not informed how "latent homosexuality" is detected.[112] One can only assume that the observer's values played a large part. In the same study, the inference that woman's desire to reverse the dominance relationship is "unnatural" and an indication of her hatred shows how thoroughly the study incorporates Freudian notions and underlying cultural standards of female masochism and passivity.

Societal Origins of Prostitution

Social factors often lead to, or result in prostitution. In some societies women may become prostitutes out of dire need, to support their families or to keep themselves from starving.[113] In affluent societies an economic basis for prostitution lies in the relatively limited opportunities for women to be economically independent of men.[114] Prostitution "flourishes in societies with strong monogamous family traditions where 'respectable' women are denied sexual, social and economic freedom for fear of defilement."[115]

Like attitudes to rape, attitudes towards prostitution are based on a double standard which labels " promiscuous" females as unnatural and deviant, while males cannot be promiscuous because they are merely fulfilling natural sexual urges. Unlike rape, however, offenses related to prostitution carry relatively little punishment. This may seem contradictory, but is actually an illustration of how laws which appear to be designed to protect women, are actually designed to protect men's property. Severe penalties for rape are punishment for the defilement of another man's property. Seen as immoral and debased parasites, prostitutes warrant no protection. Moreover, they fill a male need, so that token punishment is meted out to satisfy conventional morality and to dissuade them from encroaching on respectable neighbourhoods.

Although a re-examination of the politics of prostitution is of prime importance, Walkowitz[116] points out that commercial sex is a "hot and dangerous issue for feminists." In earlier campaigns, feminist anger was "easily diverted into repressive campaigns against male vice and sexual variation, controlled by men and corporate interests whose goals were antithetical to the values and ideals of feminism."

PORNOGRAPHY

The themes of pornographic literature are violence, domination and the conquest of women. Rape, incest and sadomascochism are commonly portrayed. Many people have noted the growing portrayal of physical and sexual violence towards women in store displays, record album covers, fashion magazines, films and novels. "Snuff" movies, involving actual and stimulated pornographic murder, have an eager market.

We regard pornography as a social control mechanism aimed at keeping women subordinate to men, and as a medium for the expression of norms about male domination and power. Society, however, assumes that pornography concerns sexuality alone. While conservative forces seek to eliminate pornography because it condones illicit and perverse sexuality and is a threat to the status quo, many contemporary social scientists, intellectuals and liberal humanists oppose any plans to control pornography. They associate pornography with free and unfettered expression, which they believe to promote growth and lead to human liberation. This position is given credence by the report of the U.S. Commission on Pornography.[117] Reflecting, presumably, the predominant view that sexual repression is bad, and that pornography is a matter of sexuality alone, they were unable to document detrimental effects of pornography. We should note that, a year earlier, the Commission on the Causes and Prevention of Violence had concluded that people can be induced to act aggressively by media violence. More recent research has indicated that presentations which combine eroticism and aggressiveness provoke aggression in the subjects.[118] Male subjects in one study were shown a rape scene after having read a sadomasochistic story. They tended to misinterpret the victim's pain as a sign of her sexual excitement. The male subjects appeared to identify with the rapist, and 51% responded that they might rape someone themselves if they were assured that they would not get caught! The linking of violence with sexual excitment "provides an unusual opportunity for conditioning of violent responses to erotic stimuli."[119]

The Danish experience is widely cited as proof of "safety outlet" theories. During the 1960s, the Danes gradually removed all legal restrictions on pornography, and claimed a dramatic decrease in sex crimes. Further research has shown that the statistics were artificially deflated by removing certain crimes such as homosexual prostitution, and that the incidence of rape had actually increased.

AN EMERGING FEMINIST CRITIQUE

The frequency of themes of male domination and female subjugation, with accompanying hostility, cruelty and contempt towards women, in literary descriptions of sexual activity was extensively documented by Millet in *Sexual Politics*.[120] Moreover, she argued that increasing sexual permissiveness during the twentieth century has allowed the expression of male hostility to flourish. Whereas Millet dealt with well-known avant-garde writers, Morgan[121] and Dworkin[122] were concurrently exposing the same themes in left-hippie underground newspapers. Examining the history of rape, Brownmiller[123] defined pornography as "the undiluted essence of anti-female propaganda" and charged that sexual aggressiveness was promoted by the open display of pornography.

With the appearance of "Snuff" in 1975, feminist activities began to focus in earnest on sexual violence in the media. Emphasizing the relationship between increasing violence in pornographic material, its overflow into more conventional books, films, magazines and store displays, and an ever-increasing rate of rape, Morgan[124] stated that "pornography is the theory and the rape the practice." Feminists postulate that increased violence is a male response to feminism. Russell[125] claims that "the great proliferation of pornography since 1970 — particularly violent pornography and child pornography — is part of the male backlash against the women's liberation movement. Enough women have been rejecting the traditional role of being under men's thumbs to cause a crisis in the collective male ego. Pornography is a fantasy solution that inspires non-fantasy acts of punishment for uppity females." This heightened interest in pornography fits conveniently with our consumer society whose economic goals are readily served by the commercialization and exploitation of sexuality.

Many feminists have called for government censorship of pornography.[126] Again, as with campaigns about prostitution, there are many pitfalls in confronting this issue. Feminist anger, energy and argument too often finds itself sandwiched between two opposing positions. On the one hand there are the moralists and fundamentalists who seek to suppress pornography along with all sexual information. On the other, are the civil libertarians who regard any form of censorship as an infringement on human rights and freedoms. The debate has thus become polarized between supporters of oppressive puritanism and advocates of total license. This leaves feminists with the difficult task of developing and advancing a complex and contentious analysis. It is an analysis which seeks to draw distinctions between positive, enhancing and erotic images of sexuality and the degrading, exploitative and sadistic images portrayed in pornography. Given the current polarization of the debate, the highly lucrative nature of the pornography business and the lack of recognition of the validity of women's perspective on this or any other issue, this is no simple task.

CONCLUSIONS

The violence towards women that we have described exemplifies age-old attitudes towards women as inferiors, non-persons who have no legal rights, have status only as men's property, are objects to be used for men's pleasure, and are destined to serve men and bolster their self-esteem. Fears of women's power are also embodied in the violence and humiliation to which women are sometimes subjected.

The various institutions of society, including the family, the criminal justice system, the health system and psychiatry, obscure and minimize the violence to which women are exposed and make it difficult for a woman to realize that she is being ill-treated, let alone to escape and claim her rights. If the abused woman does complain, she is likely to be punished, ostracized or subject to counselling that blames her for the abuse. The rape victim is treated as the offender and meets almost insuperable obstacles in a criminal justice system that protects men and discredits her. The incest victim is subject to the same suspicion, but may in addition be removed from her home and ostracized by her family. The husband of the battered wife may mete out further punishment, she may get short shrift from welfare agencies who may want to keep the family together at all costs, and from mental health workers who may urge her to change the behaviour that is, they feel, provoking the abuse. A wife who has been raped by her husband has no legal recourse, as a husband's legal, conjugal rights do not prevent forcible or coercive sex. A prostitute who refuses to comply with her pimp risks a severe beating. As we have shown in this chapter, psychiatric theories that depict these women victims as masochistic, seductive, provocative, depraved, primitive and so on, contribute to women's oppression and the perpetuation of abuse.

Theories about the male perpetrators also serve to cloak the societal origins of violence towards women. The attribution of individual pathology to the rapist, batterer, or instigator of incest places these men outside normal group membership and thus the connection between normal and violent behaviour can be avoided. Attention, for instance, is forced away from the possibility that sexual aggression may be consistent with normative male sexual behaviour. A psychodynamic formulation serves to justify or explain behaviour and divert attention from the cultural and social conditions which are the root of the problem. Rapists, woman batterers, perpetrators of incest, and users of prostitutes and pornography are all conforming, albeit in perhaps an extreme way, to male sex role expectations, beliefs in male superiority, and views of women based on property rights and archetypal images.

Obscuring the true nature and extent of the violence allows males to exercise their prerogative and, in addition, has many fiscal advantages. Policies that help battered wives to leave home would be very expensive and disruptive to the economy. Prostitution and pornography are vast industries. While the helping professions are trying to prevent incest or treat families where it has occurred, other elements in society are cashing in on incest and the sexual exploitation of children.[127] In describing recent books, films and television shows with an incest theme, a *Penthouse* article comments "Just as we seem to be running low on marketable taboos, the unspeakable predictably popped up."[128]

It is clear that many interwoven forces work to maintain a society where violence towards women is endemic. Present solutions such as policing rape-prone neighbourhoods, rape relief programs, self-defense courses for women, sex education, and groups for battered wives and battering husbands must also be accompanied by measures to remedy the deep societal roots of this problem.

≡   ≡   ≡

CHAPTER VIII

WOMEN AND DEPRESSION

STUDIES HAVE DEMONSTRATED THAT for every male diagnosed as suffering from depression, two to six times as many females are so diagnosed.[1] These figures hold in hospitals, out-patient clinics, mental health centres and private practice. Related to this, a study of the prescription of mood-modifying drugs in Saskatchewan[2] showed that anti-depressants were prescribed to at least twice as many women as men in every age group. In the 20-29 age range, the ratio was 8:1.

What is the significance of these findings? Are women more vulnerable to depression on a biological basis? Does a woman's psychological makeup render her more prone to depression? Are women's circumstances more depressing than those of men? Are women being labelled as depressed and treated with anti-depressants when their environment creates unavoidable misery and distress? What do we mean by depression? Is it merely a catch-all phrase for a vast range of distress that is not something else? How does it differ from misery and grief?

To begin to cast light on these issues we will briefly describe diagnostic frameworks, theories of depression and how these have been applied to women, the pitfalls of using models which focus on individual dysfunction, and new work which both confirms the high incidence of depression among women and points to a new understanding thereof.

CLASSIFICATION SYSTEMS AND THEORIES

A review of systems of classification and theories of depression shows a striking lack of conceptual clarity. Depression may be equated with an illness, viewed as a syndrome, thought to be a symptom, or

172

discussed as a normal affect. Writers jump confusingly from one view to another. For instance, in the *Comprehensive Textbook of Psychiatry*, Linn states that "Depression is one of the most common *illnesses* to which mankind is subject. Paradoxically, it is probably the most frequently overlooked *symptom*, and even when recognized, it is probably the single most incorrectly treated *symptom* in clinical practice. Not only are the signs and symptoms of depression multiple and complex at any given stage of the *disorder* . . ."[3]

Attempts at classification continue, with ongoing revisions, as in the draft forms of the American Psychiatric Association's *Diagnostic and Statistical Manual of Mental Disorders III*. The state of the art is revealed by a statement about the category of "affective disorders" which reads, "Big doings here. First of all Episodic Affective Disorders are now termed Major Affective Disorders. Duration of Depressive Episode is raised to at least two weeks. The exclusionary criteria (that push one into Schizoaffective) have been modified (see the text for Schizoaffective). Finally, the criteria for levels of severity have been revised to divide psychotic features into 'mood congruent' and 'mood incongruent'."[4]

Many textbooks still include four types of depression, stemming from Kraeplin's initial manic-depressive classification. These are manic-depressive illness, involutional melancholia, psychotic depressive disorder, and neurotic depression. Beginning with Kraeplin's division of depressive conditions into those arising from disorders of the brain and those caused by a stressful environment, clinicians and theoreticians have focussed on the two types of depression which may be considered to have a different etiology, pathogenesis, clinical features, and to need contrasting approaches to treatment. Depressive episodes have been divided into neurotic and psychotic, endogenous and reactive, agitated and retarded, primary and secondary, major and minor, and so on. Recently, the overall group of affective disorders has been divided into unipolar and bipolar types.[5] It can be seen that distinctions are being made on the basis of such variables as mood, activity level, severity, presumed genetic or nongenetic origin, and degree of contact with reality. Other concepts that are used to bring more distressed people under the umbrella are those of depressive equivalents, "hidden depression," "smiling depression," "depressive practices," and "depressive personality." Thus, we have a mishmash of ideas which amply illustrate our present lack of understanding of depression and how these primitive paradigms could lead to overutilization of the diagnosis.

Depression, however, although ill defined and misunderstood, is no myth. The sufferer complains of problems with sleep and appetite, lack of energy, loss of interest, feelings of inadequacy and harsh self-blame, hopelessness, indecisiveness, slowed thinking, and sometimes has suicidal thoughts. Genetic, endocrine, psychodynamic, cognitive, behavioural and social theories of depression all seek to explain these behavioural changes .

Studies demonstrate considerable evidence for a genetic factor in some types of depression, with an underlying biochemical abnormality.[6] X-linkage has been postulated as an explanation for the greater incidence of depression in females. It is hypothesized that the gene for depression is located on the X chromosome, so that females, who have two X chromosomes, will be affected more often.[7] Studies of possible X-linkage, however, have inconsistent and contradictory results.[8]

Much work has linked depression to hormonal changes during the female reproductive cycle. Writers note mood changes during the menstrual cycle and with oral contraceptives, and the greater incidence of depression during the postpartum period and at the menopause. A number of studies have shown increased irritability, anger, anxiety or depression during the paramenstruum (the period of three days prior to and during menstruation).[9] The numerous physiological hypotheses include hormone induced sodium and water retention, high levels of oestrogen, deficiency of progesterone, allergic sensitivity to oestrogens or progesterone, increased antidiuretic hormone, hypoglycaemia, increased aldosterone, increased blood levels of serotonin synergist, pelvic congestion, increased capillary permeability to protein, and changes in brain endorphins. There is no convincing evidence for any of these hypotheses.[10] It is crucial to note that much behavioural data have been gathered from deviant subgroups who do demonstrate that suicide, suicidal attempts, crimes, disorderly conduct in schools and prisons, accidents and admission to hospital for psychiatric illness are more likely to occur in the paramenstrual phase. These data can be inappropriately applied, in a biased fashion, to normal women whose performance on a variety of tasks has not been shown to fluctuate with the cycle.[11]

Evidence for the association of depression with oral contraceptive use is similarly inconclusive. There is some evidence that women who have been depressed before, or who expect adverse side effects, tend to have more depressive symptoms while on oral contraceptives.[12] In a small number of women a Vitamin B_6 deficiency, with consequent inhibition of the synthesis of biogenic amines in the central nervous system, has been attributed to oral contraceptives and assumed to cause depression.[13] Hormone levels gradually increase throughout pregnancy, so that prior to the onset of labour the various hormone levels are 10 to 1,000 times normal. The levels return to normal within ten days after the baby is born. The "new baby blues" have been ascribed to these hormone changes. In addition, the increased risk of severe depression and other disorders during the first few months postpartum is thought to be due to sudden withdrawal of the hormones which may have an effect similar to the withdrawal of psychoactive drugs, to alterations in fluid and electrolyte balance, or to the secretion of prolactin.[14]

Many medical myths surround the menopause. It is thought that women become irritable, depressed, unpredictable and irrational during this period. Medical beliefs, which continue the Victorian physician's assumption that menopause is the Rubicon of a woman's life[15] and which reflect cultural stereotypes about the desirability of eternal youth, frequently give rise to the prescription of oestrogen for supposed menopausal symptoms. Medical textbooks have "perpetuated an image of the menopausal *patient,* which new generations of physicians were free to presume was a scientific description of a menopausal *woman.*"[16] The menopause has been likened to diabetes[17] and termed a "deficiency disease."[18] Oestrogen replacement therapy continues to be popular despite the demonstration of increased risk of uterine cancer.[19] In psychiatry a special diagnosis, "Involutional Melancholia," is given to menopausal depression. Obsessional and overly conscientious people are thought to be vulnerable to this disease, for which the best treatment is said to be electroshock.[20]

Studies have shown that there is no increased risk of depression during the menopause,[21] and community surveys have demonstrated that only about 10% of women express regret about the cessation of periods.[22] Twelve years ago, in reviewing 30 years of studies, Rosenthal[23] concluded that Involutional Melancholia has never existed as a separate entity, a view which is only now being adopted in new systems for classifying mental disorders.

Psychoanalysts have found evidence that depression is rooted in the emotional experiences of the infant, namely loss of, or deep disappointment in the parents, particularly the mother. A loss later in life rekindles early feelings of worthlessness, abandonment, rage and hopelessness.[24] Depression-prone individuals suffer from excessive guilt, self-criticism, dependency, have problems with close relationships, and tend to turn hostility against themselves. Some psychodynamic theories give lack of self-esteem a central role in the genesis of depression. For example, Bibring[25] turns away from the orality inherent in the psychoanalytic framework to state that different sets of aspirations set the stage for clinical depressions. These are: the wish to be loved, appreciated and worthy, rather than inferior and unworthy; the wish to be secure, great, strong, superior, and not insecure and weak; and the wish to be good and loving, not hateful, aggressive and destructive. Depression is thus created by people's awareness of their failure to live up to these aspirations and by their helplessness and inability to change the situation.

Weissman and Klerman[26] point out the similarities between psychoanalytic theories of depression and psychoanalytic views of the personality of "normal" women who are characterized as narcissistic, masochistic, dependent, and unable to express hostility as a result of their special resolution of the Oedipus complex. Moreover, they point out that few psychoanalysts have tried to explain the frequency of depression in women by linking it to their presumed characterological conflicts. Although psychoanalytic views of depression and women's personality are widely accepted, proponents of these views draw mainly on case studies and clinical impressions; empirical evidence for their support is meagre. Weissman and Paykel's[27] study of depressed women failed to show predisposing dependency or obsessional traits, and demonstrated that depressed women were more hostile than a control group of non-depressed women. Few studies support the hypothesis that depression-prone individuals are excessively dependent on the maintenance of self-esteem.[28]

Cognitive theorists link affect to cognition and describe the negative set of depressed people who perceive their experience in distorted and idiosyncratic ways. Beck[29] characterises the vulnerability of the depression-prone person as "attributable to the constellation of enduring negative attitudes about himself, about the world, and about his future. Even though these attitudes (or concepts) may not be prominent or even discernible at a given time, they persist in a latent state like an explosive charge ready to be detonated by an appropriate set of conditions. Once activated, these concepts dominate the person's thinking and lead to the typical depressive symptomatology." Similarly, behavioural theorists, e.g., Seligman,[30] view depression as a state of "learned helplessness" where the person has repeatedly learned that passivity and helplessness are the only appropriate responses to environmental traumas and difficulties. Women's socialization to be dependent, compliant, nurturant, submissive, and reliant on affirmation from others, along with their second-class status in the world and pervasive underlying cultural beliefs about feminine evil,[31] place them in a very vulnerable depression-prone position in the models of Bibring, Beck, and Seligman.

In their widely read book, *The Depressed Woman*, Weissman and Paykel[32] take a psychosocial approach to the study of 40 depressed women who were clinic outpatients and compare them with a control group of 40 non-depressed women in the community. They investigated the social, family and community adjustment of the depressed women and found that their marriages were characterised by interpersonal friction, impaired communication, and the woman's submissiveness and dependency. There was a widespread negative impact on the children. Helplessness, neediness and hostility interfered with her ability to be a warm, giving and consistent mother. Despite Weissman and Paykel's attempt to study depression in a much broader context, their view remains traditional. They view depression as a cause rather than an effect of the woman's problems with social relationships. Therapy concentrates on the woman alone, with the husband seen occasionally and viewed as an adjunct or helper. In another article, Weissman and Klerman[33] present overwhelming evidence for the psychosocial origins of depression and little for the biological origins, but go on to propose a model with a biological base which has evolved by natural selection. Females are thought to be more sensitive to disruptions of attachment bonding, and the high incidence of depression in women is related to the frequency of disruptions of bonds by the moves, separation, divorce, diminution of family ties and loss of traditional support systems which are characteristic of modern industrial society.

IMPLICATIONS

Notwithstanding the relevance or partial relevance of some of these theories, there is a major pitfall. Depression is typically formulated as a dysfunction of the individual woman and treatment is designed to effect some change on her part such as an altered mood produced by an anti-depressant drug, working through a loss, transcending an Oedipal conflict, learning to be more assertive or undertaking a critical re-examination of her negative cognitive sets. The need to change her environment is rarely addressed, and her husband seldom included except as a help and support to her. She is almost never apprised of the role of social structures and her own socialization in creating and perpetuating her distress. A reliance on the presumed genetic origins of depression leads to impersonal and narrow appraisals, the neglect of factors in day-to-day living situations, and a reliance on drug treatment. The drawbacks of these approaches will be illustrated with case histories from the practice of P.S. Penfold.

■   A psychiatric resident presented 69-year-old Mrs. L. as a typical case of unipolar affective disorder and requested help with drug management. His formulation of the case rested solely on one previous episode of depression and failed to explore Mrs. L.'s present circumstances. Mrs. L. had been widowed three years previously, had recovered from her grief but had become upset again following the death of a close woman friend. In addition, she described being rejected by her son, and a gradually increasing handicap from arthritis which would soon necessitate nursing home placement and was interfering with her travel plans. After a discussion, the resident no longer planned drug therapy but set up meetings with Mrs. L.'s family and with the doctor who was treating her arthritis. The focus was on reducing Mrs. L.'s feelings of powerlessness and dependency, re-establishing communication with her family, and enabling her to set up a support system and meet others with similar handicaps.

A reliance on the endocrine origins of depression has a similar effect.

■   Suffering from postpartum depression, treated with a variety of drugs but never completely remitting over several years, Mrs. M. had increasing difficulties with her 4-year-old daughter, Janet. Janet was energetic, defiant, noisy, aggressive and disruptive. Mrs. M. felt alienated from Janet, hostile and resentful towards her, and sometimes jealous of Janet's relationship with her father. Mrs. M.'s previous psychiatrist had never seen Mr. M. I insisted that both parents come and assume equal responsibility for the family situation. After a few sessions the problems were clear. Mrs. M. felt trapped at home and resented Mr. M.'s freedom while he travelled all over the province. Mrs. M.'s hostile feelings towards Janet caused her to vacillate between anger and permissiveness. Mr. M. tried to act as a buffer between Mrs. M. and Janet, and was often manipulated by the little girl. Mr. M. could not understand Mrs. M.'s difficulties in coping with the family as his mother had been a strong and competent woman. Mrs. M., who had been raised to believe that women should be dependent, submissive and defer to their husband's authority, could not understand why Mr. M. would not allow her to lean on him. Rapid improvement in Janet's behaviour, Mrs. M.'s depression, and family relationships resulted from acknowledging these difficulties and devising a plan of action.

■ Ms. N.'s long-standing feelings of irritability, fatigue, insomnia and headaches were presumed to be menopausal in origin by her doctor, who prescribed oestrogen replacement therapy. There was no change, so he gave her anti-depressants which made her sleepy and unable to function on her job. She joined a woman's group and rapidly realized that her symptoms were related to an oppressive job situation. Her boss demanded punctuality, servility, perfect typing, many cups of coffee, and expected her to willingly do over-time on very short notice several nights a week.

Similarly, an emphasis on early childhood experiences and psychodynamics may obscure the problem.

■ The loss of her father when she was six was assumed to be the cause of Mrs. O.'s depression, and her unresolved Oedipal conflict was thought to underlie her husband's complaints of her frigidity. Mrs. O. lived in a suburban housing division and was totally responsible for the 24-hour-a-day, 7-day-a-week care of three preschool children. Her husband's demanding job as an air traffic controller and his assumption that he should fulfill breadwinner obligations alone precluded any help from him. Mrs. O. felt trapped, tired, overwhelmed, resentful and seething with anger towards her husband. Because of her socialization she thought she should be happy, could not acknowledge her feelings as expectable in the situation, and agreed with her doctor that she was depressed, neurotic and had sexual problems.

Behaviour modification approaches lend themselves to traditional "solutions."

■   Unresponsive to a large variety of anti-depressant drugs, Mrs. P. was referred to a psychologist who set up a behaviour modification system with her husband as cotherapist. Mr. P. reinforced Mrs. P. for competent behaviour. The "competent behaviour" list as defined by the psychologist and husband was almost exclusively made up of traditional female tasks such as making the dinner, doing the laundry, and grocery shopping. A year later, a child's school problems led to a thorough family assessment which revealed that Mrs. P. was being battered by her husband.

Sometimes the diagnosis of "depression" is very loosely used.

■   Miss Q., a university student, went to her doctor with complaints of headache, fatigue, dizzy spells, insomnia, anxiety and the conviction that she would not pass her exams. He stated that he thought she was depressed and gave her anti-depressant medication. A few weeks later she discovered that she was several months pregnant.

NEW WORK

A number of studies have examined the often raised possibility that the preponderance of depression among women is an artifact produced by women's different perception, acknowledgement and reporting of stress, and different patterns of seeking help. No difference has been found, however, between men and women in actual[34] or perceived stress.[35] Women acknowledge symptoms of distress more frequently[36] and have different patterns of health-seeking behaviour, attending doctors and clinics more often.[37] While women's greater attendance at health-care facilities may inflate the rate of depression, it cannot account for a similar preponderance of depressed women in community surveys.[38]

With regard to the relationship between depression and the menstrual cycle, Koeske and Koeske[39] have found a willingness on the part of women and men to attribute negative moods to the premenstruum, that is to blame depression and irritability on "pre-menstrual tension."

Such an attribution can lead to the discounting of situational factors and an emphasis on biology in explaining negative, but not positive moods. This can lead to a vicious circle in which guilt, self-condemnation, anxiety and depression are a function of the belief in biological explanations. The danger here is that this in turn may render unlikely any attempt to change damaging situational factors. Koeske and Koeske are also concerned that the attribution process may have a role in actually causing pre-menstrual tension.

New work is beginning to pave the way for innovative models of depression that incorporate women's experience. An example is Brown and Harris's *Social Origins of Depression: A Study of Psychiatric Disorder in Women.*[40] They concentrated on demonstrating that there *is* a link between clinical depression and a woman's daily experiences. Their study of women in Camberwell, a London borough, demonstrated that 15% of the women were depressed while and additional 18% were considered to be borderline cases. In 83%, traumatic life events or major ongoing difficulties preceded the onset of depression. The great majority of provoking events concerned the experience of loss or disappointment defined broadly to include the threat of or actual separation from a key person, a life threatening illness to a close relative, a major financial loss, an unpleasant revelation about someone close, and miscellaneous crises such as losing a job after a prolonged period of steady employment. Thus the loss or disappointment would concern a person or object, a role, or an idea. Ongoing difficulties which increased the risk of depression included bad housing and a poor marriage.

They found that among those with children at home, working-class women were four times more likely to suffer from depression. In addition to social class, they found four vulnerability factors: lack of an intimate relationship with someone to trust and confide in, particularly a husband or boyfriend; three or more children under 14 at home; loss of a mother before the age of 11; or lack of employment outside the home. Their model, incorporating vulnerability factors, provoking agents such as life events and major ongoing difficulties, and a third set of symptom-formation factors, appears to apply to all types of depression, including psychotic and neurotic forms. They note that "there was a slight hint that a sub-group of depression might exist that was without a provoking agent."

Brown and Harris say, "We have, in effect, developed a social psychological theory of depression, and at the same time made a reasonable case for the relevance of wider social processes, leaving more obscure than we like the details of this influence. Just how much, for instance, of the difficulty of women with young children stems from the circumstances of their task and how much from a sense of doing work that is undervalued in a society geared to reward through employment?"

Brown and Harris state that the understanding of untreated depressions, as in their Camberwell study, has implications for the handling of women who do reach a treatment setting. Physical treatments need to be augmented by "social therapy" aimed at raising self-esteem and increasing the availability of long-term positive reinforcement. The implication of their results for prevention includes the need for wider social and political changes so that fewer people experience provoking agents and so that fewer people are vulnerable. Backing for an increased number of preschool and daycare facilities and more part-time employment opportunities for women is also contained in their findings. They accent the loneliness and isolation that exists in our society and the role these play in family health, stating that "to combat these, and to build a sense of mastery and self-esteem, which will render every member of the community more resilient to the buffers of experience, requires more than a comforting talk in a surgery [doctor's office], although even this is all too often not available."

The need for recognition of the difficulties of woman's daily experience and how this can lead to depression is underscored by other studies. Richman[41] studied the mothers of three-year-olds, some of whom had been identified as having behaviour problems. Thirty-nine percent of the "problem" group and 26% of the control group of mothers whose children did not have problems, were found to have symptoms of depressive illness. In yet another study she found depressive symptoms of a severe or moderating degree in 41% of the mothers who lived in subsidized housing with a three-year-old and at least one younger sibling.[42] Of a sample of mothers of preschool children in inner London, Moss and Plavis[43] found that 52% of them had a moderate or severe "distress problem." Assessment of distress was made by asking about feelings of anxiety, worry, depression, tension, irritability, suicidal thoughts and functional impairment. The authors call for "better understanding of the contemporary situation of women caring for small children which may increase their susceptibility to psychiatric disorder."

A new understanding of postpartum depression arises from a focus on women's experience. The smiling madonna myths of pregnancy, and the promise of fulfillment, gratification and increased attention and respect from the husband are belied by the reality of total commitment to the demands of a new infant and the invidious effect these expectations may have on the new mother and other members of the family.[44] Stating that "there is a fourth trimester to pregnancy that we neglect at our peril," Kitzinger[45] describes a transitional period of approximately three months after birth during which women are highly vulnerable, subject to confusion, despair, anxiety and depression. The baby's demands are fierce and relentless, and "the mother easily feels resentment, irritation, even hatred and then overpowering guilt that she experiences these 'unmaternal' reactions." Basing their treatment approach on the reports, needs, feelings and experiences of women in their program, The Vancouver Postpartum Counselling Service has developed a model which incorporates societal, family and individual dimensions.[46]

At the forefront of new work on the menopuase, Bart suggests that cross-cultural studies can be used to tease out socio-cultural and physiological dimensions. She found that improved status at middle age is related to an extended family system rather than a nuclear family system, a strong tie to family of orientation and kin rather than a strong marital tie, geographical closeness to the family of orientation, an institutionalized grandmother role rather than no formal grandmother role, a constructive mother-in-law role, a strong mother-child relationship which is reciprocal in later life, and a valuing of age over youth.[47] Using this frame of reference it is evident why middle-aged women have a low status in North American society. Life is particularly difficult for women who have emphasized the maternal role or the glamour role. "Our emphasis on youth and the stipulation that mothers-in-law should not interfere can make middle age stressful for many women."[48] Studying 533 hospital records and conducting an intensive assessment of a small sample of depressed women, Bart validated her impressions from cross-cultural studies and found the highest rate of depression among housewives experiencing maternal role loss. She hypothesized that the incidence of menopausal depression was related to the lack of meaningful roles and the consequent loss of self-esteem rather than to hormone changes. Of the 20 women interviewed intensively, all those with children, when asked what they were most proud of replied, "My children." Being a good mother was the only accomplishment of their own that they mentioned.[49]

Women writers addressing a general audience have given the best description of women's daily lives and the paths to resentment, misery, frustration, boredom and fatigue. Of the present generation of feminist writers, Betty Friedan[50] was the first to give words to "the problem that has no name," the terrible tiredness that sent so many women to their doctors. The outward signs of misery, according to Germain Greer,[51] are nagging, being overweight, premature aging, headaches, backaches, loss of appetite, rheumatism and abdominal complaints. Women justify their irritability and tiredness by symptoms which they and their doctors view as illnesses. The outcome is often excessive pill consumption or unnecessary surgery. Greer relates women's misery to the monotonous and unremitting drudgery of their tasks in the home, saying that "A housewife's work has no results: it simply has to be done again." She stresses confusion and ambivalence about bringing up children, a task for which women bear full responsibility while receiving little training or guidance.

Sheila Rowbotham's book, *Woman's Consciousness, Man's World*, includes a chapter called "A Woman's Work is Never Done."[52] Emphasizing that the housewife is safe only in the bath, she describes how cleaning, tidying and cooking are inescapably interwoven with the expectation that the housewife will solves crises immediately, absorb all tensions, and miraculously create and maintain an atmosphere of calm and organization. Within the framework of their daily lives, women have devised particular resistances. "There is the switching-off, the half-there swimmy feeling, the barriers around yourself, and there is illness. Fatigue, illness, nervous complaints, agoraphobia. Tranquilizers, sleeping pills and supermarket alcohol are the remedies." Women's "neurosis of nothingness," a pervasive feeling of emptiness, of being nothing, not existing except as someone who is needed by husband and children arises from the nature of women's work in the home. Only through self-abnegation, states Rowbotham, can a woman obtain self-affirmation. Pouring herself into husband and children is the only way to gain recognition and self-realization as a good mother and a "feminine" woman.

In the first chapter of her book, *Of Woman Born*, Adrienne Rich[53] draws on entries in her own journal to vividly depict the ambivalence, anger and depression which accompany motherhood. Her relationship with three small sons included "the murderous alternation between bitter resentment and raw-edged nerves, and blissful gratification and tenderness." She writes of being "caught up in waves of love and hate, jealousy even of the child's childhood; hope and fear for its maturity; longing to be free of responsibility, tied by every fibre of one's being." The sense of entrapment was accompanied by physical exhaustion and terrible mental depression with "Anger, weariness, demoralisation. Sudden bouts of weeping, a sense of insufficiency to the moment and to eternity . . . I weep and weep, and the sense of powerlessness spreads like a cancer through my being." This sense of the experience of depression, women's invisible work and the lack of acknowledged worth, can be found in the writings of women artists and scholars. It goes beyond anything offered by the traditional psychiatric literature on women and depression.

CONCLUSIONS

There is a high incidence of depression in women, especially among mothers of young children, accompanied by a high rate of prescription of anti-depressant drugs. Although ambiguities in the definition and classification of depression may lead to an untoward number of women being assumed to have a psychiatric illness; depression is no myth and there are many women suffering from it. Despite the possible relevance of some present theories, their focus on the individual woman as the problem and the person to be treated obscures other issues. The effect of a woman's daily experience while living out her expected role in the family and subject to stresses generated by our present social structure is missed.

The need for new models and a new understanding is clear.

≡　　　　≡　　　　≡

CHAPTER IX

PSYCHOTROPIC DRUGS AND WOMEN

AN EXAMINATION OF THE HIGH PRESCRIPTION RATES OF psychoactive drugs, particularly to women, highlights how beliefs about the efficacy of these drugs have evolved and how stereotypes about women allow physicians to ignore the actual stresses of women's lives and to view those who complain or fail to cope as sick.

THE PRESCRIPTION OF PSYCHOACTIVE DRUGS

Canadian studies have shown that women receive more prescriptions for all drugs than do men. For psychotropic drugs, however, the female:male differential is highest, with 67-72% of prescriptions going to women.[1] Two recent studies designed to investigate women's health care needs and drug use in detail, reported a startlingly high consumption of tranquilizers. Of women studied in Winnipeg,[2] Manitoba, 20% had used tranquilizers during the previous two weeks. In Etobicoke,[3] Ontario, 15% of a sample of adult women said that they had used a tranquilizer within the previous two days. Other studies have shown that many more women than men use tranquilizers steadily or receive multiple prescriptions in the course of a year.[4] In a Vancouver study of visually impaired children and adolescents, 17% of the mothers and 3% of the fathers were taking psychoactive drugs. This applied to both the index group and to a control group of normal children.[5]

The historical role of the physician as the active giver of some kind of treatment has been documented over the centuries. Osler contended, in 1904, that "the doctor's visit is not complete without the prescription."[6] There have been estimates that three-fourths of visits to a physician result in the giving of a prescription, and that about one-fourth of all prescriptions are for a psychotropic substance. It is important to note that the emergence of psychotropic drugs has helped to bring the family doctor into the field of psychiatric treatment, as demonstrated by Saskatchewan statistics which show that 80% of psychiatric diagnoses are made by family physicians.[7]

The readiness with which general practitioners prescribe psychotropic drugs is shown by an Australian study[8] which used the method of pseudopatient observation in the context of general practice. Persons playing the role of a patient suffering from a depression of psychosocial origin presented themselves to a random sample of 25 general practitioners. The most common form of treatment was prescription (78% of all consultations), of which 90% contained at least one psychotropic agent. Other treatments were reassurance and discussion (42%), counselling (28%), psychiatric referrals (12%), and social agency referrals (4%). No mention of possible side effects was given on 57% of the occasions when a psychotropic drug was given;

The dilemmas of the busy doctor are outlined by Wolfe[9] who points out that some of those who write most critically about over-prescribing have never been in the frontline situation of earning a living in a busy medical practice. Busy doctors face a number of serious dilemmas. They have little training in pharmacology and are often the willing victims or accomplices of the pharmaceutical industry's propaganda.[10] Furthermore, they get little or no leadership from their medical association via journals which tend to be financed and thus influenced by drug companies' advertising. Wolfe goes on to emphasize that practising doctors may lack an awareness of important ethical issues and may not be ready to cope with the increasing demand for informed consent; to start sharing things with patients rather than directing them. It may be difficult for doctors to confront the fact that they still work, essentially, as small private entrepreneurs in situations which do not permit the sharing of skills and resources.

Adverse reactions to psychotropic drugs may be compounded by the addition of another drug to minimize the effects of the first one. Reports in the literature rarely address this problem directly, but the extent of the difficulty can be gleaned from papers speaking on other subjects. For instance, Finn,[11] in describing the field trial of a new diagnostic framework (American Psychiatric Association, *Diagnostic and Statistic Manual III*), admitted that the assessment of patients entering the hospital was made difficult by the fact that 48% of the patients had been taking drugs for months prior to admission. Many were taking a combination of drugs; one patient was taking 13 drugs, of which 11 were prescribed!

As yet, there is little insistence on the importance of telling the patient about possible risks and side effects; in fact, many physicians appear to view this as an invidious encroachment on their rights, one which will diminish the usefulness of the drug by frightening the patient about possible problems. While traditional presentations caution about the effects of antipsychotic drugs on the blood, liver, skin and other organs, and comment on problems of dizziness and drowsiness caused by anti-anxiety and anti-depressant drugs, they rarely give a full account of the range of possible adverse effects. Moreover, the reader's attention is not focussed on the impairment of efficiency at work, the dulling of senses and emotions, the effect on sexual performance, the lack of energy, and lethargy. These are more subtle vicissitudes which may obscure the possibility of other solutions for the individual, preventing them from taking initiative and using their own resources, and dulling them into accepting their predicament as inevitable and immutable.

Accidental poisoning and the use of psychotropic drugs to attempt suicide are now major problems,[12] with diazepam (Valium) the most freqently used drug.[13] The growing street use of Valium and other psychoactive drugs is another area that has gained little recognition.[14] Similarly, the addiction potential of Valium and the consequent very serious withdrawal symptoms are reaching public awareness through the media[15] rather than coming from the medical profession.

THE POWER OF BELIEFS ABOUT PSYCHOTROPIC DRUGS

Most mental health professionals believe that psychotropic drugs have a place in the management of emotional distress. Those who work in general hospital emergency departments, on admission wards, or in mental hospitals, are usually convinced that drugs are a vital part of the treatment plan for the acutely disturbed person who could not, they feel, be managed appropriately without medication. Many feel that the post-hospital adjustment of such a person depends on the continued administration of maintenance doses of the drug.

Drugs hold such a primary place in the arsenal of most psychiatrists, particularly for the treatment of severe disturbances, that papers which begin to raise some doubts about the necessity of drugs for the management of, for instance, schizophrenia, tend to be met with disbelief and defensiveness. One such paper which met with angry rebuttals in letters to the editor of the *American Journal of Psychiatry,* argues that the treatment of schizophrenia is so completely drug oriented that this is an obstacle to the exploration of alternative therepeutic approaches. As little is really known about schizophrenia, contend the authors, this narrowing of the clinical approach is alarming. They compared a group of patients treated with neuroleptic medication and the traditional hospital approach with a group of similar patients in a program emphasizing psychosocial treatment and little or no medication. Follow-up revealed a small but significantly superior outcome for the group receiving little or no medication and heavy psychosocial treatment. Moreover, the patients who had received no medication at all were faring as well as those who had received small doses.[16]

Similarly, the side effects of powerful drugs are often downplayed and the possibility of permanent damage ignored. For example, psychiatrists have been extrememly reluctant to acknowledge that long term use or high doses of phenothiazines cause tardive dyskinesia, a disabling neurological condition that is often permanent.[17] For instance, Crane[18] notes that numerous articles on tardive dyskinesia have been published in the last decade[19] and that in 1972 and 1973, package inserts of antipsychotic drugs were updated to include cautions about this problem. Despite all these cautions, Crane felt that the use of antipsychotic drugs was continuing unabated, and decided to see whether an educational approach would affect physicians' prescribing patterns. In a lecture and discussion period with the staff of a well-known hospital, he emphasized that lower doses of neuroleptics should be given to all patients. He discovered that his educational efforts had been to no avail: before the lecture patients were given an average daily dose of 250 mg. of chlorpromazine, after the lecture they received an average daily dose of 252 mg.

He then attempted to work with various ward physicians, urging them to reduce neuroleptic medication. While there was some degree of cooperation in wards housing less disturbed patients, he found that attempts to lower doses were fruitless in wards with large numbers of disturbed patients. He noted that despite the high doses of medication prescribed to them, most patients continued to be disturbed. Thus, he postulated that the amount of medication given was related to the intensity of the behavioural disturbance rather than to the effectiveness of the treatment. Crane concludes by commenting that pleas from a few concerned individuals about the need to use neuroleptic drugs with great caution have fallen on deaf ears, and that efforts to improve the quality of patient care by peer review committees, medical associations and other organizations have been equally ineffective. He stresses that "tremendous obstacles exist when some practices are based on faith instead of medical considerations."

Authors such as Schofield[20] assume that consumer expectations, related to the amount of mental health propaganda in the media and to people's expectations of happiness, result in requests for psychotropic drugs. It is not clear, however, where consumer expectations end and physicians' prescribing habits begin. In fact, one study showed that psychiatric inpatients, whose pattern of prescription would usually include regular medication several times a day, requested tranquilizers on an average of once per three day period, although given the option of requesting diazepam up to a maximum of four times a day.[21]

A study of people attending a community health facility found that women were more ready to label themselves as psychiatrically ill, that, having spoken to more people in their intimate networks, they were more ready to enter treatment, and more accepting of the patient role.[22] Women are more compliant about taking the medication prescribed for them.[23] A recent Vancouver study[24] of women's understanding of minor tranquilizer use showed that they felt that these drugs were sometimes needed to help them "cope." Coping, for them, meant the management of their role as housewife and mother. One woman in this study felt that she got a message from her doctor "that all I was expected to do was to get on with being who I was, which was a woman with two children and a husband."

Some writers argue that women's "illness behaviour" is different from that of men. They contend that women have more time to go to doctors, are more expressive of feelings, more prepared to request medication, and more likely to comply with suggested treatment. A number of surveys have shown that women consistently report more symptoms of physical and emotional discomfort than men.[25]

It seems obvious that both physician and woman patient are enmeshed in a demand for treatment. Cooperstock[26] suggests that physicians often feel frustrated and bored by women's "vague complaints" such as fatigue, headache, sleeplessness and unhappiness, and tend to view them as "trivial."[27] She emphasizes that, almost always, a prescription is given for a medication that is likely to be as non-specific as the complaint (i.e., a tranquilizer). A woman in the Vancouver study[28] said, "I feel that, essentially, when a doctor prescribes a pill for me, it's to put him out of my misery."

TRADITIONAL ACCOUNTS

Historical or cross-cultural accounts usually insist that mood-modifying substances, such as opium, peyote and alcohol, have been used throughout the centuries and across the world to blot out a bleak existence, or as a part of a ritual or religious ceremony. Jeffreys[29] states that it is "clear from anthropological and historical studies that those who did not take some 'mindbending' chemical regularly or on ritual occasions have been the exception rather than the rule in all known soceities." This account becomes an explanation which is then put forward as a reason for maintaining the status quo. People, it is contended, cannot exist without some kind of readily available chemical crutch. This argument goes on to postulate that control of one substance would merely lead to the use of something else, and ignores the difference between self-administered and prescribed drugs.

Traditional textbook presentations link drugs with specific disease states and put forward theories about the action of the drug on the brain. Specific drugs, or groups of drugs, are discussed in terms of indications for use, usual range of dosage, side effects, possible complications, and contra-indications. Some writers emphasize the importance of a correct diagnosis which enables prescription of a specific drug, while others appear to dispense with diagnosis and engage in a "therapeutic trial" where the response to a drug indicates the diagnosis. A depression which improves with tricyclic anti-depressant drugs would be labelled an endogenous depression. If it fails to improve, it would be felt to be a neurotic depression.

It appears that some textbooks are beginning to reflect controversies, but in a defensive fasion. For instance in the *Comprehensive Textbook of Psychiatry* chapter on "Minor Tranquilizers, Sedatives and Hypnotics," the author does comment on the clinical dilemma posed by the availability of effective anti-anxiety agents, asking who should they be prescribed for. He thinks that they should be used for acute, severe anxiety states or for problems of living, of which he gives some examples — the distraught divorcée, recent widows, a mother stressed by her daughter's marriage. (It is interesting that all of the concrete examples he offers are female!) He asks whether people would be better off living through their discomfort, and solving their problems without chemical help. Having made these germane comments, he goes on to invalidate them and to make some contradictory rebuttals in the next few paragraphs. He stresses that "the general belief that many physicians over-prescribe tranquilizers — a belief shared by many physicians and laymen — is really unproved," and goes on to say that to demonstrate overuse one needs clear criteria for use, and these are lacking.

WHAT IS USUALLY MISSING, OR MINIMIZED, IN TRADITIONAL ACCOUNTS

Most historical perspectives fail to mention the growing use of drugs for the control of disturbed and disturbing behaviour, thus aiding society in the suppression of deviant behaviour; behaviour which could perhaps have otherwise been viewed as an indication of the need for change in institutions or systems. Only recently has the occasional paper attempted to analyze women's status and role as a major factor in the prescription of psychotropic drugs for women.[30]

"Fads" in the prescription of psychotropic drugs are rarely mentioned, and certainly never used to illustrate how present-day beliefs about the efficacy of certain drugs might be entirely erroneous. In a recent paper Amin[31] discusses the history of the search for a perfect sleeping pill, showing that the low therapeutic index and addicting potential of barbiturates were ignored for 50 years, while cases of addiction were attributed to the "moral depravation of the people." The ideology surrounding the present-day use of benzodiazepines, he points out, repeats all the old mistakes.

When presenting information concerning the usefulness of particular drugs the "placebo effect" is often minimized, and writers fail to examine how much improvement is in fact due to the drug itself, to the passage of time, to the surrounding milieu, to the compelling expectations of the physician[32] or hospital or clinic staff, or to a multitude of other factors. When reading reviews of the studies claiming monumental effectiveness of major tranquilizers for the treatment of schizophrenia, one's attention is not drawn to the fact that about 20% of the studies demonstrated no difference between groups given the drugs and those given an inert placebo.[33] For psychoactive drugs in general it has been shown that two in five patients respond to placebo treatment and that numerous non-drug factors influence response.[34] A study of 200 general practitioners in the British Isles explored the influence of doctors' and patients' attitudes on the efficacy of drug therapy in anxious and depressed patients. The improvement recorded in response to either drug given by an optimistic doctor was more than double that obtained by pessimistic doctors. The attitude of the patient, although tending to influence the outcome somewhat if the patient was optimistic, showed a far less striking effect.[35]

There is little recognition of the need to look beyond the traditional position at the enormous self-interests of industries that promote mood-modifying substances and at the staggering growth of the pharmaceutical industry since World War II. The interests of the pharmaceutical industry in profits rather than patients, in enhancing their stock value rather than ethics, can be seen in accounts of the illicit traffic in opium which was smuggled into China by Swiss drug firms in the 1920s, and the way that powerful drugs are sold in Africa for purposes that would not be permitted in developed countries with regulations about drug safety.[36] Strong pressure groups, such as the International Federation of Pharmaceutical Manufacturers Associations, have warded off the international control of drugs.[37]

Fashions in drug use are determined, at least in part, by the pharmaceutical industry. Claims of tremendous progress in the drug treatment of emotional disorders are paralleled by increasing sophistication in drug marketing and sales promotion. The industry has promoted the universality of symptoms of emotional distress, aided the inclusion of problems of living within the scope of medicine, and reinforced popular convictions about the right to avoid suffering, the pursuit of eternal youth and constant happiness. As a result the industry has been able to be increasingly over-inclusive in its claims for products which are put forward as solutions to a vast array of life's problems. Thus, like other manufacturers of consumer goods, the industry works on creating a need for the product by defining the conditions for its use. The market is flooded with "new breakthroughs" which are only minor chemical variations of already existing drugs. The real purpose of this enterprise, however, is obscured by claims about the need for continued research for more effective remedies — when actually it represents a constant attempt to maintain market monopolies and defeat competitors by bringing out a "new improved" product.

Huge amounts of money are expended to sustain drug company sales. In Great Britain, where prescription charges vary from low to nil, there is one drug company salesman for every seven general practitioners.[38] Total marketing costs in the U.S.A. are estimated at over $6,000. per physician per year.[39] Drug companies provide "educational services"; pamphlets about new drugs constantly arrive in the mail; booths at national and international meetings provide literature and present videotapes designed to prove the efficacy of their products and are serviced by persuasive representatives who offer to send free samples or even free books if one's interest is judged to be sufficient. Drug companies finance lunches, dinners, and small, intimate, all-expense-paid meetings. So-called drug trials, in which general practitioners try a new drug on their patients in return for payment or a gift from the manufacturer, have been exposed in England and pronounced "promotional gimmicks with little scientific basis."[40]

GROWING CRITICISM

Questions are beginning to emerge in journals and textbooks. An editorial in the *Canadian Medical Association Journal* stressed that physicians "naturally fear being criticized for failure to recognize, diagnose and treat. Despite this we must . . . oppose media forces that advise analgesics for every minor pain, tranquilizers for each of life's minor day-to-day setbacks."[41] Morgan[42] emphasizes that ". . . the time has come for a critical reappraisal of the way in which they (drugs) are prescribed." Parish[43] asks, "Is it right to perform a pharmacological leucotomy on a large section of contemporary society?" Hollister,[44] in reviewing drug therapy of mental disorders, comments that the plethora of psychotherapeutic drugs has "contributed more to the confusion of physicians than to benefits for patients." He remarks that decisions about the drug to be administered to a patient are largely trial-and-error because of lack of experimental evidence on the specific indications for each drug, and notes that many patients receive absurd combinations of psychotropic drugs. He stresses that drugs used merely as a chemical straightjacket constitute an abuse.

The author of the chapter on drug dependence in the *Comprehensive Textbook of Psychiatry* remarks that "physicians are now compelled to examine the consequences of the fact that a number of therapeutic substances have been introduced with insufficient awareness of their potential for abuse." In the above-named text, however, it is in the chapter on "Socioeconomic Considerations of Psychiatry" that the issues surrounding drug use are succinctly confronted. Author Ginzberg notes that the pessimistic evaluators of psychiatry are emphasizing the dysfunctional effects of drug therapy, stressing that accumulating evidence demonstrates serious and long-term negative effects from an over-reliance on many drugs in common use.

One of the most critical series of monographs, by the U.S. Group for Advancement of Psychiatry (G.A.P.), appers to be "Pharmacotherapy and Psychotherapy: Paradoxes, Problems and Progress."[4][5] This publication, while committed to an integrated approach to pharmacotherapy and psychotherapy, highlights a number of contradictions and pitfalls. Noting the vast array of psychiatric treatment methods, the authors contend that the determinants of the type of treatment offered are rarely clear, and that they appear to be greatly influenced by the training and ideology of the personnel available for treatment. They point out that those without licence to prescribe drugs, or experience in using them, frequently oppose them vehemently. Others use drugs for the relief of symptoms or as part of the treatment plan. Still others rely on drugs exclusively, frequently in inappropriate doses, and occasionally to the detriment of the patient.

The G.A.P. emphasizes that clinicians' selection of drugs and/or psychotherapy is usually based on their training and therapeutic orientation. They may work from an implicit theoretical model, based on empirical experience and pragmatic goals. Conflicting ideas are readily apparent if clinicians are asked to explain their rationale for prescribing various therapies. The G.A.P. advances the concept of "prototheories," or ideological rationales, which underlie and justify the nature of working decisions made by practitioners. A prototheory is the mode by which professionals explain their ideological commitment to themselves, each other and the larger public.

Noting that psychiatric staff are unwilling to engage in research, the G.A.P. attributes this to the staff's reluctance "to adopt a self-critical attitude and to accept the fact that many of their procedures have never been clearly demonstrated to be useful." Psychiatric staffs may not be entirely convinced that their treatment methods are effective, yet, to justify their employment and remuneration they have to hang on to an ideological commitment to them. Evidence of the staff's commitment to their beliefs is demonstrated by their contention that patients in research programs are being deprived of effective treatment if they are assigned to an untreated control group. Stressing that psychiatrists and other physicians often prescribe psychotropic drugs in haphazard ways without appropriate follow-up, precautions or awareness of the negative effects, the G.A.P. contends that psychotropic drugs are correctedly used, underused, overused, and misused. It proposes a range of treatment studies in a variety of clinical facilities which will allow a critical examination of current beliefs and will foster a climate of scepticism about the usefulness of existing treatments.

PRESCRIPTION OF PSYCHOTROPIC DRUGS FOR WOMEN

As women are prescribed two-thirds of all psychotropic drugs, an understanding of the basis for this difference in prescription rate is crucial. It appears to be rooted in the unrecognized stresses of women's traditional role and the pervasive sentiment that women who deviate from, or complain about, their traditional role as wife, mother, sex object and self-sacrificing nurturer must be sick. We postulate that women's traditional role is maladaptive and subject to many stresses. Several studies have underscored the difficulties of women's daily experience. Moss and Plavis[46] found that in inner London, 52% of the mothers of preschool children had a moderate or severe "distress problem." Richman's[47] study of mothers of three-year-olds with behaviour problems demonstrated that 39% of the study group and 26% of the control group of mothers, whose children did not have a behavioural problem, were depressed. In another study she found depressive symptoms of a severe or moderate degree in 41% of mothers who lived in subsidised housing with a three-year-old and at least one younger sibling.[48] Brown and Harris's[49] study of women in Camberwell, England, showed that 15% of the women were clinically depressed while an additional 18% were considered to be borderline cases. Among those with children at home, working-class women were four times more likely to suffer from depression. Women who are employed outside the home are somewhat protected from depression[50] and use few psychotropic drugs. In one study, 25% of full-time housewives, 19% of women with part-time jobs, and 11% of women with full-time jobs, reported using psychotropic drugs during the previous two weeks. This study also showed that involvement in activities outside the home, such as sports, club participation and visiting friends, was also related to drug use. Less activity outside the home was related to greater drug use.[51]

The doctor's perception of a distressed woman cannot fail to have a bearing on the decision to give, or not to give, drugs. Medical school teaching still perpetuates mythology about women,[52] often presented as scientific knowledge. Clinician bias about women's mental health is illustrated by the Broverman Study[53] which demonstrated that the clinician's opinion about a mentally healthy woman paralleled the prevalent cultural assumptions that women should be nurturant, emotional, sensitive, lacking in assertion and objectivity, and lacking in competitiveness and aggressiveness in order to be considered "normal."

Further support for the contention that clinician stereotyping and expectations play a major role in shaping women's "illness behaviour" and determining physicians' prescribing patterns comes from a study of a family practice clinic.[54] The study population included everyone coming to the clinic complaining of i) unhappiness, crying, depression, ii) nervousness, iii) tension, restlessness and worrying. Women received significantly more minor tranquilizers than men, while men received slightly more laboratory tests and physical therapies. Six months later the prescribing differential had increased; women were receiving even more minor tranquilizers. This study also showed that the increased prescription of tranquilizers paralleled the total number of clinic visits for women, but not for men, for whom a number of alternate therapeutic avenues were tried.

If kept within the medical framework, women's distress is viewed as a psychiatric disorder alone, and psychotropic drugs are seen as the treatment of choice.

DRUG ADVERTISING

A few minutes spent scanning the advertising pages in medical or psychiatric journals will demonstrate that women are depicted as the patient in almost all advertisements for minor tranquilizers and anti-depressants. The portrayal of women, both in the pictures and captions, makes it immediately obvious that drug advertising plays a major role in reinforcing stereotypes and encouraging the administration of drugs to women. For instance, an advertisement for an antidepressant urges, "Don't settle for half-measures." The patient is a middle-aged woman with anguished eyes, a deeply furrowed brow, and grey-brown hair swept back severely from her face. She is entirely clothed in black. Her face, divided in half vertically, is banded horizontally with pink and yellow on one side, and vertically with yellow and green on the other. Whether she represents the mythical repressed, frustrated and unhappy spinster or a recent widow, the message is clear. She can only be half a woman, as she is, and needs medication to make her "whole."

Seidenberg[55] postulates that drug companies realize that they can sell their products most effectively by presenting physicians with a derogatory and demeaning image of women who are portrayed as bad-tempered, nagging, vain, self-centered and "irrationally" unhappy with their role in life. In addition, an advertisement may contain a sexual appeal. At a pharmaceutical display during the 1976 Canadian Psychiatric Association meeting, large advertisements for "N" featured a face of a beautiful women with eyes half-closed. After checking with colleagues of both sexes and finding that almost all immediately associated this picture with orgasm, a young female psychiatric resident told the salesman that she felt the picture was disgusting in this context. He assumed that she was a psychiatrist's wife, and replied, jokingly, "Well, it's the kind of thing that turns your old man on, and sells our products." This advertisement ran for several months in the *Canadian Psychiatric Association Journal,* claiming to improve affect and communication in schizophrenia, senility, and "all disorders of affect, irrespective of diagnosis." Smaller pictures, all of women, depicted these three conditions. A magic cure-all for woman's problems? One wonders how much the sale of "N" increased.

Drugs are often presented as the solution for women's problems, to help them cope with their traditional role. For example, a journal advertisement for an anti-depressant shows a pretty young woman going down some staris carrying a full laundry basket. The caption reads, "In depression — first get the patient moving." An advertisement for a minor tranquilizer depicts an attractive young blonde woman, dressed in a soft blue nightgown, collapsing into an armchair. The caption reads, "Some days she can't seem to function . . ." Another adverstisement portrays the tear-streaked face of an attractive young blonde woman who is said to be suffering from "Copelessness." Medication, it is suggested, will help her pull herself together and apply herself to needed tasks. Both of these advertisements strongly suggest that inability to function in a traditional female role, inability to cope with being a woman and with woman's tasks, need to be treated with medication.

Some recent advertisements are more subtle in their presentation and concede that other measures may be needed in addition to drugs. "The empty nest syndrome" is a full-page advertisement of a bored looking woman sitting on a sofa in the livingroom of the house. Also shown is a beautifully appointed diningroom, the bedroom of a school-age boy complete with flags, ball and baseball bat, and a girl's room with flowers, dolls and frills. The junk in the attic includes a tricycle, a wagon and dolls, and adds to the powerful portrayal of the woman left at home when the children are all in school. It is conceded that this woman needs activites outside of the home, but stated that this needs to be initiated with anti-depressant medication.

Contending that "chauvinism and sexism run rampant through these messages," Seidenberg adds that the bias is further illustrated by the fact that the physician, psychiatrist, or psychotherapist is never a woman. After searching through numerous advertisements in journals published in 1977 and 1978, we found only two that depicted a woman as a physician or therapist. In one, three doctors are discussing "Q." An older, conservatively dressed man appears to be in charge, while a young woman, possibly a medical student, has the hand of an older man protectively placed on her shoulder. These were the only departures we could find from the usual scene where the woman is the helpless, insecure, inadequate patient, often seated below, or looking up to, a strong paternal, male figure.

An advertisement for "T" on the back cover of the August 1977 issue of the *American Journal of Psychiatry,* shows a male hand giving a prescription to an extremely attractive, young blonde woman who looks calm, serene, adoring and grateful. "T" is "a prudent prescription for today's anxious patient," and one is urged "Maybe it's time?" If one leaves this portrayal of peace and tranquility and the message that this is the drug of choice, one with greater versatility and the same effectiveness for "today's patient," and heeds the small print at the bottom of the page ("Please see overleaf for prescribing information"), one is surprised by the host of warnings, contraindications, precautions and adverse reactions listed there. The whole advertisement, in portrayal and layout, appears to be a clever enticement to the male physician, promising admiration from pretty women, and minimizing the pitfalls of giving such a powerful, possibly addictive drug to women of child-bearing age.

Medical journals rely on funds from advertising, and so do little or nothing to expose or change these practices. Seidenberg comments that his first article on this topic was refused by twenty journals, and eventually published by a journal that does not accept drug advertising. This is, perhaps, a measure of the resistance to an embarrassing exposure, which might lead to fewer requests for space for drug advertising in the journal.

HOW PSYCHOTROPIC DRUGS AFFECT WOMEN

(Illustrations will be taken from the practice of P.S. Penfold.)

The use of psychotropic drugs as an answer to women's difficulties leads to a number of problems. The woman is put into a sick role, so that society is readily able to view her as the problem, and thus avoid taking any responsibility for needed changes.

■　Mrs. J.'s first baby was difficult, falling into that 10% of the child population described by Thomas, Chess and Birch[56] as difficult. As a baby, John was colicky, unpredictable, cried easily and slept poorly. As a "terrible two" he was impossible. As John grew older his high activity level, short attention span, distractibility, moodiness, impulsiveness and temper tantrums drove the J.s to despair. Mrs. J., however, had never heard of "difficult" children. She was convinced that the difficulty was her own inadequacy and failure as a mother. Her husband, mother-in-law, friends, neighbours, and family doctor shared this perspective. She was prescribed a variety of tranquilizers by her doctor, and viewed herself as sick, neurotic. Whenever a confrontation was brewing with her son or her husband, who shared many of the son's personality characteristcs, she took a pill and tried to placate them, usually taking responsibility for the problem herself.

Women are often given psychotropic drugs when they are facing a crisis such as death, separation, divorce or marital conflict. Medication may suppress the positive coping mechanisms which an individual brings into play after the initial phase of disorganization and turmoil. In specific situations, such as death of a loved one, the use of drugs may immobilize the person to the extent that they are unable to go through the stages of normal grieving.

■　Sixteen-year-old Kelly K. was referred to me because of depression, weight gain and promiscuity. Her father had died two years previously, yet Kelly and her mother first discussed his death in my office. They described the horror of Mr. K.'s sudden death and how both of them had been told by their priest, family doctor, friends and neighbours to put on brave faces and try to cope; "don't let your father/husband down." The family doctor accompanied his suggestions with large doses of tranquilizers, for them both, for the next few months. On withdrawal of the medication, both had experiences which they felt "showed I was going crazy." Kelly felt her father was still around; she could hear his voice and smell his pipe. Mrs. K. felt overwhelmed by angry feelings about her husband leaving her with the children. Neither could share these strange feelings with the other. Mrs. K. became withdrawn and preoccupied, and then worried about Kelly's defiance, over-eating and staying out late "with the wrong group."
Once their feelings were put into perspective as normal manifestations of the second stage of grief, the onset of which had been greatly delayed by the use of medication, mother and daughter were able to cry together, work through their feelings and begin to accept the fact of Mr. K.'s death.

Medication may affect a woman's ability to function in her work at or outside of the home, and her relationship with significant people.

■　Mr. M., an Italian immigrant, complained that his wife lay on the sofa all day and seemed not to care about her appearance, the house and the children. In his opinion she was "going through the change of life." He was inclined to accept this, but complaints from the school and visits from the public health nurse eventually drove him into bringing the two younger children to the clinic. An Italian-speaking social worker found out that Mrs. M. had been to her doctor a few months before, complaining of headaches, stomach-ache, and "nerves." The medication prescribed, which she took faithfully, had induced her zombie-like state.

■ Mrs. P., speaking to a group about postpartum depression, described her own experiences. She had been expected, by herself, her relatives and friends, to be the perfect mother. Feeling depressed, resentful and guilty, she made repeated visits to her family doctor, voicing vague complaints about her baby's health and her own state of mind. Her doctor (who seemed to be aligned with all those who thought she was a perfect mother and that there could not be anything seriously wrong) gave her Valium. She felt intermittently drowsy, even more alienated from the baby and aware of occasional, frighteningly hostile impulses (which could have been caused by Valium)[57] towards the child. Several months later, she heard of the Vancouver Postpartum Counselling Service, where she, at last, felt understood, supported and helped. She quickly recovered without the "help" of Valium.

Dependency on psychotropic drugs may erode many facets of a woman's life. She can feel powerless, helpless, and afraid to be without her chemical crutch. Drug treatment may also prevent the accurate diagnosis of medical conditions.

■ Betty, a 32-year-old professional woman who had been taking 10 mg. of Valium three or four times a day for the previous three years, admitted that she could not imagine doing without the drug. Three years before my first contact with her, she had been admitted to hospital with some rather vague complaints: lassitude, lack of energy, stomach pain. When a variety of tests were all negative, she was assumed to be neurotic and referred to a psychiatrist who put her on Valium and told her that "you will be alright when your boyfriend gets back from Africa and marries you."

She described an oppressive and unrewarding job situation in which she was expected to work 50-60 hours a week, exposed to constant criticism and blamed if anything went wrong. Her boss took all the credit for any achievements. Betty constantly chided herself for her inability to cope, and felt that her anxiety and disorganization "proved" the diagnosis of neurosis. So she continued to function, marginally, taking Valium, and unable to sustain any relationships or take part in any activities beyond the work situation.

Over the next few months, seeing me at two-week intervals, Betty quit her job (after gaining the confidence to tell her boss of her anger), found other employment and gradually decreased her Valium. Her self-confidence and ability to enjoy herself returned, and after about eight sessions she told me that she was off Valium and felt that our discussions had gone as far as she needed.

About six months later, Betty called me, in a panic. She had had another attack of the same symptoms that had caused her hospitalization four years previously. Based on the reports of her previous hospitalization, her general practitioner assumed that the problem was neurotic. I telephone the general practitioner and said that I felt that Betty had been labelled, and that I was convinced that Betty's symptoms were not "all in her head." Betty's longstanding gynecological disorder was finally diagnosed.

Multiple addiction to drugs and other substances, minimized or unmentioned in traditional accounts, generally goes unrecognized.

■ Mrs. Y., the stylishly-dressed wife of a prosperous businessman, brought in her seven-year-old son, complaining of his defiance, inability to make friends, bossiness and bedwetting. I noticed that she entered the office stiffly and sat down carefully, and that there was a faint, stale odour in the air. After gathering the usual material, I questioned her about possible drinking problems. She burst into tears and confided about her growing dependence on alcohol and Valium. Mrs. Y. described her repeated visits to the family doctor with complaints of tiredness and nervousness. She had never admitted to a drinking problem and the doctor had never inquired, prescribing Valium for her "nerves."

In addition, there are physiological effects which can be very serious. A careful examination of the literature would suggest that the risks incurred, the side-effects produced as a result of the use of psychotropic drugs, may often far outweigh any possible benefit to the woman in distress. For instance, the side-effects which can be caused by Valium include drowsiness, coordination difficulties, fatigue, dizziness, nausea, blurred and double vision, headache, slurred speech, tremors, impaired memory, confusion, depression, incontinence or retention of urine, constipation, skin rash, generalized exfoliative dermatitits, low blood pressure, rapid pulse, flushing, blood in the urine, changes in sexual desire, damage to white blood cells, jaundice, extreme hypersensitivity and reactions such as rage instead of sedation. Psychotropic drugs may cause damage to the fetus, and the affect the infant of a lactating woman. The use of benzodiazepines (e.g., Valium, Vivol, etc.) by a lactating mother causes lethargy and weight loss in the infant, and hypnotics (e.g., Dalmane, Seconal, etc.) may cause a sedative effect and impair feeding or lead to drowsiness and a rash.[58]

One might contend, then, that the prescription of drugs to women in the childbearing years should be avoided whenever possible. The assumption that administration of drugs at other phases of the life cycle is less dangerous brings up both the prevalent use of drugs for children who do not conform in school,[59] and the problems of polypharmacy in the treatment of the elderly.[60]

■   This situation was described to me by a pharmacologist. He noticed that his recently bereaved neighbour, formerly a spry, energetic and vivacious woman in her 60s, was becoming increasingly withdrawn, slow, lethargic, and loath to leave her house. He assumed that she was grieving for her dead husband, and that the eventual working through of this phase would lead to the re-emergence of her previous high level of functioning. Then he did not see her around her garden or in the street, and after some months he heard that she was bedridden. On visiting her, he was puzzled and concerned by her disorientation and apathy, but it was only after the woman had been bedridden for a year that he allowed himself to overcome his ethical qualms, confront her physician and find out that she was on an assortment of tranquilizers and sleeping pills, given to her originally for her depression following the bereavement, and increased and added to when "she did not appear to be responding." As the various medications were gradually withdrawn, the widow got up from her bed, again took charge of her house and affairs, and quickly resumed her previous level of functioning after having been in suspended animation for a year.

A DIFFERENT PERSPECTIVE

In seeking to re-examine the increase in the prescription of psycho-active drugs in general, and to women in particular, we will touch again on beliefs about the efficacy of tranquilizers, and then look further at the prescription of psychoactive drugs for women. The beginnings of community psychiatry are linked by many psychiatrists with the discovery of potent tranquilizing drugs in the early 1950s. These drugs, according to the U.S. Joint Commision on Mentall Illness and Health,[61] allowed a radically different approach to the treatment of psychotic people in hospital, promoted early discharge and made management in the community feasible for many disturbed persons who would otherwise be admitted to hospital.

In fact, studies of a number of English and U.S. mental hospitals show that new discharge patterns emerged before the introduction of these new drugs.[62] In the late 1940s and early 1950s, the emergence of efforts to control expenditure in health care and social services at a time when general expenditure on welfare programs was rapidly expanding, led some hospitals to shift their policies towards stressing the avoidance of hospitalization and emphasizing early discharge if hospitalization proved unavoidable.[63]

Postulating that the availability of psychoactive drugs gave psychiatrists a new credibility in the eyes of their medical colleagues, Scull[64] looks critically at the theory that the discovery of tranquilizers transformed the management of mental illness. He postulates that the new drugs may have had little effect on discharge patterns, but could have made the actual physical management of the disturbed behaviour much less problematic. The new drugs, he contends, may have offered a more palatable means of control and decreased the need for a variety of physical restraints. Scull shows that the emergence of community psychiatry was not a unitary phenomenon. He relates it to general policy changes which led to the parallel development of community management for other "deviant" groups such as the criminal or juvenile delinquent. The availability of psychotropic drugs was never offered as a rationale for the invovement of such groups in the decarceration process. Changes in policy and administration at governmental levels produced the potential for a wide range of welfare services and payment schemes to be delivered at a community level in a seemingly more effective and efficient manner with less financial outlay.

Perhaps the role of psychoactive drugs has been misinterpreted, and their availability has been given total credit for a change that can be partially accounted for by policy decisions made by governments faced with fiscal dilemmas. This alternate view reinforces many questions about the actual state of knowledge of drug effectiveness and the validity of the many claims of effective treatment that are made.

A powerful medical ideology has grown up around psychoactive drugs which presents them as effective and necessary for a number of conditions. Reports of side-effects and permanent damage have had a negligible dampening effect on their use. As Muller[65] stressed, the doctor's use of drugs may appear practical, problem-oriented and compassionate. In actuality, the use of drugs may be achieving the goals of other, less visible parties, such as the pharmaceutical industry. We have noted that people who do not conform to society's norms and patients whose behaviour in mental hospitals is disturbing may receive drugs as a method of control rather than as a method of treatment. We have suggested that women's expectations and their perception of their difficulties as medical problems mirror clinicians' biases about "mentally healthy women,"[66] and that the pharmaceutical industry takes advantage of the situation by deliberately reinforcing the notion that women's everyday problems of living in an oppressive society are diseases. A recent study indicates that major Canadian medical journals have not, over the years, carried the preponderance of detrimental advertising material found in studies elsewhere.[67] There is nothing to indicate, however, that Canadian women fare better with regard to the overprescription of psychoactive drugs than do women in other parts of the world.

Traditional approaches, talking about the use of drugs for an individual patient, neglect ethical considerations and do not confront the fact that drugs are a powerful modality for social control. It is unlikely that physicians think about the social consequences of thousands of people on methadone, millions of people on antipsychotic drugs, and even more millions on other potent biochemical agents. They are perhaps even less likely to realize that they are acting as agents of social control when a woman is drugged to make her more "feminine," more accepting of her traditional role, or less disturbing to her husband. Nor do physicians necessarily recognize the implications of prescribing drugs to the poor or to racial minorities when the effect may be to render them subdued and powerless.

Drug technology obscures social issues such as poverty, racism and and inequality; society is absolved from its responsibility. If children can be made to conform in the classroom by giving them drugs, then the need to rebuild and reorganize educational structures can be avoided; if addicts can be maintained on methadone, we do not need to look at ways of rebuilding gratifying human connections for them; if women are drugged into conformity, we do not have to think about their inequality in the family system and the community. If given enough drugs, mental patients can be rendered docile and maintained with their relatives or in boarding homes in the community, thus obviating the need for expensive hospital care or for a creative, innovative approach to treatment, rehabilitation and the restoration of a sense of dignity and worth.

CONCLUSIONS

Our present social structures, including the dominant-subordinate relationship between men and women, create stresses, conflicts, difficulties, and unhappiness. The ideology surrounding psychoactive drug prescription teaches us to view symptoms of distress as a manifestation of individual pathology. People are given prescriptions for, and use psychotropic drugs as an individual solution to their misery.

A rationale for the prescription of psychoative drugs to women has developed within the framework of the ideology surrounding the institution of the family, and both reflects and reinforces traditional stereotypes about women's status and role. Drug advertisements, physicians' attitudes, and women's expectations all reflect the desirability of the woman functioning well in her traditional role, or assume that her unhappiness stems from the unavailability of supposed fulfillment.

≡　　　　　≡　　　　　≡

PART THREE

ALTERNATIVES
and
DIRECTIONS

CHAPTER X

ALTERNATIVES TO TRADITIONAL TREATMENT: TOWARDS FEMINIST THERAPY

WHILE THE MAIN FOCUS OF THIS BOOK IS THE contradictions within psychiatry and their implications, it seems appropriate at this point to outline some of the changes that have taken place, largely as a result of pressure from women in the community and the work of women within their professions. Indeed, there have been some momentous improvements, particularly in the area of violence towards women, which provides the most extreme examples of female oppression and its support by sexist theories and practice. Caution is warranted, however, and feminists should refrain from concluding that we have finally been heard. Acceptance of a feminist perspective may be genuine and deeply felt, engendering far-reaching change in both clinical practice and personal life; it may also be fashionable, a new bandwagon, highly token and superficial, thus very susceptible to the needs of the profession or the dictates of the system.

Studies based on questionnaire administration, which purport to demonstrate that biases based on sex or gender no longer exist, and that therapy is value free, are highly suspect. Therepists are intelligent enough to know what they ought to answer; what they actually practice may be a different matter. Feedback from women about their therapists, and from students in the mental health professions about their teachers and their experiences within institutions indicates that actual change is limited and very slow. Another possible pitfall is the quest for the principles and techniques of feminist therapy. There is a danger that it will be accorded a place, along with the several hundred other different types of therapy, and viewed as a technique that can be learned, perhaps in a weekend workshop. Feminist therapy must be viewed as a perspective, not a technique; a way of seeing, understanding and making connections. Much remains to be written and understood about the philosophy and practice of therapy when the therapist is a feminist.

In our search for the principles of feminist therapy we have studied the characteristics of oppression, the impact of women's studies courses, and the processes of consciousness raising and self-help groups. The theoretical basis for feminist therapy also lies within the broad range of writing over the last decade which illuminates women's experience and perspective. This literature includes the work of female novelists and poets, female scholars and writers who analyse women's status, role and place; female psychiatrists, psychologists and sociologists who have developed a critique of the traditional literature of their respective disciplines.

Feminism itself embraces a variety of viewpoints which can be related to the range of alternatives to traditional treatment that women have developed. Although not exclusive, three main positions can be identified: those of liberal feminism, radical feminism, and socialist feminism. Liberal feminists assume that sexist attitudes will gradually change as a result of public education and campaigning for equal rights and opportunities for women. Problems in the health care system, they feel, would be solved by changing physicians' sexist attitudes and by facilitiating the entrance of more women into medical school, with a corresponding influx of men into nursing. Radical feminists view the patriarchal family as the primary agent of women's oppression and seek to find alternatives to existing social institutions. The radical Women's Health Movement has focussed on teaching and organising women consumers of health care, thus indirectly bringing pressure to bear on the system. Socialist feminists try to understand the oppression of women in relation to social and economic structures. They note profound inequities and biases within capitalist medicine and believe that a humane and equal medical system will only be possible within a truly democratic socialist system.

WOMEN IN THE MENTAL HEALTH PROFESSIONS

Over the last decade, women have been actively addressing a variety of issues by initiating task forces, committees and working groups within their professional associations. These issues include the status of women within the profession, the needs of female clients, an examination of mental health theories, a critique of teaching within the profession, recommendations for new teaching material or programs, and attempts to convince colleagues that various political, social and economic issues have direct relevance to women's mental health.

Several examples will be described here, with a focus on notable achievements or difficulties. The American Psychiatric Association Task Force on Women (which later became the Committee on Women) was formed in 1972, and initially appeared to be making a great deal of progress towards its objectives and to be well-accepted within the profession. The events of 1980, however, highlighted the traditional attitude of the majority of APA members and their inability to recognize the relationship between the Equal Rights Amendment (ERA) and the mental health of female patients. Although the American Psychiatric Association made a commitment, in 1973, to support the ERA and hold meetings only in those states that had ratified the ERA, this commitment by the board of Trustees was overturned three times in the subsequent years, and the APA met twice in unratified states. Reading reports of the Committee on Women during these years, it appears that the Committee initially believed that the APA members were misguided and ill-informed about women's issues, and would soon realise the crucial connection between the ERA and women's mental health.

The Committee on Women and the associated organization, Psychiatrists for ERA (which included both men and women) were well-organized at the APA annual meeting in San Francisco in May 1980. Speakers, marches, stickers, pledges and media involvement created a stirring atmosphere. During her speech, Gloria Steinem mentioned that she could publish, in *Ms.* magazine, the names of all the psychiatrists who attended the New Orleans convention. The Board of Trustees again voted to move the meeting from New Orleans. But the predicted backlash recurred, and by June 1980 the Board had once again reversed its position and voted to go to New Orleans. By this time very little doubt remained about the position of the majority of U.S. psychiatrists, and many female psychiatrists were afforded a very clear view of the challenges they faced. They could no longer make excuses for their male colleagues, or think that they "misunderstood." The *Committee on Women Newsletter* emphasized that "we have to face the reality now. We are living in a sexist country where tourism is more important a concern than human rights. We are discriminated against in our jobs, our organizations; we are still the oppressed 'majority'."[1]

The Association's decision to hold the 1981 meeting in New Orleans was a Phyrrhic victory. A massive boycott, spearheaded by the Committee on Women and Psychiatrists for ERA, led to a much-reduced attendance, several invited speakers cancelled their lectures, and many papers were withdrawn.

Formed in 1975, the Task Force on Women of the Canadian Psychiatric Association has a small number of enthusiastic adherents who have worked at both national and local levels to initiate changes in teaching, put on panels and workshops, liaise with women in the community, and reach positions of influence in the profession. A Task Force member, Judy Gold, was elected as the first female president of the Canadian Psychiatric Association for 1981-82. However, many women within the organization either feel that the Task Force is unnecessary or lack interest in its aims. It would probably take events such as those that occurred within the American Psychiatric Association to raise the consciousness of some of these women and to shake their belief that sexism either does not exist, or has been totally transcended.

Perhaps because they lack the weighty tradition of the medical establishment, psychological associations seem to have been more responsive to change. The Canadian Psychological Association Committee on the Status of Women, which was formed in 1977 as a result of the work of the Task Force on Women, has formulated the "Guidelines for Therapy and Counselling with Women." These guidelines were adopted by the Canadian Psycholgocial Association in October 1980, and have been widely circulated.

The preamble to the Guidelines emphasizes that sex-biased therapy may not be a result of deliberate impropriety, but related to the therapist's previous training and practice in which an awareness of the potentially debilitating effects of traditional roles was not fostered. Drawing on the "Ethical Standards for Psychologists," it states that psychologists should be aware of the need for continuing education, and should recognize differences among people such as those associated with ethnic background, age, sex, and socioeconomic circumstances. If necessary to assure competent service or research with such persons, training, experience or consultation should be sought. The preamble goes on to state:

"The guidelines for therapy/counselling are rooted firmly within the general principles of therapy and counselling. In all instances therapists should be knowledgeable about the life situations of their clients, and about the psychological and other literature relevant to the types of clients and the types of problems with which they deal. They should also be aware of the impact their own socialization has had on them, and recognize the potential biases against which they must guard. Those offering psychotherapy or counselling to women have an obligation to be knowledgeable about the current literature concerning sex bias and sex-role stereotyping, to continually re-assess their own values and attitudes in the light of new evidence, and to be especially sensitive to the fact that women may be especially disadvantaged by the power relationships between therapist/counsellor and client."

The guidelines state:

1. The therapist/counsellor is willing to help the woman [sic] client to explore alternative life options in addition to the culturally defined gender role. Besides marriage and motherhood, he or she acknowledges the importance of other activities in both creating and solving women's problems.

2. The therapist/counsellor realizes that women do not bear the total responsibility for the success of marriage and for childrearing.

3. The therapist/counsellor recognizes the existence of social bias against women, and explores with the client the possibility that her problems may be based on society's definition of women's role rather than entirely within herself.

4. While respecting the right of the therapist/counsellor to determine the appropriate therapeutic strategy for a client, he or she is sensitive to and avoids the use of theoretical concepts that serve to reinforce the female stereotype of dependency and passivity, or to limit the woman's personal development.

5. The therapist/counsellor avoids interpreting psychological problems that occur at times of biological change in a woman's life,

e.g., childbirth, menopause, solely in terms of her reproductive/biological functioning.

6. The therapist/counsellor avoids the use of language implying sex bias, especially sexist jokes and the use of labels derogatory or demeaning to women.

7. The therapist/counsellor recognizes physical violence and sexual abuse as crimes, and does not encourage the woman [sic] client to submit to them, to accept their legitimacy, or to feel guilty about being a victim. The therapist actively acknowledges that there is no provocation that justifies resorting to physical or sexual violence.

8. The therapist/counsellor recognizes a woman [sic] client's right to have a fully adult role in the therapist-client relationship, without guidance from or deference to a man, and helps her achieve such a role.

9. The therapist/counsellor considers the sexual activity of the client without employing a "double standard" based on gender.

10. The therapist/counsellor does not treat the woman [sic] client as a sex object.[2]

(Reprinted with the permission of the Canadian Psychological Association.)

WOMEN'S STUDIES PROGRAMMES IN UNIVERSITIES AND COMMUNITY COLLEGES

Women's studies combine the characteristics of an academic field and a social movement, and cut across the biomedical sciences, the humanities and the social sciences. The interdisciplinary field has generated research, scholarly journals, newsletters, bibliographic periodicals, annotated bibliographies, major texts and archival collections of important historical documents.

Women's studies programmes are primarily educational and seek to dispel traditional views about women's place and role, and to highlight women's lack of visibility in the various disciplines. This can be done in a variety of ways. Women's place in society and in the family can be examined from an historical and cross-cultural perspective. The attitude of professions towards women, and the experience of women who attempt to work in those profession can be studied. Sex-role stereotyping can be explored, and alternative concepts, such as androgyny, can be introduced.

In women's studies programmes, some women learn to question the assumptions and beliefs that they had previously accepted. They discover that some personal problems, which they had thought were unique to themselves, are shared by every woman and that women's "shortcomings" can usually be understood as the result of social conditioning rather than personal inadequacies. They begin to transcend their self-blame about lack of motivation, lack of achievement, sexual problems, and family difficulties. They realize that women have a right to full personhood, and begin to be able to shed their burden of self-abnegation and pervasive guilt. Women's distrust of each other is reduced as they understand that they have been taught to seek out, compete for, and maintain a relationship with an idealised male protector at any cost, including the loss of all other friendships. They develop a more critical attitude towards society's institutions, and become more objective and realistic about education, career, marriage and motherhood. Myths about the fulfillment afforded by marriage and motherhood are laid bare, and realities about career-marriage conflicts brought to light. Women's careers and job aspirations are seen to be subject to sexism and discrimination in society. For many women, a women's studies course opens up exciting and challenging new perspectives, and intitiates a process of change including more comfort with, and respect for, other women, greater self-assertion and less self-criticism.

During a women's studies course the change in women students ranges from none to considerable.[3] Most students experience some emotional turmoil, and a few may develop significant difficulties. The degree of change and ability to incorporate and integrate the material being presented depends on individual differences and the surrounding feminist milieu. If female students are to develop a feminist consciousness they need access to further women's studies courses, consciousness raising groups and support systems. Small, same-sex discussion groups increase the potential of a women's studies course, and allow students to share personal concerns and to express themselves freely. Ideally, consciousness-raising, and support and feminist therapy groups should all be available. Instructors can reduce students' anxieties by preparing them for the discomfort, anxiety, uncertainty and anger that they may feel during the course. Sometimes a few male students can dominate a women's studies course, so the instructor has an important role in encouraging female students to speak more and men to speak less. Discussions of the effect of sexism on men and of male roles, can defuse tensions between women and men in the class, and make it less likely that women's personal relationships with men will bear the brunt of their anger and discontent.

CONSCIOUSNESS-RAISING GROUPS

Like women's studies programmes, consciousness-raising groups enable women to develop a different perspective of themselves, their relationships, and society. In addition, the consciousness-raising group provides invaluable ongoing support. A group consists of a number of women, usually between six and ten, who make a commitment to meet regularly in an atmosphere of mutual trust, respect, sharing and self-disclosure. Groups are egalitarian and leaderless and each member takes responsibility for bringing up topics, issues and difficulties for discussion.

Consciousness-raising is a process of growing awareness of the implications of being a woman in a male-dominated world. Group discussions challenge traditional views that male-female relationships are merely individual interactions between two equal persons. Women become more and more aware that their relationship with men is a class relationship in which they (the women) are subordinates. As they come to perceive the many obstacles that our social structures create for women, they are able to see that the environment, rather than intrapsychic dynamics, plays a major role in their difficulties and distress. Women begin to question the medical-psychological model of behaviour based on innate, biological predispositions, and struggle to re-examine the patterns of socialization that assign them to the roles of self-sacrificing mother, perpetual nurturer and helpless patient.

The small group structure and the comparison of personal experiences leads to heightened self-awareness. Women, who may be asserting themselves for the first time in their lives, both give and receive support and gain a sense of closeness and intimacy. This can be a new and exciting experience comparied to their previous one of competition with, and alienation from, other women. Women find themselves taken seriously, perhaps for the first time. It may also be the first opportunity they have had to listen and be listened to without the interruptions that women frequently experience with male intimates and with men in work and social situations. Women develop respect for each other, so that the consciousness-raising group may become ". . . a kind of seminar in which society itself [is] analysed from this new perspective of respecting women."[4] Members learn to identify with each other, support and respect each other, stop competing with each other, and to transcend the self-rejection that is a barrier to intimacy with other women. Women often view themselves as destructive, and accept blame for their own distress and for any problems of the men and children in their lives. Groups, on the other hand, may help women to see the connection between a sense of perpetual wrongness and pervasive guilt, and the deep-rooted feeling of having been born in the "wrong" sex. They provide a forum in which to discuss the far-reaching effect of this conviction on individual women's lives.

Some processes can be identified in consciousness-raising groups. Group members quickly move towards intimacy and closeness and develop strong loyalties to each other. Dropouts usually occur early and are often caused by a woman's apprehension about the man in her life who appears to be threatened by her involvement in the group, or by changes in her behaviour. Members of a group may go through a period of depression; they have developed awareness, are making changes as individuals, but are unable to make any impact on the outside world.

Group members who do not succumb go on to develop a variety of ways of combatting feelings of frustration and apathy, and finding ways, however small, of having an impact on the outside world. The group as a whole may become involved in some form of action, protests, political lobbying or educational programmes. Each group member, in her personal life, in her place of work, or in the community, may evolve some form of activity that embodies feminist principles. The group may then become a place where women share frustrations and successes, discuss strategies and options, and define goals and priorities. At this point the consciousness-raising group takes on the characteristics of a self-help or support group, although the process of consciousness-raising itself can go on for some years and involve the individual in a wider world-view of the operations of the institutions of society.

Because of the society in which we live, and because of the obstacles that women face, many group members continue to feel torn between a pull to remain with traditional ties and a pull to move onward.

Members recognize these dilemmas; the consciousness-raising group explores issues, catalyzes assertiveness, ventilates anger and offers support for action. Ideally, however, it does not insist on actions, belittle choices, or berate a member who is vacillating, has slipped back, or whose consciousness is lower than might be expected.

Some groups are formed for the explicit purpose of consciousness-raising, others may evolve out of groups of women that decide to meet around a particular interest, problem or "cause." For example, there could be a group of faculty women who decide to meet about salary and tenure prospects, a group of women factory workers who meet about working conditions or the need for unionization, or a group of mothers who plan to organize daycare for their children.

Many women are hostile to consciousness-raising groups and view them as invidiously erosive of male-female relationships and family life. Others misunderstand the purpose of these groups and view joining one as merely exchanging one kind of dependency for another. Still others cannot comprehend that other women could offer intimacy and support, and thus illustrate their acceptance of the cultural definition of valuable time as being that which is spent in the company of men. It seems likely that many women have an inkling of the compromises they are making, but are not ready to explore these or to make the commitment to some kind of change or personal action which joining a group may represent.

SELF-HELP GROUPS AND ALTERNATIVE SERVICES

Community organiser, Saul Alinsky,[5] insisted that mental health and economic and political self-determination are inseperable, and argued that people's self-esteem is benefitted by a collective movement to obtain power. In this section we are including a wide range of mutual aid groups and services developed by women for each other and for other women. First, however, we want to focus on some general principles of self-help groups.

Over the last decade, numerous self-help groups have developed in many countries. Self-help groups have been able to deal constructively with problems that professionals have had the least success with — problems such as alcoholism, addiction, and chronic illness. They provide ". . . a mechanism whereby individuals in a collective setting with others who face similar life situations can assume responsibilities for their own bodies, psyches and behaviour, and can help others do the same."[6] As opposed to the isolation of individual therapy, people in a self-help group get a sense of common plights and problems. Playing the helper role themselves at times, they become more objective and able to use their own experience to help others. This helps them to see their own problems in a broader context. Self-help groups are often consumer initiated, peer-centered and focus on personal experience in contrast to professional training that discourages identification, concern, full involvement and deep caring. There is the implicit message that people need not be passive, that they do have power, particularly in a group. Members are expected to help each other, and the group expects action, autonomy and independence. In return, the group offers support and permits a certain amount of dependency. People feel supported and get a sense of common purpose, often going on to involvement in broader social and political issues.

Some self-help groups have maintained this original form, while others have developed in a variety of directions, including seeking government and private funding, becoming business ventures, adding professionals, and including volunteers who are not in difficulty themselves. Women's self-help groups have followed a similar pattern, with some developing into alternate services for women.

The development of women's gynaecological self-help groups and women's self-help clinics can serve as a paradigm. A self-help group usually consists of six to ten women who meet together on a regular basis to exchange information about health and experiences with doctors, learn and practice breast and vaginal self-examination, discuss contraceptive techniques and study common gynaecological conditions. A popular manual for these groups is *Our Bodies, Ourselves.*[7] A group may evolve into a self-help clinic, where services to women are provided by women who have an advanced knowledge of self-help procedures. Such clinics may treat some gynaecological problems, fit contraceptive devices, and refer women to reliable doctors for abortions. In some areas they perform menstrual extractions themselves, a procedure which removes a woman's menstrual fluid in about five minutes and which can also be used for early abortions. The clinics educate women about their bodies, about self-care, about various gynaecological procedures, and often maintain a list of doctors who are considered to be non-sexist.

Self-help clinics do not claim to replace doctors or try to imitate them. Their goal is to get women to recognize what health care they can provide for themselves and what comes within the province of the physician. They attempt to build women's autonomy and self-reliance, and lessen their dependency on professionals and institutions. Like the consciousness-raising group, the gynaecological self-help group brings women into a co-operative and sharing relationship with other women, often for the first time in their lives. The change produced by their collective efforts in demystifying health care and building autonomy and independence gives them a sense of power and control that they may not have hitherto experienced.

Probably the most widely known and accepted alternate services for women are those developed for battered women and for rape victims. Community awareness of the former problem started with the opening of Chiswick Women's Aid in London, England, in 1971. Although planned as a women's community centre, it was rapidly flooded with women and their children escaping from brutal husbands. The publication of Erin Pizzey's book, *Scream Quietly or the Neighbours Will Hear* (1974),[8] sparked international concern, and there are now shelters for battered women in many countries of the world. Shelters for these women are staffed by other women whose feminist perspective and personal experience of abuse are likely to be considered more appropriate qualifications than professional training. Battered women and their children who enter these shelters are given support and have the opportunity, both informally and in groups, to share their experiences. Their stay at the shelter is often time-limited, and they are expected to find other accomodations and make plans for the future. Unfortunately, in many communities little support is available to them when they leave the shelter and, intimidated by the prospect of poverty and single parenthood, some return to the abusive environment.

Over the last few years, rape crisis intervention and counselling centres have emerged in most large communities. Most are community-based and have self-help characteristics, while a few have developed in hospital settings.[9] They usually function as an alternative to other traditional social services and challenge traditional attitudes to rape as an individual problem or misfortune, arguing that rape is a consequence of the inequality between men and women inherent in the present structure of society. Although structure and funding vary, many centres adhere, as far as possible, to self-help principles. Some centres are structured as collectives and their activities, policies and goals are determined by the collective membership. The membership often consists of volunteers and salaried staff, all women, many of whom were rape victims themselves. In addition to crisis intervention, centres are often greatly involved in public education with regard to the problems surrounding rape and factors contributing to the high incidence of sexual assault. Centres meet the specific needs of the individual victim, working within a feminist analysis of rape. Victims are supported through medical, police and legal procedures, and helped to ventilate feelings of anger, shame, humiliation and fear.

Alternative services for alcoholic and addicted women which incorporate self-help principles and a feminist analysis of the women's difficulties allow these women to transcend their self-hate and self-loathing, to stop viewing themselves as hopeless deviants who have failed to achieve society's traditional goals for women, and to gain a new sense of power and autonomy. With a sense of self-worth, and a radically different perspective on their lives, some women are able to give up their chemical dependency and often devote themselves to the treatment of other women who are similarly afflicted, or to other courses of social action.

The Post-Partum Counselling Service in Vancouver is an example of a feminist-oriented women's service which has a small staff of paid professionals but which functions largely along self-help lines. Initially, workers sought understanding of post-partum depression from medical and psychiatric texts. Finding these virtually useless, they have gradually evolved a treatment model for post-partum depression which is based on women's experience. Women who have recovered from such a depression work as volunteers and are assigned to newly referred women on a one-to-one basis. The volunteeers are available by phone, on a 24-hour basis, to offer support, understanding and advice based on their own experience. Groups for the depressed women, for their partners, and for couples all function to alleviate the women's feelings of uniqueness and sickness, and connect their feelings of distress and depression to sex role expectations, myths that surround pregnancy and motherhood, stresses within the family, and pressures from social structures.[10]

The alternatives that women have developed are a step in the direction of helping women to see their lives in a different perspective, aiding them to seek their rights, eliminating sex role stereotyping, and avoiding the contradictions of traditional therapy that we have described. However, as they are operating within, and are to some extent dependent on our present social structure, there are the ever-present dangers of co-optation, tokenism and exploitation. Women's educational programmes and services, like wives dependent on their husbands, are often dependent on the benevolence of the male-dominated power structure of government, university or profession. If they do not stretch the limits too far, they may be proudly shown off as an example of sensitivity to women's issues and absence of discrimination. If they become too demanding and contentious, they may find their funds cut off. All too often women's studies programmes are viewed as "frills" and faculty teaching in these programmes have, in some settings, found that their contribution to women's studies courses are not considered as "serious teaching." Again using the analogy of women in the nuclear family, women's educational programmes and services, like women in the home, are not taken seriously and often find themselves set apart and isolated — easy prey for the "divide and conquer" tactics of the male power structure. Women's services are kept marginal, compete with each other for limited funds, and are often forced to exist on yearly grants. Thus, a great deal of the staff's time and energy is diverted into yearly grant applications, seeking letters of support, and trying to devise ways of existing within traditional systems.

THE THEORY OF FEMINIST THERAPY

Feminist therapy rests on a body of experiences and on perspectives about women's lives which have gradually been built up by female novelists, diarists, writers, scholars, filmmakers and artists. Although the basic principles of feminist therapy are often sought, and sometimes assumed to be similar to those of other schools of therapy, there is no way that a general framework can be set out. A prolonged process of exposure to a variety of women's work is necessary. While Clara Thompson, Karen Horney, and a recent spate of feminist female psychiatrists have written about the vicissitudes of psychiatry, it is important to be aware of other sources outside the psychiatric frame. These include, among many others, Margaret Atwood, Maire-Claire Blais, Nicole Brossard, Phyllis Chesler, Mary Daly, Simone de Beauvoir, Barbara Ehrenreich, Dierdre English, Betty Friedan, Germain Greer, Elizabeth Janeway, Margaret Lawrence, Doris Lessing, Kate Millet,

Juliette Mitchell, Robin Morgan, Anais Nin, Marge Piercy, Adrienne Rich, Sheila Rowbotham, Gabrielle Roy, Dorothy Smith, and Dorothy Tennov.

From such authors one gains a clear sense of women's daily experiences, the stresses of their lives and the problems in their relationships. The invidious effect of oppression can be seen and the basis of traditional theories readily identified. For instance, Rich illustrates women's primary responsibility for their children, and their pervasive sense of guilt. Describing the birth of her first child, she says: "Soon I would begin to understand the full weight and burden of maternal guilt, then daily, nightly, hourly, *Am I doing what is right? Am I doing enough? Am I doing too much?* The institution of motherhood finds all mothers more or less guilty of having failed their children." Related also to women's full-time responsibility for their children are the feelings of murderous anger that can arise "because there was no one and nothing else on which to discharge anger."

Rich notes that women commonly have mothering attitudes towards men. She feels that this is one of the most insidious patterns between the sexes and stresses that when women equate men with children, men are infantilized and a massive amount of female energy is lost. Rich's chapters on mother-son and mother-daughter relationships deserve careful reading. She describes how a mother is expected to facilitate her son's involvement with the male world. She notes that all women, even those who are attempting to transcend the present inequality, are afraid of alienating their male children from their culture, and asks: ". . . do we fear that they will somehow lose their male status and privilege, even as we are seeking to abolish that inequality?" A woman who cannot express her rage, Rich stresses, may foster masculine aggressiveness in her son, creating self-fulfilling expectations, so that her son becomes a typical member of the male realm that has victimized her.

Depicting ambivalent, conflicting interactions between mother and daughter, Rich comments that "the anxious pressure of one female on another to conform to a degrading and dispiriting role can hardly be termed 'mothering' even if she does this believing it will help her daughter to survive." She underscores the process by which mothers hand on their own expectations and victimization to their daughters. In the context of rape, she highlights how mothers carry over their own guilt and hatred into their daughters' experiences: "The mother knows that if

raped she would feel guilty; hence she tells her daughter she *is* guilty."
Writing about the sad and unnecessary rivalry between mothers and
daughters, she relates it to her own experience of feeling that her
mother had sacrificed her to her father's needs and theories. Many
women, Rich emphasizes, feel anger and disgust towards their mothers,
whom they view as having led and modelled a life of compromise and
self-hatred.

Some female writers have tackled the relationship between psychiatry and women's oppression more specifically. *Women Look at
Psychiatry*[12] contains personal accounts of the experiences of psychiatric patients as well as chapters on sex role stereotypes, the psychiatric
oppression of women, pitfalls inherent in drawing conclusions from official statistics on mental illness, and the development of feminist
counselling. The editors, Dorothy Smith and Sara David, aim ". . . to
make visible how current psychiatric practice affects women, and to
offer readers a chance to learn from women's experiences in doing it
differently." Their goal is to bring understanding, information, critiques,
examples, ideas and concepts to women so that they can make sense of
their psychiatric experiences. Dorothy Smith[13] has shown how women
are forced into a second-hand understanding of the world. There is a
disjunction between women's actual experience and how they are told
to interpret it. Women are trained to invalidate their own experiences,
understanding and feelings, and to look to men to tell them how to
view themselves. The ideas, concepts, images and vocabularies that are
available to women with which to think about their experiences have
been formulated from the male viewpoint by universities, professions,
industries, and other organizations. These are reinforced by images of
women in the media: women's magazines, women's novels, women as
depicted in advertisements, in children's stories, and in movies. How,
she goes on to ask, can women understand their situation? Psychiatric
ideologies, she emphasizes, teach women to see their resentment and
despair about their place in the social structure as an individual problem, an emotional disorder.

In *Women and Madness*, Phyllis Chesler[14] describes women's
"careers" as psychiatric patients, pointing out that both individual
treatment by a psychiatrist and experiences in mental hospitals mirror
the female experience in the family. She describes interviews with 60
female patients, covering a wide range of age, class and ethnicity, and
with a variety of marital, maternal, sexual and political involvements.

She emphasizes that very few of the women appeared to have a mental disturbance, "Most were simply unhappy and destructive in typically (and approved) female ways." Pointing out that help-seeking behaviour is not valued or understood in our society, she notes that people needing help are mistrusted, pitied, physically beaten, given shock therapy, lied to, yelled at and eventually left to their own devices with the conviction that it is "all for their own good." She argues that many women in American mental hospitals perform sex-role stereotyped slave labour, working as domestics for little or no reward. Many of the women she studied suffered abuse or neglect by the medical system, some were sexually exploited, some experienced ridicule and abandonment by both professionals and family, and most received little "therapy," verbal or otherwise.

Psychologist Dorothy Tennov[15] comes to similar conclusions — that psychotherapy is hazardous, that the patient may be insulted and treated with disrespect, and that ". . . the bulk of women [sic] 'patients' are not mentally ill but particularly afflicted by the 'woman's situation.'" Her book is directed particularly towards psychodynamic psychotherapy which, she contends, is being aggressively promoted by a group of professionals ". . . far from ready to concede the defeat implied by doubts and qualifications expressed within their own journals."

Some female psychiatrists have written critically about traditional psychiatry and have proposed alternate views. Karen Horney questioned many of Freud's theories about personality development. A number of her papers included reformulations of women's development, and she pointed out that ". . . psychoanalysis is the creation of a male genius, and almost all of those who developed his ideas have been men."[16] Horney questioned Freud's claim that women's castration fantasies are caused by penis envy alone, and argued that they might have a number of roots,[17] including male envy of the female.[18] She took issue with the notion that female frigidity was a disease, stressing cultural factors and arguing that our male-oriented culture is "not favorable to the unfolding of woman, and her individuality."[19] Horney dismissed the belief that men have a greater tendency towards polygamy as a "tendentious confabulation in favor of men,"[20] and pointed out how a male-oriented psychology contributes to marital conflicts.[21] It has been suggested that Freud was acutely aware of Horney's criticism and may have specifically directed at her the comment, "We shall not be so very surprised if a woman analyst who has not been sufficiently convinced of her own desire for a penis also fails to assign adequate importance to that factor in her patients."[22] Thus, her criticism was dismissed as a function of her own psychological problems, a favourite way of discounting women or any critics of psychoanalysis.

Like Horney, Clara Thompson stresses that cultural conditions underly women's inferiority. She argues that the so-called feminine traits of narcissim, passivity, masochism, rigidity and the need to be loved are caused by economic helplessness. Penis envy, she notes, can only be viewed as a symbolic wish for a penis, equated with male power.[23] Because of their socially inferior position, women are more susceptible to neurotic disorders, and they must conflict with conventional expectations and values if they wish to fully utilize opportunities. In her later work, stressing growing opportunities for women, Thompson noted women's tendency to take on male characteristics: "having no path of their own to follow women have tended to copy men. Imitating a person superior to one is by no means unusual."[24]

More recently, Anne Seiden's review articles,[25] which drew attention to the relevance of research in "women's studies" to psychiatry, have been a useful resource for feminists. Seiden describes research on sex differences, sexual and reproductive life, family structure and child rearing, and the psychology of women at work and in the community. Discussing the implications of this research for the clinical treatment of women, Seiden shows how it brings back into central focus the adverse effects of psychotherapy. She writes of the devastating effect of sexual abuse on the therapeutic relationship; the "one down" position of women in therapy which is similar to that in marriage ". . . thus encouraging the fantasy that an idealized relationship with a more powerful other is a better solution to life problems than taking autonomous actions;" theories that support stereotypical assumptions and different standards of mental health for women; how women are harmed by "blame-the-mother" theories; and lack of recognition of the occupational hazards of the housewife role.

Seiden goes on to argue that the feminist perspective could catalyze major changes in social psychology over the next decade. With the involvement of more female researchers and a focus on women's lives, "We may hope to see clinical practice . . . increasingly based on solid research findings rather than the translation into professional language of what is essentially folklore."Female psychology will, she hazards, no longer consist of the psychology of the "other," the supporting cast. Males will no longer be viewed as prototypical members of the human race.

THE CHARACTERISTICS OF OPPRESSION

There are undeniable parallels between the situation, status and so-called "nature" of women, and those of victims of oppression, discrimination, marginality and minority status. Many of the characteristics attributed to women and ascribed to their biological endowment, innate inferiority or specific psychology, can equally be accounted for as the result of a prolonged and particular subordinate status in this society. An accumulation of material from a number of sources has led to a clear recognition of the relationship between oppression and the "psychology" of women. The study of colonized peoples, peasants, minority and marginal groups has produced consistent information about the common experiences and characteristics of members of these groups.[26] Much of this information has been brought to the fore by the radical psychiatry and psychology movements. Other writers have drawn attention to the parallels which exist between popular images and stereotypes of feminine behaviour and the characteristics of oppressed peoples.[27]

Allport, in his influential work on prejudice and its active manifestation in discrimination,[28] codified a variety of what he called "ego defences" found in victims of prejudice. Among them are a number that echo the traditional images of women and the tenets of their psychology. The development of socially pleasing traits such as fawning, sycophancy, or clowning are individual responses. These imply an underlying vigilance and hypersensitivity to the dominant mode. In order to survive, slaves, prisoners and outcasts manifest withdrawal, passivity, acquiesence and the outward appearance of satisfaction. A common response to the deprivation inherent in subordination is the leading of a compartmentalized life or consciousness, compensating in dreams or fantasy. Survival through slyness or cunning has led to accusations throughout history that subordinates are dishonest or tricky. In these circumstances the common reaction of denial of membership in the oppressed group and identification with the dominant group can produce self-hate, especially if there is no pretense involved and the subordinates actually agree with the dominant group's evaluation and see themselves through the dominants' eyes. This can lead either to the self-fulfilling prophecy of acquiring the attributed traits and thus becoming the stereotype, or to aggression against one's own group. Other ways of responding to subordinate status include symbolic status-striving via flashy displays and sexual conquests. Such activities are intended to induce pride and self-respect. Subordinates may react with extreme prejudice against the oppressor or with equally extreme compassion, sympathy and understanding for others. They may fight back via militant action, or undertake enhanced striving, redoubling their efforts in any sphere open to them and sometimes evoking grudging admiration. Allport states that the anxiety and anger caused by open rebellion could lead to mental illness and collapse, and that high-achieving subordinates are often abused for being too industrious and clever. Finally, he indicates that victims of prejudice may manifest neuroticism, but feels that this label is less appropriate for them than that of occupying marginal status. He presents the example of Lewin's work with adolescents which demonstrated the storm and stress created for adolescents because they are never certain whether they will be admitted into the adult world or not.

Jean Baker Miller, herself a practising psychoanalyst, uses the understanding of relations between dominant and subordinate groups as a theme and basis for her recent book, *Toward a New Psychology of Women.*[29] She isolates certain characteristics of subordinate groups as typical of any irrationally unequal power relation based on ascribed status such as race, religion or sex. Those in a relation of subordination need to survive above all. Direct response to destructive treatment must be avoided, along with self-interested and open action, since it may be met with rejection, punishment or even death. Women who step out of line, Miller notes, can suffer a combination of social ostracism, economic hardship and psychological isolation. They may even be diagnosed as having a personality disorder.

Yet women are different from members of other oppressed groups in that they must often live in intimate and intense relationships with males. Women cannot express their resentment openly; conflict is usually covert, expressed in subtle ways such as a wife's slow and invidious deprecation of her spouse's abilities as a husband, father and breadwinner. Disguised reactions and indirect action often contain hidden defiance under the guise of pleasing or accommodating the powerful group. Television comedies of the "I Love Lucy" variety often contain elements of outwitting or manipulating the boss or husband or making covert fun of him. Because the dominant groups fail to perceive this mode of operating, they seldom have the chance to recognize their impact on others or to gain a valid understanding of subordinates. This, Miller comments, is ". . . particularly ironic since . . . the societal 'experts' in knowledge about subordinates are usually members of the dominant group."

Miller focuses on the fact that women are closely involved with, and attached to, physical, emotional and mental growth and change as their children mature. The awareness that fostering growth in others is their only valid role detracts from their ability to enjoy their children's growth, as does the isolation, loneliness and drudgery of the setting in which they work. Miller notes that women's responsibility for the emotional relationships in the family, for child care and for housework are seen to be less valued tasks. They are "essential," but are outside the "real world." She emphasizes that "women work with the pervaisve sense that what they do does not matter as much as what men do."

The subordinates, then, are the ones who have the opportunity to know and understand the dominant group. Indeed, they must do so in order to predict what will please or displease those on whom their fate depends. "Feminine wiles" and "feminine intuition" are easily seen in this context as the skills that long practice has developed into a fine art of interpretation of verbal and nonverbal cues. This focus on the powerful goup often means that subordinates know more about the dominants than they know about themselves. Self-knowledge is difficult to gain without accurate reflection or a realistic evaluation of capabilities and experiences. In these circumstances it is easy to absorb the untruths disseminated by the dominant group and to believe that any inequality is a result of inferiority and inadequacy. If there are few alternative concepts with which to explain the situation, it is even easier to internalize dominant beliefs. Yet it is also true that subordinates may have an accurate view of the injustice of their position, one which comes into conflict with the ideas they have absorbed from the dominants. This almost inevitably generates inner tension.

Psychologists and psychiatrists use the term "identification with the aggressor" to describe the way in which members of a less powerful group imitiate their oppressors or destructively treat members of their own group. Another form of this identification is to attempt to gain power by oppressing those who are in any way subordinate to one's own position. Fanon[30] describes the use of black police and torturers to enorce the rule of white colonial powers in Madagascar, while Daly[31] recounts the barbarous treatment which women inflict on their daughters to make them acceptable to men in various cultures. "Uncle Toms" have been in this position and the behaviour of some successful professional women has been sufficiently marked as both imitative of male standards and unsympathetic to other women's struggles to earn the title of "Queen Bee."

Despite the obstacles, oppressed groups have an historic tendency to strive for greater freedom. It is difficult, however, to find records of such efforts upon which to base a supporting tradition or history since the dominant culture fails to preserve them. Open conflict occurs to the extent that subordinates demand freedom of expression, expose inequalities and question the basis of its existence.

An important distinction must be made between those who realize that they belong to a subordinate group and those who do not.[32] Clear recognition of subordinate status, and one's right to challenge it, radically alters one's perspective of self and society. Most blacks now recognize their subordinate status and have made many strides towards equality. Most women still fail to perceive their minority status and may resist or impede the efforts of those women who do press for change.

For instance, in the course of the current women's movement some female psychiatrists have become aware of the male-oriented nature of their discipline, the biases and discrimination to which women patients are exposed and to which they too, are subject. Others, however, practise in a manner that is indistinguishable from that of their male colleagues. They can be heard espousing traditional psychiatric theories, they tend to decry women's services, and express irritation about women who are demanding a female therapist. These female psychiatrists never raise their voices in support of women's issues and, like many female doctors, will claim that they have never been treated unequally and never been discriminated against in medical school, residency or in practice. The presence of many "Queen Bees," women who could be described as having "identified with the aggressor," creates many problems. One cannot assume, as male psychiatrists who are sympathetic to women's concerns do, that any female psychiatrist in a position of power or influence will promote a feminist perspective, or that any female psychiatrist will bring the principles of feminist therapy to bear in her work with female patients. Simply referring female patients to a female therapist is not, unfortunately, a remedy against sexist treatment.

FEMINIST THERAPY

Because it draws on the background of women's experience, feminst therapy is a perspective rather than a technique.[33] The therapist must be a feminist with a firm commitment to feminist values; feminist therapy cannot be treated as another school of therapy with a set of "how to's." Feminist therapists come from diverse schools of psychotherapy and use a variety of techniques in their work. They are however, united by common bonds, and some general principles can be identified.

Hallmarks of feminist therapy are its commitment to feminist principles, the application of a feminist analysis to the women's current situation, and its grounding in current research about women.[34] The approach is egalitarian, with a careful avoidance of the one-down position and a recognition of the importance of the therapist as a role model.[35] Feminist therapists spell out their own values to women who seek their guidance, and make full use of self-disclosure as it relates to shared experiences.

Commitment to feminist principles leads proponents of feminist therapy to value collective rather than hierarchical structures, and to stress the equal sharing of resources, power and responsibility.[36] Feminist therapists often work in groups or collectives where each member has an equal share in decision-making and in defining goals and priorities. Group therapy is often the preferred mode. Therapeutic strategies are centred around maintaining and enhancing the woman's power and responsibility. Responsibility in this instance, however, has different connotations from those sometimes advanced by adherents of the Human Potential Movement. Most women feel guilty and responsible for their own and their families' difficulties. These feelings are constantly reinforced by the kinds of images and stereotypes which we have already considered, and by the social structures which lie behind the symbolic forms. Shedding all-pervasive guilt and recognizing the realistic limits and possibilities of responsibility are important features of the therapeutic process. Feminist therapy usually incorporates "sex role analysis"[37] with a comparison of the costs and benefits of traditional and feminist values. The woman works with the therapist, or therapist and group, to make a contract delineating her goals and objectives and the number of sessions she will attend. Open files are maintained and a woman may join her therapist in writing a progress note or a report that might be required by any outside agency. Most accounts of feminist therapy address issues for individual women or women in groups. Alternatively, feminist-oriented family therapy may enable a family to recognize and change the destructive consequences of stereotyped roles and expectations in the family.[38]

A number of accounts of feminist therapy which lay out principles and techniques are now available.[39] Rather than attempting to summarize and integrate these accounts, we have chosen to present a description of the changes that the dedication to feminist principles have brought to the work of one of the authors, P.S. Penfold.

APPLYING FEMINIST PRINCIPLES TO WORK AS A CHILD AND FAMILY THERAPIST

As I have become increasingly involved in feminism, my style of working with families has gradually changed. Many of these families come to a multidisciplinary pediatric clinic, where I work as psychiatric consultant, with a child who is the identified patient. Very few families are looking for a feminist therapist, and I do not try to impose my values on them. A feminist perspective, however, allows a different kind of understanding of family interactions and patterns, and is likely to open up some alternate ways of management.

Attempts to conceptualize my own merging of feminism and psychiatry were very painful and difficult until I realized that I tended to devalue and consider suspect those understandings which arose from my own experiences as a woman, mother and wife. This tendency is linked to my medical and psychiatric training which has deeply imbued me with the conviction that one's approach should be rational and scientific, and to my conditioning as a woman which tells me that my work isn't serious or of any value.

A review of typed reports and case notes made over the past decade shows up this deficiency and highlights my need to present my findings in a fairly traditional format. The selective process involved in writing a psychiatric case history is evident. What is written down seems bare and sterile compared with the rich set of imporessions that I have of the family and how we worked together. How I feel as people describe their problems and difficulties is absent. Little is recorded about how I identify with their situation, reach out, talk about myself and my children, and use myself and my own experiences to help clarify problems and feelings. I do not describe the process of nonverbal interaction, modelling, and giving permission to talk about feelings. I have found it difficult to set forth the multiple nuances and inter-actions which seem to leave the woman in the family feeling under-stood, cared for and less guilty. It also gives her a clearer view of how she has reached a particular place in her life and some grasp of the things she needs to do for herself, and for and with her family.

Writing this book, speaking in the community about counselling women and about feminist therapy, teaching psychiatric residents about women and psychotherapy, and my own sense of confusion about "What is feminist therapy?" have combined to force me to stop feeling apologetic about my "unscientific" and intuitive approach to families, and to acknowledge that I am able to make a constructive blend of feminism with knowledge about child development, tempera-mental endowment, family dynamics, and various methods of interven-tion.

To the therapy of women, and of women and their families, I bring an awareness of current research about women and a recognition of societal and environmental determinants as a basis for problems. Labels that have already been attached to a woman or a family are ignored. My usual practice is to get the description of the problem directly from the family without reading referral information, thus avoiding preconceived ideas. Contracts are used, with families taking part in decisions about goals, objectives and the number of sessions required. Families are given copies of reports or may help to write them, and they are included in conferences with other related professionals. Creating dependency is avoided. The emphasis is on responsibility, strengths, and the person's or the family's own support systems. The assumption that the woman in the family is competent is particularly important, as women are considered, and often consider themselves, to be weak, dependent and inadequate. Similarly, creating or reinforcing guilt or blame is avoided.

However, a woman may need to see her own responsibility for a particular pattern of behaviour in herself or in the family. When a woman is able to see her life experience from a different perspective, she can recognize how her struggles and frustrations have affected the rest of the family — without blaming herself or feeling individually and uniquely culpable.

My focus includes helping the woman to examine her own self-defeating patterns, to see how she allows herself to be victimized. Women need to understand how they can feed into their own situation of inequality and oppression. Many women have a pervasive feeling of shame, a conviction of perpetual wrongness which is induced by their birth into the "wrong sex" or "the second sex" and their socialization as a subordinate. External oppression is internalized and converted into self-oppression or even into self-hatred and self-mutilation. Women sometimes use society's romantic myths about courtship, love and marriage to combat their feelings of shame and perpetual wrongness and to blot out feelings of embarrassment, inadequacy and loneliness. In their inner fantasies they may depict themselves as beautiful, elegant, sophisticated, poised, fashionably dressed, wealthy, well-travelled and compellingly attractive to men. The harsh reality of the gap between their own lives and the romantic myths leads to further feelings of inadequacy and failure.

As a woman, mother of three children, ex-wife and single parent, I find that my personal experiences can be selectively used and discussed with a woman or a family in order to illustrate various problems and difficulties. Thus, I try to blend a feminist perspective with use of my own knowledge, various treatment techniques, and a variety of community resources to make a constructive plan with a woman and her family.

An abbreviated case report, written in an attempt to accent the therapist's role and highlight the woman and her life experiences, may serve to illustrate these points.

■   The C.s brought their seven-year-old daughter to the Clinic. Juliette was not doing well in school, was overweight, and her behaviour at home greatly irritated her mother. Juliette, she emphasized, was restless, stubborn, easily distracted, irritable and sensitive.

Mrs. C., an attractive and well-dressed woman, was tense, self-effacing, and spoke in a quiet, low tone of voice. She seemed intent on minimizing any problems at home apart from the difficulties with Juliette. Mr. C. talked about being home only four days in every two or three months. I asked Mrs. C. how she felt about this and she contended, at length, that it didn't make any difference to the family (mother, Juliette and younger sister). I commented that I felt puzzled by her apparent outer calm and lack of emotional response to a situation that I would find trying.

In obtaining Juliette's "developmental history" I discovered that Juliette had been active, restless, sensitive and easily distracted right from birth. This reminded me of my son, so I talked about how baffled and guilty I had been as a parent. I commented about children's temperamental endowment, and how some children are much harder to bring up than others.

In the process of piecing together a "family history" we moved on to talk about the parents' backgrounds. Mrs. C. described her mother as the dominant parent, who ran down her father, bossed him around, and tried to run everyone's lives by frequently telling them how grateful they should be. I was aware of similarities to my own mother and commented that parents like that could make children feel very guilty. Flashing through my head at the same time was my awareness of how easy it was to blame my mother, and how difficult it was for me to see my father's role in the problem.

Mrs. C. went on to describe how they had gone to visit with her parents, in another city, about two years ago. A few hours after their departure, and following an argument with Mrs. C., her mother had committed suicide. I was struck by Mrs. C.'s lack of observable feelings as she recounted this, and by my own feeling of how intensely guilt-producing this would be for me if my mother were to kill herself in this way. I said, emphatically, "How awful that must have been for you!" at the same time thinking about psychiatric formulations of suicide as an intensely hostile act, one aimed at producing guilt in other members of the family.

Juliette, a dumpy and rather unappealing seven-year-old, seemed disinterested and diffident as she talked about home, school and her few friends. She was uneasy and restless. I found myself feeling that she would be a hard child to like or feel spontaneous with.

After seeing Juliette, I talked with the C.s again, attempting to get an initial understanding of the problem. I commented on the child's difficult temperament and the problems that the family might be experiencing related to grandmother's suicide and father's absence, suggesting a few further sessions to talk about these issues. Mr. C. wouldn't be available but Mrs. C. agreed that she would like a few sessions to talk about Juliette, their relationship, and her own feelings. We agreed on three sessions.

During her next session, I asked Mrs. C. about female friends. She replied that she had none, and didn't need any as she was busy enough looking after the house and the girls. I expressed surprise, saying that it sounded rather lonely to me. We talked about her husband's absences; she claimed again that she didn't mind, adding that she felt he rather enjoyed being away from the family. I felt she was putting herself down, perhaps blaming herself for her husband's wish to be away, so I commented that I was puzzled by her contention that she didn't care, and wondered whether she felt she didn't deserve her husband's presence at home. We talked about ways of promoting Juliette's self-confidence, and Mrs. C. said that she was spending half-an-hour every evening, with Juliette alone, playing a game or engaging in a hobby.

On the next occasion, Mrs. C. came with her husband. I noticed them laughing and talking together in the waiting room. Mrs. C. said that she felt much better about Juliette, more relaxed with her and more tolerant of her behaviour. She told me that they were going to buy a smaller home "because my husband is rarely home and it's too much for me to keep up by myself." Hesitantly, she went on to talk about how isolated she felt from the other women in her neighbourhood, presenting this as one of the reasons she wanted to move. She commented that "They all withdrew from me after my mother's suicide, and didn't ask me to go to anything." I said that I was surprised that that would be their reaction, rather than feeling sympathetic. We talked some more about her mother's death and about relationships in the family. This time she talked resentfully about her father, saying " 'Til this year I used to think that it was all my mother's fault, as he used to make out that he was always picked on." She described how he had called up after her mother's death and blamed her for it. My reaction was to comment on the burden of guilt and blame she had gotten as a result.

Several week later Mrs. C. came back for a final session. This time she was bouncier and more open with her feelings. She said that she had done a great deal of thinking over the previous weeks. Since her mother's death she had realized "I've been in a real slump." The reaction of her neighbours was put into a different perspective and she now felt, "I don't think they really avoided me. I felt so miserable I didn't want to relate to them." She described feeling reluctant to leave the house since her mother's death, avoiding new situations, parties and friends because she felt very nervous, found her heart beating rapidly and her face flushing. Her doctor told her that she was suffering from agoraphobia and had given her tranquilizers that made her feel detached, sleepy and even less like going out. Now she felt that the only way to overcome her fears was to "Get going out into the world. I've met a few women in my new neighbourhood, I've enrolled in the tailoring course that I have put off for years, and I am taking pottery with Juliette." We spent some time talking about relationships with other women and how supportive they can be. Mrs. C. complained, "It seems to take women a long time to like me." We discussed this both in terms of her tendency to cover up her feelings, to appear cool, calm and collected and also in terms of the competition that goes on between women and how it keeps them isolated from each other. Mrs. C. commented, "Sometimes people have thought I was snobby, but I am really quite shy and take a long time to warm up to people." I suggested that Mrs. C. try to share her feelings of inadequacy and nervousness with female friends.

Mrs. C. went on to talk about her marriage. It had not gone well since her mother's death and she and her husband had thought about separating. In fact, his present job was a compromise, a trial separation in many ways. Since coming to the Clinic, emphasized Mrs. C., their relationship was much improved; "We feel we have a second chance. . . . He will soon be getting a job as supervisor much nearer home." Both Juliette and Mrs. C. had gone on a diet, and were going swimming. Mrs. C. related her own feelings of depression, apathy, isolation and lack of interest in caring for her body by exercising and keeping her weight down with the development of some of the same problems in Juliette. She felt very positively about working together on diet and exercise, and remarked again that her relationship with Juliette was warmer, more relaxed, and seemed better for both of them.

At the end of this session, Mrs. C. and I attempted to summarize what had transpired during the four sessions that she had come to the Clinic and the thinking that she had done in between. She said that she felt "understood, not so guilty, especially when you talked about your own feelings about your children. I felt treated as a person, and also sometimes stimulated and challenged." She had been particularly struck, she said, by her realization that her contention that she did not need any female friends did not seem valid and that she was walling herself off from people. She felt that "I have got enough out of this now to go on by myself," but was encouraged to call me in the future if she wanted to discuss anything.

A traditional psychodynamic formulation of this case would focus on Mrs. C.'s unresolved Oedipus complex, her hostility towards her mother, who was seen as dominating and depriving, and her guilt and self-blame when her mother killed herself. A description of her defences against anxiety would note projection ("the other women dislike me"), denial ("I don't need any friends," and "I don't mind my husband being away"), isolation of affect (her lack of emotional involvement), and displacement (agoraphobia − her anxiety stemming from inner conflicts is displaced onto outside forces). Her depression might very easily be formulated as related to the loss of her mother, to fantasized loss of her husband, to loss of self-esteem and to inturned anger. If the therapist's role was examined, her counter-transference, and her own unresolved Oedipal conflict, would doubtless come to light. Mrs. C.'s identification with her mother would be stressed, and her ambivalent relationship to Juliette noted to be similar to that of Mrs. C. and her mother. Similarly, problems in the marital relationship would be attributed to unresolved elements in Mrs. C.'s relationship to her father. Treatment approaches based on this formulation might include psychotherapy for Mrs. C., with a lengthy exploration of her feelings towards her parents, or psychotherapy for Mrs. C. and Juliette.

Alternatively, an emphasis on the biological basis of depression would lead to the prescription of anti-depressants for Mrs. C. A behaviour therapy program for her presumed "learned helplessness" might require her husband to be co-therapist. Many other approaches to this family might be suggested, depending on the orientation of the therapist, including family therapy, marital therapy, group therapy for Juliette, a mothers' group for Mrs. C., and directive parent counselling about the child's problem.

While recognizing Mrs. C.'s anxiety and depression, and the use of various coping mechanisms, I chose to work with her in a way that emphasized her strengths, competence, resourcefulness and responsibility, and put her current situation into perspective as a woman, wife and mother. Her perception of other women as critical, distant and in competition with her was questioned. My self-disclosure about my own child, and the discussion of children's temperamental endowment reduced guilt and self-blame. She did much of the work herself and was able to see how her own struggles had affected Juliette. This realization, however, did not produce guilt and blame, but mobilized energy directed towards getting both of them out of a rut.

In steering away from guilt-laden, mother-blaming theories, we have to avoid throwing the baby out with the bath water. Seeing the C. family's difficulties as entirely externally determined would not be helpful either. Mrs. C. needed help to understand the pattern of her life, and to concentrate on areas she was avoiding. My approach, focusing on her experiences as woman, wife and mother allowed her to see how these had affected both herself and other family members. Thus, needed changes became apparent.

CONCLUSION

During the last decade much light has been cast on women's experience and perspective, particularly by literature that is outside the psychiatric framework. A new psychology of women is beginning. Yet women are still attempting to frame their experiences in a language that is imbued with male terms, male expectations and male definitions. New work will have to find clear and unambiguous ways to describe women's world, and reassess from women's standpoint such concepts as shame, guilt, autonomy, actualisation, individuation and, above all, femininity and its relation to femaleness, if any.

Concurrently, women have been moving into positions of leadership and gaining influence within their professions, spearheading educational programmes in universities and community colleges, and initiating a wide range of alternate services for women. Gains, although impressive in some areas, have been limited and constrained in others, for instance in the traditional and male-dominated psychiatric establishment. Many obstacles remain and much change will have to take place before alternate services gain credibility and a secure funding base, and before women have an equal voice in the mental health professions.

A feminist perspective and the various analyses that grow out of it lead to a different view of both the problems and treatment of women from those held by traditional psychiatry. Many women seek psychiatric help because it is the only kind of help that seems valid and is also covered by medical insurance. Feminists believe that much of the misery and distress that women experience does not require therapy or treatment in the traditional sense. Women need to gain a sense of self, and to develop assertiveness, independence and an accurate perspective of the difficulties and obstacles for women in this society. For many women, enrollment in a women's study course or participation in a con-sciousness-raising group leads to the recognition of the implications of their programming as females, their place in dominant-subordinate male-female relationships, and their constant bombardment from the surrounding culture with its exhortations to be "feminine," suspicious of other women, nurturant, compliant and submissive. In most cases, the recognition and the experience of sharing with, and receiving support from other women leads to a different perspective of the world and of the self which allows for self-assertion, growth and change. Some women, however, are so paralysed by internalized, oppressive views of women's nature, so laden with self-hate, so convinced of their total inadequacy as wives or mothers, so blamed from within and without, that involvement in a women's studies course or a women's group may not suffice, and can contribute to a downward spiral of guilt, inade-quacy and self-blame. These women may need more extended forms of help and support of the kind described as feminist therapy.

≡   ≡   ≡

≡*CONCLUSION*

WE HAVE COME TO SEE THAT
as Rich points out, ". . . masculine ideologies are the creation of masculine subjectivity; they are neither objective, nor value-free, nor inclusively 'human.' Feminism implies that we recognize fully the inadequacy for us, the distortion, of male-created ideologies, and that we proceed to think, and act out of that recognition."[1] Women's perspective has provided us with a radical critique which reveals the essentially ideological nature of the psychiatric enterprise. Psychiatry uses its formulations to maintain the psychiatric version of reality and to play its part in organizing and administering segments of society, as well as seeking to serve the patient population. By doing so it obscures the possibility of understanding the actualities of certain people's lives in ways other than those offered by psychiatry. Thus it defuses the possibility of other actions or solutions to people's difficulties. We have seen that this is doubly effective for women who do not have a chance to represent their own experience in the male world. The struggle by women to begin to do this has already revealed significant gaps in our understanding of how society actually operates. We are beginning to see how our consciousness of what is "natural" and "normal" comes to us from the specific forms of organization of current society, though it is often couched in the language of myth and tradition.

Psychiatry has gone hand in hand with the rest of the medical profession, not only in supporting existing views of women, but in providing an even more comprehensive ideology to institutionalize their oppression as an inevitable "fact of life," and in developing practices that both reflect and enforce that oppression.

243

PROBLEMS WITHIN PSYCHIATRY

The institution of psychiatry presents itself as healing, benign and compassionate while obscuring its function as part of the apparatus through which society is ordered. While psychiatry's function as a social regulator can clearly be seen in the hospitalization of people who are thought to be a danger to the community, more subtle manifestations can be detected in the rationales for administering psychotropic drugs, and in the goals set in behavioural therapy and psychotherapy. Where women are concerned, most psychiatric theories and practices validate the male as prototype, legitimize women's second-class status as male property, validate dominant-subordinate relationships between men and women, re-inforce the institution of Motherhood as a sacred calling, urge women to view their identity in terms of their success as wife, mother and sexual companion, and reflect descriptions and prescriptions based on archetypal images. Thus, psychiatry is a very powerful force towards preserving a situation which works for the material gain of men.

Psychiatry sees itself as neutral and relatively independent of the state, along with business, the legal system and other professions. Like other professions, however, it can be seen to be one of the institutional forms whereby the work of organizing and administering society is ac-complished. These institutional forms are the ideological structures through which state control is exercised in the interest of those in dominant social positions. The inter-relationships become clear, for example, in the case of the pharmaceutical and alcohol industries which flourish and expand while psychiatric theories and attitudes allow the responsibility for needing psychoactive drugs or alcohol to be focused on the individual alone. By concentrating on the individual, psychiatry can also be seen to be protecting males, with theories and attitudes towards rape, wife battering, incest and prostitution which rationalize or normalize male behaviour and blame women and female children for their own victimization.

As part of scientific medicine, psychiatry claims to have a body of knowledge from which to derive an "expert-service model." In actuality it often sets forth the moral strictures of a given society and includes a confusing array of contradictory theories which may flourish if they happen to fit current social trends. As a whole it is not comprised of a well-researched and scientific body of knowledge. Although many psychiatrists are uncomfortably aware of contradictions and difficulties, the response to criticism seldom includes a re-examination of the fundamental assumptions of the discipline. Most commonly the answer is sought in such measures as bringing psychiatry closer to its "medical origins," in concentrating on "biological psychiatry," in re-defining the "medical model" *per se,* in developing new classifications of psychiatric disorder, and in attempting to create new or different methods of service delivery. These responses serve to reinforce psychiatry as a medical enterprise yet fail to confront the issue of psychiatry's implication in the process of the increasing medicalization of social problems as a form of social control.

Psychiatry purports to diagnose and classify dysfunction in an individual or a family and apply appropriate treatment. In fact, this attribution of responsibility to the individual or family often takes the form of "blaming the victim" and thus obscures the role of social systems in the production of distress and damage.

"Blame the victim" models lead to the scapegoating of mothers, blaming the rape victim and battered wife, dismissing the prostitute as primitive or deviant, accusing the alcoholic's wife of causing her husband's downfall, pointing the finger at the little girl who is assumed to have seduced her innocent father, and attributing women's addiction to tranquilizers to neuroticism and inadequacy.

Psychiatry presents itself as knowledgeable about women, focusing on women as wives and mothers and on their role in the family. In actuality, however, women's lives are invisible in many areas of theory. Little is written about the development of the female child, the adolescent girl, the single woman, the elderly woman, or the alcoholic or drug-addicted woman. Women's sexuality is seen only in conjunction with, and as an adjunct to men's. Lesbianism, at least until recently, has been seen as pathological, if considered as an issue at all. Much is written about women in their socially valuable roles as wives and mothers. The psychology of women is presented as a collection of characteristics which are biologically endowed, unique and necessary to women. They are seen to be rooted in differences between male and female brains, in different expressions of genes or hormones and to be part of the "natural order of things." Clinicians rely on the presence or absence of these traits to enable them to distinguish between mentally healthy and deviant women. These characteristics, however, are typical of any oppressed group of people. Compliance, submissiveness, lack of initiative, dependency, and sensitivity to the needs and feelings of others are qualities seen in oppressed peoples, as are the manifestations of rage and despair so often experienced as mental illness.

The consumer of psychiatry, the person who comes for help to the psychiatrist, mental health professional or general practioner who relies on the quick application of psychiatric principles, is likely to be completely unaware of the contradictions within the institution. Many consumers believe in the scientific and expert knowledge claimed by psychiatry and, moreoever, share the cultural belief systems on which the theories are based. Thus a psychiatric formulation may make sense to a consumer on several different levels. Women, for instance, are socialized to accept full responsibility for the happiness and success of the family and are subtly conditioned into their subordinate second-class role while being told this will be the source of great gratification. Women are therefore often ready to look for the cause in themselves and to accept the patient role, medication and other measures that both they and their therapist may perceive as necessary to help them cope with and adjust to their situations. Two-thirds of psychiatric patients, or persons attending general practioners' offices, who are given psychiatric diagnoses, are women. Women are prescribed two-and-a-half to six times as many psychotropic drugs as men. Women are urged to adjust to, cope and be happy with their duties as wives and mothers; or if single, are encouraged to see their problems as stemming from the lack of a husband and children. Their difficulties, distress and resentment are seen as individual problems that must be transcended. Women, who are trained to be more compliant, may fall more readily into a sick role or "patient career" and are more likely to take drugs which are prescribed for them. Clinicians are seldom aware of the social control functions that they are performing, do not appreciate the massive societal obstacles that women face, and often have little understanding of the problems that stem from dominant-subordinate relationships between men and women.

IMPLICATIONS AND DIRECTIONS

It is evident, from women's standpoint, that we need better ways of describing and accounting for the way in which society is organized and governed, and the part that psychiatry plays in this. We need theories and practices which address the actual lives of women (and of men), and the distress and dysfunction from which they suffer. Although definitive knowledge of the nature of "psychiatric" disturbance is lacking, research has begun to suggest the psycho-biological, cultural and social correlates which are implicated in the definition of mental illness. Certain altered states of consciousness, such as those described under the diagnostic categories of schizophrenia and particular forms of depression, appear to have some relationship to genetic factors. These conditions are found to exist in a small proportion of the population, historically and cross-culturally. Such people exhibit strikingly similar forms of inappropriate, bizarre or violent behaviour. It seems probable that knowledge concerning these states is at an analogous stage to the understanding of the relationship of fever to illness in the medical sciences prior to the development of germ theory and the availability of adequate technology to pursue research into epidemiology.

Much rigorous exploration is needed in order to recognize and expand upon the useful knowledge of human functioning that psychiatry has accumulated within its ideology. This is one of the issues which must be faced. Even in the best of all possible worlds it would seem, at this stage of knowledge at least, that there will be a need for true asylum, refuge and protection for those who are distressed or who cause distress and danger to others in society. It is clear that a better way of recognizing to whom this applies is necessary, and that the institution of psychiatry at this time contains too many processes of "invisible judgement" to provide the expert service which it proposes. Furthermore, an understanding of the ways in which this is a world disastrously out of tune with human needs is fundamental to revising our ideas of how to offer help and support to those who suffer, at the individual level, the damage and strain which our social structures impose.

Such an understanding is not neutral. It is, in a non-partisan sense, a political stance; one which acknowledges that this is not the best of all possible worlds for many who live in it. This acknowledgment implies a commitment to action and to change for those who purport to have at heart the interests of those who suffer the costs. A commitment of this nature would require the development of a psychiatry that would truly be *for* the patient, not one that obscures the human costs of our present forms of social organization by presenting an ideology which accounts for and contains damage and distress within the individual who experiences it. A psychiatry that is not prepared to confront these issues is clearly not on the side of the patient, and certainly not neutral, but declares its allegiance to the ruling apparatus and its commitment to the maintenance of the system at the cost of those individuals who fail to adjust to its demands and strictures. To be other than a sophisticated form of adjustment therapy requires an intensive re-evaluation and restructuring of the very ways of thinking and acting which make up psychiatry as it now stands. This will allow us to see how psychiatry can contain elements which make it helpful and healing for some and exploitative for others, and to distinguish between them.

In searching for ways to approach this mammoth and complex undertaking, women's perspectives must play a crucial part. "If we conceive our feminism as more than a frivolous label, if we conceive of it as an ethics, methodology, a more complex way of thinking about, thus more responsible acting upon, the conditions of human life, we need a self-knowledge which can only develop through a steady, passionate attention to *all* female experience."[2] It is not, however, merely a matter of including women's experience in an overall picture. The implication is broader. Women have hitherto been defined only in terms of men. Men are not the sum total of humanity (although this has been obscured); therefore what we "know" of men and of humanity is also incomplete and represents a partial reality. As Rich points out, ". . . the lives of men cannot be understood by burying the lives of women; . . . to make visible the full meaning of women's experience, to reinterpret knowledge in terms of that experience, is now the most important task of thinking."[3]

It is this task which lies ahead if women (and men) are to resolve the psychiatric paradox.

≡   ≡   ≡

I: A CRITIQUE OF THE HISTORY OF PSYCHIATRY

1. Engel, G., "The Need for a New Medical Model: A Challenge for Biomedicine," *Science*, 196, 4286 (1977), 130.
2. Watzlawick, P., Weakland, J. and Fisch, P., *Change: Principles of Problem Formulation and Problem Resolution* (New York: W. W. Norton & Co. Inc, 1974).
3. Zola, I.K., "Medicine as an Institution of Social Control," *Sociological Review*, 20 (1972), 487-504.
4. Mora, George, "Historical and Theoretical Trends in Psychiatry," in *Comprehensive Textbook of Psychiatry*, Vol. 1, 2nd Edition, Freedman, Kaplan and Sadock, eds. (Baltimore: Williams & Wilkins, 1975), pp. 1-75.
5. Khun, T.S., *The Structure of Scientific Revolutions*, 2nd Edition (Chicago: Univ. of Chicago Press, 1970), Sections I and XI.
6. Ibid., p. 1.
7. For example: Mora, "Historical and Theoretical Trends in Psychiatry"; Bromberg, W., *The Mind of Man: A History of Psychotherapy and Psychoanalysis* (New York: Harper Colophon, 1963 Edition, revision of Harper & Bros., 1937); Ackerknecht, E.A., *A Short History of Psychiatry* (New York: Hafner, 1968, First Edition, 1979); Hobbs, T., "Mental Health's Third Revolution," in *Perspectives in Community Mental Health*, A.J. Bindman and A.D. Spiegel, eds. (Chicago: Aldine Publishing, 1969); Bassuk, E.L. and Gerson, S. "Deinstitutionalization and Mental Health Seminars," *Scientific American*, 238, 2, 1978.
8. Hobbs, 1969.
9. Bromberg, 1963, p. 17.
10. Ibid., p. 28.
11. Mora, 1975, p. 24.

12. Hobbs, 1969, p. 30.

13. Rome, H.P., "Psychiatry and Foreign Affairs," *Am. J. Psychiatry*, 125 (1968), 725-730.

14. Caplan, Ruth, *Psychiatry and the Community in Nineteenth Century America* (New York: Basic Books, 1969), p. 313.

15. Ibid.

16. Mora, 1975, p. 1.

17. Ibid.

18. Ibid., p.8.

19. Kuhn, 1970, p. 3.

20. Ibid.

21. Agassi, J., *Toward a Historiography of Science* (The Hague: Moulton, 1963).

22. Mora, 1975, p. 71.

23. Ibid., p. 1.

24. Ibid., P. 72.

25. Kuhn, 1970, p. 138.

26. Cunningham, M., Review of *Textbook of Disturbances of Mental Life or Disturbances of the Soul, Canada's Mental Health*, 26 (1978), 2.

27. Bromberg, 1963, pp. 9, 76, 110.

28. Bromberg, ibid., p. 48.

29. Smith, D.E., "Women and Psychiatry," in *Women Look at Psychiatry*, D.E. Smith and S. David, eds. (Vancouver: Press Gang Publishers, 1975).

30. Ibid., and in seminar presentations and lectures in advanced Women's Studies and Sociology of Knowledge, University of British Columbia, Fall 1976 to Spring 1977.

31. Hollingshead, A.B. and Redlich, F.C., *Social Class and Mental Illness* (New York: John Wiley & Sons, 1958).

32. Rosenhan, D.L., "On Being Sane in Insane Places,"*Science*, 179 (1973).

33. Bass, M. and Paul, D., "The Influence of Sex on Tranquilizer Prescribing," paper presented at the North American Primary Care Research Group Meeting, March 1977, Williamsburg, Virginia.

34. Mr. Brown is a past presidential advisor on Mental Health in the U.S. Ms. Brown is an opposition member of the British Columbia Legislative Assembly and an outspoken feminist critic.

35. For example: See recommendations from the conference, "In the Service of the State: The Psychiatrist as Double Agent." Special Supplement, *Hastings Centre Report*, April 1978; Lazare, A., "Hidden Conceptual Models in Clinical Psychiatry," *New England Journal of Medicine*, 228, 7, (1973), 345-351; Engel, 1977.
cal Model."

36. For example: Torrey, E. Fuller, *The Death of Psychiatry* (Radnor, Pa.: Chilton Book Co., 1974); Halleck, S.L., *The Politics of Therapy* (New York: Science House, 1971); Szasz, T.S., *The Myth of Mental Illness*, revised edition (New York: Harper & Row, 1974); *The Manufacture of Madness* (New York: Delta Books, Dell Publishing Co., 1970); and many other works; Laing, R.D., *The Divided Self: A Study In Family and Madness* (Chicago: Quadrangle Books, 1960).

37. For example: Goffman, E., *Asylums: Essays on the Social Situation of Mental Patients and other Inmates* (New York: Anchor Doubleday, 1961); Schell, R., *Being Mentally Ill: A Sociological Theory* (Chicago: Aldine Press, 1962); Scull, A.T., "From Madness to Mental Illness: Medical Men as Moral Entrepreneurs," *Arch. Europ. Sociol.*, XVI (1975), pp. 218-251; and Scull, A.T., "Cyclical Trends in Psychiatric Practice: The Case of Bettleheim and Tuke," *Social Science and Medicine*, 9 (1975), 633-640; and *Decarceration* (New Jersey Prentice Hall, 1977); Braginsky, B.M., Braginsky, D.D. and Ring, K., *Methods of Madness: The Mental Hospital as a Last Resort* (New York: Holt, Rinehardt & Winston, 1969); Tennov, D., *Psychotherapy: The Hazardous Cure* (New York: Abelard-Schuman, 1975).

38. For example: Foucault, M., *Madness and Civilization: A History of Insanity in the Age of Reason* (New York: Pantheon Books, 1965); Grob, G.N., "Rediscovering Asylums: The Unhistorical History of the Mental Hospital," *Hastings Centre Report*, August 1977, 33-41; Bateson, G., *Mind and Nature* (New York: E.P. Dutton, 1979).

39. For example: Chesler, P., *Women and Madness* (New York: Doubleday, 1972); Smith, D. and David, S., ed., *Women Look at Psychiatry* (Vancouver: Press Gang, 1975); Tennov, D., *Psychotherapy: The Hazardous Cure;* Franks, V. and Burtle, V., eds. *Women in Therapy* (New York: Brunner/Mazel Publishers, 1974); Levine, S., Kamin, L. and Levine, E.L., "Sexism and Psychiatry," *Amer. J. Orthopsychiatry*, 44, (1974), 327-336; Rawlings, E.I. and Carter, D.K., eds. *Psychotherapy for Women. Treatment Toward Equality* (Springfield Illinois: Charles C.

for Women. Treatment Toward Equality (Springfield, Illinois: Charles C. Thomas, 1977).

≡   ≡   ≡

II. TOWARD A BROADER VIEW OF THE INSTITUTION

1. Kittrie, N. *The Right to be Different* (Baltimore: Johns Hopkins Press, 1971).
2. Scull, A.T., *Decarceration* (New Jersey: Prentice-Hall, 1977).
3. Ibid., p. 15.
4. Ibid., p. 23.
5. Ibid., Chapters 5 and 8.
6. Mora, G., "Historical and Theoretical Trends in Psychiatry.", in *Comprehensive Textbook of Psychiatry*, Vol. 1., 2nd Ed. Freeman, Kaplan and Sadock, eds., (Baltimore: Williams & Williams, 1975), p. 8; Kelman, S. "Toward the Political Economy of Medical Care," *Inquiry* 8, 3 (1971), 30-38.
7. Cunningham, M., Review of *Textbook of Disturbance of Mental Life or Disturbances of the Soul, Canada's Mental Health,* 26: 2, 1978; Caplan, R., *Psychiatry and the Community in Nineteenth Century America* (New York: Basic Books Inc., 1969), pp. 312-313.
8. Scull, 1977, pp. 30 and 39.
9. Navarro, V., "The Industrialization of Fetishism or the Fetishism of Industrialization," *Int. J. Health Services,* 5, 3, (1975). pp. 351-371.
10. Grob, G.N., "Rediscovering Asylums: The Unhistorical History of the Mental Hospital," *Hastings Centre Report,* August 1977, p. 39.
11. Caplan, 1969.
12. Grob, 1977, p. 36.
13. Szasz, T.S., *The Manufacture of Madness* (New York: Delta Books, 1970), pp. 140, 141, 143 & 154.
Sociology of Knowledge (New York: 1970), p. 79, cited in Scull, "From Madness to Mental Illness," p. 257.
15. Scull, A.T., "From Madness to Mental Illness: Medical Men as Moral Entrepreneurs," *Arch. Europ. Sociol.,* XVI (1975), 218-251.
16. Smith, D.E., "A Sociology for Women,"

16. Smith, D.E., "A Sociology for Women," in *The Prism of Sex: Essays in the Sociology of Knowledge*, Eds. J.A. Sherman and E. Torton Beck (Madison: Univ. of Wisconsin Press, 1979), Section 1.

17. Conrad, P., "The Discovery of Hyperkinesis: Notes on the Medicalization of Deviant Behavior," *Social Problems*, 23,1 (1975); and Newberger, E.H. and Bourne, R., "The Medicalization and Legalization of Child Abuse," paper presented at the Symposium on Violence in the Family, *Second World Conference of the International Society on Family Law*, Montreal, 1975.

18. Zola, I.K., "Medicine as an Institution of Social Control," *Sociological Review*, 20 (1972), 487-504.

19. Pitts, J., "Social Control: The Concept," *International Encyclopedia of the Social Sciences*, D. Sills, ed., Vol. 14 (New York: Macmillan, 1968).

20. Illich, I., *Medical Nemesis: The Expropriation of Health* (Toronto: McClelland and Stewart, 1975).

21. Bazelon, D.L., "The Perils of Wizardry," *Am. J. of Psychiatry*, 131, 12 (1974), 1317-1322.

22. Szasz, T., ed. *The Age of Madness* (New York: Anchor Press/Doubleday, 1973), p. 51; LaLonde, M., *A New Perspective on the Health of Canadians* (Ottawa: Government of Canada, 1974); Conrad, "The Discovery of Hyperkinesis"; Starr, P., "The Politics of Therapeutic Nihilism," *The Hastings Centre Report*, 6, 5 (1976), 24-30; Navarro, 1975.

23. Caplan, 1969, pp. 107-108.

24. Franks, V. and Burtle, V., eds., *Women in Therapy*, (New York: Brunner/Mazel, 1974).

25. Levine, S., Kamin, L., and Levine, E.L., "Sexism and Psychiatry", *Amer. J. Orthopsychiatry*, 44, 3 (1974), 327-336.

26. Zilboorg, G., *The Medical Man and the Witch During the Renaissance* (Baltimore: Johns Hopkins Press, 1935).

27. Walsh, M.R. *Doctors Wanted: No Women Need Apply* (New Haven, Conn.: Yale Univ. Press, 1977), and "The Rediscovery of The Need for a Feminist Medical Education," *Harvard Educational Review*, 49, 4, (1979), 447-466; Corea, G., *The Hidden Malpractice* (New York: William Morrow & Co., 1977); Rich, A., *Of Woman Born* (New York: W.W. Norton & Co., 1977); Ehrenreich, B. and English, D., *For Her*

Own Good: 150 Years of the Experts' Advice to Women (New York: Anchor Books, 1979), and *Complaints and Disorders: The Sexual Politics of Sickness* (Old Westbury, N.Y.: The Feminist Press, 1973); Oakley A., "Wisewoman and Medicine Man: Changes in the Management of Childbirth," in Mitchell, J. and Oakley, A., eds., *The Rights and Wrongs of Women* (Harmondworth, Middlesex: Pelican Books, 1976); Stuard, Mosher D., "Dame Trot," in *Signs,* 1, 2, (1975); Sachs, A. and Wilson, J. Hoff, *Sexism and the Law* (Oxford: Martin Robertson and Co., 1978).

28. Walsh, 1979, 449-452.

29. Smith, "Women and Psychiatry," in Smith, D. & David, S., eds. *Women Look at Psychiatry* (Vancouver: Press Gang, 1975).

30. Corea, 1977, p. 89.

31. Ibid., p. 86.

32. Rome, H.P., "Psychiatry and Foreign Affairs," *Amer. J. Psychiatry,* 125 (1968), 725-730.

33. Scull, 1977, pp. 9-10.

34. Grob, 1977, p.39.

35. Janeway, Elizabeth, "The Women's Movement" in Freedman, Kaplan and Sadock, *Comprehensive Textbook of Psychiatry,* 1975.

36. Karasu, T.B., "Psychotherapies: An Overview," *American Journal of Psychiatry,* 134, 8 (1977), 851; Seiden, A.M., "Overview: Research on the Psychology of Women, Part II," *American Journal of Psychiatry,* 133, 10 (1976), 1117, 1120.

37. Scull, A.T., "Cyclical Trends in Psychiatric Practice: The Case of Bettelheim and Tuke," *Social Science and Medicine,* 9 (1975), 633-640.

38. Ehrenreich and English, 1979, pp. 71-72.

39. Navarro, 1975, p. 364; Kelman, 1971, p. 34.
man, S., "Toward the Political Economy of Medical Care," p. 34.

≡ ≡ ≡

III: PSYCHIATRIC IDEOLOGY AND ITS FUNCTIONS

1. Smith, D.E., "Women and Psychiatry" in Smith, D.E. and David, S., eds., *Women Look at Psychiatry* (Vancouver: Press Gang Publishers, 1975), p. 2.

2. Ullman, L.P. and Krazner, L., *A Psychological Approach to Abnormal Behavior* (New Jersey: Prentice-Hall, 1969), pp. 204-205; Broverman, I.K. et al., "Sex Role Stereotypes and Clinical Judgements of Mental Health," *Journal of Consulting and Clinical Psychology*, 34, 1 (1970), 1.

3. Gaylin, W., *In the Service of the State: The Psychiatrist as Double Agent*, Conference co-sponsored by the American Psychiatric Association and the Hastings Centre, 1977. Proceedings published in *The Hastings Centre Report*, 8, 2, (1978).

4. Newberger, E.H. and Bourne, R., "The Medicalization and Legalization of Child Abuse," paper presented at the symposium: *Violence and the Family*, Second World Conference of the International Society on Family Law, Montreal, 1977, p. 7.

5. Offer, D. and Sabshin, M., "Normality," Chapter 6, Section 6, in *Comprehensive Textbook of Psychiatry*, eds. Freeman, Kaplan and Sadock (Baltimore: Williams and Wilkins, 1975).

6. Ibid., p. 459.

7. Romano, J., "Basic Orientation and Education of the Medical Student," *Journal A.M.A.*, 143 (1950), 409.

8. Offer and Sabshin, 1975, p. 460.

9. Freud, S., quoted in Offer and Sabshin, "Normality," p. 460.

10. Eysenck, H.J., *The Uses and Abuses of Psychology* (Hammondworth: Penguin Books, 1953), p. 178.

11. Ibid., p. 177; Offer and Sabshin, "Normality," p. 460.

12. Ibid.

13. Eysenck, op. cit., pp. 177-178.

14. Offer and Sabshin, 1975, p. 460.

15. Ibid.

16. Eysenck, op. cit., p. 179; Janeway, E., *Man's World, Woman's Place* (New York: Dell Publishing Co., 1971).

17. Offer and Sabshin, 1975, p. 463.

18. Sabshin, M., Diesenhaus, H. and Wilkerson, R., "Dimensions of Institutional Racism in Psychiatry," *Am. J. Psychiatry* 127 (1970), 787.

19. Watzlawick, P., Weakland, J. and Fisch, P., *Change: Principles of Problem Formulation and Problem Resolution* (New York: W.W. Norton & Co., 1974).

20. de Bono, E., *The Uses of Lateral Thinking* (Great Britain: Jonathan Cape, 1967); Kuhn, T.S., *The Structure of Scientific Revolu-*

tions, 2nd Ed. (Chicago: Univ. of Chicago Press, 1970).

21. Fanon, F., *The Wretched of the Earth* (New York: Grove Press; London: Granada, 1963).

22. Freire, P.,*The Pedagogy of the Oppressed* (New York: Seabury Press, 1973).

23. Hegel, G., *The Phenomenology of the Mind,* Wallace trans. (Oxford: Oxford Univ. Press, 1971), cited in Smith, D.E., "A Sociology for women," in *The Prism of Sex: Essays in the Sociology of Knowledge,* Eds. J.A. Sherman and E. Torton Beck (Madison: Univ. of Wisconsin Press, 1979), Sect. 1.

24. Allport, G., *The Nature of Prejudice* (Cambridge, Mass.: Addison-Wesley, 1954).

25. Miller, J. Baker and Mothner, I., "The Psychological Consequences of Sexual Inequality," *Amer. J. Orthopsychiatry,* 44, 5 (1971), 768.

26. Ibid.

27. Ibid.

28. Argyris, C. "Dangers in Applying Results from Experimental Social Psychology," *Amer. Psychologist,* 30 (1975), 469, cited in E. I. Rawlings and D.K. Carter, eds., *Psychotherapy for Women* (Springfield, Illinois: Charles C. Thoman, 1977), p. 447.

29. Smith, D.E., 1975, p. 90.

30. Ibid.,

31. Ibid., p. 91.

32. Ibid., p. 92.

33. Smith, D.E., 1975, p. 14.

34. Lazare, A, "Hidden Conceptual Models in Clinical Psychiatry," *New England Journal of Medicine,* 288, 7 (1973), 345-351.

35. Ibid., p. 347. Quoted from Alexander, F. and French, T.M., *Pschoanalytical Therapy: Principles and Application* (New York: Ronald Press, 1946).

36. Ibid.

37. Ibid.

38. Ibid., p. 345.

39. Ibid., pp. 348-349.

40. Ibid., p. 350.

41. Ibid., p. 350.

42. Fanon, F., *Black Skins, White Masks* (New York: Grove Press;

London: Granada, 1967).

43. Brooks, K., "Freudianism is Not a Basis For a Marxist Psychology," in P. Brown, ed., *Radical Psychology* (New York: Harper Colophon, 1973).

44. Smith, D.E., 1975, p. 103.

45. Smith, D.E., "A Sociology For Women," p. 19; Weber, M., *The Theory of Social and Economic Organization* (New York: Free Press, 1964).

46. *Professional Responsibilities and Peer Review,* a conference report by The American Psychiatric Association, 1977, p. 7; *In Service of the State,* Hastings Centre Report, 8, 2, (1978).

47. Rosenhan F., "On Being Sane in Insane Places," *Science,* 179 (1973), 253.

48. Chesler, P., *Women and Madnesss* (New York: Doubleday, (1972).

49. Smith, D.E., 1975, p. 5.

50. Drummond, H., "Diagnosing Marriage," *Mother Jones,* July (1979), 14-21.

51. Smith, D.E., "Women and Psychiatry," p. 4.

52. Smith, D.E., "Women and the Politics of Professionalism." Unpublished paper, 1979.

53. Caplan, N. and Nelson, S.D., "On Being Useful: The Nature and Consequences of Psychological Research on Social Problems," *Amer. Psychol.* 28 (1973), 199, cited in Rawlings and Carter, 1977 p. 448.

≡   ≡   ≡

IV: WOMAN: THE UNIVERSAL SCAPEGOAT

1. Gluckstern, N.B., "Beyond Therapy: Personal and Institutional Change" in Rawlings, E.I. and Carter, Diane K., eds. *Psychotherapy for Women. Treatment—Toward Equality* (Springfield, Illinois: Charles C. Thomas, 1977), p. 437.

2. Smith, D.E., "An Analysis of Ideological Structures and How Women Are Excluded: Considerations for Academic Women." *Rev.*

258 —

Canad. Soc. & Anth:/Canad. Rev. Soc. & Anth. 12, 4 (1975), part 1.

3. Adams, P., "Fatherlessness: Policy Suggestions", paper presented at the North American Seminar on The Impact of Change on Mental Health and Child and Family Development. Val David, Quebec, June 7, 1977.

4. Smith, D.E., "Women and Psychiatry," in D.E. Smith and S. David, eds., Women Look at Psychiatry (Vancouver: Press Gang Publishers, 1975), p. 6; Herscherberger, Ruth, *Adam's Rib* (New York: Harper and Row, 1948).

5. Morgan E., *The Descent of Woman* (New York: Bantam Books, 1973).

6. Tanner, N. and Zilman, A., "Women in Evolution. Part I: Innovation and Selection in Human Origins," *Signs,* 1, 3 (1976), 585-608; and Zilman, A., "Women in Evolution. Part II: Subsistence and Social Organization Among Early Hominoids." *Signs,* 4. 1 (1978), 4-20.

7. Clark, L. and Lewis, D., *Rape: The Price of Coercive Sexuality* (Toronto: The Women's Press, 1977) pp. 111-124.

9. Daly, M., *The Church and the Second Sex* (New York: Harper Colophon, 1968 and 1975).

10. Bianchi and Ruether, 1976.

11. Davis, N.Z., "Women's History in Transition: The European Case," *Feminist Studies* 3, 3-4 (1976) 83-103, cited in Longee, C.C., "Modern European History", *Signs* 2, 3 (1976), 630.

12. Kelly-Gadol, J., "Did Women Have a Renaissance?" in *Becoming Visible: Women in European History,* eds. Bridenthal, R. and Koonz, C. (Boston: Houghton Mifflin 1976). Cited in Longee, C.C., 1976, p. 633.

13. Rowbotham, S. *Women, Resistance and Revolution,* (London: Allen Lane, The Penguin Press, 1972).

14. de Beauvoir, S., *The Second Sex* (New York: Bantam Books, 1961), p. xv.

15. Bianchi and Reuther, 1976, p. 78.

16. Friedan, B., *The Feminine Mystique* (New York: Dell Publishing, 1963).

17. Andelin, Helen B., *Fascinating Womanhood* (Santa Barbara: Pacific Santa Barbara, March 1965.

18. Ryan, W., *Blaming the Victim* (New York: Vintage, Random House, 1976).

19. O'Connor, J., *The Fiscal Crisis of the State* (New York: St.

Martin's Press, 1973).

20. Bianchi and Reuther, 1976, "Introduction."

21. Wylie, P., *Generation of Vipers* (New York: Rinehart & Co., 1942).

22. Voth, H., *The Castrated Family* (Kansas City: Sheed, Andrews & McNeal, Universal Press, 1977).

23. For example: Erikson, E., "Once More the Inner Space: Letter to a Former Student", in Strouse, J. Ed. *Women and Analysis* (New York: Dell Publishing, 1974)

24. Bardwick, J., "Ambivalence: The Socialization of Women", in Bardwick, J., Ed., *Readings on the Psychology of Women* (New York: Harper J., ed., & Row, 1972); Rich, A., *Of Woman Born* (New York: Bantam Books, 1977), p. 190.

25. Broverman, I.K. et al, "Sex Role Stereotypes and Clinical Judgements of Mental Health", *Journal of Consulting and Clinical Psychology*, 34, 1, (1970), 1.

26. D'Arcy, Carl and Schmitz, Janet, "Sex Differences in the Utilization of Health Services for Psychiatric Problems in Saskatchewan." Paper presented at the Canadian Psychiatric Association Annual Meeting, Saskatoon, Saskatchewan, September 29, 1977.

27. For example: Gomes, B. and Abramowitz, S.I., "Sex Related Patient-Therapist – Effects on Clinical Judgements", *Sex Roles*, 2, 1 (1976); and Abramowitz, S.I., et al., "Sex Bias in Therapy: A Failure to Confirm", *Am. J. Psychiatry*, 133 (1976).

28. For example: Brown, C.R. and Hellinger, M., "Therapists' Attitudes Towards Women," *Social Work*, 20, (1975), 266-270.

29. For example: Kinzel, K.M., "A Study of the Influence of Sex-Role Stereotypes on Marriage Counsellor's Personal and Clinical Evaluation of Their Clients," Masters thesis, University of Regina, 1974.

30. Brown and Hellinger, 1975.

31. Fancher, R.E., "Freud's Attitudes Towards Women: A Survey of His Writings," *Queen's Quarterly*, 82, 3 (1975), 368-393.

32. Mitchel, J., *Psychoanalysis and Feminism* (New York: Vintage Books, 1975).

33. Freud, S., *The Standard Edition of the Works of Sigmund Freud* (London: Hogarth Press, 1953), Vol. 1, p. 270, cited in Fancher, R.E., "Freud's Attitudes Towards Women", p. 375.

34. Freud, S., *New Introductory Lectures in Psychoanalysis* (New York: W.W. Norton, 1933).

35. Fancher, 1975, p. 374.

36. Lambert, H.H., "Biology and Equality: A Perspective on Sex Differences," *Signs*, 4, 1 (1978), 104.

37. Freud, S., "The Psychology of Women," *New Introductory Lectures in Psychoanalysis* (London: Hogarth Press, 1946), p. 149.

38. Fancher, 1975, p. 383.

39. Caplan, P.J., "Problems in the Psychological Study of Sex Differences," *Canadian Newsletter of Research on Women*, VII, 2 (1978), 14.

40. Fancher, 1975, p. 387.

41. Deutsch, H., *The Psychology of Women* (New York: Grune and Stratton, 1944).

42. Interview with Helene Deutsch, cited in Mitchell, 1975, p. 298.

43. Brown and Hellinger, 1975, p. 267.

44. Erikson, E.H., *Childhood and Society*, (New York: Doubleday & Co., 1950); Sec. Ed. New York: W.W. Norton & Co., 1963), p. 231.

45. Schwartz, M.C., "Sexism in the Social Work Curriculum," *Journal of Education for Social Work*, Fall (1973).

46. Erikson, E.H., "Womanhood and the Inner Space," In Strouse, 1974, p. 337.;

47. Ibid., p. 355.;

48. Ibid., p. 337.;

49. Ibid., p. 354.

50. Caplan, P.J. "Erikson's Concept of Inner Space: A Data-Based Re-evaluation," *Am. J. Orthopsychiatry*, 42, 1, (1979), 100-108.

51. Sullivan, H. Stack., "Developmental Syndromes" and "Basic Conceptions" in Maddi, S., Ed., *Perspectives in Personality* (Boston: Little Brown & Co., 1971).

52. Maslow, A., "Some Basic Propositions of a Growth and Self-Actualization Psychology," "Deficiency Motivation and Growth Motivation" in Maddi, 1971, p. 239.

53. Ibid., p. 221.

54. Ibid., p. 227.

55. Maslow, A., *The Farther Reaches of Human Nature* (New Viking Press, 1971).

56. Maslow, A., "Self Esteem (Dominance Feeling) and Sexuality in Women," *Journal of Social Psychology*, 16 (1942).

57. Ibid., and Maslow, A., *Motivation and Personality* (New York: Harper & Row, 1954).

58. Chesler, P., *Women and Madness* (New York: Avon Books, 1973).

59. Rawlings, E. I., and Carter, D.K., "Values and Value Change in Psychotherapy," in Rawlings and Carter, 1977, p. 13.

60. Barash, D., *Sociobiology and Behavior* (New York: Elsevier Scientific Publishing, 1977), p. 310, cited in Lowe, M., "Sociobiology and Sex Differences", *Signs,* 4, 1 (1978), 124.

61. Weisstein, N., "Psychology Constructs the Female" in Gornick, V. and Moran, B.K., eds., *Woman in Sexist-Society: Studies in Power and Powerlessness* (New York: Basic Books, 1971), p. 208.

62. Rheingold, J., *The Fear of Being a Woman* (New York: Grune and Stratton, 1964), p. 714. Cited in Weisstein, 1971, p. 208.

63. Lundberg., F., and Farnham, M., *Modern Woman: The Lost Sex* (New York: The Universal Library, 1947), p. 143.

64. Haraway, D., "Animal Sociology and a Natural Economy of the Body Politic, Part I: A Political Physiology of Dominance," *Signs,* 4, 1 (1978), 25.

65. Ibid., Part II.

66. Allen, A., "Woman's Place in Nature," *Forum,* 7 (1889), 258-63. Cited in Magner, L.N., "Woman and the Scientific Idiom," *Signs,* 4, 1 (1978), 72.

67. Freud, S., *Civilization and Its Discontents* (New York: W.W. Norton & Co., 1962).

68. Haraway, 1978, p. 47.

69. Ibid., p. 43.

70. Fancher, 1975, p. 373.

71. Haraway, 1978, p. 22.

72. Ehrenreich, B. and English, D., *Complaints and Disorders, The Sexual Politics of Sickness* (Glass Mountain Pamphlet No. 2, The Feminist Press, 1973).

73. Miller, J. Baker, *Toward a New Psychology of Women* (Boston: Beacon Press, 1976).

74. Ibid., p. 22.

75. Schofield, W., *Psychotherapy: The Purchase of Friendship* (New Jersey: Prentice-Hall, 1963).

76. Chesler, 1973.

77. Chesler, P. "Patient and Patriarch: Women in the Psychotherapeutic Relationship," in Gornick and Moran, 1971, pp. 362-392.

78. Rawlings, E.I. and Carter, D.K., "Values and Value Change in Psychotherapy", in Rawlings and Carter, 1977, p. 24.

79. Sachs, A. and Wilson, J. Hoff. *Sexism and the Law, A Study of Male Beliefs and Legal Bias in Britain and the United States* (Oxford: Martin Robertson & Co., 1978), p. 51.

≡   ≡   ≡

V: SEX ROLES AND SEX-ROLE STEREOTYPES

1. Woolf, Virginia, *A Room of One's Own* (New York, Harcourt, Brace & Co. 1929), p. 5.

2. Kleeman, J.A., "Freud's Views on Early Female Sexuality in the Light of Direct Child Observation," *J. Am. Psychoanal. Assoc.*, 24 (1976), 3-27.

3. Stoller, R., "Primary Femininity," *J. Am. Psychoanal.*, 34 (1974), 27-31.

4. Landman, L., "Recent Trends Towards Unisex: A Panel" *Am. J. Psychoanal.*, 34 (1974), 27-31.

5. Rheingold, J.C., *The Fear of Being a Woman* (New York: Grune & Stratton, 1964).

6. Spitz, R., *The First Year of Life: A Psychoanalytic Study of Normal and Deviant Development of Object Relations* (New York: International Universities Press, 1965).

7. Voth, H., *The Castrated Family* (Kansas City: Sheed, Andrews & McNeal, Universal Press, 1977).

8. Bernard, J., *Women, Wives, and Mothers: Values and Options* (Chicago: Aldine Publishing, 1975).

9. Favazza, A.R. and Oman, A., "Overview: Foundations of Cultural Psychiatry," *Am. J. Psychiatry*, 135 (1978), 293-303.

10. Mead, M., *Sex and Temperament in Three Primitive Societies* (New York: William Morrow & Co., 1935).

11. Bem, S.L., "Sex Role Adaptability: One Consequence of Psychologocial Androgyny,'. *J. Personality & Social Psychology*, 31

(1975), 634-643; Consentino, F., and Heilbrun, A.B., "Anxiety Correlates of Sex-Role Identity in College Students," *Psychological Reports,* 14 (1964), 729-730; Gall M.D., "The Relationship Between Masculinity-Femininity and Manifest Anxiety," *J. Clinical Psychology,* 25 (1969), 294-295.

12. Bem, 1975; Harford, T.C., Willis, C.H. and Deabler, L., "Personality Correlates of Masculinity-Femininity," *Psychological Reports,* 21 (1967), 881-884; Mussen, P.H., "Long-term Consequents of Masculinity of Interests in Adolescence," *J. Consulting Psychology,* 26 (1962), 435-440.

13. Block, J., "Conceptions of Sex Role: Some Cross-Cultural and Longitudinal Perspectives," *American Psychologist,* 28 (1973), 512-526; Gray, S.W., "Masculinity-Femininity in Relation to Anxiety and Social Acceptance," *Child Development,* 28 (1957), 203-214; Hartley, R.A., "Sex Role Pressures and The Socialization of the Male Child," in Stacey et al., eds., *And Jill Came Tumbling After: Sexism in American Education* (New York: Dell Publishing, 1974), pp. 185-198; Sears, R. R., "Relation of Early Socialization Experiences to Self-Concepts and Gender Role in Middle Childhood," *Child Development,* 41 (1970), 267-289; Webb, A.P., "Sex-Role Preferences and Adjustment in Early Adolescents," *Child Development,* 34 (1963), 609-618.

14. Lerner, H.E., "Adaptive and Pathogenic Aspects of Sex-Role Stereotypes: Implications for Parenting and Psychotherapy," *Am. J. Psychiatry,* 155 (1978), 48-52,

15. Bakan, D., *The Duality of Human Existence* (Chicago: Rand McNally, 1966); Jung, C.G., "Anima and Animus," in *Two Essays on Analytical Psychology: Collected Works of C.G. Jung,* Vol. 7 (Bollinger Foundation, 1953), pp. 186-209.

16. Bem, S.L., "The Measurement of Psychological Androgyny," *"Consulting & Clinical Psychology,* 42 (1974), 155-162; Bem, S.L., "Probing the Promise of Androgyny," in Kaplan, A.G. and Bean, J.P., eds., *Beyond Sex Role Stereotypes: Readings Toward a Psychology of Androgyny* (Boston: Little, Brown, & Co., 1976).

17. Frieze, I., Parsons, J., Johnson, P., Ruble, D., and Zellman, G., *Women and Sex Roles: A Sociological Perspective* (Toronto: W.W. Norton & Co., 1978); Kaplan, A.G., "Androgyny as a Model of Mental Health for Women: From Theory to Therapy," in Kaplan, A.G. and Bean, J.P., eds., *Beyond Sex Role Stereotypes* (Boston,: Little, Brown, 1976), pp. 353-362; Lips, H.M., and Colwill, N.L.,

chology of Sex Differences (New Jersey: Prentice Hall, 1978); Walum, L.R., *The Dynamics of Sex and Gender: A Sociological Perspective* (Chicago: Rand McNally Publishing, 1977).

18. Kaplan, A.G., "Clarifying the Concept of Androgyny: Implications for Therapy," *Psychology of Women Quarterly,* 3 (1979), 223-230; Kelly, J., Furnam, W., and Young, V., "Problems Associated with Typological Measurements of Sex Roles and Androgyny," *J. Consulting and Clinical Psychology,* 46 (1978), 1574-76; Kelly, J., and Worrel, J., "New Formulations of Sex Roles and Androgyny: A Critical Review," *J. Consulting and Clinical Psychology,* 45 (1977), 1101-1115; Locksley, A. and Colten, M.E., "Psychological Androgyny: A Case of Mistaken Identity? *J. Personality & Social Psychology,* 37 (1979), 1017-34; Yonge, G.D., "The Bem Sex-Role Inventory: Use With Caution If At All," *Psychological Reports,* 43 (1978), 1245-1246.

19. Stark-Adamec, C., Graham, J.M., and Pyke, S.W., "Androgyny and Mental Health: The Need for a Critical Evaluation of the Theoretical Equation," *International J. Women's Studies,* 3 (1980), 490-507.

20. Stoll, C.S., *Female and Male: Socialization, Social Roles, and Social Structure* (Dubuque, Iowa: William C. Brown, 1974); Bernard, J., 1975.

21. Nadelson, C.C., "The Impact of the Changing Role of Women and the Women's Movement," paper presented at the North American Seminar on *The Impact of Change on Mental Health and Child and Family Development,* Val David, Quebec, June 7, 1977.

22. Acker, J., Book review of *Women, Wives and Mothers. Signs,* 1 (1976), 973-975.

23. Morris, Jan, *Conundrum* (New York: Harcourt, Brace, Jovanovich, 1974), p. 148.

24. Graham, J.M. and Stark-Adamec, C., "Sex and Gender: The Need for Redefinition (Double Entendre Intended)," *Resources for Feminist Research,* IX, (1980), 7; Unger, R.K., "Toward a Redefinition of Sex and Gender," *American Psychologist,* 34 (1979), 1085-1094.

25. Group for the Advancement of Psychiatry, *The Educated Woman: Prospects and Problems,* Vol. IX, Report No. 92, 1975.

26. Vaughter, R.M., "Psychology," *Signs,* 2 (1976), 120-146.

27. Stoller, 1976.

28. Stoll, 1974.

29. Block, 1973.

30. Stoller, R., "The Sense of Maleness," *Psychoanalytic Quarte*

ly, 34 (1965), 207-218.

31. Money, J., "Gender Role, Gender Identity, Core Identity: Usage and Definition of Terms," *J. Amer. Acad. Psychoanal.,* 1 (1973), 397-405.

32. Bradley, S.J. et al., "Gender Identity Problems of Children and Adolescents: The Establishment of a Special Clinic," *Can. Psychiatr. Assoc. J.,* 23 (1978), 175-183.

33. Freud, S., *New Introductory Lectures on Psychoanalysis,* Lecture 33, 1933.

34. Freud, S., *The Taboo of Virginity, Collected Papers,* Vol. IV, 1918, p. 218.

35. Freud, S., *Three Contributions to The Theory of Sex,* translated from the German by A.A. Brill (New York: Dulton, 1962).

36. Freud, S., *Civilization and Its Discontents* (London: Hogarth Press, 1930).

37. Deutsch, H., *The Psychology of Women: A Psychoanalytic Interpretation* (New York: Grune & Stratton, 1945).

38. Bonaparte, M., *Female Sexuality* (New York: Grove Press, 1965), p. 148.

39. Robinson, M.N., *The Power of Sexual Surrender* (New York: Doubleday, 1959), p. 158.

40. Erikson, E.H., *Childhood and Society* (New York: W.W. Norton, 1963). 2nd Edition, pp. 48-108.

41. Zilboorg, G., "Masculine and Feminine: Some Biological and Cultural Aspects," *Psychiatry,* 7 (1944), 257-296.

42. Marmor, J., "Changing Patterns of Femininity: Psychoanalytic Implications," in Rosenbaum, S. and Alger, I., eds,. *The Marriage Relationship* (New York: Basic Books, 1968).

43. Tooley, K.M., "Johnny, I Hardly Knew Ye: Toward Revision of the Theory of Male Psychosexual Development," *Amer. J. Orthopsychiat.,* 47 (1977), 184-195.

44. Zuger, B., "The Role of Familiar Factors in Persistent Effeminate Behavior in Boys," *Am. J. Psychiatry,* 126 (1970), 1167-1170.

45. Baker, H., Stoller, R.J., "Can a Biological Force Contribute to Gender Identity? *Am. J. Psychiatry,* 124 (1968), 1653-1658; Green, R., *Sexual Identity Conflict in Children and Adults* (Baltimore: Penguin Books, 1974); Stoller, R.J., *The Transexual Experiment* (London: Hogarth Press, 1975).

46. Money, J., "Gender Role, Gender Identity, Core Gender Iden-

tity: Usage and Definition of Terms" *J. Amer. Acad. Psychoan.,* 1 (1973), 397-405.

47. Money, J. and Ehrhardt, A.A., *Man and Woman, Boy and Girl* (Baltimore and London: Johns Hopkins Univ. Press, 1972).

48. Baker, S.W., "Biological Influences on Human Sex and Gender," *Signs,* 6 (1980), 80-96.

49. Bradley, 1978.

50. Constantinople, A. "Sex Role Acquisition: In Search of the Elephant," *Sex Roles,* 5 (1979), 121-133; Katz, P.A., "The Development of Female Identity," in Kopp, C.B. and Kirkpatrick, M., eds., *Becoming Female: Perspectives on Development* (New York & London: Plenum, 1979).

51. Mischel, W., "A Social Learning View of Sex Differences in Behavior," in Maccoby, E., ed., *The Development of Sex Differences* (Stanford: Stanford Univ. Press, 1966); Green, R., 1974.

52. Kohlberg, L. and Ullian, P.Z., "Stages in the Development of Psychosexual Concepts and Attitudes," in Friedman, R.C. et al., eds., *Sex Differences in Behavior,* (New York: John Wiley, 1974), pp. 209-222.

53. Ullian, P.Z., "The Development of Conceptions of Masculinity and Femininity," in Lloyd, B. and Archer, J., eds., *Exploring Sex Differences* (New York: Academic Press, 1976), pp. 25-47.

54. Rebecca, N., Hefner, R. and Oleshansky, B., "A Model of Sex Role Transcendence," in Kaplan and Bean, 1976, pp. 90-97.

55. Parsons, T., "The Social Structure of the Family," in Anshen, R.N., ed., *The Family: Its Function and Destiny* (New York: Harper, 1959).

56. Westley, W.A. and Epstein, N.B., *The Silent Majority* (New York: Jossey-Bass, 1969).

57. Voth, 1977.

58. Seidenberg, R., "For the Future—Equity?" in Miller, J. Bak ed., *Psychoanalysis and Women* (Middlesex, England: Penguin Books, 1973).

59. Morgan, E., *The Descent of Woman* (New York: Bantam Books, 1973).

60. Tiger, L., *Men in Groups* (New York: Random House, 1969).

61. Morris, D., *The Human Zoo,* (New York: McGraw-Hill, 1969).

62. Ardrey, R., *The Territorial Imperative: A Personal Inquiry into the Animal Origins of Property and Nations* (New York: Atheneum,

1966).

63. Carpenter, C.R., *Naturalistic Behavior in Non-human Primates* (Penn: Pennsylvania State Univ. Press, 1964); Southwick, C.H., ed. *Primate Social Behavior* (Princeton: Van Nostrand, 1965).

64. Schultz, A.H., *The Life of Primates* (New York: Universe Books, 1969), Chapter 13; Mitchell, G.D., "Paternalistic Behavior in Primates," *Psych. Bull.,* 71 (1969), 399-417.

65. Etkin, W., ed. *Social Behavior and Organization among Vertebrates* (Chicago: Univ. of Chicago Press, 1964); Tinbergen, N., *Animal Behavior* (New York: Time-Life, 1965).

66. Bleier, R., "Bias in Biological and Human Sciences: Some Comments," *Signs* 4 (1978), 159-162.

67. Wilson, E.O., *Sociobiology: The New Synthesis* (Cambridge, Mass.: Harvard Press, 1975).

68. Barash, D., *Sociobiology and Behavior* (New York: Elsevier Scientific Publishing 1977), p. 310.

69. Sahlins, M., *The Use and Abuse of Biology.* (Ann Arbor:Univ. of Michigan Press, 1976).

70. Barash, 1977, p. 283.

71. "Sociobiology: Doing What Comes Naturally" (film for high-school students), distributed by Document Associates, Inc., 880 Third Ave., New York, N.Y., 10022.

72. Money and Erhardt, 1972.

73. McDonald, P.G. and Doughty, C., "Androgen Sterilisation in the Neonatal Female Rat and its Inhibition by an Estrogen Antagonist," *Neuroendocrinology,* 13 (1973-1974), 182-188; Ryan, K.H. et al., "Estrogen Formation in the Brain," *Am. J. Obstetrics and Gynecology,* 114 (1972), 454-460.

74. Stark-Adamec, C. and Adamec, R.E., "Aggression by Men Against Women: Adaptation or Aberration?" *International Journal of Women's Studies,* 5, 1 (1982), 1-2.

75. Dixson, A.F., "Androgens and Aggressive Behavior in Primates: A Review." *Aggressive Behavior,* 6 (1980), 37-67.

76. Mead, 1935.

77. Henshel, A.M., *Sex Structure,* Canadian Social Problems Series, (Longmans, Canada, 1973).

78. Gould, R.E., "Socio-Cultural Roles of Male and Female," in Freedman, A.M., Kaplan, H.I. and Sadock, B.J., eds., *Comprehensive Textbook of Psychiatry,* 2nd Edition, Vol. 2 (Baltimore: Williams &

268 –

Wilkins, 1975), pp. 1460-1466.

79. Imperato-McGinley et al., "Androgens and the Evolution of Male-Gender Identity among Male Pseudohermaphrodites with 5-reductase Deficiency," *New England J. Medicine,* 300 (1979), 1233-1237.

80. Davis, N.Z., "Women's History' in Transition: The European Case," *Feminist Studies,* 3 (1976), 83-103.

81. Bloch, R.H., "Untangling the Roots of Modern Sex Roles: A Survey of Four Centuries of Change," *Signs* 4 (1978), 237-252.

82. Rappaport, R. and Rappaport, R., *Dual Career Families* (Middlesex, England: Penguin Books, 1971).

83. Rubin, J.Z., Provenzano, F.J. and Luria, "The Eye of the Beholder: Parents' Views of Sex of Newborns," *Am. J. Orthopsychiat.,* 44 (1974), 12-19.

84. Moss, H., "Sex Age and State as Determinants of Mother-Infant Interaction," *Merrill Palmer Quarterly,* 13 (1967), 19-36.

85. Berens, A.E., "Sex-Role Stereotypes and the Development of Achievement Motivation," *Ontario Psychologist,* 5, 2 (1973), 30-35.

86. Henshel, A.M., 1973; Rheingold, H.L. and Cook, K.V., "The Contents of Boys' and Girls' Rooms as an Index of Parents' Behavior," *Child Development,* 46 (1975), 459-463.

87. Serbin, L.A., Connor, J.M., and Iler, I., "Sex-Stereotyped and Non-Stereotyped Introductions of New Toys in the Preschool Classroom: An Observational Study of Teacher Behaviour and Its Effects," *Psychology of Women Quarterly,* 4 (1979), 261-265; Serbin, L.A., O'Leary, K.D., Kent, R.N. and Tomick, I.J., "A Comparison of Teacher Response to the Pre-Academic and Problem Behaviour of Boys and Girls," *Child Development,* 44 (1973), 796-804; Fling, S. and Manosevitz, M., "Sextyping in Nursery School Children's Play Interests," *Developmental Psychology,* 7 (1972), 146-154.

88. Margolin, G. and Patterson, G.R., "Differential Consequences Provided By Mothers and Fathers for Their Sons and Daugthters," *Developmental Psychology,* 11 (1975), 537-538.

89. Block, J.H., Block, J. and Harrington, D., "Sex-Role Typing and Instrumental Behaviour: A Developmental Study." Paper presented at the meeting of the Society of Research in Child Development, Denver, April 1975.

90. Meissner, M. et al., "No Exit for Wives: Sexual Division of Labour and the Cumulation of Household Demands," *Canad. Rev. Soc. and Anth.,* 12 (1975), 424-439.

91. Baker Miller, J., *Towards a New Psychology of Women* (Boston: Beacon Press, 1976).

92. Caplan, P.J., *Barriers Between Women* (Jamaica, New York: S. P. Medical and Scientific Publications, 1980).

93. Henshel, 1973.

94. Nichols, J., *Men's Liberation: A New Definition of Masculinity* (New York: Penguin Books, 1975).

95. Schein, L., "Man to Man", *Makara,* (Oct./Nov. 1976), 34-38.

96. Seidenberg, 1973.

97. Greenglass, E., "Fruitful Directions for Research and Theory in the 1980s", *Resources for Feminist Research,* IX, 2 (1980), 12-13.

98. Tuchman, A., "Women's Depiction by the Mass Media", *Signs,* 4 (1979), 528-542; Rickel, A.U. and Grant, L.M., "Sex Role Sterotypes in the Mass Media and Schools: Five Consistent Themes", *International J. Women's Studies, 2 (1979), 164-179.*

99. Callahan, S.C., *Parenting: Principles and Politics of Parenthood* (Baltimore: Penguin Books, 1974).

100. Women on Words and Images, "Look Jane Look. See Sex Stereotypes", in Stacey et al., eds., 1974, pp. 159-184.

101. Weitzman, L.J. et al., "Sex Role Socialization in Picture Books for Preschool Children," *Am. J. Sociology,* 47 (1972), 1125-1150.

102. Voth, 1977.

103. Mill, John Stuart. *The Subjection of Women* (M.I.T. Press, 1970; originally published in London by Longmans, Green, Reader and Dyer, 1869).

104. Rappaport and Rappaport ,1971.

105. Toffler, A., *Future Shock* (New York: Bantam Books, 1972).

106. Henshel, 1973.

107. Baker Miller, 1976.

108. Stephenson, S., "The Impact of the Women's Movement: Implications for Child Development, Mental Health and Family Policy," *Canada's Mental Health,* 26, Supplement: Child and Family Mental Health Services: Future Policy Issues, pp. 10-13, March 1978.

109. Fitzhugh, G., *Sociology for the South, or the Failure of a Free Society* (Richmond, Va: A. Morris, 1854); Nott, J.C., "Statistics of the Southern Slave Population," *De Bow's Commercial Rev.,* 4 (1875), 275-290.

110. Meigs, C., Lecture on "The Distinctive Characteristics of the Female," Jefferson Medical College, Philadelphia, T.K. and P.G. Collins, 1847; Carpenter, W., *Principles of Human Physiology,* fourth ed. (Philadelphia 1850); Tracy, S., *Principles of Human Physiology,* fourth ed. (Philadelphia, 1860).

111. O'Neill, J., "Observations of the Occipital and Superior Maxillary Bones of the African Cranium," *Am. J. Medical Science,* 19 (1850). 78-83; Peacock, T.B., "On the Weight of the Brain in the Negro." *Memoirs of the Anthropological Society,* 1 (1853), 65-72; Merrill, A.P., "An Essay on Some of the Distinctive Peculiarities of the Negro Race," *Memphis Medical Recorder,* 4 (1855), 1-17.

112. Newman, L.E., "Treatment for the Parents of Feminine Boys," *Am. J. Psychiatry,* 133 (1976), 683-687.

113. Group for the Advancement of Psychiatry, 1975.

114. Vaughter, 1976.

115. Haraway, D., "Animal Sociology and a Natural Economy of the Body Politic, Part II: The Past is the Contested Zone: Human Nature and Theories of Production and Reproduction in Primate Behaviour Studies," *Signs,* 4 (1978), 37-60.

116. Haraway, D., "Animal Sociology and a Natural Economy of the Body Politic, Part I: A Political Physiology of Dominance," *Signs,* (1978), 21-36.

117. Lowe, M., "Sociobiology and Sex Differences," *Signs,* 4 (1978), 118-125.

118. Zilboorg, 1944.

119. Stewart, A.J. and Winter, D.G., "The Nature and Causes of Female Suppression," *Signs,* 2 (1977), 531-553; Lamphere, L., "Anthropology," *Signs,* 2 (1977), 612-627.

120. Longee, C.C., "Modern European History," *Signs,* 2 (1977) 628-650; Rapp, R. "Review: Anthropology," *Signs,* 4 (1979), 497-513.

121. Stewart and Winter, 1977.

122. Rosenburg, M., "The Biologic Basis for Sex Role Stereotypes in Kaplan, A.G. and Bean, J.P., 1976.

≡   ≡   ≡

— 271

VI: WOMEN AND THE FAMILY

1.   Ruskin, J., "Of Queens Gardens," in *Sesame and Lilies* ([n.c.] : Hammond Publishing, 1902).

2.   Galbraith, J.K., *Economics and the Public Purse* (Boston: Houghton-Mifflin, 1973).

3.   Myrdal, A. and Klein, F., *Women's Two Roles,* second edition (London: Routledge and Kegan Paul. 1968).

4.   Meissner, M. et al., "No Exit for Wives: Sexual Division of Labour and the Cumulation of Household Demands," *Rev. Canad. Soc. & Anthr.,* 12 (1975), 424-439.

5.   Weisner, T.S., "Some Cross-Cultural Perspectives on Becoming Female," in Kopp, C.B., ed., *Becoming Female: Perspectives on Development* (New York & London: Plenum Press, 1979).

6.   Apoko, A., "At Home in the Village: Growing up in Acholi," in Fox, L.K., ed., *East African Childhood: Three Versions* (Nairobi: Oxford Univ. Press, 1967).

7.   Whiting, B. and Edwards C.A., "Cross-Cultural Analysis of Sex Differences in the Behaviour of Children Aged Three Through Eleven," in LeVine, R.A., ed., *Culture & Personality, Contemporary Readings* (Chicago: Aldine, 1974).

8.   Brusegard, D., "Health," *Perspectives Canada III,* Ottawa, no date, p. 48.

9.   Berman, D., *Death on the Job: Occupational Health & Safety Struggles in the United States* (New York: Monthly Review Press, 1978).

10.   Brenner, M.H., "Personal Stability and Economic Security," *Social Policy,* 8 (1977), 1.

11.   Hinkle, E. et al., "Occupation, Education and Coronary Heart Disease," in Hart, E. and Sechrist, W., eds., *Dynamics of Wellness,* (Belmont: Wadsworth Publishing, 1970), pp. 396-414.

12.   Boston Women's Health Book Collective *Ourselves & Our Children* (New York: Random House, 1978).

13.   Hannerz, U., *Soulside: Inquiries into Ghetto Culture and Community* (New York: Columbia Univ. Press, 1969); Stack, C., *All Our Kin: Strategies for Survival in a Black Community* (New York: Harper & Row, 1974).

14.   Useem, M. & Miller, S.M., "The Upper Class in Higher Education," *Social Policy,* 7 (1977), 4; Bowles, S. & Gintis, H., *Schooling in*

Capitalist America (New York: Basic Books, 1977); Bowles, S., Unequal Education and the Reproduction of the Social Divsion of Labor," in Carney, M., ed., *Schooling in a Corporate Society: The Political Economy of Education in America and the Alternatives Before Us* (New York: David McKay & Co., 1972).

15.   Stephenson, P.S., "Project Toddler — a drop in the bucket?" *J. of the Division of Early Childhood,* 1 (1979), 115-122.

16.   "Poor Kids", a Report by the National Council of Welfare on Children in *Poverty in Canada,* March 1975, p. 41.

17.   Manuel, G. and Posluns, M., *The Fourth World: An Indian Reality* (Collier-MacMillan Canada, Ltd., 1974); Cardinal, H., *The Unjust Society: The Tragedy of Canada's Indians* (Edmonton: M.G. Hunting Ltd., 1969).

18.   "Women and Poverty," A Report by the National Council of Welfare, Ottawa, October 1979.

19.   Davin, A., *"Imperialism and Motherhood," History Workshop,* 5 (1978), 9-65.

20.   Stephenson, P.S., "Society's Changing Attitude to the Idiot," *Canadian Psychiatric Association J.,* 12 (1967), 83-84.

21.   Taylor, J.W., "The Diminishing Birthrate and What is Involved in It," Presidential Address to Inaugural Meeting of British Gynaecological Society, *British Medical Journal,* 20 Feb., (1904), 427.

22.   Key, E., *The Century of the Child* (New York: G.P. Putnam, 1909), pp. 100-101.

23.   Editorial, *J. American Medical Association,* 32 (1899), 1183.

24.   Roback, A.A., *History of American Psychology* (New York: Appleton-Century-Crofts, 1950), p. 569.

25.   Watson, J.B., *Behaviorism* (New York: W.W. Norton, 1924).

26.   Liddiard, M., *The Mothercraft Manual* (London: J.A. Churchill, eigth edition, 1931).

27.   Mitchell, J., *Psychoanlaysis and Feminism* (New York: Random House, 1974).

28.   Ilg, F.L. and Ames, L.B., *Child Behavior* (New York: Harper & Row, 1951).

29.   Anthony, E.J. and Benedek, T., *Parenthood: Its Psychology and Psychopathology* (Boston: Little, Brown, 1970).

30.   Wylie, P., *Generation of Vipers* (New York: Rinehart & Co., 1950).

31.   Erikson, E., *Childhood and Society* (New York: W.W. Nor-

ton & Co., 1950).

32. Bowlby, J., *Maternal Care and Mental Health* (Geneva: World Health Organization monograph, 1951).

33. Spitz, R., "Hospitalism: An Inquiry into the Genesis of Psychiatric Conditions in Early Childhood, Part I," *Psychoanalytic Study of the Child,* 1 (1945), 53-74.

34. Bowlby, 1951.

35. Spitz, R., *The First Year of Life: A Psychoanalytic Study of Normal and Deviant Development of Object Relations* (New York: International Universities Press, 1965).

36. Wolins, M., "Group Care: Friend or Foe?" *Social Work,* 14 (1969), 35-53.

37. Levy, D.M., *Maternal Overprotection* (New York: Columbia Univ. Press, 1943).

38. Miller, M.L., "Allergy and Emotions," *International Archives of Allergy and Applied Immunology,* 1 (1950), 40-49.

39. Harris, I.D. et al., "Observations on Asthmatic Children," *American Journal of Orthopsychiatry,* 20 (1950), 490-505; Miller, H. and Baruch, D.W., "A Study of Hostility in Allergic Children," *American Journal of Orthopsychiatry,* 20 (1950), 506-519.

40. Weiss, E. and English, O.S., *Psychosomatic Medicine* (Philadelphia: W.B. Saunders, 1957), p. 374.

41. French, T.M. and Alexander, F., *Psychogenic Factors in Bronchial Asthma* (Washington: National Research Council, 1941).

42. Karpman, B. ed., *Symposia on Child and Juvenile Delinquency* (Washington: Psychodynamics Monograph Series, 1959).

43. Berkovitz, P. and Rothman, E., *The Disturbed Child* (New York: New York Univ. Press, 1960); Levy, D.M., "Primary Affect Hunger," *American Journal of Psychiatry,* 94 (1937), 643-652; Levy, D.M., *Maternal Over-Protection* (New York: Columbia Univ. Press, 1943).

44. Bowlby, J., "Forty-Four Juvenile Thieves: Their Character and Home Life," *International Journal of Psychoanalysis,* 25 (1944), 19-53, 107-127; Spitz, R.A., "Possible Infantile Precursors of Psychopathy," *American Journal of Orthopsychiatry,* 20 (1950), 240-248.

45. Sullivan, H.S., *The Interpersonal Theory of Psychiatry* (New York: Norton, 1953); Mullahy, P., *Oedipus Myth and Complex* (New York: Hermitage, 1948).

46. Stephenson, P.S., "Myths about Juvenile Delinquency,"

Canadian Journal of Criminology and Corrections, 15, 1 (1973), 83-92.

47.   Fromm-Reichman, F., "Transference Problems in Schizophrenia," *Psychoanalysis,* 8 (1936), 412-426.

48.   Arieti, S., *Interpretation of Schizophrenia* (New York: Brunner, 1955).

49.   Wilman, B.B., "Schizophrenia in Childhood," in Wolman, B. B. ed., *Manual of Child Psychopathology* (New York: McGraw-Hill, 1972.

50.   Hill, L.B., *Psychotherapeutic Intervention in Schizophrenia* (Chicago: Univ. of Chicago Press, 1955).

51.   Lidz, T., Fleck, S. and Cornelison, A., *Schizophrenia and the Family* (New York: International Universities Press, 1965).

52.   Bateson, G. et al., "Towards a Theory of Schizophrenia," *Behavioural Science,* 1 (1958), 251-264.

53.   Waring, E.M., "Family Therapy and Schizophrenia," *Canadian Psychiatric Association Journal,* 23 (1978), 51-58.

54.   Wilson, L., *This Stranger, My Son* (London: John Murray, 1969), pp. 74-75.

55.   Despert, J.L., "Some Considerations Relating to the Genesis Of Autistic Behaviour in Children," *American Journal of Orthopsychiatry,* 21 (1951), 335-350; Kanner, L., "Autistic Disturbances of Affective Contact," *The Nervous Child,* 2 (1943), 217-250.

56.   Bettelheim, B., *Infantile Autism and the Birth of the Self* (New York: Free Press, 1967).

57.   Mahler M.S., *On Childhood Psychosis and Schizophrenia: Autistic and Symbiotic Infantile Psychoses, Psychoanalytic Study of the Child,* Vol. 7 (New York: International Universities Press, 1952), pp. 286-305.

58.   Kysar, J.E., "The Two Camps in Child Psychiatry," *Am. J. Psychiat.,* 125 (1968), 141-147.

59.   Powell, G.J., "Growing up Black and Female," in Kopp, C. B., ed., *Becoming Female,* 1979.

60.   Rutter, M., "Psychological Development: Predictions from Infancy," *Journal of Child Psychiatry and Psychology,* 11 (1970), 49-62; Sameroff, A.J., "Early Influences on Development: Fact or Fancy?" *Merrill-Palmer Quarterly,* 20 (1975), 275-301; Caldwell, V.M., "The Effects of Infant Care," in Hoffman, M.L. and Hoffman, L.W., eds., *Review of Child Development Research,* Vol. I (New York: Russell Sage, 1965), pp. 9-88; Yarrow, L.J., "Separation from Parents in Early

Childhood," in Hoffman and Hoffman, 1965, pp. 89-136.

61. Bronson, W.C., "Mother-Toddler Interaction: A Perspective on Studying the Development of Competence," *Merrill-Palmer Quarterly*, 20 (1974), 275-301.

62. Rathbun, C., DiVirgilio, L. and Waldfogel, S., "The Restitutive Process in Children Following Radical Separation from Family and Culture," *Am. J. Orthopsychiatry*, 28 (1958), 408-415; Winick, M., Meyer, K.K. and Harris, R.C., "Malnutrition and Environmental Enrichment by Early Adoption," *Science*, 190 (1975), 1173-1175.

63. Rutter, M., *Maternal Deprivation Reassessed* (Middlesex, England: Penguin Books, 1972).

64. Herzog, E. and Sudia, C.E., "Fatherless Homes: A Review of Research," *Children*, September-October 1968, 177-182.

65. Earls, F., "The Fathers (Not the Mothers): Their Importance and Influence with Infants and Young Children," in Chess, S. and Thomas, A., eds., *Annual Progress in Child Psychiatry and Child Development* (New York: Brunner/Mazel, 1977).

66. Kagan, J., Kearsley, R.B. and Zelazo. P.R., *Infancy: Its Place In Human Development* (Cambridge Mass.: Harvard Univ. Press, 1978).

67. Ehrenreich, B. and English, P., *For Her Own Good: 150 Years of Experts' Advice to Women* (New York: Anchor Books, 1979).

68. Toffler, A., *Future Shock* (New York: Random House, 1970).

69. Umana, R.F., Gross, S.J. & McConville, M.T., *Crisis in the Family: Three Approaches* (New York: Gardner Press,1980), p. 92.

70. Sonne, J.C. and Lincoln, G., "The Importance of a Heterosexual Co-therapy Relationship in the Construction of a Family Image," in Cohen, I.M. ed., *Family Structure, Dynamics & Therapy, Psychiatric Research Report No. 20* (Washington, D.C.,: American Psychiatric Association, 1966), p. 200.

71. Umana et al., p. 100.

72. Ibid., p. 108.

73. Bowen, M., "The Use of Family Theory in Clinical Practice," in Haley, J., ed., *Changing Families* (New York: Grune & Swatton, 1971).

74. Voth, H., *The Castrated Family* (Kansas City: Sheed, Andrews & McNeal, Universal Press, 1977).

75. Rheingold, J.C., *The Fear of Being a Woman* (New York: Grune & Stratton, 1964).

76.   Rheingold, J.C., *The Mother, Anxiety, Death and the Catastrophic Death Complex* (London: V & A Churchill, 1967).

77.   Stephenson, P.S., "The Impact of the Women's Movement – Implications for Child Development, Menatl Health, and Family Policy," *Canada's Mental Health,* 26, 1, Supplement (1978), 10-13.

78.   Ryan, W., *Blaming the Victim* (New York: Vintage, Random House, 1976).

79.   Featherstone, J., "Family Matters," *Harvard Educational Review,* 49 (1979), 20-52.

80.   Labonte, R. and Penfold, P.S., "Canadian Perspectives in Health Promotion: a Critique." Health Education 19 (3,4), 4-9, 1981.

81.   Janeway, E., *Man's World, Woman's Place* (New York: Delta Books, 1971), p. 190.

82.   Jan, J.E., Freeman, R.D. and Scott, E.P., *Visual Impairment in Children and Adolescents* (New York: Grune & Stratton, 1977).

83.   De Myer, M.K., *Parents and Children in Autism* (New York: John Wiley & Sons, 1979).

≡   ≡   ≡

VII: VIOLENCE TOWARDS WOMEN

1.   Statistics Canada, *Crime and Traffic Enforcement Statistics,* 1976.

2.   Clark, L.M.G. and Lewis, D.J., *Rape: The Price of Coercive Sexuality* (Toronto: Women's Press, 1977), p.151; Clark, L.M.G. and Lewis, D.M., "A Study of Rape in Canada – Phases C & D," *Report to the Donner Foundation of Canada,* April 30, 1977.

3.   Johnson, A.G., *On the Prevalence of Rape in the United States, Signs* 6 (1980), 136-146.

4.   Burt, M.R., "Cultural Myths & Supports for Rape," *J. of Personality & Social Psychology,* 38, 2 (1980), 217-30.

5.   Smart, C., *Women, Crime and Criminology: A Feminist Critique* (London: Routledge and Kegan Paul, 1976), p. 94.

6.   Brownmiller, S., *Against Our Will: Men, Women and Rape* (New York: Simon & Schuster, 1975), p. 12.

7.   LeGrand, C.E., "Rape and Rape Laws: Sexism in Society and

Law," *California Law Review*, 16 (1973), 932-945.

8.   Brownmiller, 1975, pp. 165-184.

9.   Ibid., pp. 23-118.

10.   Glueck, S., *Mental Disorders and the Criminal Law* (New York: Little Brown, 1925).

11.   Karpman, B., "The Sexual Psychopath." *J. Criminal Law & Criminology*, 42 (1951), 184-198.

12.   Reinhardt, J. and Fisher, E., "The Sexual Psychopath and the Law." *J. Criminal Law & Criminology*, 42 (1951). 184-198.

13.   Glueck, S., 1925; Leppman, F., "Essential Differences Between Sex Offenders," *J. Criminal Law & Criminology* 32 (1941), 366-380.

14.   Karpman, 1951.

15.   Karpman, B., *The Sexual Offender and His Offences* (New York: Julian Press, 1954).

16.   East. W., "Sexual Offenders — A British View," *Yale Law Review*, 55 (1946), 527-557.

17.   Ibid.; Karpman, 1951; Guttmacher, M., *Sex Offences: The Problem, Causes and Prevention* (New York: Norton, 1951).

18.   Littner, N., "Psychology of The Sex Offender: Causes, Treatment, Prognosis, *Police Law Quarterly*, 3 (1973), 5-31.

19.   Mendelsohn, B., "The Origin of the Doctrine of Victiminology," in Drapkin, I. and Viano, E., eds., *Victimology* (Lexington, Mass.: D.C. Heath & Co., 1974), p. 3.

20.   Deutsch, Helene, *The Psychology of Women* (New York: Grune & Stratton, 1944).

21.   Hollander, B., *Psychology of Misconduct, Vice and Crime* (New York: MacMillan, 1924).

22.   Von Hentig, H., "Remarks on the Interaction of Perpetrator and Victim," *J. Criminal Law & Criminology*, 31 (1940), 303-309.

23.   Amir, M., "Victim Precipitated Forcible Rape," *J. Criminal Law, Criminology and Police Science*, 58, 4 (1967), 493.

24.   MacDonald, J.M., *Rape Offenders and Their Victims* (Springfield, Illinois: Charles C. Thomas, 1971).

25.   Littner, 1973.

26.   Abrahamsen, D., *The Psychology of Crime* (New York: Columbia Univ. Press, 1960).

27.   Factor, M., "A Women's Psychological Reaction to Attempted Rape," *Psychoanalytic Quarterly*, 23 (1954), 243-244.

28. Abrahamsen, 1960.

29. Roberts, L. and Pacht, A., "Termination of Inpatient Treatment for Sex Deviates: Psychiatric, Social and Legal Factors," *Am. J. Psychiatry*, 121 (1965), 873-880.

30. McCaldon, R.J., "Rape," *Canadian J. Corrections*, 9 (1957), 37-59.

31. Kasdener, S., "Rape Fantasies," *J. Religion and Health*, 14 (1975), 50-57.

32. Hartman, A., Nikolay, R., "Sexually Deviant Behaviour in Expectant Fathers," *J. Abnormal Psychology*, 71 (1966), 232-234.

33. Amir, M., *Patterns in Forcible Rape* (Chicago: Univ. of Chicago Press, 1971); East, 1946; Guttmacher, 1951; Leppman, 1941; Rada, R., "Alcoholism and Forcible Rape," *Am. J. Psychiatry*, 132 (1975), 444-446.

34. Clark and Lewis, *Rape: The Price of Coercive Sexuality*, 1977.

35. Hilberman, E., *The Rape Victim* (Washington, D.C.: American Psychiatric Association, 1976).

36. Clark and Lewis, "A Study of Rape in Canada — Phases C & D."

37. Freud, S., *Femininity, New Introductory Lectures in Psychoanalysis,* translated by W.J.H. Sprott, 1933.

38. Bonaparte, M., *Female Sexuality* (New York: Grove Press, 1965), p. 80.

39. Millet, K., *Sexual Politics* (Garden City, N.Y.: Doubleday, 1970).

40. Sutherland, E., "Sexual Psychopathy Laws," *J. Criminal Law & Criminology*, 40 (1950), 543-554.

41. Amir, 1971; Clark and Lewis, *Rape: The Price of Coercive Sexuality*, 1977.

42. Clark and Lewis, *Rape: The Price of Coercive Sexuality*, 1977, p. 107.

43. Brownmiller, 1975, pp. 218-225.

44. Russell, D. *The Politics of Rape: The Victim's Perspective* (New York: Stein and Day, 1975), p. 260.

45. Clark and Lewis, *Rape: The Price of Coercive Sexuality*, 1977, p. 101.

46. Amir, 1967.

47. Geller, S., "The Sexually Assaulted Female; Innocent Victim

or Temptress?" (Toronto: Employee Health Services Branch, Parliament Buildings, 1974).

48.   Mulvihill, D.J., Tumin, M.M. and Curtis, L.A., *Crimes of Violence*, Vols. 11 & 12, a staff report to the National Commission on the Causes and Prevention of Violence (Washington, D.C.: U.S. Government Printing Office, 1969).

49.   Gebhard, O.P. et al., *Sex Offenders: An Analysis of Types* (New York, 1965).

50.   Carpenter, J. and Armanti, N., "Some Effects of Ethanol on Human Sexual and Aggressive Behaviour": in B. Hessin and H. Begleiter, eds., *The Biology of Alcoholism*, Vol. 2 (New York: Plenum Press, 1972).

51.   Rada, 1975.

52.   Hilberman, E., 1976; Notman, M.T. and Nadelson, C.C.," The Rape Victim: Psychodynamic Considerations, *Am. J. Psychiatry*, 133 (1976), 408-413.

53.   Metzger, D., "It is Always the Woman who is Raped," *Am. J. Psychiatry*, 133 (1976), 405-408; Russell, D., *The Politics of Rape: The Victim's Perspective* (New York: Stein and Day, 1976).

54.   McCombie, S.L., et. al., "Development of a Medical Center Rape Crisis Intervention Program," *Am. J. Psychiatry*, 133 (1976), 418-421; Neufeld, S. and Uit den Bogard, B., "Characteristics of Rape," *Report to the Non Medical Use of Drugs Directorate*, Health and Welfare Canada. Project No. 1216-9-70; Goldsberry, N., "Rape in British Columbia: a Report to the Ministry of Attorney-General," Victoria, B.C., March 1979.

55.   Metzger, 1976.

56.   Groth, A.N. Burgess, A.W. and Holmstrom, L.L., "Rape: Power, Anger and Sexuality,"

57.   Hilberman, 1976.

58.   Smart, 1976. p. 107.

59.   Clark and Lewis, "A Study of Rape in Canada — Phases C & D," 1977.

60.   De Francis, V., ed., *Sexual Abuse of Children* (Denver: Children's Division of the American Humane Association, 1967).

61.   Weinberg, S.K., *Incest Behaviour* (New York: Citadel Press, 1955).

62.   Sgroi, S.M., " 'Kids with Clap': Gonorrhea as Indicator of

Child Sexual Assault," *Victimology,* 2 (1977), 251-267.

63.   Branch, G. and Paxton, R., "A Study of Gonococcal Infections Among Infants and Children," *Public Health Reports,* 80 (1965), 347-352.

64.   Sgroi, 1977.

65.   Revitch, F. and Weiss, R., "The Pedophilic Offender," *Diseases of the Nervous System,* 23 (1962), 73-78.

66.   Abraham, K., "The Experiencing of Sexual Traumas as a Form of Sexual Activity," in Abraham, K., ed., *Selected Papers on Psychoanalysis,* (London: Hogarth Press, 1942), pp. 47-63; Bender, L. and Blau, A., "The Reaction of Children to Sexual Relations with Adults," *Am. J. Orthopsychiatry,* 7 (1937), 500-518.

67.   Goodwin, J. and Sahd, D. "Incest Hoax: False Accusations and False Denials," paper presented at the American Psychiatric Association Annual Meeting, Toronto, May 4, 1977; McDonald, J.M., *Rape: Offenders and Their Victims* (Springfield: Charles Thomas, 1971), pp. 209-230, 284-291.

68.   Lustig, N., Dresser, J.W., and Spellman, S.W., "Incest: a Family Group Survival Pattern," *Archives of General Psychiatry,* 14 (1966), 31-40.

69.   Kaufman, I., Peck A.L. and Tagiuri, C.K., "The Family Constellation and Overt Incestuous Relationships Between Father and Daughter," *American J. Orthopsychiatry,* 24 (1954), 266-279.

70.   Rosenfeld, A.A., et al., "Incest and Sexual Abuse of Children" *J. American Academy of Child Psychiatry,* 16 (1977), 327-339.

71.   Brant, R.S.T. and Tisza, V.G., "The Sexually Misused Child *Am. J. Orthopsychiatry,* 47 (1977), 80-90.

72.   Weiner, I.B., "Father-Daughter Incest: A Clinical Report," *Psychiatric Quarterly,* 36 (1962), 607-632.

73.   Yogoguchi, L., "Children not Severely Damaged by Incest with a Parent," *J. American Academy of Child Psychiatry,* 5 (1966), 111-124; Weiner, J.B., "Father-Daughter Incest," *Psychiatric Quarterly,* 36 (1962), 1132-1138.

74.   Lukianowitz, N., "Incest," *British J. Psychiatry,* 120 (1972), 301-313.

75.   Sloane, P. and Karpinski, E., "Effects of Incest on the Participants," *Am. J. Orthopsychiatry,* 12 (1942), 666-673; Kaufman, I., Peck, A. and Tagiuri, L. 1954.

76.   Benward, J. and Densen-Gerber, J., *Incest as a Causative Fac-*

tor in Anti-Social Behaviour: An Exploratory Study (New York: Odyssey Institute, 1975).

77.   Herman, J. and Hirschman, L., "Father-Daughter Incest," *Signs,* 2 (1977), 735-756.

78.   Gelles, R.J., *The Violent Home* (Beverly Hills, Ca: Sage Publications, 1972).

79.   Statistics Canada, *Homicide in Canada,* 1974.

80.   Gropper, A. and Marvin, J., "Violence Begins at Home," *The Canadian,* November 20, 1976.

81.   Downey, J. and Howell, J., "Wife Battering: a Review and Preliminary Enquiry into Local Incidence, Needs and Resources," *United Way of Greater Vancouver,* September 1976.

82.   Segal, J., "Violent Men-Embattled Women" *Cosmopolitan,* May (1976), 238-241.

83.   Hilberman, E. and Munson, K., "Sixty Battered Women," *Victimology,* Special issue on spouse abuse, 2 (1977-78), 460-471.

84.   Van Stolk, M., "Beaten Women, Battered Children," *Children Today,* March-April (1976), 9-12; Gelles, R.J., "Violence and Pregnancy: A Note on the Extent of the Problem and Needed Services," *Family Coordinator,* January (1975).

85.   Whitehurst, R.N., "Alternative Family Structures and Violence Reduction," in Steinmetz, S. and Straus, M. eds., *Violence in the Family* (New York: Dodd, Mead, 1974).

86.   Van Stolk, 1976.

87.   Gould Davis, E., *The First Sex* (New York: Platinum, 1971).

88.   Lystad, M.H., "Violence at Home: A Review of the Literature," *Am. J. Orthopsychiatry,* 45 (1975), 328-345.

89.   Gil, D., *Violence Against Children: Physical Child Abuse in the United States* (Cambridge: Harvard Univ. Press, 1970).

90.   Miller, N., *Battered Spouses* (London: G. Bell & Sons, 1975).

91.   Schultz, L.G., "The Wife-Assaulter," *J. Social Therapy,* 6 (1960), 103-112.

92.   Goode, W.J. and Whitehurst, R.N., in Steinmetz, S.K. and Straus, M.A., *Violence and the Family,* 1974.

93.   Goode, W., "Violence Among Intimates," U.S. National Commission on the Causes and Prevention of Violence. Task Force on Individual Acts of Violence, *Crimes and Violence,* 13 (1969), 941-977.

94.   Storr, A., *Human Aggression* (New York: Bantam, 1970).

95.   Gropper and Marvin, 1976.

96.   Gropper, A. and Currie, J., *A Study of Battered Women, M.A. Thesis,* School of Social Work Library, Univ. of British Columbia, March 1976.

97.   Morrissey, M. "Why a Transition House for Women", paper presented at symposium, Alternatives to Psychiatric Treatment for Women, *Canadian Psychiatric Association Annual Meeting,* Halifax, Nova Scotia, 1978.

98.   Pizzey, E., *Scream Quietly or the Neighbours Will Hear* (Middlesex, England: Penguin Books, 1974).

99.   Ibid., p. 102.

100.   Downey and Howell, 1976.

101.   Gayford, J.J., "Wife Battering: A Preliminary Survey of a Hundred Cases," *British Medical J.,* January (1975), 195-197.

102.   Martin, D., *Battered Wives* (San Francisco: Glide 1976).

103.   Downey and Howell, 1976, p. 24.

104.   Tidmarsh, M., "Violence in Marriage," *Social Work Today,* 7, 2 (1976), 36-38.

105.   Gelles, 1972.

106.   Lombroso, C. and Ferrero, W., *The Female Offender* (London: Fisher Unwin, 1895).

107.   Rolph, C.H., *Women of the Streets* (London: Secker & Warburg, 1955).

108.   Gibbens, T.C.N., "Juvenile Prostitution," *British J. Delinquency,* 8 (1957).

109.   Gibbens, 1957; Greenwald, H. *The Call Girl* (New York: Ballantine Books, 1958).

110.   Ibid.

111.   Henriques, F., *Modern Sexuality,* Vol. III, *Prostitution and Society* (London: MacGibbon and Kee, 1968).

112.   Gibbens, 1957.

113.   Bullough, V.L., *The History of Prostitution* (New York: University Books, 1964).

114.   Smart, C., *Women, Crime and Criminology: A Feminist Critique* (London: Routledge and Kegan Paul, 1976).

115.   Davis, K. "Prostitution" in Merton, R.K. and Bisbet, R., eds., *Contemporary Social Problems* 3rd Edition, (New York: Harcourt Brace Jovanovich, 1971).

116.   Walkowitz, J.R., "The Politics of Prostitution" *Signs* 6 (1980), 123-135.

117. The Commission on Obscenity and Pornography. *The Report of the Commission on Obscenity and Pornography*, (Washington, D.C.: U.S. Government Printing Office, 1970.

118. Diamond, I., "Pornography and Repression: A Reconsideration *Signs* 5 (1980), 686-701.

119. Fesbach, S. and Malamuth, N., "Sex and Aggression: Proving the Link," *Psychology Today*, 12 (1978), 111-117.

120. Millet, K., *Sexual Politics* (New York: Doubleday & Co., 1969), pp. 42-45.

121. Morgan, R., "Goodbye to All That", in Martin, W., eds, *The American Sisterhood* (New York: Harper & Row, 1972), p. 361.

122. Dworkin, A., *Woman Hating* (New York: E.P. Dutton, p. 78.

123. Brownmiller, 1975.

124. Morgan, R., *Going Too Far* (New York: Random House, 1977), p. 169.

125. Russell, D., "On Pornography," *Chrysalis* 4 (1977), 12.

126. Brownmiller, 1975; Lewis, D.J., "Pornography: Developing Feminist Perspectives," Kinesis, *Vancouver Status of Women*, October 1978.

127. Steinem, G., "Is Child Pornography About Sex? *Ms.* 6, 2 (1977), 42-44.

128. Nobile, P., "The Last Taboo," *Penthouse*, December (1977).

VIII: WOMEN AND DEPRESSION

1. Weissman, M.M. and Klerman, G.L., "Sex Differences and the Epidemiology of Depression," *Arch. Gen. Psychiat.*, 34 (1977), 98-111; Statistics Canada, Mental Health Statistics Annual Reports; Silverman, C., *The Epididemiology of Depression* (Baltimore: Johns Hopkins Press, 1968); Wing, J.K. and Hailey, A.M., eds., *Evaluating a Community Psychiatric Service* (London: Oxford Univ. Press, 1972).

2. Research Divison, Saskatchewan Alcoholism Commission. *A Socio-Demographic Profile of People Prescribed Mood-Modifiers in Saskatchewan.* Final Report, January, 1978.

3. Linn, L., "Clinical Manifestations of Psychiatric Disorders," in Freedman, A.M., Kaplan, H.I. and Sadock, B.J., *Comprehensive Textbook of Psychiatry II* (Baltimore: Williams and Wilkins, 1975), p. p. 811.

4. The Task Force on Nomenclature and Statistics of the

American Psychiatric Association, Micro-D. Revisions in the Diagnostic Criteria of the DSM III 1/15/78 Draft; Second Printing 1/2/79.

5.　　Garfinkel, P.E., Walsh, J.J., Stancer, H.C., "Depression: New Evidence in Support of Biological Differentiation," *Am. J. Psychiat.*, 136 (1979), 535-539.

6.　　Kety, S. and Schildkraut, J.J., "Biogenic Amines and Emotion," *Science*, 156 (1967), 21.

7.　　Slater, E. and Cowie, V., "The Genetics of Mental Disorders" *Oxford Monographs in Medical Genetics* (London: Oxford Univ. Press, 1971).

8.　　Goetze, U., Green, R., Whybrow, P., et al., "X-Linkage Revisted," *Arch. Gen. Psychiat.*, 31 (1974), 665-672.

9.　　Blank, A.M., Goldstein, S.E., Chatterjee, N., "Premenstrual Tension and Mood Changes," *Can. J. Psychiatry*, 25 (1980), 577-585; Dalton, K., *The Premenstrual Syndrome* (Springfield, Ill.: Charles C. Thomas, 1964); Dalton, K., *The Menstrual Cycle* (New York: Pantheon Books, 1969); McClure, J., Reich, T., Wetzel, R., "Premenstrual Symptoms as an Indicator of Bipolar Affective Disorder," *Br. J. Psychiat.*, 119 (1971), 527-528; Wetzel, R., Reich, T., McClure, J., et al., "Premenstrual Affective Syndrome and Affective Disorder," *Br. J. Psychiat.* 127 (1975), 219-221.

10.　　Reid, R.L. and Yen, S.S.C., "Premenstrual Syndrome," *Am. J. Obstet. Gyn.*, 139, 1 (1981), 85-104.

11.　　Friedman, R.C., Hurt, S.W., Arnoff, M.F., and Clarkin, J., "Behaviour and the Menstrual Cycle, *Signs*, 5 (1980), 719-738.

12.　　Weissman, M.M. and Slaby, A.E., "Oral Contraceptives and Psychiatric Disturbance: Evidence From Research." *Br. J. Psychiat.*, 123 (1973), 513-518.

13.　　Adams, P.W., et al., "Effect of Pyridoxine Hydrochloride (Vitamin B_6) upon Depression Associated with Oral Contraception." *The Lancet*, April (1973), 897-904.; Winston, F., "Oral Contraceptives, Pyridoxine and Depression." *Am. J. Psychiat.*, 130 (1973), 1217-1221.

14.　　Koran, L.M. and Hamburg, P.A., "Psychophysiological Endocrine Disorders," in Freedman, A.M., Kaplan, H.I., and Sadock, B.J., eds., *Comprehensive Textbook of Psychiatry II* (Baltimore: Williams & Wilkins, 1975), pp. 1673-1684.

15.　　Haller, J.S. Jr., and Haller, R.M., *The Physician and Sexuality in Victorian America* (Urbana: Univ. of Illinois Press, 1975), p. 135.

16.　　Goodman, M., "Toward a Biology of Menopause," *Signs*, 5

(1980), 739-753.

17.   "Medical Sexism." *Healthright*, 6 (1975-76).

18.   Wilson, R.A., *Feminine Forever*, (New York: M. Evans, 1966).

19.   Ziel, H.K., and Finkle, W.D., "Increased Risk of Endometrial Carcinoma Among Users of Conjugate Oestrogens, *New Eng. J. Med.*, 293 (1975), 1167-1170.

20.   Ford, H., "Involutional Melancholia," in Freedman, Kaplan. and Sadock, 1975, pp. 1025-1042.

21.   Hallstrom, T., *Mental Disorder and Sexuality in the Climacteric* (Goteberg, Sweden: Orstadius Biktryckeri AB, 1973); Winokur, G., "Depression in the Menopause," *Am. J. Psychiat.*, 130 (1973), 92-93; Silverman, C., *The Epidemiology of Depression* (Baltimore: Johns Hopkins Press, 1968); Adelstein, A.M., Downham, P.Y., Stein, Z., et al., "The Epidemiology of Mental Illness in an English City." *Social Psychiatry*, 3 (1964), 455-468; Sorenson, A. and Stromgren, E., "Frequency of Depressive States within Geographically Limited Population Groups, *Acta Psychiatrica Scandinavica*, 37 (1961), 32-68.

22.   McKinlay, S.M. and Jeffreys, M., "The Menopausal Syndrome," *Br. J. Preventive Social Med.*, 28 (1974), 108-115; Neugarten, B., *Middle Age and Aging* (Chicago: Univ. of Chicago Press, 1968); Hallstrom, T., 1973.

23.   Rosenthal, S.H., "The Involutional Depressive Syndrome," *Am. J. Psychiat.* (Suppl.), 124 (1968), 21-35.

24.   Robertson, B.M., "The Psychoanalytic Theory of Depression," *Can. J. Psychiat.*, 24 (1979), 341-352.

25.   Bibring, E., "The Mechanism of Depression," in Greenacre, P. ed., *Affective Disorders: Psychoanlytic Contributions to their Study* (New York: International Universities Press, 1961), pp. 13-48.

26.   Weissman, M.M. and Klerman, G.L., "Sex Differences and the Epidiology of Depression," in Gomberg, E.S. and Franks, V., *Gender and Disordered Behavior: Sex Differences in Psychopathology* (New York: Brunner/Mazel, 1979).

27.   Weissman, M.M. and Paykel, E.S., *The Depressed Woman: A Study of Social Relationships* (Chicago: Univ. of Chicago Press, 1974).

28.   Chodoff, P., "The Depressive Personality: A Critical Review," *Arch. Gen. Psychiat.*, 27 (1972), 666-673.

29.   Beck, A.T., *Depression: Clinical, Experimental and Theoretical Aspects* (London: Staples Press, 1967).

30. Seligman, M.E.P., "Learned Helplessness," *Ann. Rev. Med.,* 23 (1972), 407.

31. Hays, H.R., *The Dangerous Sex: The Myth of Feminine Evil.* (New York: Putman, 1964).

32. Weissman, M.M. and Paykel, E.S., 1974.

33. Weissman, M.M. and Klerman, G.L., 1979.

34. Horowitz, M., "New Directions in Epidemiology," *Science,* 188 (1975), 850-851.

35. Paykel, E.S., Prusoff, B.A., and Uhlenhuth, E.H., "Scaling of Life Events," *Arch. Gen. Psychiat.,* 25 (1971), 340-347.

36. Blumenthal, M.D., "Measuring Depressive Symptoms in a General Population," *Arch. Gen. Psychiat.,* 32 (1975), 971-978.

37. Mazer, M., "People in Predicament: A Study in Psychiatric and Psychosocial Epidemiology," *Social Psychiatry,* 9 (1974), 85-90; Silverman, C., 1968.

38. Sorenson and Stromgren, 1961; Paykel, E.S., et al., "Life Events and Depression: a Controlled Study," *Arch. Gen; Psychiat.,* 21 (1969), 753-760; Schwab, J.J., McGinnis, N.H., and Warheit, G.J., "Social Psychiatric Impairment: Racial Comparisons" *Am. J. Psychiat.,* 130 (1973), 183-187; Martin, F.F., Brotherston, J.H.F., and Chave, S. P.W., *Br. J. Preventive Social Med.,* 11 (1957), 196-202.

39. Koeske, R.K. and Koeske, G.F., "An Attributional Approach to Mood and the Menstrual Cycle," *J. of Personality and Social Psychology,* 31 (1975), 473-478.

40. Brown, G.W. and Harris, T., *Social Origins of Depression: A Study of Psychiatric Disorder in Women* (London: Tavistock Publications, 1978).

41. Richman, N., "Depression in Mothers of Preschool Children." *J. Child Psychol. Psychiat.,* 17 (1976), 75-78.

42. Richman, N., "The Effect of Housing on Preschool Children and Their Mothers," *Develop. Med. Child Neurol.,* 16 (1974), 53-58.

43. Moss, P. and Plavis, I., "Mental Distress in Mothers of Preschool Children in Inner London *Psychol. Med.,* 7 (1977), 641-652.

44. *Postpartum Depression* National Film Board, Canada, 1979.

45. Kitzinger, S., "The Fourth Trimester," *Midwife, Health Visitor, and Community Nurse,* 11 (1975), 118-121.

46. Robertson, J.M., "A Treatment Model for Postpartum Depression," *Canada's Mental Health,* 28, 2 (1980), 16-17.

47. Bart, P.B., "Why Women's Status Changes in Middle Age,"

Sociological Symposium, 3 (1969), 1-18.

48.   Bart, P.B. and Grossman, M., "Menopause," in Notman, M.T. and Nadelson, C.C., eds., *The Woman Patient* (New York: Plenum, 1978).

49.   Bart, P.B., "Mother Portnoy's Complaints," *Trans-Action,* 8 (1970), 69-74; Bart, P.B., "Depression in Middle-Aged Women," in Gornick, V., Moran, B.K., *Women in Sexist Society: Studies in Power and Powerlessness* (New York: Basic Books, 1971), pp. 99-117.

50.   Friedan, B., *The Feminine Mystique* (New York: Dell Publishing, 1963), pp. 11-27.

51.   Greer, G., *The Female Eunuch* (St. Albans, Great Britain: Paladin, 1971).

52.   Rowbotham, S., *Woman's Consciousness, Man's World,* (Middlesex, England: Penguin Books, 1973), pp. 67-80.

53.   Rich, A., *Of Woman Born: Motherhood As Experience and Institution* (New York: W.W. Norton, 1976).

≡   ≡   ≡

IX: PSYCHOTROPIC DRUGS AND WOMEN

1.   Parish, P.A., "The Prescribing of Psychotropic Drugs in General Practice," *Journal of Royal College of General Practitioners,* Supplement No. 4, 21 (1971), 1-77; Parry, H.J., Balter, M.B., Mellinger, D., Cisin, I.H., and Manheimer, D.I., "National Patterns of Psychotherapeutic Drug Use," *Archives of General Psychiatry* 28 (1973), 760-783; Cooperstock, R. and Sims, M., "Mood-Modifying Drugs Prescribed in a Canadian City: Hidden Problems," *American Journal of Public Health,* 61 (1971), 1007-1016.

2.   Guse, L., Morier, G., and Ludwig, J., "Winnipeg Survey of Prescription (Mood-Altering) Use Among Women," *Technical Report, N.M.U.D.D.* Manitoba Alcoholism Foundation, October, 1976.

3.   Committee Concerned with Women's Health Issues in Etobicoke, Ontario, "The Use of Prescription Medication by Women 18 Years and Over in Etobicoke," Study in Progress.

4.   Cooperstock, R., "Psychotropic Drug Use Among Women" *Canadian Medical Association Journal,* 115 (1976), 760-763; Skegg, D.G., Doll, R., and Perry, J., "Use of Medicines in General Practice,"

288 –

British Medical Journal, 1 (1977), 1561-1563; Dumonchel, T. "Maudites droguées," in *Tu prends-tu une jolie Madame chose"* (Montreal: Les Editions de la pleine lune).

5.   Jan, J.E., Freeman, R.D., Scott, E.P., *Visual Impairment in Children and Adolescents* (New York: Grune and Stratton, 1977).

6.   Osler, Sir William *Aequanimitas, with Other Addresses to Medical Students, Nurses, and Practitioners Of Medicine* (London: H.K. Lewis, 1939).

7.   D'Arcy, Carl and Schmitz, Janet, "Sex Differences in the Utilization of Health Services for Psychiatric Problems in Saskatchewan," Paper presented at symposium "The Woman Patient," *Annual Meeting, Canadian Psychiatric Association,* Saskatoon, September 29, 1977.

8.   Owen, Allen and Winkler, Robin C., "General Practitioners and Psychosocial Problems: An Evaluation Using Pseudopatients," *Medical Journal of Australia,* 2 (1974), 393-398.

9.   Wolfe, Samuel, "The Social Responsibility of the Physician in Prescribing Mind-Affecting Drugs," Social Aspects of the Medical Use of Psychotherapeutic Drugs, op. cit., Ruth Cooperstock, ed., p pp. 53-62.

10.   Lasagna, L., *The Doctor's Dilemmas* (New York: Harper, 1962).

11.   Finn, Richard "In-patient Field Trial," paper presented at special session "DSM III on trial: Some of the Evidence," *Annual Meeting, American Psychiatric Association,*Toronto, May 4, 1977.

12.   Morgan, H. G., et al., "Deliberate Self-Harm: Follow-up Study of 279 Patients," *British Journal of Psychiatry,* 128 (1976), 361-368; O'Brien, J. Patrick, "A Study of Low-Dose Amitriptyline Overdoses," *American Journal of Psychiatry,* 13 (1976), 66-68.

13.   Cooperstock, Ruth, Presentation given at workshop, "The Chemically-Dependent Woman," Toronto, June 4, 1977.

14.   Woody, G.E., O'Brien, C.P. and Greenstein, R, "Misuse and Abuse of Diazepam: Increasingly Common Medical Problem," *International Journal on Addiction,* 10 (1975), 843-848.

15.   *An Easy Pill to Swallow,* National Film Board, Canada; Gordon, Barbara, *I'm Dancing as Fast as I Can* (New York: Harper & Row, 1979).

16.   Carpenter, William T., McGlashan, Thomas H., Strauss, John S., "The Treatment of Acute Schizophrenia Without Drugs: An Investigation of Some Current Assumptions," *American Journal of Psychiatry,*

134 (1977), 14-20.

17.   Quitkin, F., et al., "Tardive Dyskinesia: Are First Signs Reversible?" *American Journal of Psychiatry,* 134 (1977), 84-87.

18.   Crane, George E., "The Prevention of Tardive Dyskinesia," *American Journal of Psychiatry,* 134 (1977). 756-758.

19.   American College of Neuropsychopharmacology — Food and Drug Administration Task Force, "Neurological Syndromes Associated with Antipsychotic Drug Use," *Archives of General Psychiatry,* 28 (1973), 463-467.

20.   Schofield, William *Psychotherapy: The Purchase of Friendship* (Englewood Cliffs, N.J.: Prentice-Hall, 1964).

21.   Winstead, D., Blackwell, B., and Eilers, M.K., "Diazepam on Demand: Drug Seeking Behaviour in Anxious Inpatients," *Archives of General Psychiatry,* 30 (1974), 349-351.

22.   Horwitz, A., "The Pathways into Psychiatric Treatment: Some Differences Between Men and Women," *Journal of Health and Social Behaviour,* 18 (1977), 169-178.

23.   Greenberg, Roger P., Fisher, Seymour, and Shapiro, Jeffrey, "Sex Role Development and Response to Medication by Psychiatric In-patients," *Psychological Reports,* 33 (1973), 675-677.

24.   Boulter, Alison and Campbell, Marie, "An Ethnography of Minor Tranquilizer Use in Selected Women's Groups in Vancouver," *Report prepared for N.M.U.D.D.,* September 1, 1977.

25.   Phillips, D.L. and Segal, B.E., "Sexual Status and Psychiatric Symptoms," *American Sociological Review,* 34 (1969), 58-72; Wadsworth, J.E.J., Butterfield, W.J.H., and Blaney, R., *Health and Sickness: The Choice of Treatment* (London: Tavistock Publications, 1971); Dunnell, K. and Cartwright, A., *Medicine Takers, Prescribers and Hoarders* (London: Routledge and Kegan Paul, 1972).

26.   Cooperstock, Ruth, "Women and 'Excessive' Use of Psychotropic Drugs," paper presented at *Annual Meeting, Canadian Psychiatric Association,* Saskatoon, September 29, 1977.

27.   Mechanic, D., "Correlates of Frustration Among British General Practitioners," *Journal of Health and Social Behaviour,* 11, 2 (1970), 87-104.

28.   Boulter and Campbell, 1977.

29.   Jeffreys, Margot, "Medicine Takes in the Medical Use of Psychotropic Drugs," *Supplement to Journal of Royal College of General Practioners,* 23, 1973.

30. Cooperstock, R., "Sex Differences in the Use of Mood-Modifying Drugs: An Explanatory Model," *Journal of Health and Social Behaviour,* 12 (1971), 238-244.

31. Amin, M.M., "Sleeping Pill – A Review in Historical Perspective," paper presented at *Annual Meeting, Canadian Psychiatric Association,* Saskatoon, September 28, 1977.

32. Cartwright, Ann, "Prescribing and the Relationship Between Patients and Doctors," *Social Aspects of the Medical Use of Psychotropic Drugs,* Ruth Cooperstock, ed., (Toronto: Addiction Research Foundation of Ontario, 1974).

33. Davis, John M., and Cole, Jonathan O., "Antipsychotic Drugs," *Comprehensive Textbook of Psychiatry,* Volume 2, Second Edition, Alfred M. Freedman, Harold I. Kaplan, and Benjamin J. Sadock, eds., (Baltimore: Williams and Wilkins, 1975).

34. Joyce, C.R.B., "Psychopharmacology – Dimensions and Perspective," *Mind and Medicine Monographs* (London: Tavistock Publications, 1968).

35. Wheatley, David, *Nonspecific Factors in Drug Therapy,* Carl Rickels, ed., (Springfield, Illinois: Charles C. Thomas, 1968).

36. Gillie, O., " 'Hazardous' Drugs Sold For Use in Africa by International Companies," London, *Sunday Times,* August 13, 1978.

37. Bruun, Keltie, "International Drug Control and the Pharmaceutical Industry," *International Symposia on Alcohol and Drug Addiction* Ruth Cooperstock, ed., (Toronto: Addiction Research Foundation, 1974).

38. Parish, 1971.

39. Mendelsohn, R., *Confessions of a Medical Heretic* (New York: Warner Books, 1980), p. 73.

40. Cowhig, J., "Minister Demands Clean-up of Doctors' Trials for Drugs," *London Observer,* January 28, 1979.

41. Cooperman, Earl M., "Antibiotics: No Panacea," editorial, *Canadian Medical Association Journal,* 116 (1977), 229-230.

42. Morgan, 1976.

43. Parish, P.A., "Is it Right to Perform a Pharmacological Leucotomy on a Large Section of Contemporary Soceity?" *Drugs and Society,* 1(1972), 11-14.

44. Hollister, Leo E., "Drug Therapy: Mental Disorders – Antipsychotic and Antimanic Drugs," *New England Journal of Medicine.* 286 (1972), 984-987.

45.   Committee on Research, Group for the Advancement of Psychiatry, *Pharmacotherapy and Psychotherapy; Paradoxes, Problems and Progress*, Vol. IX, Report No. 93, March 1975.

46.   Moss, P. and Plavis, I., "Mental Distress in Mothers of Preschool Children in Inner London," *Psychological Medicine*, 7 (1977), 641-652.

47.   Richman, N., "Depression in Mothers of Preschool Children, *Journal of Child Psychology and Psychiatry*, 17 (1976), 75-78.

48.   Richman, N., "The Effect of Housing on Preschool Children and Their Mothers," Developmental Medicine and Child Neurology, *16 (1974), 53-58.*

49.   *Brown, G.W.* and Harris, T., *Social Origins of Depression: A Study of Psychiatric Disorders in Women* (London: Tavistock Publications 1978).

50.   Mostow, E. and Newberry,P., "Work Role and Depression in Women: A Comparison of Workers and Housewives in Treatment," *American Journal of Orthopsychiatry*, 45 (1975), 538-548; Radloff, Lenore, "Sex Differences in Depression: The Effects of Occupation and Marital Status," *Sex Roles*, 1 (1975), 249-265.

51.   Guse et al., 1976.

52.   Howell, Mary C., "What Medical Schools Teach about Women," *New England Journal of Medicine*, 291 (1974), 305-307.

53.   Broverman, Ingae K. et al., "Sex Role Stereotypes and Clinical Judgements of Mental Health," *Journal of Consulting and Clinical Psychology*, 34 (1970), 1-7.

54.   Bass, M. and Paul, D., "The Influence of Sex on Tranquilizer-Prescribing," paper presented at the North American Primary Care Research Group Meeting, March 1977, Williamsburg, Virginia.

55.   Seidenberg, Robert, "Images of Health, Illness and Women in Drug Advertising," *Journal of Drug Issues*, 4 (1974), 264-267.

56.   Thomas, A., Chess, S., and Birch, H.G., *Temperament and Behaviour Disorders in Children*, (New York: New York Univ. Press 1968).

57.   Stein, Larry, Belluzzi, James D., and Wise, C. David, "Benzodiazepines: Behavioural and Neurochemical Mechanisms," *American Journal of Psychiatry*, 134 (1977), 665-672.

58.   Shore, M.F., "Drugs Can Be Dangerous During Pregnancy and Lactation," *Canadian Pharmaceutical Journal*, 103 (1970), 358-367; "Drugs in Breast Milk," *Therapeutics Bulletin*, 6 (1975), 8-9; Bar-

tig, D. and Cohon, M.S., "Excretion of Drugs in Human Milk," *Hospital Formulary Management,* 4 (1969), 26-27.

59.　Schrag, Peter and Divoky, Diane, *The Myth of the Hyperactive Child and Other Means of Child Control* (New York: Laurel Books, 1976).

60.　Prien, R.F., Klett, C.J. and Caffey, E.M., "Polypharmacy in Psychiatric Treatment of Elderly Hospitalized Patients: Survey of 12 Veterans Administration Hospitals," *Diseases of the Nervous System,* 37 (1977), 333-336.

61.　Joint Commission on Mental Illnesss and Health. *Action for Mental Health: Final Report* (New York: Basic Books, 1961).

62.　Mechanic, David, "Some Factors in Identifying and Defining Mental Illness," *Mental Hygeine,* 46 (1972), 66-74; Joenig, J. and Hamilton, M.W., *The Desegregation of the Mentally Ill* (London: Routledge and Kegan Paul, 1969).

63.　Wing, J.K. and Brown, G.W., *Institutionalism and Schizophrenia* (Cambridge: Cambridge Univ. Press, 1970).

64.　Scull, Andrew, *Decarceration* (Spectrum Books, Prentice-Hall 1977).

65.　Muller, Charlotte, "Economic Aspects of the Medical Use of Psychotropic Drugs," in Cooperstock, 1974, pp. 35-52.

66.　Broverman et al., 1970.

67.　Richie, Elizabeth, and Burwell, Elinor J., "Sex Bias in Canadian Medical Journals," paper presented at the Meetings of the Canadian Psychological Association, Calgary, 1980.

≡　　　　　　≡　　　　　　≡

IX: ALTERNATIVES TO TRADITIONAL TREATMENT: TOWARDS FEMINIST THERAPY

1.　Rice, M.M., ed., *Neswletter of the American Psychiatric Association Committee on Women,* October-December, 1980.

2.　Canadian Psychological Association, "Guidelines for Therapy and Counselling with Women," Short Version: *Canadian Psychologist,* 21 (1980), 4; Long Version: *The Ontario Psychologist,* 13 (1981), 2. Permission to reprint guidelines obtained from CPA, 14-03-82.

3. Guzell, M.C., "Problems of Personal Change in Women's Studies Courses," in Rawlings, E.I. and Carter, D.K., eds., *Psychotherapy For Women: Treatment Toward Equality* (Springfield, Illinois: Charles C. Thomas, 1977).

4. Tennov, D., *Psychotherapy: The Hazardous Cure* (Garden City, N.Y.: Anchor Books, 1976).

5. Alinsky, S.D., "The Poor and the Powerful," *Int. J. Psychiat.* 4 (1967), 308-317.

6. Sidel, V.W. and Sidel, R., "Beyond Coping," *Social Policy,* September/October (1976), 67.

7. Boston Women's Health Collective, *Our Bodies, Ourselves* (New York: Simon & Schuster, 1975).

8. Pizzey, E., *Scream Quietly or the Neighbours Will Hear* (Middlesex, England: Penguin Books, 1974).

9. McCombie, S.L., et al., "Development of a Medical Center Rape Crisis Intervention Program." *Am. J. Psychiat.,* 133 (1976), 418-421.

10. Robertson, J.A., "A Treatment Model for Postpartum Depression," *Canada's Mental Health,* 28, 2 (1980), 16-17.

11. Rich, A., *Of Woman Born* (New York: W.W. Norton, 1976).

12. Smith, D.E. and David, S., eds., *Women Look at Psychiatry* (Vancouver: Press Gang Publishers, 1975).

13. Smith, D.E., "Women, the Family and Corporate Capitalism" in Stephenson, M., ed., *Women in Canada* (Toronto: New Press, 1973).

14. Chesler, P., *Women and Madness* (New York: Avon Books, 1972).

15. Tennov, 1976.

16. Horney, K., "The Flight from Womanhood: The Masculinity Complex in Women As Viewed by Men and by Women." *Int. J. Psycho-Anal.,* 7 (1926),324-329.

17. Horney, K., "On the Genesis of the Castration Complex In Women," *Int. J. Psycho-Anal.,* 5 (1924), 50-65.

18. Horney, 1926.

19. Horney K., "Inhibited Feminity: Psychoanalytical Contribution to the Problem of Frigidity," in Horney, K., *Feminine Psychology* (New York: W.W. Norton, 1967), pp. 71-83.

20. Horney, K., "The Problem of the Monogamous Ideal." *Int. J.*

Psycho-Anal., 9 (1928), 318-331.

21.   Horney, 1967, pp. 119-132.

22.   Freud, S., "An Outline of Psychoanalysis," in Collected Papers, Vol. 23 (London: The Hogarth Press, 1956).

23.   Thompson, C., "Penis Envy in Women" (1943), in Miller, J.B. ed., Psycho-Analysis and Women (Baltimore: Penguin Books, 1973).

24.   Thompson, C., On Women (New York: Mentor Books, 1964).

25.   Seiden, A.M., "Overview: Research on the Psychology of Women in Families, Work, and Psychotherapy." Am. J. Psychiat., 133: (1976), 995-1007, 1111-1123.

26.   Fanon, F., The Wretched of the Earth (New York: Grove Press, London: Granada, 1963), Freire, P. The Pedagogy of the Oppressed (New York: Seabury Press, 1973); Sartre, J-P., Anti-Semite and Jew (New York: Grove Press, 1960).

27.   Rubin, G., Woman as Nigger, Ann Arbor, Michigan The Argus, (March 28 – April 11; April 14-28, 1969), 71-15; 14; Myrdal, G., "A Parallel to the Negro Problem," Appendix 5, in An American Dilemna (New York: Harper, 1944), pp. 1073-1078.

28.   Allport, G., The Nature of Prejudice (Cambridge, Mass.: Addison-Wesley, 1954).

29.   Miller, J.B., Toward a New Psychology of Women (Boston: Beacon Press, 1976).

30.   Fanon, F., Black Skins, White Masks (New York: Grove Press, London: Granada 1967).

31.   Daly, M., Gyn/Ecology: The Metaethics of Radical Feminism (Boston: Beacon Press, 1978).

32.   Hacker, H.M., Women as a Minority Group, in Roszack, B. and Roszack, T., (New York, Evanston, and London: Harper and Row, 1969), pp. 130-148.

33.   Griffith, A., "Feminist Counselling: A Perspective," in Smith, D.E. and David, S., eds., Women Look at Psychiatry (Vancouver: Press Gang Publishers, 1976).

34.   Seiden, A.M., Overview: Research on the Psychology of Women.

35.   Tennov, D., Psychotherapy: The Hazardous Cure, pp. 190-195.

36.   Maracek, J. and Kravetz, D., "Women and Mental Health: A

Review of Feminist Change Efforts," *Psychiatry*, 40 (1977), 323-329.

37. Rawlings, E.I. and Carter, D.K., eds., *Psychotherapy for Women: Treatment Toward Equality* (Springfield, Illinois: Charles C. Thomas, 1977), pp. 49-76.

38. Hare-Mustin, R.T., "A Feminist Approach to Family Therapy," *Family Process*, 17 (1978), 181-194.

39. David, S., "Becoming a Nonsexist Therapist," in Smith, D.E. and David, S., eds., *Women Look at Psychiatry* (Vancouver: Press Gang Publishers, 1976), pp. 165-174; David, S., "Working Effectively with Women," *Canada's Mental Health*, 28, Summer, 1980; Hare-Mustin, 1979; Mander, A.V., *Feminism as Therapy* (New York: Random House, 1974); Rawlings and Carter, 1977; Sturdivant, S., *Therapy with Women: A Feminist Philosophy of Treatment* (New York: Dell Books, 1977); Wyckoff, H., *Solving Women's Problems* (New York: Grove Press, 1977).

≡   ≡   ≡

CONCLUSIONS

1. Rich, A., in Ruddick, S. and Daniels, P., eds., *Working It Out* (New York: Pantheon Books, 1977), p. XVII.

2. Ibid., p xxiii.

3. Ibid.

Abraham, K. "The Experiencing of Sexual Traumas as a Form of Sexual Activity." Ed. K. Abraham. *Selected Papers on Psychoanalysis.* London: Hogarth Press, 1942, pp. 47-63.

Abrahamsen, D. *The Psychology of Crime.* New York: Columbia Univ. Press, 1960.

Abramowitz, S.I., et al. "Sex Bias in Therapy: A Failure to Confirm." Am. J. Psychiatry, 133 (1976).

Acker, J. Book review of *Women, Wives and Mothers. Signs,* 1 (1976), 973-975.

Ackerknecht, E.A. *A Short History of Psychiatry.* 1st ed., 1959; rept. New York: Hafner, 1968.

Adams, P. "Fatherlessness: Policy Suggestions." Paper presented at the North American Seminar of the Impact of Change on Mental Health and Child and Family Development. Val David, Quebec, 7 June 1977.

Adams, P.W., et al. "Effect of Pyridoxine Hydrochloride (Vitamin B_6) upon Depression Associated with Oral Contraception." *The Lancet,* 28 (1973), 897-904.

Adelstein, A.M., Downham, P.Y., Stein, Z., et al. "The Epidemiology of Mental Illness in an English City." *Social Psychiatry,* 3 (1964), 455-468.

Agassi, J. *Toward a Historiography of Science.* The Hague: Moulton, 1963.

Alinsky, S.D., "The Poor and the Powerful." *Int. J. Psychiat.,* 4 (1967), 308-317.

Allen, A. "Woman's Place in Nature." *Forum,* 7 (1889), 258-263.

Allport, G. *The Nature of Prejudice.* Cambridge, Mass.: Addison-Wesley, 1954.

American College of Neuropsychopharmacology — Food and Drug Administration Task Force. "Neurological Syndromes Associated with

Antipsychotic Drug Use." *Archives of General Psychiatry,* 28 (1973), 463-467.

Amin, M.M. "Sleeping Pills — A Review in Historical Perspective." Paper presented at Annual Meeting, Canadian Psychiatric Association, Saskatoon, 28 September 1977.

Amir, M. *Patterns in Forcible Rape.* Chicago: Univ. of Chicago Press, 1971.

Amir, M. "Victim Precipitated Forcible Rape." *J. Criminal Law, Criminology and Police Science,* 58, 4 (1967), 493.

An Easy Pill to Swallow. National Film Board, Canada.

Andelin, Helen B. *Fascinating Womanhood.* Santa Barbara, CA: Pacific Santa Barbara, 1965.

Anthony, E.J. and Benedek, T. *Parenthood: Its Psychology and Psychopathology.* Boston: Little, Brown, 1970.

Apoko, A. "At Home in the Village: Growing Up In Acholi." Ed. L.K. Fox. *East African Childhood: Three Versions.* Nairobi: Oxford Univ. Press, 1967.

Ardrey, R. *The Territorial Imperative: A Personal Inquiry into the Animal Origins of Property and Nations.* New York: Atheneum, 1966.

Argyris, C. "Dangers in Applying Results from Experimental Social Psychology." *Amer. Psychologist,* 30 (1975), 469.

Arieti, S. *Interpretation of Schizophrenia.* New York: Brunner, 1955.

Bakan, D. *The Duality of Human Existence.* Chicago: Rand McNally, 1966.

Baker, H., Stoller, R.J. "Can a Biological Force Contribute to Gender Identity?" *Am. J. Psychiatry,* 124 (1968), 1653-1658.

Baker, S.W. "Biological Influences on Human Sex and Gender." *Signs,* 6 (1980), 80-96.

Barash, D. *Sociobiology and Behavior.* New York: Elsevier Scientific Publishing, 1977.

Bardwick, J. "Ambivalence: The Socialization of Women." Ed. J. Bardwick. *Readings on the Psychology of Women.* New York: Harper & Row, 1972.

Bart, P.B. "Depression in Middle-Aged Women." Ed. V. Gornick and B. K. Moran. *Women in Sexist Society: Studies in Power and Powerlessness.* New York: Basic Books, 1971.

Bart, P.B. "Mother Portnoy's Complaints." *Trans-Action,* 8 (1970), 69-74.

Bart, P.B. "Why Women's Status Changes in Middle Age." *Sociological Symposium*, 3 (1969), 1-18.

Bart, P.B. and Grossman, M. "Menopause." Ed. M.T. Notman and C.C. Nadelson. *The Woman Patient.* New York: Plenum, 1978.

Bartig, D. and Cohon, M.S. "Excretion of Drugs in Human Milk." *Hospital Formulary Management,* 4 (1969), 26-27.

Bass, M. and Paul, D. "The Influence of Sex on Tranquilizer Prescribing." Paper presented at the North American Primary Care Research Group Meeting, Williamsburg, VA, March 1977.

Bassuk, E.L. and Gerson, S. "Deinstitutionalization and Mental Health Seminars." *Scientific American,* 238, 2 (1978).

Bateson, G. *Mind and Nature.* New York: E.P. Dutton, 1979.

Bateson, G. et al. "Towards a Theory of Schizophrenia." *Behavioural Science,* 1 (1958), 251-264.

Bazelon, D.L. "The Perils of Wizardry." *Am. J. of Psychiatry,* 131, 12 (1974), 1317-1322.

Beck, A.T. *Depression: Clinical, Experimental and Theoretical Aspects.* London: Staples Press, 1967.

Bem, S.L. "Probing the Promise of Androgyny." Ed. A.G. Kaplan and J.P. Bean. *Beyond Sex Role Stereotypes: Readings Toward a Psychology of Androgyny.* Toronto: Little, Brown, 1976.

Bem, S.L. "Sex Role Adaptability: One Consequence of Psychological Androgyny." *J. Personality and Social Psychology,* 31 (1975), 634-643.

Bem, S.L. "The Measurement of Psychological Androgyny." *J. Consulting and Clinical Psychology,* 42 (1974), 155-162.

Bender, L. and Blau, A. "The Reaction of Children to Sexual Relations with Adults." *Am. J. Orthopsychiatry,* 7 (1937), 500-518.

Benward, J. and Densen-Gerber, J. *Incest as a Causative Factor in Anti-Social Behaviour: An Exploratory Study.* New York: Odyssey Institute, 1975.

Berens, A.E. "Sex-Role Stereotypes and the Development of Achievement Motivation." *Ontario Psychologist,* 5, 2 (1973), 30-35.

Berkovitz, P. and Rothman, E. *The Disturbed Child.* New York: New York Univ. Press, 1960.

Berman, D. *Death on the Job: Occupation Health and Safety Struggles in the United States.* New York: Monthly Review Press, 1978.

Bernard, J. *Women, Wives and Mothers: Values and Options.* Chicago: Aldine Publishing, 1975.

Bettelheim, B. *Infantile Autism and the Birth of the Self*. New York: Free Press, 1967.

Bianchi, E.C. and Ruether, R.R. *From Machismo to Mutuality*. New York: Paulist Press, 1976.

Bibring, E. "The Mechanism of Depression." Ed. P. Greenacre. *Affective Disorders: Psychoanalytic Contributions to their Study*. New York: International Universities Press, 1961, pp. 13-48.

Bleier, R. "Bias in Biological and Human Sciences: Some Comments." *Signs*, 4 (1978), 159-162.

Bloch, R.H. "Untangling the Roots of Modern Sex Roles: A Survey of Four Centuries of Change." *Signs*, 4 (1978), 237-252.

Block, J. "Conceptions of Sex Role: Some Cross-Cultural and Long-itudinal Perspectives." *American Psychologist*, 28 (1973), 512-526.

Block, J.H., Block, J., and Harrington, D. "Sex-Role Typing and Instrumental Behaviour: A Developmental Study." Paper Presented at the meeting of the Society of Research in Child Development Denver, April 1975.

Blumenthal, M.D. "Measuring Depressive Symptoms in a General Population." *Arch. Gen. Psychiat.*, 32 (1975), 971-978.

Bonaparte, M. *Female Sexuality*. New York: Grove Press, 1965.

Boston Women's Health Collective. *Ourselves and Our Children*. New York: Random House, 1978.

Boston Women's Health Collective. *Our Bodies, Ourselves*. New York: Simon & Schuster, 1975.

Boulter, Alison and Campbell, Marie. "An Ethnography of Minor Tranquilizer Use in Selected Women's Groups In Vancouver." Report prepared for N.M.U.D.D., September 1, 1977.

Bowen, M. "The Use of Family Theory in Clinical Practice." Ed. J. Haley. *Changing Families*. New York: Grune & Stratton, 1971.

Bowlby, J. "Fourty-four Juvenile Thieves: Their Character and Home Life." *International Journal of Psychoanalysis*, 25 (1944), 19-53, 107-127.

Bowlby, J. *Maternal Care and Mental Health*. Geneva: World Health Organization monograph, 1951.

Bowles, S. "Unequal Education and the Reproduction of the Social Division of Labor." Ed. M. Carney. *Schooling in a Corporate Society: The Political Economy of Education in America and the Alternatives Before Us*. New York: David McKay & Co., 1972.

Bowles, S. and Gintis, H. *Schooling in Capitalist America.* New York Basic Books, 1977.

Bradley, S.J. et al. "Gender Identity Problems of Children and Adoles cents: The Establishment of a Special Clinic." *Can. Psychiatric Assoc. J.,* 23 (1978), 175-183.

Braginsky, B.M., Braginsky, D.D. and Ring, K. *Methods of Madness. The Mental Hospital as a Last Resort.* New York: Holt, Rinehard & Winston, 1969.

Branch, G. and Paxton, R. "A Study of Gonococcal Infections Among Infants and Children." *Public Health Reports,* 80 (1965), 347-352

Brant, R.S.T. and Tisza, V.G. "The Sexually Misused Child." *Am. J. Orthopsychiatry,* 47 (1977), 80-90.

Brenner, M.H. "Personal Stability and Economic Security." *Social Policy,* 8 (1977), 1.

Bromberg, W. *The Mind of Man: A History of Psychotherapy and Psy choanalysis.* 1937; New York: Harper Colophon, 1963.

Bronson, W.C. "Mother-Toddler Interaction: A Perspective on Studying the Development of Competence." *Merrill-Palmer Quarterly,* 20 (1974), 275-301.

Brooks, K. "Freudianism is Not a Basis for a Marxist Psychology." Ed. P. Brown. *Radical Psychology.* New York: Harper Colophon, 1973.

Broverman, Inge K. et al. "Sex Role Stereotypes and Clinical Judge- ments of Mental Health." *Journal of Consulting and Clinical Psy chology,* 34, 1 (1970), 1-7.

Brown, C.R. and Hellinger, M. "Therapists' Attitudes Towards Wo- men." *Social Work,* 20 (1975), 4.

Brown, G.W. and Harris, T. *Social Origins of Depression: A Study of Psychiatric Disorder in Women.* London: Tavistock, 1978.

Brownmiller, S. *Against Our Will: Men, Women and Rape.* New York: Simon & Shuster, 1975.

Brusegard, D. "Health." *Perspectives Canada III.* Ottawa, n.d.

Bruun, Keltie. "International Drug Control and the Pharmaceutical Industry." Ed. R. Cooperstock. *International Symposia on Alcohol and Drug Addiction.* Toronto: Addiction Research Foundation, 1974.

Bullough, V.L. *The History of Prostitution.* New York: University Books, 1964.

Caldwell, V.M. "The Effects of Infant Care." Ed. M.L. Hoffman and L. W. Hoffman. *Review of Child Development Research,* Vol. I. New

York: Russell Sage, 1965, pp. 9-88.

Callahan, S.C. *Parenting: Principles and Politics of Parenthood.* Baltimore: Penguin Books, 1974.

Canadian Psychological Association. "Guidelines for Therapy and Counselling with Women." Short version: *Canadian Psychology,* 21 (1980), 4. Full version: *The Ontario Psychologist,* 13 (1981), 2.

Caplan, J.J. "Erikson's Concept of Inner Space: A Data-Based Reevaluation." *Am. J. Orthopsychiatry,* 41, 1 (1979).

Caplan, P.J. *Barriers Between Women.* Jamaica NY: S.P. Medical and Scientific Publications, 1980.

Caplan, P.J. "Problems in the Psychological Study of Sex Differences." *Canadian Newsletter of Research on Women,* VII, 2 (1978).

Caplan, Ruth. *Psychiatry and the Community in Nineteenth Century America.* New York: Basic Books, 1969.

Cardinal, H. *The Unjust Society: The Tragedy of Canada's Indians.* Edmonton: M.G. Hunting, 1969.

Carpenter, C.R. *Naturalistic Behavior in Non-Human Primates.* Penn: Pennsylvania State Univ. Press, 1964.

Carpenter, J. and Armanti, N. "Some Effects of Ethanol on Human Sexual and Aggressive Behaviour." Ed. B. Hessin and H. Begleiter. *The Biology of Alcoholism,* Vol. 2. New York: Plenum Press, 1972.

Carpenter, W. *Principles of Human Physiology.* 4th ed. Philadelphia, 1850.

Carpenter, William T., McGlashan, Thomas H., and Strauss, John S. "The Treatment of Acute Schizophrenia without Drugs: An Investigation of Some Current Assumptions." *Am. J. Psychiatry,* 134 (1977), 14-20.

Cartwright, Ann. "Prescribing and the Relationship Between Patients Ed. R. Cooperstock. *Social Aspects of the Medical Use of Psychotropic Drugs.* Toronto: Addiction Research Foundation of Ontario, 1974.

Chesler, P. "Patient and Patriarch: Women in the Psychotherapeutic Relationship." Ed. Gornick and Moran. *Woman in Sexist Society.*

Chesler, P. *Women and Madness.* New York: Avon Books, 1973.

Chodoff, P. "The Depressive Personality: A Critical Review." *Arch. Gen. Psychiat.,* 27 (1972), 666-673.

Clark, L.M.G. and Lewis, D.J. *Rape: The Price of Coercive Sexuality.* Toronto: Women's Press, 1977.

Clark, L.M.G. and Lewis, D.J. "A Study of Rape in Canada — Phases C and D." Report to the Donner Foundation of Canada, 30 April, 1977.

Commission on Obscenity and Pornography. *The Report of the Commission on Obscenity and Pornography.* Washington, D.C.: U.S. Government Printing Office, 1970.

Committee Concerned with Women's Health Issues in Etobicoke, Ont. "The Use of Prescription Medication by Women 18 Years and Over in Etobicoke."

Committee on Research, Group for the Advancement of Psychiatry, *Pharmacotherapy and Psychotherapy: Paradoxes, Problems and Progress.* Vol. IX, Report No. 93, March 1975.

Conference: "In the Service of the State: The Psychiatrist as Double Agent." Special Supplement, *Hastings Centre Report,* April, 1978.

Conrad, P. "The Discovery of Hyperkinesis: Notes on the Medicalization of Deviant Behavior." *Social Problems,* 23, 1 (1975).

Consentino, F. and Heilbrun, A.N. "Anxiety Correlates of Sex-Role Identity in College Students." *Psychological Reports,* 14 (1964), 729-730.

Constantinople, A. "Sex Role Acquisition: In Search of the Elephant." *Sex Roles,* 5 (1979), 121-133.

Cooperman, Earl M. "Antibiotics: No Panacea." Editorial. *Canadian Medical Association Journal,* 116 (1977), 229-230.

Cooperstock, Ruth. Presentation given at workshop. "The Chemically Dependent Woman." Toronto, 4 June 1977.

Cooperstock, Ruth. "Psychotropic Drug Use Among Women." *Canadian Medical Association Journal,* 115 (1976), 760-763.

Cooperstock, Ruth. "Sex Differences in the Use of Mood-Modifying Drugs: An Explanatory Model." *Journal of Health and Social Behaviour,* 12 (1971), 238-244.

Cooperstock, Ruth. "Women and 'Excessive' use of Psychotropic Drugs." Paper presented at Annual Meeting of the Canadian Psychiatric Association, Saskatoon, 29 September 1977.

Cooperstock, R. and Sims, M. "Mood-Modifying Drugs Prescribed in a Canadian City: Hidden Problems." *American Journal of Public Health,* 61 (1971), 1007-1016.

Corea, G. *The Hidden Malpractice.* New York: William Morrow & Co., 1977.

Cowhig, J. "Minister Demands Clean-Up of Doctors' Trials for Drugs." *London Observer*, 28 January 1979.

Crane, George E. "The Prevention of Tardive Dyskinesia." *Am. J. Psychiatry*, 134 (1977), 756-758.

Cunningham, M. Review of *Disturbances of Mental Life or Disturbances of the Soul. Canada's Mental Health*, 26 (1978), 2.

Dalton, K. *The Menstrual Cycle*. New York: Pantheon Books, 1969.

Dalton, K. *The Premenstrual Syndrome*. Springfield, IL: Charles C. Thomas, 1964.

Daly, M. *Gyn/Ecology: The Metaethics of Radical Feminism*. Boston: Beacon Press, 1978.

Daly, M. *The Church and the Second Sex*. 1968; New York: Harper Colophon, 1975.

D'Arcy, Carl and Schmitz, Janet. "Sex Differences in the Utilization of Health Services for Psychiatric Problems in Saskatchewan." Paper presented at the Canadian Psychiatric Association Annual Meeting, Saskatoon, Saskatchewan, 29 September 1977.

David, S. "Becoming a Nonsexist Therapist." Ed. D.E. Smith and S. David. *Women Look at Psychiatry*. Vancouver: Press Gang Publishers, 1976, pp. 165-174.

David, S. "Working Effectively with Women." *Canada's Mental Health*, 28 (1980).

Davin, A. "Imperialism and Motherhood." *History Workshop*, 5 (1978), 9-65.

Davis, John M. and Cole, Jonathan O. "Antipsychotic Drugs." Ed. A.M. Freedman, H.I. Kaplan and B.J. Sadock. *Comprehensive Textbook of Psychiatry*, Vol. 2. 2nd ed. Baltimore: Williams & Wilkins, 1975.

Davis, K. "Prostitution." Ed. R.K. Merton and R. Nisbet. *Contemporary Social Problems*. 3rd ed. New York: Harcourt Brace Jovanovich, 1971.

Davis, N.Z. "Women's History in Transition: The European Case." *Feminist Studies*, 3, 3-4 (1976), 83-103.

de Beauvoir, S. *The Second Sex*. New York: Bantam Books, 1962, p. xv.

de Bono, E. *The Uses of Lateral Thinking*. Great Britain: Jonathan Cape, 1967.

De Francis, V., ed. *Sexual Abuse of Children*. Denver: Children's Division of the American Humane Association, 1967.

De Myer, M.K. *Parents and Children in Autism*. New York: John Wiley & Sons, 1979.

Despert, J.L. "Some Considerations Relating to the Genesis of Autistic Behaviour in Children." *Am. J. Oethopsychiatry*, 21 (1951), 335-350.

Deutsch, H. *The Psychology of Women: A Psychoanalytic Interpretation.* New York: Grune & Stratton, 1945.

Diamond, I. "Pornography and Repression: A Reconsideration." *Signs*, 5 (1980), 686-701.

Dixson, A.F. "Androgens and Aggressive Behaviour in Primates: A Review." *Aggressive Behaviour*, 6 (1980), 37-67.

Downey, J. and Howell, J. "Wife Battering: A Review and Preliminary Enquiry into Local Incidence, Needs and Resources." United Way of Greater Vancouver, September 1976.

"Drugs in Breast Milk." *Therapeutics Bulletin*, 6 (1975), 8-9.

Drummond, H. "Diagnosing Marriage." *Mother Jones*, July 1979, 14-21.

Dumonchel, T. "Maudites droguées." *Tu Prends-tu une jolie Madame chose?* Montreal: Les Editions de la Pleine Lune.

Dunnell, K. and Cartwright, A. *Medicine Takers, Prescribers and Hoarders.* London: Routledge and Kegan Paul, 1972.

Dworkin, A. *Woman Hating.* New York: E.P. Dutton, 1974.

Earls, F. "The Fathers (Not the Mothers): Their Importance and Influence with Infants and Young Children." Ed. S. Chess and A. Thomas. *Annual Progress in Child Psychiatry and Child Development.* New York: Brunner Mazel, 1977.

East, W. "Sexual Offenders — A British View." *Yale Law Review*, 55 (1946), 527-557.

Editorial. *J. American Medical Association*, 32 (1899), 1183.

Ehrenreich, B. and English, D. *Complaints and Disorders, The Sexual Politics of Sickness.* Glass Mountain Pamphlet No. 2. The Feminist Press, 1973.

Ehrenreich, B. and English D. *For Her Own Good: 150 Years of Experts' Advice to Women.* New York: Anchor Books, 1979.

Engel, G. "The Need for a New Medical Model: A Challange for Biomedicine." *Science*, 196, 4286 (1977).

Erikson, E.H. *Childhood and Society.* New York: Doubleday & Co., 1950. 2nd ed. New York: W.W. Norton & Co., 1963.

Erikson, E. "Once More the Inner Space: Letter to a Former Student." Ed. J. Strouse. *Women and Analysis.* New York: Dell Publishing, 1974.

Etkin, W., ed. *Social Behavior and Organization Among Vertebrates.* Chicago: Univ. of Chicago Press, 1964.

Eysenck, H.J. *The Uses and Abuses of Psychology.* Hammondsworth: Penguin Books, 1953, p. 178.

Factor, M. "A Woman's Psychological Reaction to Attempted Rape." *Psychoanalytic Quarterly,* 23 (1954), 243-244.

Fancher, R.E. "Freud's Attitudes Towards Women: A Survey of His Writings." *Queen's Quarterly,* 82, 3 (1975), 368-393.

Fanon, F. *Black Skins, White Masks.* New York: Grove Press. London: Granada, 1967.

Fanon, F. *The Wretched of the Earth.* New York: Grove Press. London: Granada, 1963.

Favazza, A.R. and Oman, A. "Overview: Foundations of Cultural Psychiatry." *Am. J. Psychiatry,* 135 (1978), 293-303.

Featherstone, J. "Family Matters." *Harvard Educational Review,* 49 (1979), 20-52.

Fee, E. "Women and Health Care: A Comparison of Theories." *Int. J. Health Services,* 5 (1975), 397-415.

Fesbach, S. and Malamuth, N. "Sex and Aggression: Proving the Link." *Psychology Today,* 12 (1978), 111-117.

Finn, Richard. "In-Patient Field Trial." Paper presented at special session "DSM III on Trial: Some of the Evidence." Annual meeting of the American Psychiatric Association, Toronto, 4 May 1977.

Fitzhugh, G. *Sociology for the South, or the Failure of a Free Society.* Richmond VA: A Morris, 1854.

Fling, S. and Manosevitz, M. "Sextyping in Nursery School Children's Play Interests." *Developmental Psychology,* 7 (1972), 146-154.

Ford, H. "Involutional Melancholia." Ed. Freedman, Kaplan and Sadock. *Comprehensive Textbook of Psychiatry.* Baltimore: Williams & Wilkins, 1975, pp. 1025-1042.

Foucault, M. *Madness and Civilization: A History of Insanity in the Age of Reason.* New York: Pantheon Books, 1965.

Franks, V. and Burtle V., ed. *Women in Therapy.* New York: Brunner Mazel, 1974.

Freiere, P. *The Pedagogy of the Oppressed.* New York: Seabury Press, 1973.

French, T.M. and Alexander, F. *Psychogenic Factors in Bronchial Asthma.* Washington: National Research Council, 1941.

306 –

Freud, S. "An Outline of Psychoanalysis." *Collected Papers,* Vol. 23. London: Hogarth Press, 1956.

Freud, S. *Civilization and Its Discontents.* London: Hogarth Press, 1930. New York: W.W. Norton & Co., 1962.

Freud, S. "Femininity." *New Introductory Lectures in Psychoanalysis.* Trans. W.J.H. Sprott. 1933.

Freud, S. *New Introductory Lectures in Psychoanalysis.* New York: W. Norton & Co., 1933.

Freud, S. "The Psychology of Women." *New Introductory Lectures in Psychoanalysis.* London: Hogarth Press, 1946.

Freud, S. *The Standard Edition of the Works of Sigmund Freud.* London: Hogarth Press, 1953.

Freud, S. "The Taboo of Virginity." *Collected Papers,* Vol. IV, 1918.

Freud, S. *Three Contributions to the Theory of Sex.* Trans. A.A. Brill. New York: Dulton, 1962.

Friedan, B. *The Feminine Mystique.* New York: Dell Publishing, 1963.

Freidman, R.C., Hurt, S.W., Arnoff, M.F. and Clarkin, J. "Behaviour and the Menstrual Cycle." *Signs,* 5 (1980), 719-738.

Frieze, I., Parsons, J., Johnson, P., Ruble, D. and Zellman, G. *Women and Sex Roles: A Sociological Perspective.* Toronto: W.W. Norton & Co., 1978.

Fromm-Reichman, F. "Transference Problems in Schizophrenia." *Psychoanalysis,* 8 (1936), 412-426.

Galbraith, J.K. *Economics and the Public Purse.* Boston: Houghton-Mifflin, 1973.

Gall, M.D. "The Relationship Between Masculinity-Femininity and Manifest Anxiety." *J. Clinical Psychology,* 25 (1969), 294-295.

Garfinkel, P.E., Walsh, J.J. and Stancer, H.C. "Depression: New Evidence in Support of Biological Differentiation." *Am. J. Psychiatry,* 136 (1979), 535-539.

Gayford, J.J. "Wife Battering: A Preliminary Survey of a Hundred Cases." *British Medical Journal,* January (1975), 195-197.

Gaylin, W. "In the Service of the State: The Psychiatrist as Double Agent." Conference co-sponsored by the American Psychiatric Association and the Hastings Centre, 1977. Proceedings published in *The Hastings Centre Report,* 8, 2 (1978).

Gebhard, O.P. et al. *Sex Offenders: An Analysis of Types.* New York, 1965.

Geller, S. "The Sexually Assaulted Female, Innocent Victim or Temptress?" Toronto: Employee Health Services Branch, Parliament Buildings, 1974.

Gelles, R.J. *The Violent Home.* Beverley Hills, Ca: Sage Publications, 1972.

Gelles, R.J. "Violence and Pregnancy: A Note on the Extent of the Problem and Needed Services. *Family Coordinator,* January, 1975.

Gibbens, T.C.N. Juvenile Prostitution, *British J. Delinquency,* Vol. 8, 1957.

Gibbens, T.C.N. Greenwald, H., *The Call Girl.* New York: Ballantine Books, 1958.

Gil, D. *Violence Against Children: Physical Child Abuse in the United States.* Cambridge: Harvard Univ. Press, 1970.

Gillie, O. " ' Hazardous' Drugs Sold for use in Africa by International Companies." London: *Sunday Times,* August 13, 1978.

Gluckstern, N.B., "Beyond Therapy: Personal and Institutional Change." Ed. E.I. Rawlings, and D.K. Carter., *Psychotherapy for Women. Treatment — Toward Equality.* Springfield, Ill. : Charles C. Thomas, 1977.

Glueck, S. *Mental Disorders and the Criminal Law* New York: Little Brown, 1925.

Goetze, U., Green, R., Whybrow, P., et al. "X-Linkage Revisited." *Arch. Gen. Psychiat.,* 31 (1974), 665-672.

Goffman, E. *Asylums: Essays on the Social Situation of Mental Patients and Other Inmates.* New York: Anchor Doubleday, 1961.

Gropper, A. and Currie, J. "A Study of Battered Women." *M.A. Thesis.* School of Social Work Library, Univ. of British Columbia, March 1976.

Gropper, A. and Marvin, J. "Violence Begins at Home." *The Canadian,* November 20, 1976.

Groth, A.N., Burgess, A.W. and Holmstrom, L.L. "Rape: Power, Anger, and Sexuality." *Am. J. Psychiatry,* 134 (1977), 1239-1243.

Group for the Advancement of Psychiatry. *The Educated Woman: Prospects and Problems,* Vol. IX, Report No. 92, 1975.

Guse, L., Morier, G., and Ludwig, J. "Winnipeg Survey of Prescription (Mood-Altering) use Among Women." *Technical Report, N.M.U.D.D.* Manitoba Alchoholism Foundation, October 1976.

Guttmacher, M. *Sex Offences: The Probelm, Causes and Prevention.* New York: Norton, 1951.

Guzell, M.C. "Problems of Personal Change in Women's Studies Courses." Ed. E.T. Rawlings and D.K. Carter. *Psychotherapy for Women: Treatment Toward Equality.* Springfield, Ill.: Charles C. Thomas, 1977.

Hacker, H.M. *Women as a Minority Group.* Ed. B. Roszack and T. Roszack. New York: Evanston and London, Harper and Row, 1969, pp. 130-148.

Halleck, S.L. *The Politics of Therapy.* New York: Science House, 1971.

Haller, J.S. Jr., and Haller, R.M. *The Physician and Sexuality in Victorian American.* Urbana, Ill.: Univ. of Illinois Press, 1975.

Hallstrom, T. *Mental Disorder and Sexuality in the Climateric.* Goteberg, Sweden: Orstadius Biktryckeri AB, 1973.

Hannerz, U. *Soulside: Inquiries into Ghetto Culture and Community.* New York Columbia Univ. Press, 1969.

Haraway, D. "Animal Sociology and a Natural Economy of the Body Politic, Part I: A Political Physiology of Dominance." *Signs,* 4, 1 (1978).

Haraway, D. "Animal Sociology and a Natural Economy of the Body Politic, Part II: The Past is the Contested Zone: Human Nature and Theories of Production and Reproduction in Primate Behavioural Studies." *Signs,* 4, 1 (1978).

Hare-Mustin, R.T. "A Feminist Approach to Family Therapy." *Family Process,* 17 (1978), 181-194.

Harford, T.C., Willis, C.H. and Deabler, H.L. "Personality Correlates of Masculinity-Femininity." *Psychology Reports,* 21 (1967), 881-884.

Harris, I.D. et al. "Observations on Asthmatic Children." *American Journal of Orthopsychiatry,* 20 (1950), 490-505.

Hartley, R.A. "Sex Role Pressures and the Socialization of the Male Child." Ed. Stacey et al. *And Jill Came Tumbling After: Sexism in American Education.* New York: Dell Publishing, 1974, pp. 185-198.

Hartman, A., Nikolay, R. "Sexually Deviant Behaviour in Expectant Fathers." *J. Abnormal Psychology,* 71 (1966), 232-234.

Hays, H.R. *The Dangerous Sex: The Myth of Feminine Evil.* New York: Putman, 1964.

Hegel, G. *The Phenomenology of the Mind* Trans. Wallace., Oxford: Oxford Univ. Press, 1971.

Henriques, F. *Modern Sexuality, Vol. III, Prostitution and Society.* London: MacGibbon and Kee, 1968.

Henshel, A.M. *Sex Structure.* Canadian Social Problems series. Toronto: Longmans, Canada, 1973.

Herman, J. and Hirschman, L. "Father-Daughter Incest." *Signs,* 2 (1977). 735-756.

Herscherberger, Ruth. *Adam's Rib.* New York: Harper & Row, 1948.

Hersohn, H.L., Kennedy, P.F., McGuire, R.J. "Persistence of Extra-Pyramidal Disorders and Psychiatric Relapse after Long-Term Phenothiazine Therapy." *British Journal of Psychiatry,* 120 (1972), 41-50.

Herzog, E. and Sudia, C.E. "Fatherless Homes: A Review of Research." *Children,* September-October 1968, 177-182.

Hilberman, E. *The Rape Victim.* Washington, D.C.: American Psychiatric Association, 1976.

Hilberman, E. and Munson, K. "Sixty Battered Women." *Victimology,* Special issue on spouse abuse, 2 (1977-78), 460-471.

Hill, L.B. *Psychotherapeutic Intervention in Schizophrenia.* Chicago: Univ. of Chicago Press, 1955.

Hinkle, E. et al. "Occupation, Education and Coronary Heart Disease." Ed. E. Hart and W. Sechrist. *Dynamics of Wellness.* Belmont: Wadsworth Publishing, 1970, pp. 396-414.

Hobbs, T. "Mental Health's Third Revolution." Ed. A.J. Bindman and A.D. Spiegel. *Perspectives in Community Mental Health.* Chicago: Aldine Publishing, 1969.

Hollander, B. *Psychology of Misconduct, Vice and Crime.* New York: MacMillan, 1924.

Hollingshead, A.B. and Redlich. F.C. *Social Class and Mental Illness.* New York: John Wiley & Sons, 1958.

Hollister, Leo E. "Drug Therapy: Mental Disorders — Antipsychotic and Antimanic Drugs." *New England Journal of Medicine,* 286 (1972), 984-987.

Horney, K. "Inhibited Feminity: Psychoanalytical Contribution to the Problem of Frigidity." In Horney, K., *Feminine Psychology.* New York: W.W. Norton, 1967, pp. 71-83.

Horney, K. "On the Genesis of the Castration Complex in Women." *Int. J. Psycho-Anal.,* 5 (1924), 50-65.

Horney, K. "The Flight from Womanhood: The Masculinity Complex in Women as Viewed by Men and by Women." *Int. J. Psycho-Anal.,* 7 (1926), 324-329.

Horney, K. "The Problem of the Monogamous Ideal." *Int. J. Psycho-*

Anal., 9 (1924), 318-331.

Horowitz, M. "New Directions in Epidemiology." *Science,* 188 (1975), 850-851.

Horowitz, A. "The Pathways into Psychiatric Treatment: Some Differences Between Men and Women." *Journal of Health and Social Behaviour,* 18 (1977), 169-178.

Howell, Mary C. "What Medical Schools Teach about Women." *New England Journal of Medicine,* 291(1974), 305-307,

Ilg, F.L. and Ames, L.B. *Child Behaviour.* New York: Harper & Row, 1951.

Illich, I. *Medical Nemesis: The Expropriation of Health.* Toronto: McClelland & Stewart, 1975.

Imperato-McGinley et al. "Androgens and the Evolution of Male-Gender Identity among Male Pseudohermaphrodites with 5-reductase Deficiency." *New England J. Medicine,* 300 (1979), 1233-1237.

"In the Service of the State." *Hastings Centre Report,* 8, 2 (1978).

Jan, J.E., Freeman, R.D., and Scott, E.P. *Visual Impairment in Children and Adolescents.* New York: Grune & Stratton, 1977.

Janeway, E. *Man's World, Women's Place.* New York: Dell Publishing, 1971.

Janeway, E. "The Women's Movement." Ed. Freedman, Kaplan and Sadock. *Comprehensive Textbook of Psychiatry,* 1975.

Jeffreys, Margot. "Medicine Takes in the Medical Use of Psychotropic Drugs." *Supplement to Journal of Royal College of General Practitioners,* 23, 1973.

Joenig, J. and Hamilton, M.W. *The Desegregation of the Mentally Ill.* London: Routledge & Kegan Paul, 1969.

Johnson, A.G. "On the Prevalence of Rape in the United States." *Signs,* 6 (1980), 136-146.

Joint Commission on Mental Illness and Health. *Action For Mental Health: Final Report.* New York: Basic Books, 1961.

Joyce, C.R.B. "Psychopharmacology — Dimensions and Perspective." *Mind and Medicine Monographs.* London: Tavistock Publications, 1968.

Jung, C.G. "Anima and Animus." *Two Essays on Analytical Psychology: Collected Works of C.G. Jung,* Vol. 7. Bollinger Foundation, 1953, pp. 186-209.

Kagan, J., Kearsley, R.B. and Zelazo, P.R. *Infancy: Its Place in Human Development.* Cambridge, Mass.: Harvard Univ. Press, 1978.

Kanner, L. "Autistic Disturbances of Affective Contact." *The Nervous Child*, 2 (1943), 217-250.

Kaplan, A.G. "Androgyny as a Model of Mental Health for Women: From Theory to Therapy." Ed. A.G. Kaplan and J.P. Bean. *Beyond Sex Role Stereotypes*. Boston, Mass.: Little, Brown, 1976.

Kaplan, A.G. "Clarifying the Concept of Androgyny: Implications for Therapy." *Psychology of Women Quarterly*, 3 (1979), 223-230.

Karasu, T.B. "Psychotherapies: An Overview." *American Journal of Psychiatry*, 134 (1977), 8.

Karpman, B. ed., *Symposia on Child and Juvenile Delinquency*. Washington: Psychodynamics Monograph Series, 1959.

Karpman, B. *The Sexual Offender and His Offences*. New York: Julian Press, 1954.

Karpman, B. "The Sexual Psychopath." *J. Criminal Law and Criminology*, 42 (1951), 184-198.

Kasdener, S. "Rape Fantasies." *J. Religion and Health*, 14 (1975), 50-57.

Katz, P.A. "The Development of Female Identity." Ed. C.B. Kopp, and M. Kirkpatrick *Becoming Female: Perspectives on Development*. New York and London: Plenum, 1979.

Kaufman, I., Peck, A.L. and Tagiuri, C.K. "The Family Constellation and Overt Incestuous Relationships Between Father and Daughter." *American J. Orthopsychiatry*, 24 (1954), 266-279.

Kelly, J., and Worrel, J. "New Formulations of Sex Roles and Androgyny: A Critical Review." *J. Consulting and Clinical Psychology*, 45 (1977), 1101-1115.

Kelly, J., Furnam, W., and Young V. "Problems Associated with Typological Measurements of Sex Roles and Androgyny." *J. Consulting and Clinical Psychology*, 46 (1978), 1574-76.

Kelly-Gadol, J. "Did Women Have a Renaissance?" Ed. R. Bridenthal and C. Koonz. *Becoming Visible: Women in European History*. Boston: Houghton Mifflin, 1976.

Kelman, S. "Toward the Political Economy of Medical Care." *Inquiry*, 8, 3 (1971), 30-38.

Kety, S. and Schildkraut, J.J. "Biogenic Amines and Emotion." *Science*, 156 (1967), 21.

Key, E. *The Century of the Child*. New York: G.P. Putnam, 1909.

Kinzel, K.M. "A Study of the Influence of Sex-Role Stereotypes on Marriage Counsellor's Personal and Clinical Evaluation of Their

312 —

Clients." Masters Thesis, Univ. of Regina, 1974.

Kittrie, N. *The Right to be Different*. Baltimore: Johns Hopkins Press, 1971.

Kitzinger, S. "The Fourth Trimester." *Midwife, Health Visitor, and Community Nurse*, 11 (1975), 118-121.

Kleeman, J.A. "Freud's Views on Early Female Sexuality in the Light of Direct Child Observation." *J. Am. Psychoanal. Assoc.*, 24 (1976), 3-27.

Koeske, R.K., and Koeske G.F. "An Attributional Approach to Moods and the Menstrual Cycle." *Journal of Personality and Social Psychology.* 31 (1975), 473-478.

Kohlberg, L. and Ullian, P.Z. "Stages in the Development of Psychosexual Concepts and Attitudes." Ed. R.C. Friedman, et al. *Sex Differences in Behavior.* New York: John Wiley, 1974, pp. 209-222.

Koran, L.M. and Hamburg, P.A. "Psychophysiological Endocrine Disorders." Ed. Freedman, Kaplan and Sadock. *Comprehensive Textbook of Psychiatry II.* Baltimore: Williams & Wilkins, 1975, pp. 1673-1684.

Kuhn, T.S. *The Structure of Scientific Revolutions.* 2nd Edition. Chicago: Univ. of Chicago Press, 1970, Sections I and XI.

Kysar, J.E. "The Two Camps in Child Psychiatry." *Am. J. Psychiat.*, 125 (1968), 141-147.

Labonte, R. and Penfold, P.S. "Canadian Perspectives in Health Promotion: A Critique." *Health Education* 19: (3, 4) 4-9, 1981.

Laing, R.D. *The Divided Self: A Study in Family and Madness.* Chicago: Quadrangle Books, 1960.

LaLonde, M. *A New Perspective on the Health of Canadians.* Ottawa: Government of Canada, 1974.

Lambert, H.H. "Biology and Equality: A Perspective on Sex Differences" *Signs,* 4, 1 (1978).

Lamphere, L. "Anthropology." *Signs,* 2 (1977), 612-627.

Landman, L. "Recent Trends Towards Unisex: A Panel." *Am. J. Psychoanal.*, 34 (1974), 27-31.

Lasangna, L. *The Doctor's Dilemmas.* New York: Harper, 1962.

Lazare, A. "Hidden Conceptual Models in Clinical Psychiatry." *New England Journal of Medicine,* 288 , 7 (1973), 343-351.

LeGrand, C.E. "Rape and Rape Laws: Sexism in Society and Law." *California Law Review,* 16 (1973), 932-945.

Leppman, F. "Essential Differences between Sex Offenders." *J. Criminal Law and Criminology*, 32 (1941), 366-380.

Lerner, H.E. "Adaptive and Pathogenic Aspects of Sex-Role Stereotypes: Implications for Parenting and Psychotherapy." *Am. J. Psychiatry*, 155 (1978), 48-52.

Levine, S., Kamin, L. and Levine, E.L. "Sexism and Psychiatry." *Amer. J. Orthopsychiatry*, 44, 3 (1974), 327-336.

Levy, D.M. *Maternal Overprotection*. New York: Columbia Univ. Press, 1943.

Levy, D.M. "Primary Affect Hunger." *American J. of Psychiatry*, 94 (1937), 643-652.

Lewis, D.J. "Pornography: Developing Feminist Perspectives." *Kinesis*, Vancouver Status of Women, October 1978.

Liddiard, M. *The Mothercraft Manual*. 8th Edition. London: J.A. Churchill, 1931.

Lidz, T., Fleck, S. and Cornelison, A. *Schizophrenia and the Family*. New York: International Universities Press, 1965.

Linn, L. "Clinical Manifestations of Psychiatric Disorders." Ed. Freedman, Kaplan, and Sadock. *Comprehensive Textbook of Psychiatry II*. Baltimore: Williams & Wilkins, 1975.

Lips, H.M., and Colwill, N.L. *The Psychology of Sex Differences*. New Jersey: Prentice Hall, 1978.

Littner, N. "Psychology of the Sex Offender: Causes, Treatment, Prognosis." *Police Law Quarterly*, 3 (1973), 5-31.

Locksley, A. and Colten, M.E., "Psychological Androgyny: A Case of Mistaken Identity?" *J. Personality & Social Psychology*, 37 (1979), 1017-1034.

Lombroso, C. and Ferrero, W. *The Female Offender*. London: Fisher Unwin, 1895.

Longee, C.C. "Modern European History." *Signs*, 2 (1977), 628-690.

Lowe, M. "Sociobiology and Sex Differences." *Signs*, 4, 1 (1978).

Lukianowitz, N. "Incest." *British J. Psychiatry*, 120 (1972), 301-313.

Lundberg, F., and Farnham, M. *Modern Woman: The Lost Sex*. New York: The Universal Library, 1947.

Lustig, N., Dresser, J.W. and Spellman, S.W. "Incest: A Family Group Survival Pattern." *Archives of General Psychiatry*, 14 (1966), 31-40.

Lystad, M.H. "Violence at Home: A Review of the Literature." *Am. J. Orthopsychiatry*, 45 (1975), 328-345.

314 —

McCaldon, R.J. "Rape." *Canadian J. Corrections,* 9 (1957), 37-59.

McClure, J., Reich, T., Wetzel, R. "Premenstrual Symptoms as an Indicator of Bipolar Affective Disorder." *Br. J. Psychiat.,* 119 (1971), 527-528.

McCombie, S.L. et al. "Development of a Medical Center Rape Crisis Intervention Program." *Am. J. Psychiat.,* 133 (1976), 418-421.

MacDonald, J.M. *Rape Offenders and Their Victims.* Springfield, Ill: Charles C. Thomas, 1971.

McDonald, P.G. and Doughty, C. "Androgen Sterilisation in the Neonatal Female Rat and its Inhibition by an Estrogen Antagonist." *Neuroendocrinology,* 13 (1973-74), 182-188.

McKinlay, S.M. and Jeffreys, M. "The Menopausal Syndrome." *Br. J. Preventive Social Med.,* 28 (1974), 108-115.

Magner, L.N. "Woman and the Scientific Idiom." *Signs,* 4, 1 (1978).

Mahler, M.S. "On Childhood Psychosis and Schizophrenia: Autistic and Symbiotic Infantile Psychoses." *Psychoanalytic Study of the Child,* Vol. 7. New York: International Universities Press, 1952, pp. 286-305.

Mander, A.V. *Feminism as Therapy.* New York: Random House, 1974.

Manuel, G. and Posluns, M. *The Fourth World: An Indian Reality.* Toronto: Collier-MacMillan Canada, 1974.

Maracek, J. and Kravetz, D. "Women and Mental Health: A Review of Feminist Change Efforts." *Psychiatry,* 40 (1977), 323-329.

Margolin, G. and Patterson, G.R. "Differential Consequences Provided by Mothers and Fathers for Their Sons and Daughters." *Developmental Psychology,* 11 (1975), 537-538.

Marmor, J. "Changing Patterns of Femininity: Psychoanalytic Implications." Ed. S. Rosenbaum and I. Alger. *The Marriage Relationship.* New York: Basic Books, 1968.

Martin, D. *Battered Wives.* San Francisco Ca: Glide Publications, 1976.

Martin, F.F., Brotherston, J.H.F., and Chave, S.P.W. *Br. J. Preventive Social Med.,* 11 (1957), 196-202.

Maslow, A. "Self Esteem (Dominance Feeling) and Sexuality in Woman." *Journal of Social Psychology,* 16 (1942).

Maslow, A. *Motivation and Personality.* New York: Harper & Row, 1954.

Maslow, A. "Some Basic Propositions of a Growth and Self-Actualization Psychology." "Deficiency Motivation and Growth Motivation." Ed. S. Maddi. *Perspectives in Personality,* 1971.

Maslow, A. *The Farther Reaches of Human Nature*. New York: Viking Press, 1971.

Mazer, M. "People in Predicament: A Study in Psychiatric and Psychosocial Epidemiology." *Social Psychiatry*, 9 (1974), 85-90.

Mead, M. *Sex and Temperament in Three Primitive Societies*. New York: William Morrow & Co., 1935.

Mechanic, D. "Correlates of Frustration Among British General Practitioners." *Journal of Health and Social Behaviour*, 11, 2 (1970), 87-104.

Mechanic, David. "Some Factors in Identifying and Defining Mental Ill Illness." *Mental Hygiene*, 46 (1972), 66-74.

Medical sexism. *Healthright*, 6 (Winter 1975-76).

Meigs, C. Lecture on "The Distinctive Characteristics of the Female." Jefferson Medical College. Philadelphia: T.K. and P.G. Collins, 1847.

Meissner, M. et al. "No Exit for Wives: Sexual Division of Labour and the Cumulation of Household Demands." *Canad. Rev. Soc. and Anth.*, 12 (1975), 424-439.

Mendelsohn, B. "The Origin of the Doctrine of Victimology." Ed. I. Drapkin and E. Viano. *Victimology*. Lexington, Mass.: D.C. Heath & Co., 1974.

Mendelsohn, R. *Confessions of a Medical Heretic*. New York: Warner Books, 1980.

Merrill, A.P. "An Essay on Some of the Distinctive Peculiarities of the Negro Race." *Memphis Medical Recorder*, 4 (1855), 1-17.

Metzger, D. "It is Always the Woman who is Raped." *Am. J. Psychiatry*, 133 (1976), 405-408.

Mill, John Stuart. *The Subjection of Women*. M.I.T. Press, 1970. London: Longmans, Green, Reader & Dyer, 1869.

Miller, H. and Baruch, D.W. "A Study of Hostility in Allergic Children." *American Journal of Orthopsychiatry*, 20 (1950), 506-519.

Miller, J. Baker. *Toward a New Psychology of Women*. Boston: Beacon Press, 1976.

Miller, J. Baker and Mothner, I. "The Psychological Consequences of Sexual Inequality." *Amer. J. Orthopsychiatry*, 4, 5 (1971), 768.

Miller, M.L. "Allergy and Emotions." *International Archives of Allergy and Applied Immunology*, 1 (1950), 40-49.

Miller, N. *Battered Spouses*. London: G. Bell & Sons, 1975.

Millet, K. *Sexual Politics*. Garden City, Doubleday, 1970.

Mischel, W. "A Social Learning View of Sex Differences in Behavior." Ed. E. Maccoby. *The Development of Sex Differences.* Stanford Ca: Stanford Univ. Press, 1966.

Mitchell, G.D. "Paternalistic Behavior in Primates." *Psych. Bull,.* 71 (1969), 399-417.

Mitchell, J. *Psychoanalysis and Feminism.* New York: Random House, 1974.

Money, J. "Gender Role, Gender Identity, Core Identity: Usage and Definition of Terms." *J. Amer. Acad. Psychoanal.,* 1 (1973), 397-405.

Money, J. and Ehrhardt, A.A. *Man and Woman, Boy and Girl.* Baltimore and London: Johns Hopkins Univ. Press, 1972.

Mora, George. "Historical and Theoretical Trends in Psychiatry." Ed. Freedman, Kaplan and Sadock. *Textbook of Psychiatry,* Vol. 1. 2nd Edition. Baltimore: Williams & Wilkins, 1975, pp. 1-75.

Morgan, E. *The Descent of Woman.* New York: Bantam Books, 1973.

Morgan, H.G., et al. "Deliberate Self-Harm: Follow-up Study of 279 Patients." *British Journal of Psychiatry,* 128 (1976), 361-368.

Morgan, R. *Going Too Far.* New York: Random House, 1977.

Morgan, R. "Goodbye to All That." Ed. W. Martin. *The American Sisterhood.* New York: Harper & Row, 1972.

Morris, D. *The Human Zoo.* New York: McGraw-Hill, 1969.

Morris, Jan. *Conundrum.* New York: Harcourt, Brace, Jovanovich, 1974.

Morrissey, M. "Why a Transition House for Women." Paper presented at symposium on Alternatives to Psychiatric Treatment for Women, Canadian Psychiatric Association Annual Meeting Halifax, Nova Scotia, 18 October 1978.

Moss, H. "Sex, Age and State as Determinants of Mother-Infant Interaction." *Merrill Palmer Quarterly,* 13 (1967), 19-36.

Moss, P. and Plavis, I. "Mental Distress in Mothers of Preschool Children in Inner London." *Psychological Medicine,* 7 (1977), 641-652.

Mostow, E. and Newberry, P. "Work Role and Depression in Women: A Comparison of Workers and Housewives in Treatment." *American Journal of Orthopsychiatry,* 45 (1975), 538-548.

Mullahy, P. *Oedipus Myth and Complex.* New York: Hermitage, 1948.

Muller, Charlotte. "Economic Aspects of the Medical Use of Psychotropic Drugs." Ed. R. Cooperstock. *Social Aspects of the Medical Use of Psychotropic Drugs.* pp. 35-52.

Mulvihill, D.J., Tumin, M.M. and Curtis, L.A. "Crimes of Violence," Vols. 11 & 12. A staff report to the National Commission on the Causes and Prevention of Violence. Washington, D.C.: U.S. Government Printing Office, 1969.

Mussen, P.H. "Long-Term Consequents of Masculinity of Interests in Adolescence." *J. Consulting Psychology,* 26 (1962), 435-440.

Myrdal, A. and Klein, F. *Women's Two Roles.* 2nd edition. London: Routledge & Kegan Paul, 1968.

Myrdal, G. "A Parallel to the Negro Problem." Appendix 5. *An American Dilemma.* New York: Harper, 1944, pp. 1073-1078.

Nadelson, C.C. "The Impact of the Changing Role of Women and the Women's Movement." Paper presented at the North American Seminar on *The Impact of Change on Mental Health and Child and Family Development,* Val David, Quebec, June 1977.

Navarro, V. "The Industrialization of Fetishism or the Fetishism of Industrialization: A Critique of Ivan Illich." *Int. J. Health Services,* 5, 3 (1975), 351-371.

Neufeld, S. and Uit den Bogard, B. "Characteristics of Rape." Report to the Non-Medical Use of Drugs Directorate. Health and Welfare Canada, Project No. 1216-9-70.

Neugarten, B. *Middle Age and Aging.* Chicago: Univ. of Chicago Press, 1968.

Newberger, E.H. and Bourne, R. "The Medicalization and Legalization of Child Abuse." Paper presented at the symposium on *Violence and the Family.* Second World Conference of the International Society on Family Law, Montreal, 1977.

Newman, L.E. "Treatment for the Parents of Feminine Boys." *Am. J. Psychiatry,* 133 (1976), 683-687.

Nicholls, J. *Men's Liberation: A New Definition of Masculinity.* New York: Penguin Books, 1975.

Nobile, P. "The Last Taboo." *Penthouse,* December 1977.

Notman, M.T. and Nadelson, C.C. "The Rape Victim: Psychodynamic Considerations." *Am. J. Psychiatry,* 133 (1976), 408-413.

Nott, J.C. "Statistics of the Southern Slave Population." *De Bow's Commercial Rev.,* 4 (1875), 275-290.

Oakley, A. "Wisewoman and Medicine Man: Changes in the Management of Childbirth." Ed. J. Mitchell, J. and A. Oakley. *The Rights and Wrongs of Women.* Harmondsworth, Middlesex: Pelican Books, 1976.

O'Brien, J. Patrick. "A Study of Low-Dose Amitriptyline Overdoses." *American Journal of Psychiatry,* 134 (1976), 66-68.

O'Connor, J. *The Fiscal Crisis of the State.* New York: St. Martin's Press, 1973.

Offer, D. and Sabshin, M. "Normality." Ed. Freedman, Kaplan and Sadock. *Textbook of Psychiatry.* Baltimore: Williams & Wilkins, 1975.

O'Neill, J. "Observations of the Occipital and Superior Maxillary Bones of the African Cranium." *Am. J. Medical Science,* 19 (1850), 78-83.

Osler, Sir William. *Aequanimitas, with Other Addresses to Medical Students, Nurses, and Practitioners of Medicine.* London: H.K. Lewis, 1939.

Owen, A. and Winkler, R.C. "General Practitioners and Psychosocial Problems: An Evaluation Using Pseudopatients." *Medical Journal of Australia,* 2 (1974), 393-398.

Parish, P.A. "Is it Right to Perform a Pharmacological Leucotomy on a Large Section of Contemporary Society?" *Drugs and Society,* 1 (1972), 11, 14.

Parish, P.A. "The Prescribing of Psychotropic Drugs in General Practice." *Journal of Royal College of General Practitioners,* Supplement No. 4, 21 (1971), 1-77.

Parry, H.J., Balter, M.D., Mellinger, G.D., Cisin, I.H., and Manheimer, D.I. "National Patterns of Psychotherapeutic Drug Use." *Archives of General Psychiatry,* 28 (1973), 760-783.

Parsons, T. "The Social Structure of the Family." Ed. R.N. Anshen. *The Family: Its Function and Destiny.* New York: Harper, 1959.

Paykel, E.S. et al. "Life Events and Depression: A Controlled Study." *Arch. Gen. Psychiat.,* 25 (1971), 340-347.

Peacock, T.B. "On the Weight of the Brain in the Negro." *Memoirs of the Anthropological Society,* 1 (1853), 65-72.

Phillips, D.L. and Segal, B.E. "Sexual Status and Psychiatric Symptoms." *American Sociological Review,* 34 (1969), 58-72.

Pitts, J. "Social Control: The Concept." Ed. D. Sills. *International Encyclopedia of the Social Sciences.* Vol. 14 New York: Macmillan, 1968.

Pizzey, E. *Scream Quietly or the Neighbours Will Hear.* Middlesex, England: Penguin Books, 1974.

"Poor Kids." A Report by the National Council of Welfare on Children.

Poverty in Canada, March 1975.

Postpartum Depression, National Film Board, Canada, 1979.

Powell, G.J. "Growing up Black and Female." Ed. C.B. Kopp. *Becoming Female,* 1979.

Prien, R.F., Klett, C.J., and Caffey, E.M. "Polypharmacy in Psychiatric Treatment of Elderly Hospitalized Patients: Survey of 12 Veterans Administration Hospitals." *Diseases of the Nervous System,* 37 (1977), 333-336.

Quitkin, F. et al., "Tardive Dyskinesia: Are First Signs Reversible?" *American Journal of Psychiatry,* 134 (1977), 84-87.

Rada, R. "Alcoholism and Forcible Rape." *Am. J. Psychiatry,* 132 (1975), 444-446.

Radloff, Lenore, "Sex Differences in Depression: The Effects of Occupation and Marital Status." *Sex Roles,* 1 (1975), 249-265.

Rapp, R. "Review: Anthropology." *Signs,* 4 (1979), 497-513.

Rappaport, R. and Rappaport, R. *Dual Career Families.* Middlesex, England: Penguin Books, 1971.

Rathbun, C., DiVirgilio, L. and Waldfogel, S. "The Restitutive Process in Children Following Radical Separation from Family and Culture." *Am. J. Orthopsychiatry,* 28 (1958), 408-415.

Rawlings, E.I. and Carter, D.K., eds., *Psychotherapy for Women: Treatment Toward Equality.* Springfield, Ill. Charles C. Thomas, 1977.

Rawlings, E.I., and Carter, D.K. "Values and Value Change in Psychotherapy." Ed. Rawlings and Carter. *Psychotherapy For Women.*

Rebecca, N., Hefner, R. and Oleshansky B. "A Model of Sex Role Transcendence." Ed. Kaplan and Bean. *Beyond Sex Role Stereotypes.* Boston, Mass.: Little Brown, 1976, pp. 90-97.

Reinhardt, J. and Fisher, E. "The Sexual Psychopath and the Law." *J. Criminal Law & Criminology,* 42 (1951), 184-198.

Research Division, Saskatchewan Alcoholism Commission. *A Socio-Demographic Profile of People Prescribed Mood-Modifiers in Saskatchewan.* Final Report, January 1978.

Revitch, F. and Weiss, R. "The Pedophilic Offender." *Diseases of the Nervous System,* 23 (1962), 73-78.

Rheingold, H.L. and Cook, K.V. "The Contents of Boys' and Girls' rooms as an Index of Parents' Behaviour." *Child Development,* 46 (1975), 450-463.

Rheingold, J.C. *The Fear of Being a Woman.* New York: Grune & Stratton, 1964.

Rheingold, J.C. *The Mother, Anxiety, Death and the Catastrophic Death Complex.* London: V & A Churchill, 1967.

Rich, A. *Of Woman Born: Motherhood As Experience and Institution.* New York: W.W. Norton, 1976.

Rich, A. Ed. S. and P. Daniels. *Working It Out.* New York: Pantheon Books, 1977.

Richie, E. and Burwell, E.J. "Sex Bias in Canadian Medical Journals." Paper presented at the Canadian Psychological Association Convention, Calgary, 1980.

Richman, N. "Depression in Mothers of Preschool Children." *Journal of Child Psychology and Psychiatry,* 17 (1976), 75-78.

Richman, N. "The Effect of Housing on Preschool Children and Their Mothers." *Developmental Medicine and Child Neurology,* 16 (1974), 53-58.

Rickel, A.U. and Grant, L.M. "Sex Roles Stereotypes in the Mass Media and Schools: Five Consistent Themes." *International J. Women's Studies,* 2 (1979), 164-179.

Roback, A.A. *History of American Psychology.* New York: Appleton Century Crofts, 1959.

Roberts, L. and Pacht, A. "Termination of Inpatient Treatment for Sex Deviates: Psychiatric, Social and Legal Factors." *Am. J. Psychiatry,* 121 (1965), 873-880.

Robertson, B.M. "The Psychoanalytic Theory of Depression." *Can. J. Psychiat.,* 24 (1979), 341-352.

Robertson, J. "A Treatment Model for Postpartum Depression." *Canada's Mental Health,* 28 (1980), 16-17.

Robinson, M.N. *The Power of Sexual Surrender.* New York: Doubleday, 1959, p. 158.

Rolph, C.H. *Women of the Streets.* London: Secker & Warburg, 1955.

Romano, J. "Basic Orientation and Education of the Medical Student." *Journal A.M.A.,* 143 (1950), 409.

Rome, H.P. "Psychiatry and Foreign Affairs." *Am. J. Psychiatry,* 125 (1968), 725-730.

Rosenburg, M. "The Biologic Basis for Sex Role Stereotypes." Ed. A.G. Kaplan. and J.P. Bean. *Beyond Sex Role Stereotypes,* Boston, Mass.: Little, Brown, 1976.

Rosenfeld, A.A. et al. "Incest and Sexual Abuse of Children." *J. American Academy of Child Psychiatry,* 16 (1977), 327-339.

Rosenhan, D.L. "On Being Sane in Insane Places." *Science,* 179 (1973).

Rosenthal, S.H. "The Involutional Depressive Syndrome." *Am. J. Psy-*

chiat., Supplement, 124 (1968), 21-35.

Rowbotham, S. *Woman's Consciousness, Man's World.* Middlesex, England: Penguin Books, 1973.

Rowbotham, S. *Women, Resistance and Revolution.* London: Allen Lane, The Penguin Press, 1972.

Rubin, G. *Woman as Nigger.* Ann Arbor Michigan: The Argus. March 28-April 11; April 14-28, 1969, pp. 7-15; 14.

Rubin, J.Z., Provenzano, F.J. and Luria. "The Eye of the Beholder: Parent's Views of Sex of Newborns." *Am. J. Orthopsychiat.*, 44 (1974), 12-19.

Ruskin, J. "Of Queens Gardens." *Sesame and Lilies.* (n.c.): Hammond Publishing, 1902.

Russell, D. "On Pornography" *Chrysalis,* 4 (1977), 12.

Russell, D. *The Politics of Rape: The Victim's Perspective.* New York: Stein and Day, 1975.

Rutter, M. *Maternal Deprivation Reassessed.* Harmondsworth, Middlesex, England: Penguin Books, 1972.

Rutter, M. "Psychological Development: Predictions from Infancy." *Journal of Child Psychiatry and Psychology,* 11 (1970), 49-62.

Ryan, K.H. et al. "Estrogen Formation in the Brain." *Am. J. Obstetrics and Gynecology,* 114 (1972), 454-460.

Ryan, W. *Blaming the Victim.* New York: Vintage, Random House, 1976.

Sabshin, M., Diesenhaus, H. and Wilkerson, R. "Dimensions of Institutional Racism in Psychiatry." *Am. J. Psychiatry,* 127: 787, 1970.

Sachs, A. and Wilson, J. Hoff. *Sexism and the Law: A Study of Male Beliefs and Legal Bias in Britain and the United States.* Oxford: Martin Robertson & Co., 1978.

Sahlins, M. *The Use and Abuse of Biology.* Ann Arbor: Univ. of Michigan Press, 1976.

Sameroff, A.J. "Early Influences on Development: Fact or Fancy?" *Merrill-Palmer Quarterly,* 20 (1975), 275-301.

Sartre, J.P. *Anti-Semite and Jew.* New York: Grove Press, 1960.

Schein, L. "Man to Man." *Makara,* October/November (1976), 34-38.

Schell, R. *Being Mentally Ill: A Sociological Theory.* Chicago: Aldine Press, 1962.

Schofield, W. *Psychotherapy: The Purchase of Friendship.* Englewood Cliffs: Prentice-Hall, 1963.

Schrag, P. and Divoky, D. *The Myth of the Hyperactive Child and*

Other Means of Child Control. New York: Laurel Books, 1976.

Schultz, A.H. *The Life of Primates.* New York: Universe Books, 1969, Chapter 13.

Schultz, L.G. "The Wife-Assaulter." *J. Social Therapy,* 6 (1960), 103-112.

Schwab, J.J., McGinnis, N.H., and Warheit, G.J. "Social Psychiatric Impairment: Racial Comparisions." *Am. J. Psychiat.,* 130 (1973), 183-187.

Schwartz, M.C. "Sexism in the Social Work Curriculum." *Journal of Education for Social Work,* Fall (1973).

Scull, A.T. "Cyclical Trends in Psychiatric Practice: The Case of Bettelheim and Tuke." *Soical Science and Medicine,* 9 (1975), 633-640.

Scull, A.T. *Decarceration.* New Jersey: Prentice-Hall, 1977.

Scull, A.T. "From Madness to Mental Illness: Medical Men as Moral Entrepreneurs." *Arch. Europ. Sociol.,* XVI (1975), 218-251.

Sears, R.R. "Relation of Early Socialization Experiences to Self-Concepts and Gender Role in Middle Childhood." *Child Development,* 41 (1970), 267-289.

Segal, J. "Violent Men — Embattled Women." *Cosmopolitan,* May (1976), 238-241.

Seiden, A.M. "Overview: Research on the Psychology of Women. I. Gender Differences and Sexual and Reproductive Life. II. Women in Families, Work, and Psychotherapy." *Am. J. Psychiat.,* 133 (1976), 995-1007, 1111-1123.

Seidenberg, R. "For the Future — Equity?" Ed. J.B. Miller. *Psychoanalysis and Women.* Middlesex, England: Penguin Books, 1973.

Seidenberg, R. "Images of Health, Illness and Women in Drug Advertising." *Journal of Drug Issues,* 4 (1974), 264-267.

Seligman, M.E.P. "Learned Helplessness." *Ann. Rev. Med.,* 23 (1972), 407.

Serbin, L.A., Connor, J.M., and Iler, I., "Sex-Stereotyped and Non-Stereotyped Introductions of New Toys in the Preschool Classroom: An Observational Study of Teacher Behaviour and its Effects." *Psychology of Women Quarterly,* 4 (1979), 261-265.

Serbin, L.A., O'Leary, K.D., Kent, R.N. and Tomick, L.J. "A Comparision of Teacher Response to the Pre-Academic and Problem Behaviour of Boys and Girls." *Child Development,* 44 (1973), 796-804.

Sgroi, S.M. " 'Kids with Clap': Gonorrhea as Indicator of Child Sexual

Assault." *Victimology,* 2 (1977), 251-267.

Shore, M.F. "Drugs Can Be Dangerous During Pregnancy and Lactation." *Canadian Pharmaceutical Journal,* 103 (1970), 358-367.

Sidel, V.W. and Sidel, R. "Beyond Coping." *Social Policy,* September/October (1976), 67.

Silverman, C. *The Epidemiology of Depression.* Baltimore: Johns Hopkins Press, 1968.

Skegg, D.C.G., Doll, R., and Perry, J. "Use of Medicines in General Practice." *British Medical Journal,* 1 (1977), 1561-1563.

Slater, E. and Cowie, V. "The Genetics of Mental disorders." *Oxford Monographs in Medical Genetics.* London: Oxford Univ. Press, 1971.

Sloane, P. and Karpinski, E. "Effects of Incest on the Participants." *Am. J. Orthopsychiatry,* 12 (1942), 666-673.

Smart, C. *Women, Crime and Criminology: A Feminist Critique.* London: Routledge & Kegan Paul, 1976.

Smith, D.E. "A Sociology for Women." Ed. J.A. Sherman and E. Torton Beck. *Sociology of Knowledge.* Madison: Univ. of Wisconsin Press, 1979, Section 1.

Smith, D.E. "An Analysis of Ideological Structures and How Women are Excluded: Considerations for Academic Women." *Rev. Can. Soc. & Anth. / Can. Rev. Soc. & Anth.,* 12, 4 (1975), part 1.

Smith D.E. and David, S., *Women Look at Psychiatry.* Vancouver: Press Gang Publishers, 1975.

Smith, D.E. "Women, the Family and Corporate Capitalism." Ed. M. Stephenson, *Women in Canada.* Toronto: New Press, 1973.

Sociobiology: Doing What Comes Naturally. Film for Highschool Students distributed by Document Associates, Inc., 880 Third Avenue New York, N.Y., 10022.

Sonne, J.C. and Lincoln, G. "The Importance of a Heterosexual Co-Therapy Relationship in the Construction of a Family Image." Ed., I.M. Cohen. *Family Structure, Dynamics and Therapy, Psychiatric Research Report No. 20.* Washington, D.C.: American Psychiatric Research Association, 1966.

Sorenson, A., and Stromgren, E. "Frequency of Depressive States Within Geographically Limited Population Groups." *Acta Psychiatrica Scandinavica,* 37 (1961), 32-68.

Southwick, C.H., ed. *Primate Social Behavior.* Princeton: Van Nostrand 1965.

324 —

Spitz, R. "Hospitalism: An Inquiry into the Genesis of Psychiatric Conditions in Early Childhood, Part I." *Psychoanalytic Study of the Child*, 1 (1945), 53-74.

Spitz, R. *The First Year of Life: A Psychoanalytic Study of Normal and Deviant Development of Object Relations*. New York: International Universities Press, 1965.

Spitz, R.A. "Possible Infantile Precursors of Psychopathy." *American Journal of Orthopsychiatry*, 20 (1950), 240-248.

Stack, C. *All Our Kin: Strategies for Survival in a Black Community*. New York: Harper & Row, 1974.

Stark-Adamec, C. and Adamec, R.E. "Aggression by Men Against Women: Adaptation or Aberration?" *International Journal of Women's Studies* 5, 1 (1982), 1-21.

Stark-Adamec, C., Graham, J.M., and Pyke, S.W. "Androgyny and Mental Health: The Need for a Critical Evaluation of the Theoretical Equation." *International J. Women's Studies*, 3 (1980), 490-507.

Starr, P. "The Politics of Therapeutic Nihilism." *The Hastings Centre Report*, 6, 5 (1976), 24-30.

Statistics Canada. *Homicide in Canada*. 1974.

Statistics Canada. *Crime and Traffic Enforcement Statistics*. 1976.

Statistics Canada. *Mental Health Statistics*. Annual Reports.

Stein, L., Belluzzi, J.D., and Wise, C.D. "Benzodiazepines: Behavioral and Neurochemical Mechanisms." *American Journal of Psychiatry*, 134 (1977), 665-672.

Steinem, G. "Is Child Pornography About Sex?" *Ms.* 6, 2 (1977), 42-44.

Stephenson, P.S. "Myths about Juvenile Delinquency." *Canadian Journal of Criminology and Corrections*, 15, 1 (1973), 83-92.

Stephenson, P.S. "Project Toddler — A Drop in the Bucket?" *J. of the Division of Early Childhood*, 1 (1979), 115-122.

Stephenson, P.S. "Society's Changing Attitude To the Idiot." *Canadian Psychiatric Association Journal*, 12 (1967), 83-84.

Stephenson, P.S. "The Impact of the Women's Movement: Implications for Child Development, Mental Health and Family Policy." *Canada's Mental Health*, Supplement: Child and Family Mental Health Services: Future Policy Issues, 26 (1978), 10-13.

Stewart, A.J. and Winter, D.G. "The Nature and Causes of Female Suppression." *Signs*, 2 (1977), 531-553.

Stoll, C.S. *Female and Male: Socialization, Social Roles, and Social*

Structure. Dubuque, Iowa: William C. Brown, 1974.

Stoller, R. "Primary Femininity." *J. Am. Psychoanal. Assoc.,* 24 (1976), 59-78.

Stoller, R. "The Sense of Maleness." *Psychoanalytic Quarterly,* 34 (1965), 207-218.

Stoller, R.J. *The Transexual Experiment.* London: Hogarth Press, 1975.

Storr, A. *Human Aggression.* New York: Bantam, 1970.

Stuard, M.D. "Dame Trot." *Signs,* 1, 2 (1975).

Sullivan, H.S. "Developmental Syndromes" and Basic Conceptions." Ed. S. Maddi. *Perspectives in Personality.* Boston: Little Brown & Co., 1971.

Sullivan, H.S. *The Interpersonal Theory of Psychiatry.* New York: Norton, 1953.

Sutherland, E. "Sexual Psychopathy Laws." *J. Criminal Law & Criminology,* 40 (1950), 543-554.

Szasz, T.S., ed. *The Age of Madness.* New York: Anchor Press/Doubleday, 1973.

Szasz, T.S. *The Myth of Mental Illness.* Revised edition. New York: Harper & Row, 1974. *The Manufacture of Madness.* New York: Delta Books, Dell Publishing Co., 1970; and many other works.

Tanner, N. and Zilman, A. "Woman in Evolution. Part I: Innovation and Selection in Human Origins." *Signs* 1, 3 (1976), 585-608.

Taylor, J.W. "The Diminishing Birthrate and What is Involved in It." Presidential Address to Inaugural Meeting of British Gynaecological Society. *British Medical Journal,* 20 February 1904.

Tennov, D. *Psychotherapy: The Hazardous Cure.* Garden City, Anchor Books, 1976.

The Task Force on Nonenclature and Statistics of the American Psychiatric Association, Micro-D. Revisions in the Diagnostic Criteria of the DSM III. 1/15/78 Draft; Second Printing 1/2/79.

Thomas, A., Chess, S., and Birch, H.G. *Temperament and Behaviour Disorders in Children.* New York: New York Univ. Press, 1968.

Thompson, C. *On Women.* New York: Mentor Books, 1964.

Thomspon, C. "Penis Envy in Women." Ed. J.B. Miller. *Psychoanalysis and Women.* Baltimore: Penguin Books, 1973.

Tidmarsh, M. "Violence in Marriage." *Social Work Today,* 7, 2 (1976), 36-38.

Tiger, L. *Men in Groups.* New York: Random House, 1969.

Tinbergen, N. *Animal Behavior.* New York: Time-Life, Inc., 1965.

Toffler, A. *Future Shock*. New York: Random House, 1970.

Tonks, C. "Premenstrual Tension." *Br. J. Hosp. Med.*, 7 (1968), 383-387.

Tooley, K.M. "Johnny, I Hardly Knew Ye: Toward Revision of the Theory of Male Psychosexual Development." *Amer. J. Orthopsychiat..* 47 (1977), 184-195.

Torrey, E.F. *The Death of Psychiatry*. Radnor, Pa.: Chilton Book Co., 1974.

Tuchman, A. "Women's Depiction by the Mass Media." *Signs*, 4 (1979), 528-592.

Tracy, S. *Principles of Human Physiology*. 4th ed. Philadelphia, 1860.

Ullian, P.Z. "The Development of Conceptions of Masculinity and Femininity." Ed. B. Lloyd and J. Archer. *Exploring Sex Differences*. New York: Academic Press, 1976, pp. 25-47.

Ullman, L.P. and Krazner, L. *A Psychological Approach to Abnormal Behavior*. New Jersey: Prentice-Hall, 1969, pp. 204-205.

Umana, R.F., Gross, S.J. and McConville, M.T. *Crisis in the Family: Three Approaches*. New York: Gardner Press, 1980.

Unger, R.K. "Toward a Redefinition of Sex and Gender." *American Psychologist*, 34 (1979), 1085-1094.

Useem, M. and Miller, S.M. "The Upper Class in Higher Education." *Social Policy*, 7 (1977), 4.

Van Stolk, M. "Beaten Women, Battered Children." *Children Today*, March-April (1976), 9-12.

Vaughter, R.M. "Psychology." *Signs*, 2 (1976), 120-146.

Von Hentig, H. "Remarks on the Interaction of Perpetrator and Victim." *J. Criminal Law & Criminology*, 31 (1940), 303-309.

Voth, H. *The Castrated Family*. Kansas City: Sheed, Andrews & McNeal, Universal Press, 1977.

Wadsworth, J.E.J., Butterfield, W.J.H., and Blaney, R. *Health and Sickness: The Choice of Treatment*. London: Tavistock Publications, 1971.

Walkowitz, J.R. "The Politics of Prostitution." *Signs*, 6 (1980), 123-135.

Walsh, M.R. "The Rediscovery of the Need for a Feminist Medical Education." *Harvard Educational Review*, 49, 4 (1979), 447-466.

Walsh, M.R. *Doctors Wanted: No Women Need Apply*. New Haven, Conn: Yale University Press, 1977.

Walum, L.R. *The Dynamics of Sex and Gender: A Sociological Perspective*. Chicago: Rand McNally Publishing, 1977.

Waring, E.M. "Family Therapy and Schizophrenia." *Canadian Psychiatric Association Journal,* 23 (1978), 51-58.

Watson, J.B. *Behaviorism.* New York: W.W. Norton, 1924.

Watzlawick, P., Weakland, J. and Fisch, P. *Change: Principles of Problem Formulation and Problem Resolution.* New York: W.W. Norton & Co., 1974.

Webb, A.P. "Sex-Role Preferences and Adjustment in Early Adolescents." *Child Development,* 34 (1963), 609-618.

Weinberg, S.K. *Incest Behaviour.* New York: Citadel Press, 1955.

Weiner, J.B. "Father-Daughter Incest." *Psychiatric Quarterly,* 36, (1962).

Weisner, T.S. "Some Cross-Cultural Perspectives on Becoming Female." Ed. C.B. Kopp. *Becoming Female: Perspectives on Development.* New York & London: Plenum Press, 1979.

Weiss, E. and English, O.S. *Psychosomatic Medicine.* Philadelphia: W. B. Saunders, 1957, p. 374.

Weissman, M.M. and Klerman, G.L. "Sex Differences and the Epidemiology of Depression." Ed. E.S. Gomberg and V. Franks. *Gender and Disordered Behaviour: Sex Differences in Psychopathology.* New York: Brunner/Mazel, 1979.

Weissman, M.M. and Paykel, E.S. *The Depressed Woman: A Study of Social Relationships.* Chicago: University of Chicago Press, 1974.

Weissman, M.M. and Slaby, A.E. "Oral Contraceptives and Psychiatric Disturbance: Evidence from Research." *Br. J. Psychiat.,* 123 (1973). 513-518.

Weisstein, N. "Psychology Constructs the Female." Ed. V. Gornick and B.K. Moran. *Woman in Sexist-Society: Studies in Power and Powerlessness.* New York: Basic Books, 1971.

Weitzman, L.J. et al. "Sex Role Socialization in Picture Books for Preschool Children." *Am. J. Sociology,* 47 (1972), 1125-1150.

Westley, W.A. and Epstein, N.B. *The Silent Majority.* New York: Jossey-Bass, 1969.

Wetzel, R., Reich, T., McClure, J., et al. "Premenstrual Affective Syndrome and Affective Disorder." *Br. J. Psychiat.,* 127 (1975), 219-221.

Wheatley, D. *Nonspecific Factors in Drug Therapy.* Ed. Carle Rickels. Springfield, Illinois: Charles C. Thomas, 1968.

Whitehurst, R.N. "Alternative Family Structures and Violence Reduction." S. Steinmetz and M. Straus. *Violence in the Family.* New

York: Dodd, Mead, 1974.

Whiting, B. and Edwards, C.A. "Cross-Cultural Analysis of Sex Differences in the Behaviour of Children Aged Three Through Eleven." Ed. R.A. LeVine. *Culture & Personality, Contemporary Readings*. Chicago: Aldine, 1974.

Williams, E.F. *Notes of a Feminist Therapist*. New York: Dell Books, 1977.

Wilman, B.B. "Schizophrenia in Childhood." Ed. B.B. Wolman. *Manual of Child Psychopathology*. New York: McGraw-Hill, 1972.

Wilson, E.O. *Sociobiology: The New Synthesis*. Cambridge, Mass.: Harvard Univ. Press, 1975.

Wilson, L. *This Stranger, My Son*. London: John Murray, 1969.

Wilson, R.A. *Feminine Forever*. New York: M. Evans, 1966.

Wing, J.K. and Brown, G.W. *Institutionalism and Schizophrenia*. Cambridge: Cambridge Univ. Press, 1970.

Wing, J.K. and Hailey, A.M. eds. *Evaluating a Community Psychiatric Service*. London: Oxford Univ. Press, 1972.

Winick, M., Meyer, K.K. and Harris, R.C. "Malnutrition and Environmental Enrichment by Early Adoption." *Science*, 190 (1975), 1173-1175.

Winokur, G. "Depression in the Menopause." *Am. J. Psychiat.*, 130 (1973), 92-93.

Winstead, D., Blackwell, B., and Eilers, M.K. "Diazepam on Demand: Drug Seeking Behaviour in Anxious Inpatients." *Archives of General Psychiatry*, 30 (1974), 349-351.

Winston, F. "Oral Contraceptives, pyridoxine and depression." *Am. J. Psychiat.*, 130 (1973), 1217-1221.

Wolfe, S. "The Social Responsibility of the Physician in Prescribing Mind-Affecting Drugs." Ed. R. Cooperstock. *Social Aspects of the Medical Use of Psychotherapeutic Drugs*. pp. 53-62.

Wolins, M. "Group Care: Friend or Foe?" *Social Work*, 14 (1969), 35-53.

"Women and Poverty." A Report by the National Council on Welfare. Ottawa, October 1979.

Woody, G.E., O'Brien, C.P. and Greenstein, R. "Misuse and Abuse of Diazepam: Increasingly Common Medical Problem." *International Journal on Addiction*, 10 (1975), 843-848.

Woolf, V. *A Room of One's Own*. New York: Harcourt, Brace & Co., 1929.

Wyckoff, H. *Solving Women's Problems.* New York: Grove Press, 1977.

Wylie, P. *Generation of Vipers.* New York: Rinehart & Co., 1942.

Yarrow, L.J. "Separation from Parents in Early Childhood." Ed. Hoffman, M.L. and Hoffman, L.W., *Review of Child Development Research,* Vol. I, New York, Russell Sage, 1965.

Yogoguchi, L. "Children not Severely Damaged by Incest with a Parent." *J. American Academy of Child Psychiatry,* 5 (1966), 111-124.

Yonge, G.D. "The Bem Sex-Role Inventory: Use with Caution if At All." *Psychological Reports,* 43 (1978), 1245-1246.

Ziel, H.K. and Finkle, W.D. "Increased Risk of Endomentrial Carcinoma Among Users of Conjugated Oestrogens." *New England Journal of Medicine,* 293 (1975), 1167-1170.

Zilboorg, G. "Masculine and Feminine: Some Biological and Cultural Aspects." *Psychiatry,* 7 (1944), 257-296.

Zilboorg, G. *The Medical Man and the Witch During the Renaissance.* Baltimore: Johns Hopkins Press, 1935.

Zola, I.K. "Medicine as an Institution of Social Control." *Sociological Review,* 20 (1972), 487-504.

Zuger, B. "The Role of Familiar Factors in Persistent Effeminate Behavior in Boys." *Am. J. Psychiatry,* 126 (1970), 1167-1170.